AMERICA IN TWO CENTURIES:
An Inventory

AMERICA IN TWO CENTURIES:
An Inventory

Advisory Editor

DANIEL J. BOORSTIN

*See last pages of this volume
for a complete list of titles*

A
TOPOGRAPHICAL DESCRIPTION

OF THE DOMINIONS OF

THE UNITED STATES OF AMERICA

Thomas
T[homas] Pownall

EDITED BY *Lois Mulkearn*

ARNO PRESS
A New York Times Company
1976

Editorial Supervision: ANDREA HICKS

Reprint Edition 1976 by Arno Press Inc.

Copyright © 1949, by The University
   of Pittsburgh Press
Reprinted by permission of
   The University of Pittsburgh Press

Reprinted from a copy in
   The Princeton University Library

AMERICA IN TWO CENTURIES: An Inventory
ISBN for complete set: 0-405-07666-5
See last pages of this volume for titles.

Manufactured in the United States of America

Library of Congress Cataloging in Publication Data

Pownall, Thomas, 1722-1805.
   A topographical description of the dominions of the
United States of America.

   (America in two centuries, an inventory)
   "A revised and enlarged edition of A topographical
description of such parts of North America as are
contained in the (annexed) map of the middle British
colonies, &c. in North America."
   Reprint of the ed. published by the University of
Pittsburgh Press, Pittsburgh.
   Bibliography: p.
   1. United States--Description and travel--To 1783.
2. Pownall, Thomas, 1722-1805. I. Title. II. Series.
E163.P88 1976   917.4'04'2   75-22835
ISBN 0-405-07706-8

TOPOGRAPHICAL DESCRIPTION

OF THE DOMINIONS OF THE

UNITED STATES OF AMERICA

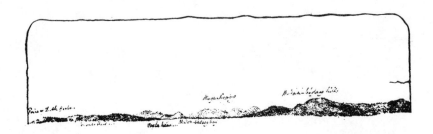

A topographic sketch by Thomas Pownall—among the large amount of manuscript material he tipped into his own copy of the first edition (published 1776), anticipating a second edition for 1779, an edition which is published only now—170 years later.

A

TOPOGRAPHICAL DESCRIPTION

OF THE DOMINIONS OF

THE UNITED STATES OF AMERICA

[BEING *A REVISED and ENLARGED EDITION of*]
A TOPOGRAPHICAL DESCRIPTION
of SUCH PARTS of NORTH AMERICA
as are CONTAINED in
THE (Annexed) MAP of the MIDDLE BRITISH COLONIES, &c.
in
NORTH AMERICA

By *T. POWNALL*, M.P.
Late GOVERNOR, CAPTAIN-GENERAL, VICE-ADMIRAL
and COMMANDER IN CHIEF of His Majesty's Provinces now States,
Massachusetts Bay and South Carolina,
and LIEUTENANT GOVERNOR of New Jersey.

EDITED BY *Lois Mulkearn*, LIBRARIAN
DARLINGTON MEMORIAL LIBRARY
UNIVERSITY OF PITTSBURGH

PITTSBURGH:
UNIVERSITY OF PITTSBURGH PRESS
1949

To Jim

FOREWORD

OF all the British administrators who served in America in the eighteenth century none showed a more sustained and lively interest in New World developments than did Thomas Pownall. The year after his arrival in New York we find him present at the Albany Congress of 1754 in an unofficial capacity and presenting to the consideration of the delegates a plan for the defense of the colonial frontiers, for which he received the thanks of the Congress. The following year he was at Alexandria, Virginia, also in an unofficial capacity, in attendance at the Governors' Conference called by General Braddock. Among the friendships he formed in America those with Benjamin Franklin and Lewis Evans were of more than usual significance. Through these various contacts he was introduced intimately to a host of problems connected with British colonial Indian relations, westward expansion, and Anglo-French rivalry in North America. In 1754 he drew up a plan for regulating Indian trade and land purchases and in 1755 he prepared his "Considerations on yᵉ Means, Method & Nature of Settling a Colony on yᵉ Lands South of Lake Erie" and a map with elaborate notations to accompany it—which are among the Loudoun Papers in the Huntington Library at San Marino, California. Both as Lieutenant Governor of New Jersey and as Governor of Massachusetts Bay he was actively and officially concerned in the war in North America that was waged from 1754 to 1763 and, especially in his latter capacity, wrote voluminous reports to his superiors in London on the progress of events in New England and also made various suggestions to both Loudoun and Abercromby—each in turn serving as commander-in-chief of the British forces in North America—for the successful prosecution of hostilities. Although he returned to England before the close of the war, his attention continued to be centered on the colonies and, among other publications credited to him, there appeared in 1764 *The Administration of the Colonies* that went through six editions; in 1776 the *Topographical Description of North America;* in 1780 *A Memorial to the Sovereigns of Europe on the present state of affairs between the old and new world;* and, finally, in 1783, the year of the Peace of Paris, *A Memorial addressed to the Sovereigns of America.*

Among Thomas Pownall's various works none has greater interest for the present-day student in the field of either American colonial history or American historical geography than the *Topographical Description.* The book, however, has been out of print and is therefore not easily available. Moreover, Pownall thoroughly revised it in the year 1784, and also made many additions to it, with the expectation of its being reissued from the press, but this was not done. Happily, Mrs. Lois Mulkearn, librarian of the Darlington Library of the University of Pittsburgh, was in a position to set herself the task of editing the revised work, which, after the lapse of so many years, is now presented to the public by the University of Pittsburgh Press.

The lives and reputations of Thomas Pownall, the colonial administrator and political theorist, and Lewis Evans, the Pennsylvania cartographer and geographer, were closely linked from the year 1754. Pownall spent some time in Philadelphia assisting Evans with the latter's famous *General Map of the Middle British Colonies* and his equally famous *Analysis* to accompany it, both of which appeared in 1755. Although Evans passed away the following year Pownall continued his interest in his friend's map and geographical guide to it and ultimately used them as the basis for both the map and the *Topographical Description* that he himself issued. In view of the fact that both the Evans' *Map* and *Analysis* were reissued in the writer's *Lewis Evans*, published in 1939 by the Historical Society of Pennsylvania, it is perhaps not inappropriate that he should write this Foreword to this revised edition of the *Topographical Description.*

There are many ways of editing a document. No two people are apt to approach the task in quite the same manner. In this instance Mrs. Mulkearn was content to give her efforts largely to the important and sometimes baffling work of identifying eighteenth-century incidents, places, and persons—letting the reader arrive at his own opinion of the soundness of Pownall's occasional excursions into the realm of scientific hypothesis respecting the origins of the topography of North America. In view of the fact that valid criticisms of such hypotheses call for very different training than that possessed by most students of colonial history, the writer is persuaded that the editor of this volume chose wisely not to attempt to enter a field in which theories, as against ascertainable facts, still so largely dominate discussion. Nevertheless, for those interested in the history of science the *Topographical Description* is at least now readily available and it will be a matter of surprise if advantage is not taken of this fact to explore some of the scientific theories embodied in it. The book, however, will doubtless make its chief appeal to those who seek rather to recapture the American eighteenth-century scene. For such it is a mine of information.

LAWRENCE HENRY GIPSON

Lehigh University

EDITOR'S PREFACE

THOMAS POWNALL, in 1753, came to America to serve as Secretary to the newly appointed royal Governor of the Province of New York, Sir Danvers Osborne. The death of the Governor, only a few days after Pownall's arrival, relieved him of his official duties. Nevertheless, he remained in America and interested himself in colonial affairs. It is said that this early interest, especially in the French-English controversy, caused him to make a thorough study of the waterways which could be used in the transportation of troops in the open conflict that he recognized as inevitable.

When Pownall assumed his duties as royal Governor of the Massachusetts Bay Colony in 1757, the French had become a real threat to the very existence of the English colonies. His intimate knowledge of the topography of the country and his constant study of the "Scouts Journals" helped much in the planning of the strategy against the French.

Late in 1759, when the American part of the "Seven Years' War" had been won by the British, Governor Pownall was transferred from the governorship of Massachusetts Bay to that of South Carolina. Instead of going from New England to South Carolina, he returned to England, and although he did not resign his position in South Carolina for almost a year, he remained in Great Britain. In fact, he never returned to America.

After a brief withdrawal from activity in colonial affairs Pownall resumed his unofficial interest, in 1764, with the publication of *The Administration of the Colonies*. This book was designed to influence public opinion on the treatment of the American colonies. In it he set forth not only his plan to knit more tightly the interests of the Colonies with those of the mother country, but also his belief that the Americans were loyal Englishmen, who, if treated fairly, were a great asset to the mother country.

* * * *

A Topographical Description of Such Parts of North America as are Contained in the (Annexed) Map of the Middle British Colonies, &c., in

North America by Thomas Pownall was published in 1776. The book was a detailed topographical description of New England and the Middle Colonies. The *Map* within the volume was a revised edition of Lewis Evans' *Map* of 1755, and the information about the Ohio Country was quoted from Lewis Evans' *Analysis* of his map of 1755. In 1779 Pownall began a revision of this work. By 1784 he had completed the revision and had written the preface to his self-styled third edition, which is this book, published now as Pownall's revised and enlarged edition.

Why this edition was not published in 1784 is unknown to the present editor. In 1854 the manuscript was sold.[1] It came later into the possession of William M. Darlington, the collector of the basic collection of books in the Darlington Memorial Library, University of Pittsburgh, Pittsburgh, Pennsylvania. The additions to the first, or 1776 edition, add about one-third in volume to the publication. Pownall made corrections and minor additions on almost every page, especially in the first part of the work. The large additions are descriptions of New York City, Boston, and the Connecticut Valley and "Extracts" from a Journal of his travels through New Jersey to Bethlehem and Philadelphia, Pennsylvania. Facsimiles of some of the holograph additions are used to illustrate this book.

* * * *

The 1949 publication has been projected to make available at reasonable cost to students of history Pownall's authentic, contemporary topographic description of the American colonies in an edition augmented by his own hitherto unpublished writings.

The editor's notes are intended to make Pownall's work more intelligible to the modern reader; they identify proper names, names of places, topographic features, and events, familiar to the reader in Pownall's time, but often unfamiliar or even unknown today. Since Pownall's work is chiefly topographical, the annotations, for the most part, are limited to identifying (according to present and past location) forts, Indian towns, early settlements, and theaters of activity during the French and Indian War. Explanations of historical matters are given only when they are judged necessary to explain Pownall more fully.

When the spelling of the names of persons, places, and topographic features is different from today's, the correct or modern spelling is placed

---

[1] "This interesting volume was sold by Messrs. Bangs, Bros., & Co., at New York, in 1854." Joseph Sabin, *A Dictionary of Books Relating to America, From its Discovery to the Present Time* (New York, J. Sabin, 1868-1936), No. 64835.

in small brackets ([]) within the body of the work; when names are completely different, the modern equivalent is given in a footnote. Since
names of persons and places given in the marginal notes appear in the
body of the book, no bracketed respellings appear in the marginal notes.

Source material has been used, whenever possible, for the location
and identification of persons, places, and events mentioned by Pownall;
secondary material has been used for the identification of modern
equivalents or present sites of colonial settlements, forts, Indian towns,
and trails. No citations are given for information obtained from general
reference works. Identification of topographic features described by
Pownall, but not named, has been made from modern maps. Names of
places and topographic features that appear in the same form in any of
the general reference works given in the bibliography receive no comment.

Pownall's corrected publication and holograph additions are
faithfully copied. His errors in spelling, punctuation, and sentence
structure are printed as they appear in the manuscript and printed
composite.

It is, of course, difficult to indicate typographically the very great
number of changes Pownall made in his edition of 1776; therefore, no
attempt has been made to do this.

The footnotes in this edition include those made by Pownall, for
both the published and unpublished editions; those made by Lewis
Evans, which were copied by Pownall; and those contributed by the
present editor. It is advisable, therefore, for the reader to examine carefully the *Guide to Footnotes* printed on page xvi.

* * * *

For typing the manuscript the editor thanks Miss Ann Retterer and
Mrs. Mildred Winner; for assistance in obtaining materials, members of
the staff of the University of Pittsburgh Library, Carnegie Library of
Pittsburgh, William L. Clements Library, Massachusetts Historical
Society Library, New England Historical and Genealogical Society
Library, Massachusetts Archives, New York Public Library, New York
Historical Society Library, Lehigh University Library, Henry E.
Huntington Library, Historical Society of Delaware Library, and the
Library of the Historical Society of Pennsylvania. Special thanks go to
the following individuals at the University of Pittsburgh: Dr. John W.
Oliver, head of the history department; and Drs. Russell J. Ferguson,
Leland D. Baldwin, and A. P. James of the same faculty; Dr. Arthur M.
Young, head of the classics department; Dr. Putnam F. Jones, head of

the English department; Dr. O. E. Jennings, director of the Carnegie Museum, Pittsburgh; and Mrs. Agnes L. Starrett, editor of the University of Pittsburgh Press. These special thanks go, too, to Dr. Douglas Adair, College of William and Mary; Dr. Julian P. Boyd, librarian of Princeton University; and Dr. Howard N. Eavenson of Pittsburgh, Pennsylvania. Particular gratitude goes to Dr. Lawrence H. Gipson, of Lehigh University, whose *Foreword* appears in this volume, and whose untiring interest and constructive criticism have been a chief source of inspiration; to Dr. A. L. Robinson, acting librarian, University of Pittsburgh, who made this publication a library project; and to my husband whose patience made the whole work possible.

LOIS MULKEARN

University of Pittsburgh,
Pittsburgh, Pennsylvania
July 17, 1948

GUIDE TO FOOTNOTES

Thomas Pownall's note } Pownall's note	Footnotes copied from 1776 edition.
Pownall's note for revised } and enlarged edition	Additions and corrected notes made by Pownall for revised edition.
Lewis Evans' note } Evans' note	Lewis Evans' notes published in Pownall's 1776 edition.

THE
PREFACE
TO THE FIRST EDITION[1]

Philadelphia. Aug. 9, 1755.

THE Map,[2] which these Sheets accompany, and which they are intended to explain, is presented to the Public, when a longer Time was indeed necessary to have given it the Degree of Correctness that was intended it. But the Conjuncture of Affairs in America,[3] and the generous Assistance of the Assembly of Pennsylvania,[4] have brought it to Light, when the Public will, it is hoped, receive Advantages from it, that will render an Apology for its premature Publication needless; and think it worthy the Encouragement of a Body who devote the Public Money to the Public Service.

It comprizes such an Extent, as is connected with that very valuable Country on the Ohio, which is now the Object of the British and French Policy, and the different Routs of both Nations thither. The Lake Ontario is equally open to both; to the One by the River St. Lawrence; to the other by the Rivers Hudson, Mohocks [Mohawk], and Seneca. But the French having, 30 Years ago, fixed themselves on the Streights of Niagara, by building Fortresses on Lands confessedly British, secured the Key on that Side to all the Country Westward. Those in Power see at last its Consequence, and are projecting the Recovery of it; and with great Judgement, for that Purpose, are establishing[5] a Naval Force on

---

[1]This preface is a copy of the preface to Lewis Evans' *Geographical, Historical, Political, Philosophical and Mechanical Essays. The First, Containing an Analysis of a General Map of the Middle British Colonies in America* . . . (Philadelphia, B. Franklin and D. Hall, 1755), pp. iii-iv. This essay is reprinted in Lawrence H. Gipson's *Lewis Evans* . . . (Philadelphia, Historical Society of Pennsylvania, 1939), preface, pp. 143-144. Thomas Pownall has made a few minor changes in words and phrases.

[2]*A General Map of the Middle British Colonies, in America* . . . By Lewis Evans, 1755. Engraved by Ja⁸ Turner in Philadelphia. Published according to Act of Parliament, by Lewis Evans, June 23. 1755 and sold by R. Dodsley, in Pall-Mall, London, & by the Author in Philadelphia.

[3][Thomas Pownall's note for revised and enlarged

edition] At the commencement of the last Warr in America, 1755.
"No doubt refers to the rapidly increasing encroachments of France on the back settlements." Henry N. Stevens, *Lewis Evans. His Map of the Middle British Colonies in America* (3d ed., London, H. Stevens, Son and Stiles, 1924), p. 9.

[4]The Province of Pennsylvania voted Lewis Evans £50 toward the expense of having this map engraved and printed. Pennsylvania (Colony) General Assembly. House of Representatives, *Votes and Proceedings of the House of Representatives of the Province of Pennsylvania* . . . *from 15th Day of October, 1744 to September 30, 1758* (Phila., Henry Miller, 1744), IV, 330, 334, 481.

[5][Pownall's note for revised and enlarged edition] Vida *Appendix* to the *Administration of the British*

Lake Ontario, as very necessary in the Recovery and securing of it. The Issue of this Enterprize will have great Influence on our Affairs, and of all Things it becomes the Colonies to push it on with Vigour. If they succeed here, the Remainder of the Work will be easy; and nothing so, without it. The English have several Ways to Ohio; but far the best is by Potomack[1] [Potomac].

By reason of the little Acquaintance the Public has with these remoter Parts, where the Country is yet a Wilderness, and the Necessity of knowing the Ways of travelling there, especially by Water, in the Map is pointed out the Nature of the several Streams; as where rapid, gentle, or obstructed with Falls, and consequently more or less fitted for Inland Navigation with Canoes, Boats, or larger Vessels; and where the Portages are made at the Falls, or from one River, Creek, or Lake to another. And for distinguishing the Extent of the Marine Navigation, the Places that the Tide reaches, in the several Rivers, are pointed out. And in these sheets, both the Marine and Inland Navigation are treated of at Length.

As the Nature of the Soil and Streams depend upon the Elevation and Depression of the Land, I have particularly explained here the different Stages that it is divided into. It were to be wished, that we had like Accounts of all Countries; as such would discover to us great Regularity, where an inattentive Observer would imagine there was nothing but Confusion; and at the same Time explain the Climates, the Healthiness, the Produce, and Conveniences for Habitations, Commerce, and Military Expeditions, to a judicious Reader in a few Pages, better than Volumes of Remarks on Places, drawn without these Distinctions.

To render this Map useful in Commerce, and in ascertaining the Boundaries of Lands, the Time of High Water at the Full and Change of the Moon, and the Variation of the Magnetical Needle, are laid down. But as these deserve particular Explanations, I have, for want of Room, concluded to treat of them at large in a separate Essay.[2]

Along the Western Margin of the Map is drawn a Line representing

---

Colonies where the Reader will see the Proposition of this measure as made to the Congress mett at Albany by Governor Pownall.

[1]For criticism and Evans' defense of this statement read Lewis Evans' *Geographical, Historical, Political, Philosophical and Mechanical Essays Number II containing a Letter Representing the Impropriety of sending Forces to Virginia . . . Published*

in the New York Mercury, No. 178, January 5, 1756. With an Answer to so much thereof as concerns the Public (Philadelphia, Printed for the Author, 1756) and reprinted in Gipson's *Lewis Evans . . . op. cit.*, pp. 177-219.

[2]This essay was never written, for Lewis Evans died on June 11, 1756, a few days after the publication of his Essay Number II. Gipson, *op. cit.*, p. 77.

the greatest Lengths of Days and Nights (without Allowance for the Refraction) which will assist Travellers in forming some Judgment of the Latitude of Places, by the Help of their Watches only.

Though many of these Articles are almost peculiar to the Author's map, they are of no less Importance than any Thing that has yet had a Place amongst Geographers. But want of Room in the Plate has obliged me to leave out what would have very much assisted my Explanation of the Face of the Country, I mean a Section of it in several Directions; such would have exhibited the Rising and Falling of the Ground, and how elevated above the Surface of the Sea; what Parts are level, what rugged; where the Mountains rise, and how far they spread. Nor is this all that a perpendicular Section might be made to represent; for, as on the superficial Line, the Elevations, Depressions, outer Appearances, and Names of Places may be laid down; so within the Area of the Section, the Nature of the Soil, Substrata, and particular Fossils may be exprest. It was with Regret I was obliged to omit it. But in some future Maps of separate Colonies, I hope to be furnished with more Room.[1]

The present, late and antient Seats of the original Inhabitants are expressed in the Map; and though it might be imagined that several Nation are omitted, which are mentioned by Authors, it may be remarked, that Authors, for want of Knowledge in Indian Affairs, have taken every little Society for a separate Nation; whereas they are not truly more in Number than I have laid down. I have been something particular in these Sheets in representing the Extent of the Confederates or Five Nations; because whatever is theirs, is expressly acceded to the English by Treaty with the French.[2]

[1][Pownall's note for revised and enlarged edition] The Materials, so far as taken from the Itinerary Observations of the present Editor, which were in Part to have composed those Sections, are now inserted in the following *Topographical Description*.

[2]By the Treaties of Breda (1667) and Westminster (1673) the English gained control over all the Dutch lands in North America. These possessions included the land of the Iroquois. The Iroquois reaffirmed their possession by the Dongan Treaty (1684) and the sale of their lands to the English in 1701. Again this English sovereignty was reaffirmed in particular at their Lancaster Treaty (1744). The terms of the Treaties of Utrecht (1713) and Aix-la-Chapelle (1748) returned the French and English territory in North America, which was gained by Wars between them, to the respective owners before their conquests.

PREFACE

TO THE

SECOND AND THIRD EDITIONS[1]

Albemarle Street 1775

THE Western Division of this present Map was composed and published at the Commencement of the late War in America.[2] It was found by the Officers and Servants of the Crown to have such a Degree of Precision, that it was used by them both in England and in America,[3] and served every practical Purpose during the Warrs. Those who have served and travelled in America, have had few Occasions of correcting it; on the contrary, its Exactness as far as a general Map means to go, has generally been confirmed by Experience on the Spot. In any Transactions since the War, where local Precision has been necessary, this Map has been referred to, not simply in private but public Transactions, such as the great Indian Purchase and Cession.[4] The Boundaries by which the Propositions for the Purchase of Lands on the Ohio were made to the Boards of Trade and Treasury, were marked and settled on this Map.[5] When the Servants of the Crown proposed in the House of Commons the Clause for the Limits of the Government of Quebec; and when the Line of those Limits were there opposed, both Sides, with this Map in their Hands, argued from it.[6]

[1]This preface is in two parts. The first part (Albemarle Street, 1775) published in Pownall's *Topographical Descriptions* ... (1776), is here greatly revised and enlarged. The second part or preface to his self-styled third edition (Richmond Hill, 1784), is printed for the first time in this, a revised and enlarged edition.

[2]1755.

[3]*Evans' Maps* figured largely in Braddock's Campaign. The 1752 edition was used both in England and America. Prepublication copies of the 1755 edition were rushed to Braddock on his arrival in Virginia. Hazel Shields Garrison, "Cartography of Pennsylvania" in *Pennsylvania Magazine of History and Biography* (Philadelphia, Publication Fund of the Historical Society of Pennsylvania, 1877—), LIX (1935), 269.

[4]See "Map of the Frontiers of the Northern Colonies with the Boundary Line Established Between Them and the Indians at the Treaty Held by Sr. Will Johnson at Fort Stanwix in Nov'r 1768, Corrected and Improved from Evans Map. By Guy Johnson, Agt Indian Affairs." Sir William Johnson, *Papers of* . . . (Albany, University of the State of N.Y., 1921-39), VI, map opposite 450.

[5]See "Vandalia as Originally Plotted on Evans' Map." Thomas Perkins Abernethy, *Western Lands and the American Revolution* (N.Y., D. Appleton-Century Co., 1937), map opposite p. 39.

[6]Published debates on the Quebec Act are not in accord with this statement. See title page: Great Britain (1760-1820, George III) House of Commons, ... *Debates of the House of Commons in the Year 1774*, *of the Bill for Making More Effectual Provision for the Government of the Province of Quebec. Drawn up from the notes of Sir Henry Cavendish. With a Map of Canada, copied from the Second Edition of Mitchell's Map of North America referred to in the Debates* (London, Ridgway, 1839).

In Mr. Evans's First Publication of this Map, the Parts within Virginia were copied from Fry and Jefferson's Map[1] of that Province, a Work of great Merit, composed from actual Surveys, and published by Jefferys in 1751. It has in this Edition been improved by later Informations. A Map engraved by Jefferys, and called, 'A new and accurate Map of Virginia,' by John Henry,[2] was published 1770. I was in Hopes to have derived Information from this, but upon Examination of it, it appears to me to be a very inaccurate Compilation; defective in Topography; and not very attentive even to Geography; The Draughtsman or the Engraver has totally omitted the South Branch of Potômack [Potomac] River: Nor is that curious and interesting Piece of Information, the Communication between the Waters of Virginia and the Waters of the Ohio, which were known when this was published, marked in it. This Map of Mr. Henry has indeed the Division Lines of the Counties of the Province drawn on it, and if they are rightly drawn, it is certainly an Improvement: But while I doubt the Accuracy of the Geography, I cannot be assured of these.

If there be any Map of Maryland published since this of Evans's, I have never seen such. There have been many new Settlements and many Improvements made in that Country since this Map was published: I have applied to Quarters whence, I did suppose, there might be derived Information in these Matters, but without Success.

Mr. Scull[3] in 1770, published a new Edition[4] of his Uncle Nic. Scull's[5] Map of Pennsylvania,[6] published in 1759. Mr. Evans in his First Edition of his Map was greatly assisted by Mr. N. Scull. The western Parts of

[1]*A Map of the most inhabited part of Virginia containing the whole province of Maryland with part of Pensilvania, New Jersey and North Carolina.* Drawn by Joshua Fry and Peter Jefferson in 1751. Printed for Robt. Sayer at No. 53 in Fleet Street & Thos. Jefferys at the Corner of St. Martins Lane, Charing Cross, London.

[2]*A New and Accurate Map of Virginia Wherein most of the Counties are laid down from Actual Surveys. With a Concise Account of the Number of Inhabitants, the Trade, the Soil, and Produce of that Province* by John Henry. Engraved by Thomas Jefferys, Geographer to the King. London, February 1770, Published according to act of Parliament for the author, by Thos. Jefferys at the corner of St. Martins Lane, in the Strand.

[3]William Scull. Birth and death dates are unknown. Evidently he was a native Pennsylvanian who was assistant to Robert Erskine, geographer and surveyor general for the Continental Army under Washington, and was, in 1755, sheriff in Northumberland County, Pennsylvania. Garrison, *op. cit.*, pp. 277-78.

[4]*To the honourable Thomas Penn and Richard Penn, esquires, true and absolute proprietors and Governors of the Province of Pennsylvania and the territories thereunto belonging and to the honorable John Penn, esquire, lieutenant governor of the same, this map of the province of Pennsylvania is humbly dedicated by their most obedient serv't W. Scull.* Philadelphia, James Nevil, for the author, April 1st, 1770.

[5]Nicholas Scull (1687-1762) surveyor general of Pennsylvania, was William Scull's grandfather not his uncle. *Pennsylvania Archives*, 1st series (Phila., Joseph Severns & Co., 1852-56), VIII, 94.

[6]*To the honourable Thomas Penn and Richard Penn, this map of the improved part of the province of Pennsylvania is humbly dedicated by Nicholas Scull.* Philadelphia, J. Davis for the author, 1759.

this Province were in Evans's Map done with a Degree of Accuracy, which I do not find this New Map can any where essentially correct or amend. The Names of new Counties, Settlements, and Townships, erected since the First Publication, are in this Edition added from the New Map of 1770.[1]

I do not know of any printed Map of New Jersey in particular. A Projection of that Province, done by Mr. Alexander,[2] Surveyor General, in which were laid down all the Stations that have been occasionally fixed by Astronomical Observation, and all the Lines which have been run by actual Survey, in the Course of the several Disputes in which that Province was involved between the East and Western, the Eliza-beth Town, and other Proprietaries, as also with the Province New York, was very obligingly copied for and given to me by his Son Lord Sterling.[3] The Parts of Mr. Evans's Map within that Province have been corrected from these Papers. The Boundary Line betwixt this Province and New York was drawn on this Map by Capt. Holland,[4] who was employed to run it.

There has, (in 1778) since the time[5] of the publication of this work, been published by Mr. Faden A Map of New Jersey[6] which is said to be laid down in ye parts near the boundary Line betwixt that Province & New York from a survey made by Lieut. Ratzer[7] under ye Orders of the Commissioners appointed to settle it & in the Northern Parts in general from a Survey by Gerard Barker, in the possession of the Earl of Dunmore.[8] I have examined this and compared with Mr. Alexander's

[1]William Scull's *Map, op. cit.*

[2]James Alexander (1691-1756), surveyor general for the Province of New Jersey.

[3]William Alexander (1726-1783), son of James Alexander.

[4]Samuel Holland, British surveyor general of lands for the Northern district of America. In 1767 while serving in this capacity Captain Holland was one of the Commissioners appointed to settle the controversy concerning the boundary line between the provinces, New York and New Jersey. *Documents relating to the Colonial history of the state of New Jersey* (Newark, Daily Advertiser Printing House, *et al.*, 1880-1928), IX, 624. (Hereafter cited as *New Jersey Archives*). Holland's appointment to service in North America may have been made in 1765 for by 1772 he had spent seven years in survey-ing part of the coast of North America. In a letter to General Thomas Gage he estimates the survey will take five years longer. Thomas Gage, *The Correspondence of . . .* , edited by Clarence Edwin

Carter (New Haven, Yale University Press, 1933), II, 601.

[5]1776.

[6]First published in 1777. "The province of New Jersey, divided into east and west, commonly called the Jerseys. Drawn from the survey made in 1769 by order of the commissioners appointed to settle the partition line between the provinces of New York & New Jersey by Bernard Ratzer, and from another large survey of the northern parts by Gerard Barker, Engraved by Wm. Faden. London, W. Faden, Dec. 1, 1777." Wm. Faden, *The North American Atlas* (London, for W. Faden, 1777), no. 22.

[7]Bernard Ratzer, British Army engineer. Leland DeWitt Baldwin, *Pittsburgh, the Story of a City* (Pittsburgh, University of Pittsburgh Press, 1938), p. 57.

[8]John Murray, *4th Earl of Dunmore* (1730-1809). Lord Dunmore was governor of New York, 1770-71, governor of Virginia, 1771-76, and governor of the Bahamas, 1787-96.

Surveys of Lines & Patents and find nothing new or more detailed than what I had seen.[1]

A Map of New York and New Jersey,[2] published by T. Jefferys, to which Publication the Name of Capt. Holland is put,[3] without his Knowledge or Consent, is little more than a Copy of those Parts contained in Evans's Map, or, if not a Copy, a Compilation from the same Materials on a larger Scale, without any essential Amendment, without scarce a Difference, except in the County of Albany, corrected from a Map of that County which Capt. Holland copied for me in 1756, from Draughts of Mr. Bleecker,[4] Deputy Surveyor in that County. The only Parts contained in the Map, thus published by Jefferys, which were surveyed by Capt. Holland are, "the Passage of the Hudson's [Hudson] River through the Highlands, "and the Parts on the Banks from Viskill[5] to Croton's [Croton] River," a Distance of about 20 Miles; and even in these Parts the Compiler has omitted to notice that remarkable Pass Martlaer's Rock.[6] The Boundary Lines of the great Patents and Manors; of some of the Counties; and some of the new Townships are drawn over this Map in their Squares: But I am not able to collect any Improvement in it either as to Topography or Geography. The present Jefferys[7] is, as I understand, in Possession of an excellent Draught of the Province of New York,[8] done under the Direction of Governor Tryon:[9] I hope the Publication will be made in a Manner worthy of it. This Map[10] is now (1779) published by Mr. Faden, a very accurate, industrious

[1]This paragraph is a 1784 addition to the 1776 publication of Pownall's *Topographical Descriptions*.

[2]"The Provinces of New York and New Jersey with part of Pensilvania, and the Province of Quebec Drawn by Major Holland, Surveyor General of the Northern District in America, Corrected and Improved from the original materials by Governor Pownall, M.P. 1776. London, printed for Robert Sayer & John Bennett 17 Aug., 1776." Thomas Jefferys, *The American Atlas* ... (London, R. Sayer and J. Bennett, 1776), no. 17.

[3][Pownall's note] Advertisement published by Capt. Holland, "Nor have I at any Time published or given my Consent to the publishing of any Plan, Map, or Survey now extant, that bears my Name. Sam. Holland."

[4]John Rutger Bleeker, (bap. 1713-1800), surveyor of Albany County and deputy surveyor for the Northern Department under Samuel Holland. The name is written both Bleeker and Bleecker.

[5]Fishkill Creek, New York.

[6]Now Constitution Island. This island projects halfway across the Hudson River and forms the left bank opposite West Point. Edward C. Boynton, *History of West Point* ... (London, Sampson Low, Son, & Marston, 1864), pp. 20-21.

[7]Evidently William Jefferys to whom Library of Congress, Division of Maps attributes *The American Atlas. op. cit.*, for T. Jefferys died in 1771. U.S. Library of Congress. Division of Maps, *A List of Maps of America in the Library of Congress* (Washington, Government Printing Office, 1901), p. 505. Hereafter cited as Phillips, *List of Maps*.

[8]*A Chorographical map of the province of New York, divided into Counties, Manors, etc. Compiled from actual surveys deposited in the patent office at New York by order of Gen. William Tryon*, by Claude Joseph Sauthier. London, W. Faden, Jan. 1, 1779.

[9]William Tryon (1729-1788) lieutenant governor North Carolina, 1765-1771, and governor New York, 1771 to the Revolution. In 1777 Tryon obtained permission to command a force of Loyalists in America, a commission he carried until 1780 when he was forced by ill health to retire and return to England.

[10]See *note 8*, above.

young Man. I saw some of the Proofs of it & made some few corrections in it. Mr. Faden has done it Justice in his attention to accuracy & by his skill in the engraving. As the scale gives room for such, I wish the Soundings up ye Hudson's [Hudson] R^r & several noted points of land on Long Island & in the Sound had been marked on it. Perhaps before any future impression these things may be putt into the plate.

Of New England there has been no new Map[1] published since that by Dr. Douglas,[2] dedicated to the several Assemblies of Messachuset's [Massachusetts] Bay, New Hampshire, Connecticut, and Rhode Island. So far as that went it was composed from actual Surveys of the Boundary Lines of the several Provinces, Colonies, Grants, and Townships: The Courses of the Rivers and the remarkable Mountains were traced and fixed with great Care and Attention. What there was wanting to a compleat Map of New England, is now added from later Information, and from later Draughts and Surveys[3] deposited at the Board of Trade, which the Earl of Dartmouth[4] permitted me to have copied for the Benefit of the Public. These new Parts which I have added are plotted down in the Form in which I think every Map which can offer to give the Face of the Country, should be drawn, tracing the Features of it, and not in Default of that, filling up the Map with Writing. Instead of Writing I have put *Figures of Reference*, and the Writing is put in the Margin and in other blank Places. The Surveys which give this Map its Accuracy in the Maritime Parts of New England were chiefly made by Capt. Holland,[5] or by his Deputies under his Direction.

Many Tracks which the Geographer will see marked in the western Parts of the Map, as it was first published at Philadelphia in 1755, were mere Indian or Traders Paths through the Wilderness,

. . . . .per avia quâ Sola nunquam

Trita rotis. . . . .

but are now in the Course of a very few Years become great Waggon Roads, & are here mark'd as such.

Et modo quae fuerat Semita, facta via.

[1]Map of New England published by Dr. Douglass. *Plan of the British Dominions of New England in North America Composed from Actual Surveys.* By Dr. William Douglas. Engraved by R. W. Seale, London, 1753. "Published by the executors of dr. William Douglas from his original draft." Phillips, *List of Maps, op. cit.,* p. 469.

[2]William Douglass (1691-1752).

[3]See Great Britain. Board of Trade and Plantations, *List of Maps, Plans, &c belonging to the Right*

Honble the Lords Commissioners for Trade and Plantations under the care of Francis Aegidius Assiotti, Draughtsman, 1780. P. R. O. CO 326/15.

[4]William Legge, *2nd Earl of Dartmouth* (1731-1801). Dartmouth was President of the Board of Trade and Plantations, 1765-66, Secretary of State for the Colonies and President of the Board of Trade and Plantations, 1772-1775, Lord privy seal, 1775-1782.

[5]See *note* 4, p. 7.

Many *Indian Settlements*, being then merely a *Collection of Wigwams* or Cabins, must now in this Edition of 1755[1] marked as COUNTY TOWNS. Many other Particulars marked in the Map, and noticed in the original Analysis, which were, 20 Years ago, Matter of practical Information, and useful to the Service, ceasing, perhaps now to have that Use, may yet be amusing as *Matters of curious Antiquity*, become so at this early Period. It will be curious in a few Years, as the Face of the Country changes and is totally altered, to view in this Map, and to read in this Description, what it was in its natural State, and how the Settlements began to expand, and had extended themselves in 20 Years.

A pirated Copy of this Map, soon after it came to England, was in a most audacious Manner published by the late Thomas Jefferys,[2] under a false Pretence of Improvements, Lewis Evans's Name was put to it; and this Plagiarism was falsely sold as Evans's Map improved; by which that very laborious and ingenious, but poor Man, was deprived of the Benefit of his Work. The Engraver was so totally ignorant of the Principles on which the Original was formed, that although he traced the Lines of the Rivers and Roads in the usual Way, yet it can scarce be called a Copy. The Mountains in America, which give the real Features to the Face of it, run in Ridges of a specific Direction, do in Places here and there run up into Peaks; do in others end abruptly in Knobs and Bluff-points; do interlock and have Gaps; all which Particulars were in the Original with a scrupulous Attention plotted and set down; as also the Parts where these Ridges spread into hilly Land. The Officer or the Geographer will look in vain for this Precision in the pirated Copy. The blundering Copyist thought, that the filling the Places where he happened to meet with the Word, *Mountains*, with the Engraver's common Marks scratched in at random, was doing the Business, by which he has put Mountains where they are not; and has converted great Swamps into Mountains; and in other Parts has totally omitted the Marks of high Ground, because he did not understand those Marks which were used to express such high Ground, without presuming to give the Range and Form, where that was not yet known. So far as respects the Face of the Country, this Thing of Jefferys might as well be a Map of the Face of the Moon. Further, in the Original there was

---

[1]Since this is a correction made in 1784, Pownall may have intended the date, 1785.

[2]*A General Map of the Middle British Colonies in America: viz. Virginia, Maryland, Delaware, Pensilvania . . . By Lewis Evans. Corrected and improved in the addition of the line of forts on the back settlements*, by Thomas Jefferys. London, R. Sayer & T. Jefferys, 1758.
Henry Stevens says that Pownall unjustly accused Jefferys, for he, Jefferys, merely reissued T. Kitchin's 1756 edition of Evans' *Map*. Stevens, *op. cit.*, p. 16.

observed a scrupulous Caution not to deceive; the Parts which were drawn from Report and Computation, and collected from Journals, are in the Original engraved in a slighter Manner, and very differently from those Parts which are laid down from actual Surveys; neither the Eye, the Ideas, nor the Spirit of the Copyist went to the Marking this; and all Parts stand equal in Authority in his false Copy.

The Plate of this blundering Copy has, in the Course of Trade, by Purchase, fallen into the Hands of Mr. Sayer[1] of Fleet-Street, a Man of Reputation in a very extensive Line of Business. He very honourably told me, that if the Plate[2] stood as a single Article in his Shop, he would destroy it directly; but that it made Part of an Atlas[3] already published by him; and was also Part of another very soon to be published[4] by him, which cost many thousand Pounds; and that he did not know how to take it out of these Collections. I can only say, it will disgrace any Collection in which it stands, and that I am sorry it is to disgrace any coming from a Shop in which there are so many valuable Maps and Charts.[5]

Richmond hill, 1784.

The very great Sale which the following Work has experienced hath intirely taken off the last impression; although it consisted of Double the number of Copies usually put into one Edition. It has been now three or four years out of Print. I have been applied to repeatedly from abroad as well as in England, to put out another Edition. In the year 1779 I undertook to revise it. I look'd out my own papers. I applied also to Lord George Germain[6] at that time the Secretary of State to whom his Majesty had assigned the American department, for leave of access to such geographical papers, & surveys of different parts in the Southern Colonies, were in his office. He granted this Favor with a degree of politeness & liberality which I beg here to make my acknowledgements to. I collated and . . . [The remainder of this preface is missing.]

[1]Robert Sayer.

[2]See *note* 2, page 10.

[3]Thomas Jefferys, engraver, *A General Topography of North America and the West Indies* (London, for R. Sayer & T. Jefferys, 1768). Lewis Evans' *Map* is number 32.

[4]T. Jefferys, engraver, *The American Atlas . . .* (London, R. Sayer & J. Bennett, 1775). It is interesting to note that the 1776 edition of this atlas, unlike the 1775 edition, does not include the Lewis Evans *Map*. See U.S. Library of Congress. Division of Maps, *A List of Geographical Atlases in the Library of Congress . . .* compiled under the direction of Philip Lee Phillips (Washington, Government Printing Office, 1909-20), I, nos. 1165-1166. Hereafter cited as Phillips, *List of Atlases*.

[5][Pownall's note for revised and enlarged edition] He has had it since corrected from my Map for the purpose of making part of a Collection in a Pocket Atlas of North America. R. Sayer and J. Bennet, *The American Military Pocket Atlas . . .* London, for R. Sayer & J. Bennet 1776. Known as the "Holster Atlas" since it was made for the use of mounted British officers. Phillips *List of Atlases, op. cit.*, I, no. 1206—Ed.

[6]George Sackville Germain (1716-1785). Known as Lord George Sackville, 1720-1770, and as Lord George Germain, 1770-1782.

A

TOPOGRAPHICAL DESCRIPTION

Of Such Parts Of

NORTH AMERICA

As Are Contained In

THE MAP

The Parts of this Work marked with inverted Commas[1] are reprinted from Mr. Lewis Evans's Analysis, printed in Philadelphia 1755; the other Parts are by Governor Pownall.

"AS different Parts of this Map are done with very different Proportion of Exactness, Justice to the Public, requires my distinguishing the Degree of Credit every Part deserves; and to make some Recompence for the Defects of those Places, where no actual Surveys have been yet made, by giving such a Description as the Nature of the Subject will admit; which may, at this Time, be of as much Consequence as the nicest Surveys destitute of this Advantage.

"The British Settlements are done, for the greater Part, from actual Surveys. The Latitudes of many Places taken with good Instruments, and the Longitudes of Philadelphia and Boston, observed by different Persons, and well agreeing, give a Foundation for the Projection of the Map. And as Philadelphia is a fine City, situate near the Center of the British Dominions on this Continent; and as, whether it is inferior to others in Wealth, or Number of Houses, or not, it far excels in the Progress of Letters, mechanic Arts, and the public Spirit of its Inhabitants; I thought this Reason sufficient for paying it the particular Distinction of making it the first Meridian of America. And a Meridian here I thought the more necessary, that we may determine the Difference of the Longitude of Places by Mensuration; a Method far excelling the best astronomical Observations; and as we may be led into several Errors by always reckoning from remote Meridians, those who have only seen the Plans and Maps of this City, must be cautioned not to give

Philadelphia made the first Meridian.

---

[1]In this present edition the inverted commas have been replaced by quotation marks.

any of them Credit, for it extends only on the West Side of Delaware,[1] about a Mile and a Half in Length, and about Half a Mile in its greatest Breadth. Near the Western Extremity is the Statehouse, the Spot proposed for my Meridian to be drawn through.[2]

"The Longitude at the Top is computed from Philadelphia; at Bottom from London, according to the late Mr. Thomas Godfrey's Observations[3] and my own at Philadelphia. And I was induced to give these the Preference to that made at New York by Mr. Burnet,[4] because of their Agreement with Mr. Th. Robie's Observations[5] at Boston. The Distance from Philadelphia to Conohasset [Cohasset], at the Mouth of Bound Brook, on Massachuset [Massachusetts] Bay, has, the far greater Part, been measured in long Lines, on public Occasions, and the Rest is supplied by Surveys[6] of particular Tracts of Land and Roads. And if Bound Brook is 19 or 20 Miles Eastward of the Meridian of Boston, as I imagine it is, there is no sensible Difference between the Observations, but what arises from the Difference of 4° between the Two Places, as laid down.

"The principal Observations of Latitude are these,

Boston, – – – – – – –	42 : 25	
N. Boundary of Connecticut, –	42 : 2	} By Governor Burnet[7]
New York, – – – – – –	40 : 42	
N. Station Point, – – – –	41 : 40	By the Jersey and N. York Commissioners 1719[8]
Philadelphia, – – – – –	39 : 57	
Shamokin, – – – – – –	40 : 40	
Owege, – – – – – –	41 : 55	} By L. Evans[9]
Onondaga, – – – – – –	42 : 55	
Oswego, – – – – – –	43 : 17	
Sandy Hook, – – – – –	40 : 28	

[1][Pownall's note] This was written in 1755.

[2]Quoted from Evans' *Analysis, op. cit.*, p. 1; reprinted in Gipson's *Lewis Evans, op. cit.*, p. 145.

[3]Thomas Godfrey (1704-1749). Godfrey's observations are recorded by Lewis Evans. *A Map of Pensilvania, New Jersey, New York . . . By Lewis Evans,* 1749. Published by Lewis Evans March 25, 1749, According to Act of Parliament, Philadelphia, Benjamin Franklin? 1749.

[4]William Burnet (1688-1729), colonial governor of New York, New Jersey, and Massachusetts. "Observations" in Royal Society of London, *Philosophical Transactions . . .* (London, The Society, 1665-date), no. 385 (1724).

[5]Thomas Robie (died 1729). "Meteorological Observations," *ibid.*, nos. 270-272 (1701).

[6][Evans' note] We call nothing *Surveys* but actual Mensurations with a Chain, and the Course taken with a good surveying Instrument. Courses with a Pocket Compass and computed Distances we call *Computations.*

[7]See *note* 4, this page.

[8]Read "Tripartite Indenture settling the North Partition Point between New Jersey & New York," in New Jersey *Archives, op. cit.*, IV, 349-99.

[9]These observations may have been made in 1743 when Lewis Evans traveled with John Bartram to Onondaga. John Bartram, *Observations on the Inhabitants, Climate, Soil, Rivers, Productions, Animals and other matters worthy of Notice . . . In his Travels from Pensilvania to Onondaga, Oswego and the Lake Ontario* (London, J. Whiston and B. White, 1751).

Ray's Town,	– – – – –	39 : 59	}	By Col. Fry[1]
Shanoppen's Town,	– – –	40 : 26		
S. Side of S. St. Louis	– – –	45 : 18	}	By Champlain, in 1603[2]
Ville Marie	– – – – – –	45 : 27		

"Though there have been many other Observations made in several Places in the Settlements, I have always chosen to adjust their Situations by Actual Mensurations; because many of the Instruments yet used are not sufficiently accurate to determine the Latitude of Places with Nicety."[3]

Many very accurate Observations of the Latitude and Longitude of many Places have been since made, which chiefly confirm the Positions in this Present Map—where they differed materially it has been corrected by them.

"A Map I published of PENNSYLVANIA, NEW JERSEY, NEW YORK, and DELAWARE[4] in 1749,[5] is reduced to a smaller Scale in this,[6] and forms those Four Colonies. The Errors are rectified, the principal of which were, Albany placed too far North, Shamokin too far West, and all the Route thence to Oswego Five Miles altogether too much North; besides several Imperfections in Places which later Observations and Discoveries have given us Knowledge of. In the first Impression[7] of my former Map I committed some Mistakes in the Names of Places near the Entrance of Delaware Bay on the West Side[d8]

Capes of
Delaware.
d H d

[1]Joshua Fry (1700?-1754). William West reported this observation by Col. Fry to be 40°27'. Pennsylvania (Colony). Provincial Council, *Minutes of . . . from its organization to the termination of the Proprietary Government* (Phila., Jo Severns & Co. [and others], 1852-53) V, 761. Hereafter cited as *Colonial Records of Pennsylvania*.

[2]Samuel de Champlain (1567-1635). The latitude for the vicinity of Ville Marie is given by Champlain in 1603 as "45° and some minutes." Samuel de Champlain. *The Works of . . .* translated . . . by H. P. Biggar (Toronto, Champlain Society, 1922), I, 153. The latitude for the south side or end of Lake St. Louis is given by Champlain in 1613 as 45°18' *ibid.* (1925), II, 261.

[3]Quoted from Evans' *Analysis*, pp. 2-3; reprinted in Gipson's *Lewis Evans*, pp. 146-47.

[4][Evans' note] So the *Three Lower Counties of Newcastle, Kent, and Sussex, upon Delaware*, were called before they were annexed to Pennsylvania, when this Name was given in Contradistinction to the *Three Upper* Counties of Chester, Philadelphia, and Bucks. As this Name exceeds in Length and Barbarity all the Savage Ones in my Title put together,

I have restored the Colony its old Name of *Delaware*.

[5]*A Map of Pensilvania, New Jersey, New York and the Three Delaware Counties. By Lewis Evans, 1749, op. cit.*

[6]Refers to Evans' *Map* of 1755.

[7]*A Map of Pensilvania . . . , By Lewis Evans, 1749, op. cit.*

[8][Pownall's note] Upon this first Reference, by Letters in the Margin, it may be proper to acquaint the Reader, that the Reference is to the Letters H and d in the Margin of the Map. The Capitals are on the eastern Margin between the Parallels of Latitudes; the small Letters in the upper Margin between the Meridians of Longitude. They are meant to direct the Reader (without perpetually repeating Degrees and Minutes of Latitude and Longitude) to a ready Manner of finding any Place mentioned in these Sheets. For instance, in this first Case: Look for H in the eastern Margin, and for d in the Northern; and in the Square where the Parallels of Latitude between which H is, intersect with the Meridians of Longitude between which d is, the Reader will find the Place referred to.

and in my Attempt to rectify them, in the second Edition,[1] did but add to the Confusion. I have since had an Opportunity of making a thorough Enquiry into this Affair, and conclude, that the Names which the Places thereabouts are now called by, and are the same as laid down in my general Map, are the only Names they ever had,[2] and still retain amongst those acquainted with them; as Lewes, Whorekill Road, Cape Hinlopen, False Cape, and Fenwick's Island: Excepting, that Mr. William Penn called Cape Hinlopen by the Name of Cape *James;* and Whorekill *Lewes,* on his first Arrival in 1682; the former is scarce known at this Day, and the Name *Lewes* is confined to the Town, while the Creek still retains the Name of *The Whorekill.*

"All must admit that the present Names are rightly laid down; but what is related in regard to the ancient Names must be Understood as only my Opinion. There are others who think, on no less Opportunity of forming a Judgement, that Cape Hinlopen was formerly called Cape Cornelius; and that *Fenwick's Island* was the *False Cape,* or *Cape Hinlopen* of the Dutch, and others, till the Arrival of the English in those Parts under Mr. Penn.

"To complete what was left imperfect in my former Map, especially in *New York,* I have been in a particular Manner assisted by Mr. William Alexander,[3] whose numerous Observations and Collections add greatly to the Merit of this Part of the present One, as they will Authority with all who know him."[4]

The upper Part of the County of Albany, in New York, together with the Country on the Mohawks [Mohawk] River, is corrected and rendered more perfect in its Topography, from a Map[5] laid down by John Rulse Bleecker,[6] Deputy to the Surveyor of the Province, which Map is composed from actual Surveys as far up the River as Orhiscony [Oriskany], the rest is traced by the Journals of the Oswego Traders, and of this Deputy Surveyor himself.

[1] *A Map of Pensilvania, New Jersey, New York and the Three Delaware Counties: By Lewis Evans, 1749, The Second Edition, July 1752;* Reprinted in Gipson, *op. cit.*

[2] Read Gipson, *ibid.,* p. 47.

[3] [Pownall's note for the revised and enlarged edition] This Gentleman afterward took the Title of Earl of Sterling and was a General Officer in the Service of the States.

[4] Quoted from Evans' *Analysis,* pp. 3-4; reprinted in Gipson's *Lewis Evans,* pp. 147-48.

[5] Probably a "Map of Albany County with the Country of the Five Nations," 1750-1770?, By Jno. R. Bleecker. Manuscript map in the New York Historical Society.

[6] [Pownall's note for the revised and enlarged edition] This Man though a good practical surveyor being no Draughtsman, Capt. Holland drew the Map for me at Albany in 1756. It was the first Draught he made in America.

John Rutger Bleecker. Here Mr. Pownall has confused the middle name, Rutger, with the middle name of the Indian interpreter, John Rulse Bleecker—Ed.

The Parts about Lake George, Wood Creek, and the Drowned Lands are corrected from a Draught[1] of that Part given to me by my Friend the late Sir William Johnson;[2] the Figures on it are placed for Reference to the Names written in a vacant Part of the Map, as also to the Account that I shall give of it in this Description, as there was not room to write the long Indian Names by which the several Parts here were marked; this Draught was made for Practice while he commanded there, and has on it all the Indian Paths and Tracks of the Scouts; I have examined it by the Journals of the Scouts which I have by me,[c] Two or Three of which I shall annex, as giving the best Account of the Face of the Country in those Parts; I have also compared it with the Surveys, since made, which lie at the Board of Trade, but find nothing which exceeds this in its Topography. The River St. Francis, and the Communication by Land between that River and the River Connecticut, is corrected and laid down in the present Map from an actual Survey[3] given to me by Capt. Holland.[4] It was made by Mr. Grant[5] his Deputy.

    When Mr. Evans rectified the northerly Projection of some Parts, in his Map published in 1749, and placed Albany lower (and right as now is confirmed by the Observations made by Order of the Governor of New York) in Lat. 42° 36'. He omitted to bring down the Parts of the Hudson River above Albany, by which Means the Distance betwixt Albany and Saratoga remained Five Miles too great, and the Distance betwixt Saratoga and Fort Edward a Mile at least. I have in this Edition corrected the upper Parts of this River from Bleecker's Survey, which Corrections fortunately coincided with my Friend Sir William Johnson's Map; as also with a Sketch wherein the Courses and Distances between Fort Edward,[6] the Old Fort Ann,[7] and Lake George, are laid down by Mr. Grant who ran them. The relative Distances are thus rectified to great Exactness; but the Whole of this Map in these Parts (as also Lake

c Vide Appendix

C c

[1] "Johnson's Map of Lake George and Vicinity." William Johnson *Papers . . . op. cit.,* II, opp., 422.

[2] Sir William Johnson (1715-1774), superintendent of Indian Affairs in the Northern department.

[3] Probably "A Plan of a Survey made to explore the Country for a road between Connecticut River & St. Francis," attributed to Hugh Finlay. Manuscript map, in Library of Congress, Map Division. Phillips, *List of Maps, op. cit.,* p. 248.

[4] [Pownall's note] Capt. Holland is surveyor general of Canada, and of the Northern District of America.

[5] James Grant, deputy surveyor under Samuel Holland, surveyor general for the Northern department.

[6] Built in 1755 at the Great Carrying Place on the Hudson River, about 45 miles north of Albany. On the present site of Fort Edward, New York.

[7] At the Wood Creek terminus of the Great Carrying Place between Hudson River and Lake Champlain. Built about 1709. On the present site of Fort Ann, New York.

Champlain and Montreal)[1] remaining still projected near Three Miles too much to the North, the South End of Lake George is about Three Miles more Northward than the New York Observations place it, being in North Latitude 43° 16′ 12″. It was proper I should mark this, but I believe it will not be thought of much Consequence.

The Observations were as follow, which I insert, that where there is any Difference the Reader may compare them, and decide for himself.

	°	′	″
Light-house at Sandy-hook – – – – – – –	40	27	40
New York Fort – – – – – – – – – –	40	41	50
Albany – – – – – – – – – – – – –	42	36	0
South End of Lake George – – – – – –	43	16	12
Crown Point – – – – – – – – – – –	43	50	7
Windmill Point – – – – – – – – – –	44	59	18
Point au Pines – – – – – – – – – – –	44	58	48
Moor's Point – – – – – – – – – – –	45	0	0

"Besides a general Map of Connecticut, which the Rev. Mr. Clap[2] favoured me with, I have been assisted in drawing the EASTERN COL-ONIES now States by Memorials, preserved in Douglas's [Douglass'] Summary,[3] of the Colony Lines, as actually run round Three Sides of CONNECTICUT and RHODE ISLAND, and between NEW HAMP-SHIRE and MASSACHUSET [TS]; and the Extension of these Lines in Two Places to Hudson's [Hudson] River. As for that said to be run from Deerfield to this River, there is certainly a Mistake of several Miles in the length of it. These, with several Surveys by Messieurs Helm, Kellog, and Chandler, amongst which is an entire one of Connecticut River from No. 4[e] to the North Side of Connecticut Colony,[f] given me by Mr. Pownall,[4] *together with his own itinerary Observations on the Face of the Country, the Ranges and Bearings of the Hills, and Distances of Places*, contribute to give these Parts a great Degree of Exactness. Nor am I obliged, in these Parts alone, to this Gentleman, but for the Corrections of many Articles, which had escaped me in the former Map, and for some other valuable Papers he procured me."[5]

e C b   f D b

[1][Pownall's note] According to an Observation made by Monsieur Gillion, Montreal is in North Lat. 45 27. Variation 10 38 West.

[2]Rev. Thomas Clap (1703-67) president of Yale College, 1740-1764.

[3]William Douglass, *A Summary, Historical and Political of the First Planting, Progressive Improvements, and Present State of the British Settlements in North America* (Boston, New England, printed: London, reprinted for R. Baldwin, 1755), 2v. Dr. Douglass summarizes the surveys and settlements of boundary lines between several New England Colonies.

[4]Thomas Pownall.

[5]Reprinted from Evans' *Analysis*, p. 4; reprinted in Gipson's *Lewis Evans*, p. 148.

The Remainder of Connecticut River to its Spring Head is now first published and added to this Map: It is laid down from an actual Survey made of it by Mr. Grant, one of Capt. Holland's Deputies, which is deposited at the Board of Trade, a Work of great Labour and Merit.

The Provinces now States Massachuset's [Massachusetts] Bay and New Hampshire are now first added to this Map. The Parts contained within the Old Province, and within the Colony of Plymouth, are laid down from Dr. Douglas's [Douglass'] Map[1] corrected by myself from particular Surveys and other local Informations which came to my Knowledge during my residence therein. Capt. Holland's Surveys do not extend to these Parts. Dr. Douglas's [Douglass'] original Map is the *Fond* for the Interior Parts of New Hampshire. Capt. Holland's Surveys[2] of those Parts correct this, and give it its Accuracy. The Maritime Parts of New England from Rhode Island to Kenebaëg [Kennebec] River, and from Penobskaëg [Penobscot] River to Passam-aquâda [Passamaquoddy] are copied in Part from Surveys made by Order of Governor Bernard,[3] and in Part from Capt. Holland's Survey,[4] a Work of the very Highest Degree of Merit.

The Kenebaëg [Kennebec] and Penobskaëg [Penobscot] Rivers, with the Country contained between them, are plotted down from Journals of the Officers of the Scouting Parties, and from the Draughts of Surveyors sent out by me to examine and make a rough Survey of those Parts.

The Earl of Dartmouth, in a Manner most obliging, permitted me to have Captain Holland's Surveys, lying at the Board of Trade, copied, that the Public might Profit of the Knowledge which they give. Mr. Lewis, a Clerk at the Board of Trade, made the Copies; as he is an exceedingly neat and accurate Draughtsman they will be found to have, although on so small a Scale, a Degree of Precision and Accuracy which many larger Maps will not pretend to.

The following Observations of Latitudes were made by Capt. Holland in the Years 1773 and 1774, in the Course of this Work;

	$\circ$	$\prime$	$\prime\prime$
The most southerly Part of Mount Desert Island	44	12	0
Fort Pownall on Penosbcot [Penobscot] River –	44	24	30

[1] *Plan of the British Dominions of New England . . . , op. cit.*

[2] *A Topographical Map of the Province of New Hampshire surveyed by Mr. Thomas Wright and others. Author S. Holland*, London, 1784. Printed for William Faden Mar. 1, 1784. Great Britain, Board of Trade and Plantations. *List of Maps . . . , op. cit.,* p. 27.

[3] Sir Frances Bernard (1712-1779), colonial governor of New Jersey and Massachusetts.

[4] See *note* 4, p. 7.

	°	′	″
Pemaquid Point – – – – – – – – –	43	48	15
Cape Elizabeth – – – – – – – – –	43	33	0
Cape Porpoise – – – – – – – – –	43	21	0
Cape Neddock – – – – – – – – –	43	9	30
Thatcher's Island Lights – – – – – –	42	38	0
Cape Ann Harbour East Point – – – – –	42	35	0
Cape Cod Most northerly Point – – – –	42	4	20

In Addition to the Topographical Notices which these Surveys give, I have been able, by my new method of putting Figures of Reference instead of writing the Names of Towns and Places, to fill up the interior Parts with a Delineation of the Face of the Country, such as will be sought for in vain in the great Maps of the largest Scale hitherto published, such perhaps for the Future will be inserted in other mapps.[1] The Ranges of the Mountains and the Bearings of the high Pikes in them are pretty accurately laid down from Observations begun long ago by Dr. Douglas [Douglass], and from others made by myself: The Returns made on the plan of Instructions I gave for that Purpose, by the Officers of the Scouting Parties, which I kept as a Guard ranging on the back Parts of the Province during the Whole of the late War; as also by Surveyors which I sent out to search and examine the Routs which the Country offered, and particularly that by Kenebëag [Kennebec] to Chaudiere; as also to examine the East Branches thereof, and the Inter-locking of those with the West Branches of Penobscëag [Penobscot], are the Authorities for the rest. The Description given of the Face of the Country will be found in the following Treatise. Accurate and detailed as these Maps are they should always be accompanied by this Descrip-tion in the Hands of those who wish to have a practical Knowledge of the Country.

Fry and Jefferson's Map of Virginia.

"The greatest Part of VIRGINIA is composed with the Assistance of Messieurs Fry[2] and Jefferson's[3] Map[4] of it, and as this had the Assist-ance of actual Surveys of the Division Line with *Carolina*, and of the Rivers *Rapahannock* [Rappahannock] and *Potomack* [Potomac] from their Entrances to their Heads, joined to the Experience of Two skilful Persons, it would have been Affectation to have omitted the Advantage

---

[1][Pownall's note] I should not have ventured to have inserted these in this Map, had I not found them to coincide with those Parts of Capt. Holland's Surveys, wherein any Notice is taken of the Moun-tains, these are indeed very few, but the Coincidence is a corroborating Authority which justifies me.

[2]Joshua Fry, (d. 1754) master in the College of William and Mary and member of the House of Burgesses of Virginia.

[3]Peter Jefferson (1708-1758), father of Thomas Jefferson.

[4]Fry and Jefferson *Map*, 1751. *op. cit.*

of it. But however, an actual Survey from Philadelphia to the Mountains, near the great Bent of Potomack [Potomac], by the Pennsylvania Surveyors in 1739,[1] enabled me to give the just Longitude of that Place from Philadelphia, which they mistook by 10 or 12 Miles; and this obliges me to give Potomack [Potomac], and the whole Country, a Position something different. As that Performance is very valuable, I contrived mine to interfere as little as possible with it; and omitted the Counties and numerous Gentlemens Seats that it contains, to give room for the Roads, Inspection-houses, Court-houses, and the Seats of some Half a Dozen Gentlemen noted in the literary Way.

"I am obliged to the Same Map and Capt. Hoxton's Chart of *Chesopeak* [Chesapeake], Bay for MARYLAND.[2] But this Colony is the worst done of all the Settlements in mine, yet the Bay from Annapolis to the Head I have lately had an Opportunity of adjusting; as well as to measure the Isthmus across from the Head of Elk to Delaware River, about Three Miles below Newcastle. There is a considerable Error in my General Map, which came Time enough to my Knowledge to be mentioned here, though not to be rectified; and that is, I make the Breadth of the Peninsula from Fenwick's Island to the South Side of Little Choptank 65 Miles, whereas Mr. Parsons,[3] One of the Surveyors, who ran the Line across, informs me, that it should have been 70."[4]

Whoever shall trace the Country along which the Line, that divides the Provinces, now States, Maryland and Pennsylvania, runs, will find every River and Mountain, every Creek, Hill, and Road of any Consequence crossing it in their Courses exactly in the Point where the actual Survey made by Authority, and engraved by J. Smither,[5] places them: The western Parts of this Line where it should become the Boundary between Virginia and Pennsylvania remain yet unsettled and a disputed Point.

The Map[6] of the Southern Colonies is an exact Copy of a large

Maryland but imperfect.

[1] *A Map of Part of the Province of Pennsylvania and of the Counties of New Castle, Kent, and Sussex on Delaware: Showing the Temporary Limits of the Jurisdiction of Pennsylvania and Maryland. Fixed According to an Order of His Majesty in Council Dated the 25th Day of May in the Year 1738. Surveyed in the Year 1739.* Phillips, *List of Maps, op. cit.,* p. 672.

[2] Walter Hoxton, *To the Merchants of London Trading to Virginia & Maryland This Mapp of the Bay of Chesepeack, with the Rivers Potomack, Potapsco North East, and Part of Chester,* London: W. Beitts and E. Baldwin, 1735.

[3] William Parsons (d. 1757), surveyor general for Pennsylvania and founder of Easton.

[4] Quoted from Evans' *Analysis,* pp. 4-5; reprinted in Gipson's *Lewis Evans,* pp. 148-49.

[5] *A Plan of the West Line or Parallel of Latitude which is the Boundary between the Provinces of Maryland and Pennsylvania engraved by J. Smither 1770.* Great Britain. Board of Trade and Plantations, *List of Maps . . . , op. cit.,* p. 33.

[6] *A General Map of the Southern British Colonies in America . . . By B. Romans, 1776.* London. Printed for R. Sayer and J. Bennett, 15th Oct[r] 1776. This map is reproduced in this book.

Map in Manuscript at the Office of the American Secretary composed from diverse works of Persons employed by Government.

Delaware Colony. "The DELAWARE Colony," now State, "is adjusted by Part of a Circle of 12 Miles Radius, run round Newcastle as a Center, and an actual Mensuration of the whole Length of the Colony, by the late Mr. Thomas Noxon.[1]

The Author's Acknowledgment of Assistance given him. "To recount all the Surveys of Roads, Tracts of Land, and general Lines that I have been favoured with in the Composition of my Map" of 1749, "which makes so considerable a Part of this, would be endless: But I must not omit here to repeat, with Gratitude, my Thanks, not only for the Favours many Gentlemen did me, but the Chearfulness they shewed in assisting in a Design intended for public Service. It would have been almost impossible to have succeeded in the Composition, notwithstanding all These Helps, without my personal Knowledge also of almost all the Country it contained. One of the greatest Mistakes in it arose from my going from Kinderhook to Albany by night, where the Skipper deceived me in the Distance."[2] The Passage of the River through the Highlands is in this Edition corrected by Capt. Holland's Draught; he surveyed these Parts from Croton River to Vish-kill [Fishkill]: The rest is corrected by the Courses which I noticed, and more than once revised, in my Passages up and down this River.

[1]Thomas Noxon, planter and gristmiller who, in 1740, built *Noxon House* near present Noxontown Pond and Silver Lake, Delaware. Federal Writers' project. Delaware, *Delaware, A Guide to the First State* (N.Y., Viking Press, 1938), p. 465.

[2]Quoted from Evans' *Analysis*, p. 5; reprinted in Gipson's *Lewis Evans*, p. 149.

SECT. I.

Of the Face of the Country

HAVING given an Account of the Authorities whereon the several Parts of this Map rest, the Editor[1] now proceeds to describe the Face of the Country in its natural State; its Mountains and Rivers, and its Vegetation, which is always the most natural and just Description of the Powers of its Soil.

This Globe, the Earth which we inhabit, is, in its natural State, in a continued Progress of Exsiccation, and is universally, wherever the Waters do not prevail, covered with Woods, so that viewing this great Continent America (as yet a new World to the Land-workers of Europe) we see it a Country of Woods and Lakes or Rivers. Except where the Land is worn to the Bone, and nothing remains on the Surface but bare Rocks, every Soil, even the poorest, hath its peculiar Cloathing of Trees and Shrubs. There are Spots here and there scattered over the Face of this Country, which, seen amongst the Woods from a Distance, seem as though they were Plains of clear'd Land, but these are covered with a Species of Dwarf of Shrub Oak which grows about the Height of a Man's Shoulder, and bears very good Acorns. There are also in many, I might say most, Places, between the Banks of the Rivers and the Hills or Mountains through which these Rivers run, Margins of rich Meadow Land clear of Trees; this peculiar State is owing to the annual Inundations that these Meadows are covered with, and to a constant Accretion of Soil which is left on the Surface after the Waters retire; these the Settlers call, by a very expressive Name, *Interval Lands*.[2] In some Parts, as on the Mohawk and Connecticut River, these Interval Lands are of a Soil so rich that they may be tilled, some have been tilled incessantly for a Century or more, and yet continue as rich as the Vale of Egypt itself. I know but of one Place which is totally without Trees, and that is a Tract of Land upon Long Island, in New York State called Jamaica or Hampstead Plain, on which a shrubby Kind of Heath only grows.

[1]Thomas Pownall.

[2]A New England colloquialism. "That extent of ground, which lay between the original bank of the river and the river itself. The New Englander relishes it (interval) more than flats or bottoms." Timothy Dwight, *Travels in New England and New York* (London, W. Baynes & Sons, 1823), II, 310.

23

The particular Kind of Tree which grows in each Tract is always determined by the peculiar Soil or Nidus which is suited to produce it in Preference to other Species. This does not exclude other Species also from growing at the same Time, but some one Species always predominates in each Tract; the Soil therefore is best known and always described by the European Settlers from its peculiar Vegetation, as Oak Land, Birch, Beech, or Chestnut Land; Pine-Barren, Maple Swamps, Caedar Swamps. Walnut or Hickory, Firs, White and Red Elm, Magnolias, Locusts, Sassafras, and various other Trees are mixed with all these.

The Fruits which grow wild, as far as my Observations went, I here set down from my Journals. The Wild Vine of different Sorts, in general produce a very small sour thick-skin'd Grape, but the Plants themselves are in their Growth luxuriant beyond the Conception of those who have not seen them. The Wild Cherry, a Tree of which I saw near Scenectady [Schenectady], appeared to me One of the largest Trees I ever saw. Mulberry Red and White, but these latter are scarce. Hickory or Walnuts of several Sorts, Hazel, Wild Prune or Plumb, Chestnuts of different Sorts, Wild Pear and Crab, a Sort of Cervice or Medlar, Bilberry, Gooseberry, and Strawberry. The individual Trees of those Woods grow up, have their Youth, their old Age, and a Period to their Life, and die as we Men do: You will see many a Sapling growing up, many an old Tree tottering to its Fall, and many fallen and rotting away, while they are succeeded by others of their Kind, just as the Race of Man is: By this Succession of Vegetation this Wilderness is kept cloathed with Woods just as the human Species keeps the Earth peopled by its continuing Succession of Generations. As it happens to Man in the Course of Fate that sometimes epidemic Distempers, Deluges, or Famine have swept whole Nations off at once, so here, by a like Fate, Epidemic Distempers, to which even the Forests are liable, have destroyed whole Tracts of Woods at once. Deluges in the Vallies, Fire & Hurricanes on the mountains have also in their course often done the same. Wherever this at any Time hath happened, one sees a new Generation bearing all the Appearance of an European new Plantation growing up. If the Soil has suffered no great Change, Woods of the same Genus arise; if it hath undergone any Change, either for the better or for the worse, then, as from a Nidus prepared for a new Brood, we see Woods of a different Species which before appeared rarely, and as Aliens in the Place, now from a new power of Vegetation, springing up and possessing the Land as the predominant Wood.

If here I should attempt to describe the Colouring of these Woods, I should be at a Loss what Season of the Year to choose, whether the sober Harmony of Greens that the Woods in all their various Tints give in Summer; or whether the flaunting Blush of Spring, when the Woods glow with a thousand Tints that the flowering Trees[1] and Shrubs throw out. If I should persuade the Painter to attempt the giving a real and strict Portrait of these Woods in Autumn, he must mix in upon his Canvass all the Colours of the Rainbow, in order to copy the various and varied Dyes which the Leaves at the Fall assume: The Red, the Scarlet, the bright and the deep Yellow, the warm Brown, the White, which he must use, would give a prismatic motley Patch-work that the Eye would turn away from, and that the Judgement would not bear; and yet the Woods in this embroidered Garb have in real Nature a Richness of Appearance beyond Conception. But this is not the only Instance, there are many which I, who have used myself to draw from Nature, have observed, wherein Nature will not bear a Portrait, and wherein she is never less imitated than when she is attempted to be literally copied.

Some few Observations in these Matters, corrected on Enquiry, which I noted and set down, although they be those of a very unskilful Naturalist, may yet suggest some Hints to those who know how to derive Advantages from the meerest Trifles.

The Grapes of European Vines which are transplanted to America do not so well bear the sudden Changes of the Weather, nor the Extreams of the Dry and Wet which the Climate is liable to, as the native Grapes. If there be much Thunder, and that attended with heavy Showers, and followed by Gleams of excessive Heat, at the Time that the Exotic Grapes are growing to their Maturity, such Grapes are apt to burst; whereas the thick Skin of the native Grapes preserve them against this Mischief; When therefore I have seen with what abundant Luxuriancy these native Vines grow, and have been taught that the coarsest Fruits by Cultivation may be meliorated even into Sorts which are delicious; When I have read how Change of Soil and Cultivation have succeeded, I have always thought that the American Settlers would do more wisely in trying to cultivate and meliorate their native Vines,

---

[1][Pownall's note] I am no Botanist, but I will here transcribe from my Journal the Names of some of the flowering Trees and Shrubs which I find inserted there; the Red Flowering Maple, the Sassafras, the Locust, the Tulip Tree, Chestnut, the Wild Cherry, Prune, Crab, Sloe, Pear, Dogwood, Hawthorn, Elm, Leather Tree, a Sort of Gilder Rose, Swamp Laurel or Magnelia Honeysuckle; there were Multitudes of Flowers which I saw in the Pine-barrens and Swamps, but which I know not the Names of.

small and sour as their Grapes may appear at present, than by endeavouring to force the Nature of the foreign Vine. It takes always a great Time to accommodate an Exotic to a foreign Clime, and does not always succeed at last; the Native, whose Nature is already assimilated to its own Clime, might sooner, and with better Hopes of Success, be improved under the present State and Progress of American cultivation.[1]

Mr. Gist,[2] in his Journal (vide Appendix N° VI.)[3] says, that in some of the Plains of the Oïilinois [Illinois] Country, a Species of *Wild Rye*[4] grows spontaneously, that it shoots in Winter so as to appear Green through the Snow, though Two Feet deep; I have heard the same from others, but as neither they nor I were Botanists, I never was able to ascertain what this Plant so called was. The very first and most learned of Botanists in England never heard any Thing of it. I have oftentimes, on the same Principles as above, wished that Experiments were made as to the Cultivation and Melioration of it. The Wheat Plant, which now in its cultivated State gives Bread to great Part of the human Species, was most likely brought to this State by some such Cultivation, from some such humble wild Plant: It is singular, and a curious Fact, that no History gives us any Account of the native Place of this Plant as indigenous.

Since the Paragraph above was written I have received from Lieut. Governor Mercer,[5] a Native of Virginia, who has seen the Plant growing, and has eaten the Seed of it, the following Account: "The Wild Rye, which grows every where in the Ohio Country, is a Species of the Rye which is cultivated by the Europeans. It has the same bearded Ear, and produces a farinaceous Grain. The Ear and Grain, in the wild State of this Plant, are less, and the Beard of the Ear is longer than those of the cultivated Rye, which makes this wild Plant resemble more the Ryegrass in its Appearance; but it differs in no other Respect from the Rye, and it shoots in its spontaneous Vegetation about the Middle of November as the cultivated Rye doth." The Fact ascertained as above, that

[1][Pownall's note] Vide Mr. Anthill's Observations on the Culture of the Vine in the *Transactions* of the Philosophical Society at Philadelphia, Vol. I.
See "An Essay on the Cultivation of the Vine, and the Making and Preserving of Wine, suited to the different Climates in North America, by Edward Anthill" American Philosophical Society, *Transactions* . . . (Phila., Wm. and Thomas Bradford, 1771), I, Section II, 117-197.

[2]Christopher Gist (*ca.* 1706-1759), surveyor and agent for the Ohio Company of Virginia.
[3]Read entry dated January 27, 1751, p. 181 this work.
[4]Wild rye was indigenous grass growing along the Atlantic Coast from Virginia northward. The grass beards resemble wheat or rye. Lyman Carrier, *The Beginnings of Agriculture in America* (New York, McGraw Hill, 1923), pp. 27-28.
[5]George Mercer (1733-1784), agent for the Ohio Company of Virginia, later lieutenant-governor of North Carolina.

there is in this Part of the World a Plant of spontaneous Growth which produces Bread-corn, lead me to inquire a little more into the History of the Plant called *Wheat*, hitherto, as I said above, unnoticed and unknown; and I found in Diodorus Siculus a *Traditionary* Piece of History which almost gives the Form of a Fact to what I had before put down merely as an Opinion; he says,[1] "That Isis was the Discoverer to Mankind of the Fruit of Wheat and Barley (growing perchance amongst the other wild Plants of the Earth unknown to Men) and that Osiris taught them the Manner of cultivating this to Use." But Polyhistor (as quoted by Eusebius) giving an Account, which he took from Berosus of the ancient natural State of Mesopotamia where Babylon was built, says, that in the earliest Times it abounded with *Wild Wheat* (Πυροὺς ἀγρίους) amongst the other indigenous Plants. There is a passage in Diodorus Siculus which asserts that wheat[2] *grows wild* in Sicily, & that it was so even in the Author's time. This very circumstance leads me to think, that Although such wheat might *grow wild*, yet that it was but the self sown remains of fields once cultivated. It is not at least to me a proof, of its being *indiginous* in those parts. These passages however in History respecting the original State of the Ancient World throw a kind of reflected light of Truth on the accounts which I have receiv'd & which I here give, of the New One.

From the Accounts I have had of the Indian wild Hemp, from the Specimens which have been sent to me; from the Judgment which some of our Ropemakers of the first Class here in England have given of it; I have persuaded myself that something more might be done in America by the Cultivation of the Native than by the transplanting of a foreign species.

The Bark of the Bass or Leather Tree, with a little more Attention than is at present given to it, might be applied to all the ordinary Purposes of Country Tackle with great Benefit.

There is a Sweet Maple, from the Juice of which, extracted from the Tree, the Indians and Back Settlers make a Sugar, and from which many of the German Settlers make a rich Liqueure. I have had a considerable Quantity of this Sugar, it is very sweet, and even in its first State of Granulation has, though a peculiar, yet no unpleasing Taste:

---

[1]Εὑρούσης μὲν Ἴσιδος τόν τε τοῦ πυροῦ καὶ τῆς κριθῆς καρπὸν (φυόμενον μέν, ὡς ἔτυχε, κατὰ τὴν χώραν μετὰ τῆς ἄλλης βοτάνης, ἀγνοούμενον δὲ ὑπὸ τῶν ἀνθρώπων) τοῦ δὲ Ὀσίριδος ἐπινοησαμένου τὴν τούτων κατεργα- σίαν τῶν καρπῶν. Diodorus Sic. Lib. I, 14.

[2]Ἔν τε τῷ Λεοντίνῳ πεδίῳ καὶ κατὰ πολλοὺς ἄλλους τόπους τῆς Σικελίας, μέχρι τοῦ νῦν, φύεσθαι τοὺς ἀγρίους ὀνομαζομένους πυρούς. *Ibid.*, Lib. 2, [?]

These Trees properly cultivated, and the Sugar carefully manufactured and refined, would supply that Article of Consumption, in some degree to the people inhabiting the interior parts of the Country.

My Friend Mr. Pratt,[1] than whom there was not a wiser or more knowing Man in the Country, was always of Opinion, that the Juice which can be drawn, by Incision, from the Poison Vine is that Material which the Chinese and Japonese make their Vernice with.

He also recommended it to his Countrymen, that instead of attempting to breed the Silkworm of Asia, they should make many Trials on various Species of Spinning worms, with which the Woods in America abound. His necessary Attention to his Business as a Lawyer, and his very disinterested meritorious Labours in the public Service as a Representative of ye Town of Boston & a leading Member of the House of Assembly did not permit him to follow his Biass to the Study of Nature; but he used to tell me, that from Trials he had made he was sure a native Silk-worm would some Day or other be found in America; such when found, he said, might turn to practical Account, whereas the Thunder, the boisterous and sudden Changes of Weather, under the present State of the Climate of America, disturbed the foreign Silkworm, so as that it would never be cultivated to any Advantage equal to what the native Silk-worms might be. At the Time that these Things were with us in New England a Subject of Speculation, they were, by the Experiments made by Madam Hubert, a Provençal settled in Louisiana, become actual Facts; This lady made many comparative Experiments on the native and foreign Silk-worm, fed on different Leaves of different Mulberry Trees; the native Worm of America, though larger and stronger, yet being wild and not settled like the domiciliated Worm of Europe, did not produce an equal Quantity of Silk; but she imputed this wholly to its wild unsettled Nature; their Silk, although coarse, was strong and thick. Since the Remark above was set done, I have been informed that 10,000 Weight of Cocoons of the *native* Silk-worm of America was sold in 1771[3] at the public Filature in Philadelphia, and that the Silk produced from them was of a good Quality, and (a Sample being sent to England) was much approved of in London. I find also in the Transactions of the American Philosophical Society

Monsieur de Ptatz. Hist. de Louisiana[2] Liv. 2., Ch. 2.

---

[1]Benjamin Pratt (1710-1763), representative of Boston, in the Massachusetts Bay General Assembly, and later chief justice of the province of New York.

[2]Le Page du Pratz, *Histoire de la Louisiane . . .* (Paris, De Bure, 1768).

[3]"About 1770 the planting of mulberry trees to feed silk worms had quite a boom in Pennsylvania. A public filature for unwinding cocoons was established in Philadelphia. Prizes were given and £850 was raised for the enterprise." Carrier, *op. cit.*, pp. 178-79.

held at Philadelphia, printed in 1768, that Mr. Moses Bertram [Bartram] had made many curious Experiments on the native Silk-worm.[1]

The fine soft Hair which grows on the Bunch of the Buffalo is of that woolly or rather silken Texture, which from the Corruption of a Dutch Word we call *Mohaire*. Mrs. Wright,[2] a Woman of very uncommon Ingenuity, and possessing an uncommon Share of Science, one of a Quaker Family, that lived and had a fine Farm at the Ferry on Susquahanna [Susquehanna] River, which bears their Name, gave me, when I was at their House, a Pair of Muffeties, and shewed me a Pair of Stockings, which she had spun and knit of it. This Manufacture made of these Materials as much exceeded in Pliability, Softness, and Warmth any Woollen or Cotton, as the East Indian Fabrick called the *Shaul*[3] doth silk. The finest and most luxurious Fabricks might be made of this.

Asbestos is very common in America; and this same Gentlewoman had contrived a Method of spinning the Thread-like Fibres of this Stone into a continued consistent Thread, of which she made a Purse; she mingled and, in the Spinning, twisted it in with Flax, and of the Thread so spun knitted or netted her Work. The Whole, when finished, was thrown into the Fire, the Flax burnt away, the Fabrick remained firm and wholly of Asbestos. I mention this merely as a Curiosity, because it has been a Kind of Desideratum with the Antiquaries how the Cloth of Asbestos, which was used by the Ancients to wrap the Corps when burnt, so as to preserve the remains in the Ashes, was fabricated.

From the Nature of the Surface and interior Contexture of this American Part of our Earth, the Mountains, as we in our relative Language call them, do all run in Ridges, with almost even Tops in parallel Lines; those to the West of Hudson's [Hudson] River N.E. and S.W. those to the Eastward of it nearly N. and S. between which, in like parallel Lines, run the great Rivers.

As the general Surface of the Land slopes to the S.E. and as the Heights of the Tops of the Mountains decrease gradually on the Eastern Side, so the general Flow of the great Rivers have a Course which such a Face of Country naturally gives: While they continue to run in any one Vale their Course is S.W. whenever through the Gaps or Intersections of the Mountains they can force a Way Eastward they do, tumbling over Rocks, Rifts, and Precipices in continual Falls and Cataracts South Easterly, and so along each Stage, and so from one

[1] See American Philosophical Society, *op. cit.*, I, Section II, 224-230.
[2] Mrs. John Wright. John Wright was a justice of the peace in Lancaster County, Pennsylvania and owner of Wright's Ferry across the Susquehanna.
[3] Probably cashmere.

Stage to another, is their Course in great Zigzags S.W. and S.E. Such is the Course (speaking generally) of the Delaware, Susquehanna, and Potomack [Potomac] Rivers. The lesser Rivers, which run only from off the Eastern Slope of these Mountains (such as Rapahanoch [Rappahannock], James River, Roanoch [Roanoke] and the other Rivers of the Carolina's) urge their Course in all Ways and Windings to the Sea at S.E.

The Vales between the Ridges of these Mountains have all one and the same general Appearance, that of an Amphitheatre enclosing, as it were, an Ocean of Woods swelled and depressed with a waving Surface like that of the great Ocean itself: Though the Ridges of the Mountains run, as I have said, in nearly parallel Lines, yet at Times, by the Means of Branchings and Spurs of Mountains, they every here and there seem to close, and where they do so, the Land of the Vale also rises in irregular hilly Land, which is the Circumstance that gives this general Appearance of an Amphitheatre to these Vales, when from any of the Mountains above one looks down into them. If the Spectator hath gotten a Stand on some high Mountain so as to look across any Number of the Ridges which may be less high than that he stands on, he then sees a repeated Succession of Blue and Purple parallel waving Lines behind each other, with here and there a Breaking-off or Gap in them; here and there sudden Endings of them in perpendicular bluff Points and Knobs, as they are by the People called; and here and there high elevated Peaks; all which, together with the general Direction of the Ridges, are Points which mark the Geography of the Country to the Indians, and even in a very sufficient practical Way the general Bearings to the Geographical Surveyor. In like Manner the Courses and the Currents of the great Rivers, with their attendant Streams and Rivulets, by the Line of their Course, and by the Nature of the Current with which they flow, mark the Height of the Land, the Declination of its Sides, and its abrupt Descents or its level Plains. Those who have attentively studied this Subject, and who have accustomed themselves to apply the Knowledge, which it gives, to Cases in Fact, will soon derive from it such Information respecting a Country as will answer every Purpose of Practice; and very often such a Precision of Acquaintance with the Face of the Country, as will astonish even those who have resided in it: To give this Knowledge, as far as Information went at the Time[1] that the First Edition of this Map was published, to those whose Duty it was to know these Matters, the Ranges of the Mountains, the

[1] 1755.

Gaps in them, and the Knobs where they end, are laid down with great Attention, and, where it could be obtained, with great Precision by the Compass. The Point to which the Tide Flows, on the Rivers, the swift currents, the Rifts, the Falls, the still Water or the slowly flowing Course, are either marked in the Map or described in the following Sheets. As the general, and I had almost said, the only Way of travelling this Country in its natural State is by the Rivers and Lakes, the Portages or Carrying-places from one Water to another, or along the Shores where the Navigation is obstructed by Rifts or Falls in the same River, are particularly and pretty exactly marked and set down. The general Face of the Country, when one travels it along the Rivers through Parts not yet settled, exhibits the most picturesque Landscapes that Imagination can conceive, in a Variety of the noblest, richest Groupes of Wood, Water, and Mountains. As the Eye is lead on from Reach to Reach, at each Turning of the Courses, the Imagination is in a perpetual Alternative of curious Suspense and new Delight, not knowing at any Point, and not being able to discover where the Way is to open next, until it does open and captivates like Enchantment.

Ignotas tentare Vias, atque inter opacum
Allabi nemus——
Olli Remigio Noctemque Diemque fatigant,
Et longos superant Flexus, variisque teguntur,
Arboribus, viridasque secant placido Æquore Sylvas.

But while the Eye is thus catching new Pleasures from the Landscape, with what an overflowing Joy does the Heart melt, while one views the Banks where rising Farms, new Fields, or flowering Orchards begin to illuminate this Face of Nature; nothing can be more delightful to the Eye, nothing go with more penetrating Sensation to the Heart. To any one that has the Habit of Drawing from Nature, the making Sketches of these picturesque Scenes would be ample Employment: Some are so astonishingly great, that none but those who have made the Trial know how difficult it is to bring up the Scale of the ordinary Objects to this, which is (as it were) beyond the Garb of Nature. I made many Draughts and Sketches; some few, which were characteristic, I let the Public have in Engravings: I have seen since many fine Drawings done by our Officers and Engineers, a Collection of Engravings from all which got together would surely be curious, and not unuseful. So much for the Coup d'Oeïl of the Païsage of this Country. But pursuing the Line which I laid down of a practical Knowledge of it, we must proceed in another Train of Ideas.

SECT. II.

Description of the Tract which divides this Continent into two distinct Parts

The Two distinct Tracts of this Continent.

WHEN we proceed to a more exact Detail of this Country, so as to examine it in its Parts, we must observe, that as the Country in general is divided into different Stages, so the general Face of it contained in this Map is divided into Two distinct and very different Tracts of Country, viz. Into that Part which lies W. and S.W. of Hudson's [Hudson] River, and that which is E. and N.E. of Hudson's [Hudson] River and Lake Champlain. This specific Difference will be marked in the Descriptions which I shall give of each Part. It will be sufficient here to say, that the Mountains of the Western Division, beginning from an immense high Tract of Land lying in the Angle formed by the Mohawks [Mohawk] and Hudson's [Hudson] Rivers, go off from Hudson's [Hudson] River in one general Trending in parallel Lines and in uniform Ranges of Ridges South Westerly to West Florida and Louisiana. The Mountains of the other Division on the East Side of the River run in like uniform Ranges, but in a Direction almost due North and South parallel to the River, and end in steep Ridges and bluff Heads at or near the Coast on Long Island Sound: And in the Latitude 45 or thereabouts, turning Eastward run away to the Gulf of St. Lawrence. The Hudson's [Hudson] River, and the Lakes George and Champlain, and the River Sorel form the very peculiar Line of this Division of the Country. The Bed of the Hudson's [Hudson] River (as if it were a great deep Chasm formed in the Body of the Country by its being split down to the Level of the Sea) is a strait deep Channel running (to speak generally) North and South betwixt Two Tracts of very high Land, and admits, amidst and through high Mountains, the Flow of the Tide more than 180 Miles up it. Where it lies thus (180 Miles from the Ocean) on a Level with the Flow of the Tide, the Rivers which have their Sources in the high Lands on each Side of it, the Delaware and Susquehanna Rivers particularly, which are very great Rivers, run tumbling with a precipitate Course over Rifts and Falls for many hundred Miles S. and S.E. before they reach the same Level; even the

D c

The very particular Nature of this Division.

Connecticut River on the east of it & parallel to it runs with many a Swift and over many Falls above 100 Miles South before it reaches the same Level.

The Northern Part of this peculiar Division of the main Continent is formed by a Succession of deep Lakes, the Lakes George and Champlain, which issue the Waste of their Waters through the little River Sorel into Canada[1] River; the Bed of these Lakes is likewise formed by a deep Chasm amidst Mountains, running North and South, as continuing the same Line of the Hudson's [Hudson] River.

This River is usually, & especially by the Dutch Inhabitants of this Country, called *North River*. As I do not recollect to have seen anywhere the reason for this name given, I will insert it in this Edition. The Tract of Country lyeing between This River & the Delaware River inclusive was possessed by the Dutch under the Name of New Netherlands. They gave the two relative names of North & South River to this & the Delaware River. Their Chief Post & Town was New-Amsterdam which the English afterwards called New-York.

The Hudson's [Hudson] River arises from Two main Sources derived by Two Branches which meet about Ten Miles above Albany, the one called the Mohawk's [Mohawk] River (rising in a flat level Tract of Country, at the very Top or Height of the Land to Westward) comes away E. and S.E. at the Foot, on the North Sides of the Mountains, which the Indians call by a Name signifying the Endless Mountains.[2] It runs in a Vale, which it seems to have worn itself, with Interval Lands on each Side, for about 100 miles. Hudson's River Mohawk Branch.

The soil at the height of the Land & at the head of this River doth appear to be Low Land, that is, It is flatt, & a deep Rich Soil not yet worn away & full of bogs, ponds, & springs from whence not only this Mohawk River But the Onondaga[3] River which empties itself into Lake Ontario at Oswego derive. The River keeps on with a quiet still Stream to Burnet's field[4] having Lands of a deep & rich soil on both sides. At Burnet's field (a very fine settlement so called from Gov' Burnet) The Vale & Interval Lands form a Space from y⁰ west or upper end to y⁰ Falls about 11 miles long & from 2½ to 3½ miles wide. This Settlement[5] in 1754 consisted of about 120 Houses. The Stream after this quickens

[1]St. Lawrence.
[2]Read description by Evans. Printed on his *Map*, 1749, *op. cit.*
[3]Oswego.
[4]Burnet's Field patent (1725) extended 24 miles

from Little Falls, New York, west along both sides of the Mohawk River. Nathaniel S. Benton, *A History of Herkimer County* . . . (Albany, J. Munsell, 1856), p. 42.
[5]*Ibid.*

in its motion & begins to Wear a Valley by washing away the soil of the Lands through which it runs, but has however rich *interval Lands* on both sides which Produce Wheat Peas & Hemp without Dunge or Manure. The lands were said in 1754 to be worth 45 £ p^r Acre. About six or seven miles below Burnet's field the River running across a Rocky Stratum tumbles in a Fall by which the Navigation is interrupted. There is a good road on the side of the River by means of which all Goods & Batteaus also are carried over Land for about a mile. At this Place the Vale is narrow & the river runs close under the Hills on ye southside. After this The Vale widens again to the breadth of a mile & half or two miles, as ye River passes the Indian Castles,[1] till it comes to Schyelers[2] & Zimmermans[3] where the River runs rapid, through a narrow between three Islands: After this the Vale widens to a Triangular space of about 5½ miles long & 3¼ broad a little above, or west of Stoney-Arabia [Stone Arabia], a fine settlement so called. From hence the River runs about 7½ miles till it comes round a high point of Land called Anthony's Nose in a narrower vale of about a mile over. From hence to the Settlements at Fort Hunter[4] the Vale widens again to two & four mile breadth. After this till it comes to the west or upper End of the Precinct of Schenectady Township. The Vale is again narrow but begins to Widen at Van Eps's Farm.[5] At the Scite of Schenectady. The Vale forms the most pleasing prospect one can Imagine. The Eye from ye Hills with which it is surrounded Views is one Landschape an amphitheatre of about 4 or 5 miles long & about 2 miles broad with level lands & inclosing a rich Vale of Corn & Meadow of ye most Luxurious vegetation watered by a Beautifull River running in two Streams through it; on ye Banks of which stands a Pretty & Regular built Little Town of about 150 Houses with a Fort, a Dutch Church, & Stadthouse, in three Streight Streets parrallel to ye River & 4 at right angles with these. I speak of it in 1754. The Hills which surround this Fertile delightfull opening of the Vale rise in two ridges. The first consists of Pine Land and the second of Oak Land rising behind it.

It appeared to me seen from the little Lake by Major Glen's[6] not

[1]Mohawk Castles.

[2]Colonel Peter Schuyler was one of the grantees for the Oriskany Patent lands along the Mohawk near the mouth of Oriskany Creek. George W. Schuyler, *Colonial New York*, (New York, Charles Scribner's Sons, 1885), II, 133. Near the present site of Utica, New York.

[3]Probably near the mouth of Zimmermans Creek.

[4]Fort Hunter (1710-1776?), a frontier military post situated at the junction of the Schoharie and Mohawk rivers. Present site of Fort Hunter, New York.

[5]John J. Van Eps, one of the first land owners in the vicinity of Schenectady. John F. Watson, *Annals and occurrences of New York City and State in the Olden Time* . . . (Phila., H. F. Anners, 1846), p. 32.

[6]Jacob Glen. Johnson, *Papers, op. cit.*, I, 122;

unlike in form to the Vale between Hartford & Ware, but infinitely more picturesque in its dress as not yet totally derobed of its Native Ornaments. This Vale is narrow'd below & again widened into a lesser but somewhat similar Spott. And the River being near Two Furlongs broad, falls over a Ledge of Rocks 75 Feet perpendicular in one Fall; these Falls the Indians call by the expressive Name *Cohoes:* This is so singular an Object, that I will here insert a Description as I take it from my Journal noted down, 1754, on the Spot.

Going from Albany one rides along the banks of the Hudson river for six miles through most delightfull meadows, that is what we should call meadows in England, but all in tillage form. The river is on the right hand: The bank on the opposite shore is high woodlands sloping gently down to the Waters edge; on the left are these meadows from half to three quarters of a mile in breadth, then hilly woodlands rising gently. For two miles further through the commencement of settlements but in part clear'd. Then through Woods, Oak, Chestnut Walnut, Chesnut-oak & Elm & so for the rest of the way about four or five miles more. Here one begins to hear the *Pouiflosboish* noise of the Tumultuous rushing & dashing of Waters which amidst the stillness of the Woods is like the roar of a Storm at Sea heard from the Land in the dead of night.

I went Twice to view this; the first Time there was but little Water in the River, and what came over the Fall ran in the Cliffs and Gullies of the Rocks in Three or Four different Channels. The View of them in this State given in Mr. Calm's [Kalm] Account of America[1] would have been pretty exact, had the Draughtsman in the Composition known how to have given a Scale to them; as it is, they appear to have a Magnitude not much more than that of a Mill-dam. D c Cohoes Falls

Upon a great Flood coming down the River on the 25th of June, I went a second Time to view these Falls; they were then a most tremendous Object. The Torrent, which came over, filled the whole Space from Side to Side; before it reached the Edge of the Fall it had acquired a Velocity which the Eye could scarce follow; and although at the Fall the Stream tumbled in one great Cataract: yet it did not appear like a Sheet of Water; it was a tumultuous Conglomeration of Waves foaming, and at Intervals bursting into Clouds of Vapour, which fly off in rolling Eddies like the Smoak of great Guns. In that Part of the Fall where

William Shirley, *Correspondence* . . . , ed. by Charles Henry Lincoln (New York, Macmillan Co., 1912), II, 177.

[1]Per Kalm, *Travels in North America* . . . , translated into English by John Reinhold Forster (London, the Editor, 1770-71), II, 275-77.

the large Rock shoots forward, the Torrent as it falls into the Angle formed by it seems to lose the Property of Water; if the Eye tries to pursue it in its Fall, the Head will turn giddy; the great and ponderous Mass with which it ingulfs itself makes the Weight of it (one may almost say) visible, however it makes itself felt by keeping the whole Body of the Earth on the Banks on each Side in a continued Tremulation; after having shot down as though it would pierce to the Center, it rebounds again with astonishing Recoil in large Jets and Columns of Water to the very Height from which it fell,

⸻Ter Gurgite vastos

Sorbet in abruptum Fluctus, rursusque sub auras,

Erigit alternos⸻

This is not Poetry but Fact, and a natural Operation. In other Parts, where it shoots over in a Sheet of Water, there is a peculiar Circumstance which struck me, and which I will endeavour to explain; there are every now and then violent Explosions of Air which burst through the Surface of the Torrent, and as I considered it attentively on the Spot, I explained it as follows to myself; the Air which is contained and pent in between the Rock and the Arch of the Torrent, which shoots over it must, by the violent Motion of this Torrent, be heated and rarefied, and if so, will of course break out in Explosions; however the Fact was as I state it, and better Philosophers than I pretend to be may give better Accounts of it.

The Vapours which fly off from this Fall disperse themselves and fall in heavy Showers for near Half a Mile round the Place. Whenever the Spectator can gain a Position in a proper Angle between the Falls and the Sun, he will always see it reflected in a Rainbow.

While we are contemplating this Object, there came on a most violent Thunder Storm: Any one who has been in America knows how exceeding loud the Sound of these Explosions of the Thunder are: Yet so stunned were we with the incessant hoarse Roar of this Cataract that we were totally insensible to it.

I made a Sketch of this Fall upon the Spot, I afterwards composed a Drawing from it, wherein I was happy enough, after several Trials and Devices, to succeed in giving it it's proper Scale. Mr. P. Sanby[1] made a coloured Drawing for me from this, and an Engraving[2] has been made after it and published.

The Mohawk River runs hence with a tumbling rapid Course till

[1] Paul Sandby was the first engraver to practice aquatint engraving in England (1775).

[2] "A view of the Great Cohoes Falls on the Mohawk River; the Fall about Seventy feet; the River near a

it falls into the main River called Hudson's [Hudson]. Many little Rivers and Streams fall into this Branch; those which come from the North rise in a Tract of Country called Couxsachrâgé,[1] the Principal of which is that called Canada Creek: Those which fall into it from the South C d rise in and tumble from the high Ranges of the Endless Mountains, and interlock with the Heads of the Delaware and Susquehanna Rivers: One of these high Ridges, in which the Canajohary [Canajoharie] Creek C d rises, is called Brimstone Hill.[2] It has not run farr before it falls from a Cliff 300 feet in height. Schohary [Schoharie], which falls into the Mohawk's [Mohawk] River a little below Canajohary [Canajoharie], rises in the western Parts of the highest of the Mountains call Kaat's-kill D c [Catskill] Mountains, and runs through a deep Vale for 50 or 60 Miles. But this River is so intirely obstructed from one end to the other (except a Tract of Land about Five Miles long, 14 Miles from the Mouth) with Rifts and Falls that the Inhabitants do not use even Canoes. As the Mountains which close in this Vale are very high, the Settlements are confined to the Interval Land: These Settlers had no Communication with Hudson's [Hudson] River but by Albany, and this was by Land over the *Helleberg*,[3] in Winter Time only, with Sledges. When I was there they had proposed to make a new Road from a Point about 40 Miles up the River to a Point on the South Line of Renslaer's Manor,[4] where that Line at 12 Miles Distance from Hudson's [Hudson] River strikes the River called Kaat's-kill [Catskill].

The other or northern main Branch of this River Hudson rises from Lakes in the Mountains of Couxsachrâgé to the West of Lake Champlain, and is called Sacondaga [Sacandaga] River; it comes from the Sacondaga North with a direct southern Course till it comes within 12 Miles of the Branch Mohawk Branch,[5] then turns short back to the North, till it comes with-

Quarter of a Mile broad, Sketched on the spot by Governor Pownall, painted by Paul Sandby and Engraved by William Elliott." In *Scenographia Americana; or, A Collection of Views in North America and the West Indies. Neatly Engraved by Messrs. Sandby, Grignion, Rooker, Canot, Elliot, and others; from Drawings on the Spot, by several Officers of the British Navy & Army* . . . , (London, Printed for John Bowles, Robert Sayer, Thomas Jefferys, Carington Bowles & Henry Parker, 1768). There is, in the Map Division of Library of Congress, a manuscript pen and ink sketch, "A View of the Cohoes or Great Falls of the Mohawk River," which may be by Thomas Pownall. Phillips, *List of Maps*, *op. cit.*, p. 239.

[1]The early settlers around Albany knew this region as the "proper hunting grounds" for the Five Nations. Watson, *Annals of . . . New York*, *op. cit.*, p. 15.
[2][Pownall's note] Bituminous springs here.
[3]A ridge in the Catskill Mountains.
[4]Rensselaerwyck, a Dutch manor of about 700,000 acres on the Hudson, comprising most of the present New York counties of Albany and Rensselaer.
[5][Pownall's note] I find in my Journal of 1755 the following Observation, written down from Sir William Johnson's Information on the Spot. A convenient and advantageous Communication may be opened between the Mohawks [Mohawk] and

in Five or Six Miles of the South End of Lake George, and then winds round to the South till it meets the Western or Mohawk Branch. Where this River, about Four Miles above Fort Edward, descends from the Oak-land Tract to the Pine-land, there are Falls upon it which obstruct Navigation, above these Falls it is navigable not only for Canoes but for large Boats. There are also Two other Falls below Fort Edward. In this Bend is included the Tract of Country which the Indians call Kaiaderossoras.[1] From the Junction of these Branches, under the Name of Hudson's [Hudson] River, it runs nearly South, and passing what is called the Narrows, between Long Island and Staten Island, runs out to Sea by Sandy Hook; in its Course it passes by the City of Albany.

Albany

This City is a Corporation. It consisted in 1755 of 378 Houses, of 2972 Regular Inhabitants in Families. It has two Streets running parrallel to the bank of the River & one very broad noble Street at Right Angles with these. There is a Dutch Church & an English one; a Statehouse; & on the ground rising above it at the upper end of ye broad Street a Fort[2] which Commands the Town; but which is itself Commanded by the Ground that rises behind it, & is not tenable against a proper regular Force. The Whole Town except a Few New Houses, is intirely built after the Dutch mode. While ye Dutch had it it was called Orange. When the Duke of York had it granted to him, It took ye Name of Albany. It arose into a Town from being originally the most advanced Trading Post, in the Indian trade which the Dutch had, & which they, called by a name signifying, The Fore-sail. The River runs hence by Kinderhoëk [Kinderhook] and then under the eastern Foot of the Kaat's-kill [Catskill] Mountains and the Highlands of 'Sopos [Esopus]; but the extraordinary and very singular Passage which it has, is through a Range of very high and mountainous Lands, about 12 Miles across, called the Highlands, running directly athwart its Course; for as though a Chasm had been split in this Range of Mountains to make Way for it,

E c

it passes in a deep Channel near a Mile broad, with one Zigzag only,

---

Sacondaga [Sacandaga] Branch by cutting a Road of only Seven Miles from Johnson-hall to Sacondaga [Sacandaga] Creek; the Half of this Road next to Sacondaga [Sacandaga] is sandy Land, of White Poplars, and White and Black Pine, like the Sand betwixt Albany and Sckenectada [Schenectady]. The other Half is hilly, the Growth on the Ridges Beech and some Oak, in the Bottoms Maples. There is good Navigation from this Creek to the Falls of Sacondaga [Sacandaga].

[1]Kayaderosseras or Cayaderossoras. A large tract of Indian land beginning at the Half Moon (Waterford) to the third fall, then west to Canada Creek. *Documents relative to the Colonial History of the State of New York ...*, ed. by E. B. O'Callaghan (Albany, Weed, Parsons & Co., 1853-87), VI, 866. Hereafter cited as *N.Y.C.D.* This tract was the most valuable part of the Mohawks' hunting ground. *Ibid.*, VII, 576-77.

[2]Fort Frederick (Albany).

through these Mountains piled up almost perpendicular to a most astonishing Height on each Side of it.

> Hinc atque hinc vastae Rupes, geminique minantur
> In Coelum Scopuli: quorum sub vertice latè
> Æquora tuta silent; tum Sylvis scena coruscis
> Desuper.—

Just after having entered into this Pass, a very peculiar Rock called Martler's Rock[1] projects from the East Side into the River; and at the Foot of these immensely high Mountains, although it is as high as a Sloop's Mast, looks like a Wharf or Mole. The Eddy which this occasions in the Current, and the Wind which is always flittering here, makes this a puzzled Pass. This I find marked down in my Journal 1755, October 22, as a Spot on which a Fort placed would have great Command of this Pass; and I understand now, 1775, that the Americans have taken post and built a Fort[2] upon it. They however found afterward other positions for forts equally commanding & less commanded.[3]

After emerging out of this Pass, it spreads itself in the Form of a great Lake 15 Miles in Length by one Way of reckoning,[4] and by another 20, and about Four Miles broad, and is called the Topang [Tappan] Sea: The western Banks are perpendicular rocky Cliffs of an immense Height, Covered with Woods at the Top, which from the great Height of the Cliff seem like Shrubs. The Eastern Coasts are formed by a gently rising Country, Hill behind a Hill, of fruitful Vegetation at the back of which lye the White-plains: It then again for 20 Miles more or thereabouts takes the Form of a River, but above a Mile and Half broad, and passes by New York.

The Reader may imagine that the Scenes on this River must exhibit some of the finest Landscapes in the World; I thought so, and made many Sketches of the different Scenes, particularly of Windy Gate, the Entrance of the Highlands,[5] with a View of Martler's Rock, and of others[6] which the Passage through the Highlands gives. The Islands which may be said to lie at the Mouth of this great River, are first New York Island,[7] about 12 Miles long and scarce Two broad in the greatest

Margin notes: E c, E c, F C New York Island

---

[1]See *note* 6, p. 8.

[2]Read *American Archives, Fourth Series, Containing a Documentary History of the English Colonies in North America . . . By Peter Force.* (Wash., M. St. Clair Clarke and Peter Force, Dec. 1840), III, 1657. The fortress was called Fort Constitution.

[3]*American Archives, op. cit.,* III, 1657.

[4][Pownall's note] This is reckoning Haverstraw Bay as Part.

[5]"A View of Hudson's River of the Entrance of What is Called the Topan Sea . . ." In *Scenographia Americana . . . , op. cit.*

[6]"A View of Hudson's River of the Pakepsey and the Catts-kill Mountains from Sopos Island in Hudson's River." In *Scenographia Americana . . . , op. cit.*

[7]Present Manhattan Island.

Breadth of it, lying in the Course of the River North and South; it is at the north end separated from the Continent which forms the eastern Banks of the River by a very narrow Channel, through which the Tides flow with great Rapidity; there is a Bridge built over it, a Toll-bridge,[1] of private Property: This Island is in general of a rocky stony Texture, with a light Soil, scarce enough to cover the Rocks, and yet from rich Bottoms which there are in it, and from a certain Moisture which Stones retain in the Soil amidst which they lie, it is of a very kindly Vegetation. There is remarkable fine Water in many Parts of this little Island. From its Scite and Position it rather may be described as forming the eastern Banks of this lower Part of the River, than that it can be said to lie in New York the Mouth of it. After passing by this Island and the southern Point of it, at which the City of New York stands, the River opens again into a wide Bay 10 or 12 Miles broad, with Two or Three little Islands in it, and then passing between Long Island and Staaten [Staten] Island, through a Straight called the Narrows; it then forms a second Bay, and thence issues out between Sandy Hook and Long Island to Sea.

There is a certain affectation of prudent secrecy always observed by Writers of all Nations, that avoids the giving of too particular descriptions of the principal Ports & Harbours of their own Country. Although I believe that a knowledge of these parts of any Country may be had & are had by their Enemies: & that ignorance in these matters never remains but from indolence: Yet I restrained myself in the first editions[2] of this work from all descriptions of Ports or Harbours or Towns. Now that They cannot be any longer supposed to be unknown to other nations One may venture to give a description of them so farr as they come within the Geography and Topography of the Country. The account so farr as respects the navigation, of the Port & Harbour of New York I shall give as I received it from the regulated Pilots of that Port signed by them in the year 1755, which I brought over to England for the information of our own Government, which at that time would not be persuaded that large Shipps of Warr could with safety enter there. The General Descriptions of these as well as of the City I take from my own remarks & notes.

In approaching the Coast at about 20 leagues SW distant from the Hoëk,[3] The sounding are 35 fathoms a gritty mud with very small

[1][Pownall's note] A free Bridge has been built at the Public's Expense since I was there.

[2]Here Thomas Pownall appears to take full credit for Lewis Evans' *Analysis . . .* , *op. cit.*

[3]Sandy Hook, New Jersey. Hereafter in the text *Hook.*

at the Aspect at this work ⟨☞⟩ in regard.

There is a certain affectation of prudent secrecy always observed by Writers of all Nations, that avoids the giving of too particular descriptions of the principal ports & Harbours of their own country. Although I believe that a knowledge of these ports of any country may be had & are had, & that ignorance in these matters never arises but from indolence: Yet I restrained myself in the first editions of this work from all descriptions of Ports or Harbours or Towns. Now that they cannot be any longer supposed to be unknown to other nations I now may venture to give a description of them so far as they come within the Geography and Topography of the country. The account of the Port & Harbour of New-York I shall give as I received it from the regulated Pilots of that Port signed by them in the year 1756. Which I brought over to England for the information of our own Government which at that time would not be persuaded that large Ships of War could with safety enter there. The General Descriptions of these as well as of the City I take from my own remarks & notes.

In approaching the Coast at about 20 leagues SW distant from the Hoek. The soundings are 35 fathoms a gritty mud with very small shining particles: at 25 fathom gravel of very small round pebbles red & black: in 23 fathom the ground partakes more of white sand. The soundings shoal very regularly as you advance from 20 to 4 fathom which it is off the river.

The first land you discover in coming from sea is the High-land of the Neve-sinks, called by its Indian name, but vulgarly called nevesink or neversunk. These land in a rocky high manner

The new material added by Pownall, anticipating a second edition,
is among the most interesting in the book.

shining particles: at 25 fathom gravel of very small round pebbles red & black: in 23 fathom the ground partakes more of white sand. The soundings shoal pretty regularly as you advance from 20 to 4 fathom, which it is off the barr.

The first Land you discover in coming from Sea is the high-land of the *Nave-sinks* so called by its Indian name, but vulgarly called *Neversink* or *never sunk*. These Lands are a rocky high Hummock covered with Woods. As you approach you begin to see on the right hand faintly the line of the land of Long island: also under the Nave-sinks stretching from their foot for about 4 miles to the right or northward of this high land a neck of low sandy hills coverd with Cedars & holly, ending in a low sandy point. Between this neck called the Cedars & the Navesink is a beach which the sea sometimes breaks through so as to seperate the Cedars from the Navesink.

This was the first land of America that I saw & here I first landed. My Eye was upon the watch, and everything struck it. My imagination was all suspense & every thing made a vivid impression on my mind. I made a scetch of these Highlands & Hoëk [Hook] & the approach: there is not much picturesque matter in the view but it would make a pretty back ground to a Sea-piece of shipping. There was a trifling circumstance scarce worth remark, but as it struck my senses & I putt it down in my notes, I will transcribe it. My senses, as I advanced up towards the City were struck with a high odorous smell of burning of cedar. The inhabitants I found light their fires with cedar chips. The boatmen who row'd me up when I noticed this were insensible to it being nothing uncommon to them. In like manner when an American first comes to England, His senses are struck with the suffocating smell of our Coal Fires to which we dwellers are insensible. Having at that time my School-books in my head I recollected that Homer had thought this peculiar though trifling circumstance worthy notice in his description of Calypso's Island τηλόθι δ᾽ ὀδμὴ κέδρου τ᾽ εὐκεάτοιο θύου τ᾽ ἀνὰ νῆσον ὀδώδει δαιομένων and that Virgil thought fitt to copy this in his description of the Island of Circe.

Urit odoratam nocturna in Lumina Cedrum

Eneid. Lib. 7. line 13

The Cedar point which runs like a mole from the Navesinks was with the Navesinks called by the Dutch Sandy-Hoëk. It forms one side of the Entrance of Hudson's [Hudson] or North River & Long Island which is about 8 or 9 miles distant from this point the other. As a large Bank of Sand runs off from Long-island to within a mile & half of the

Hoëk [Hook] the entrance into the River is between this bank (called
the east-bank) and a shoal which lyes E, off the Hoëk [Hook] & runs
parrallel to it, called middle-ground, a thread of Sand about half a mile
over, runs from the E bank to this middle ground, which forms a kind of
barr at the entrance, over which the soundings were, in my time, one or
two & twenty feet. I remember striking on this in passing over in a
twenty-gun ship. There is another very narrow passage between the
middle-ground & the Hoëk [Hook]. After a Ship is over the barr it soon
finds 5, 6, or 7 fathom water. The course up to the Narrows (a narrow
pass between two bluff points of Staten & Long Islands) in the way to yᵉ
City is round the East-bank & must be kept on, W Southerly, five or
six miles. It then rounds Northward Easterly to go up to the Narrows,
Between this E bank & the W bank (A long bank running off Staten
Island 5 miles). The Narrows are about three quarters of a mile across
from point to point. The pass not a furlong. The soundings in these
narrows are 13 & 14 fathom. As some of these soundings & some of these
courses here in before mentioned may have changed in a period of near
30 years, the nautical reader is desired to compare these with later
observations.

After having passed the Barr & come from sea within the Hoëk
[Hook], & under the pleasant feel of still Water, the Eye is delighted with
the View of a most noble bay. On the left are the rocky & high woodlands of the Navesink wild & Picturesque, contrasted by the settlements
& cultivated land of Long Island on the right. The Farms on Staten
Island & the very Peculiar View of the Narrows meet your Eye upon
the Ships bow, the bay & harbour of Amboy lyeing right before you.
These pleasing & thus varied Objects form the sides of this Noble Bay.
As you advance through the Narrows the Eye expands its view again
into a still more pleasing second bay, a kind of Amphitheatre, to appearance Circular, of about 12 Miles Diameter. This being constantly
Covered with Boats Sloops & every kind of Shipping passing & repass-
ing through it & across it in all directions seems all alive with bustle &
buisness. As you advance you see in the center of the Background on the
Point of an Island the City of New York having the opening of Hudson
or North River with the high lands of Bergen & New-Jersey on the right
of it & the opening of the Harbour & Quays in the East River bounded
by the bluff points of Red Hoëk [Hook] & Yellow Hoëk [Hook] & the
Heights of Brook line[1] in Long Island on the left of it. This populous &

[1]Present Brooklyn Heights.

well built Town with the Fort[1] in front with the many steeples of its Churches the Turret of the Stadthouse & [Ex] Change dispersed amidst its buildings & the multitude of Shipping with which it is thronged perpetually makes a very striking appearance & alltogether as fine & as pleasing a View as I ever saw. I made a Scetch of this View taken from the narrows as the Foreground, correcting the bearings of all the points by the Compass. I never look at it but with a revived feel of the many pleasing daies I spent at New-York; but a certain painful regrett has always at the same time so wrought upon my mind that I have never yet found myself in a disposition to finish a drawing from it. I also copied from a Dutch Picture, and keep by me as a matter of Curiosity & Antiquity, a View of this town as it was, when a Dutch Town called Nieu-Amsteldam. One sees in this old view rows of the Gabel-ends of Houses, built under the Fort also repeated rows of the like Gabel-ends rising on the rising ground behind it mixed with the high roofed Churches & Stadthouse. On the Parapets of the Fort one sees a Flag staff of the Beacon-kind, & a Windmill. All the Houses & Public buildings were of the Dutch taste. Since it came into the hands of the English New Churches & New Houses have been built in a more modern taste & many of the Gabel-ends of y[e] old houses, just as is done in Holland, have been new fronted in the Italian stile. The City however still retains the general appearance of a Dutch-town with its row of Gabel-ends & the rows of Trees on the sides of the Streets. It is Cheifly in its publick as well private buildings built with brick & neatly paved.

There are four Principal Streets as nearly parallel to each other as the uneaveness of the ground will permitt, all the cross streets the lesser & secondary streets are at right angles with these & in general run from shore to shore across the narrow point whereon the town stands. The Principal Street is a noble broad Street 100 feet wide called Broad Way. It commences at the north gate of the Fort by a kind of Square or Place formerly a Parade[2] now (1755) a bowling green railed in, & runs directly in a strait line NE better than half a mile where it Terminates by another intended square. On the west side[3] of the Street are Several very

---

[1]Fort George 1726-1788. *N.Y.C.D.*, V, 782; John F. Watson, *Annals of Philadelphia* (Philadelphia, For sale by Uriah Hunt, 1830), Appendix, p. 29.
[2]Known as The Parade. *Valentine's Manual of Old New York, 1924*. Edited by Henry Collins Brown ... (N.Y., Gracie Mansion, c. 1923), p. 58.
[3][Pownall's note for revised and enlarged edition]

This west side, The Churches & other buildings mentioned here have been burnt down since this was written.
The great fire of 1776 burned up Broadway on the Western side from the wharf near White Hall slip to St. Paul's Church at the entrance to The Common. Watson, *Annals of Philadelphia, op. cit.*, Appendix, p. 57.—Ed.

handsome spacious Houses of the principal Inhabitants, the Lutheran Church & the English Church called Trinity Church a very large plain brick Building, but within as spacious commodious & handsome a Place of Worship as I ever saw belonging to a private Parish. In the S.E. part of the City there is another handsome modern built Church called St. George's Chapel.[1] I am told that a third English Church called St. Pauls[2] was built in broad Way: & that the intended Square above mentioned hath been built. How much of these have been burnt down I don't know.

The next principal Street called broad street being about 80 feet wide commences at the landing at west dock, where stand the [Ex] Change[3] & runs about a quarter of a mile up to the Stadthouse[4] or Town-house, An old Dutch building very spacious & well adapted to all the Offices kept therein, In apartments within which the Council Assembly & Courts of Justice hold their Sessions.

The third principal Street is called Hanover Street[5] & runs from Hanover-square,[6] in the form of an S running in its course round the sides of a high piece of ground.

The fourth principal Street like Tower Street[7] in London runs along the Vlys Quays wharfs & docks on the eastern bank of the town. The numbers of Houses & Buildings in the year 1753 were as follows:

Publick Buildings	25
Dwelling Houses	1991
Store-houses	207
Stables	150
Distilling houses	10
Sugar Houses	2
Brew houses	4
Rope Walks	4
Total	2393

The Inhabitants of the City extending through out the Island were about 15,000. The average of the Rent of the Buildings were estimated

---

[1]At Beekman and Cliff Street. *Plan of the City of New York in North America. Surveyed in the years 1766 & 1767. To His Excellency Sir Henry Moore ... is dedicated ... this Plan of the City of New York and its Environs ... B. Batzer .... Surveyed in the years 1766 & 1767.* London, Jefferys & Faden, 1776. Hereafter cited as Ratzer's *Map of New York.*

[2]On Broadway between Partition and Veasyes Streets, at the entrance to The Common, Ratzer's *Map of New York, op. cit.*

[3]Over Broad Street at Dock Street. *Ibid.*

[4]Corner Broad Street and Wall Street. *Ibid.*

[5]Hanover Street, or Queen Street. Queen Street is now Pearl Street. Watson, *Annals of Philadelphia, op. cit.,* Appendix, p. 36.

[6][Pownall's note for revised and enlarged edition] Those broad openings in a Town, which the French call Places, We call Squares. This Appellation becomes ridiculous as all these Squares are Triangles.

[7]Water Street. Ratzer's *Map of New York, op. cit.*

at 25£ p^r Ann. To give some idea of the manner in which their Houses were furnished I here insert from a speculative estimate made for me by the Vendue-master[1] extracts of the averages of the value of the Plate and furniture of the First, Middling and lower Class of Householders. He averaged the first at 700£, The second at 200£, The third he subdivided into two Classes & averaged the value of the furniture of the first of these at 40£ the second at 20£.

This pleasant City standing in a most charming situation, & enjoying the most delicious Climate in the world was inhabited by an hospitable cheerfull social people living by their extensive fortune Landed & Commercial & from the plenty & cheapness of every article of living better & more hospitably without parades than I ever saw any people in the old world live.

The North or Hudsons [Hudson] river, at opening which into the bay this City stands, is of the most perfect navigation; is seldom frozen up in Winter which the Delaware on which Philadelphia stands generally is, as also often the harbour of Boston. This North River carries from New-York to Kinder-hoëk [Kinderhook] which about 20 miles below Albany pretty uniformly 7 fathom water except where it passes through the Highlands there its depth is from 15 to 30 fathom. From Kinder-hoëk [Kinderhook] to the overslough (a barr of shallows) the depth is from 7 to 12 feet. After you are over the shallows of the overslough it deepens somewhat again up to Albany. The Navigation from New York to Albany was intirely carried on in a kind of Sloop of about 60 tons called a Yacht. The Dutch Schippers of Albany are the Cheif Navigators. They had in 1754 twenty three of these Vessels in constant employ. From the Commodiousness & Cleanliness of these Vessels one enjoys the most agreeable passage that can be wished. These Yachts brought down the Produce of Albany County Wheat Flour Pease. The Produce of the Indian Trade &c to New York & their Back carriage was all sorts of European Goods & Produce Rum Sugar Salt & every article of manufacture both for the use of the Inhabitants & for the Indian Trade.

Staaten [Staten] Island is included within the Province of New York, and is of itself one of the Counties of that Province called Richmond: This Island is about 12 Miles long, and about Six Miles broad, it is high, dry, and hilly, pleasant and fruitful; the County Town Richmond lies near the Center of it.

[1][Pownall's note for the revised and enlarged edition] A Public Auctioneer Commissioned by Government.

Long Island, formerly called by the Dutch Nassau Island, (separated from New York by the East River of Half a Mile Breadth, over which is a Ferry) is included within the Province of New York, and contains Three Counties,[1] viz. King's, Queen's, and Suffolk Counties: This Island lies nearly East and West, is more than 100 Miles long, and taking one Place with another at a Medium about 16 Miles broad. When Lewis Evans describes this Island as formed by and consisting of Sand only, he was not apprized that a Ridge of Hills beginning from the Ferry at the Narrows runs rounding across the West End of the Island to the North Side, and continues in a Range along that Side almost to the End: This Ridge forms the substantial Part of the Island; it is said that there is a Straum of Coal in this Island. The South Side of it is indeed a level Plain formed by the Accretion of Silt and Sand at the Foot of this more elevated Ridge; this Plain extends with a long slope to the Ocean, but has (as Land thus formed always has) a high Beach or Bar in the Front of it, a little below Low Water Mark.

"Hudson's [Hudson] River, at whose Entrance stands the City of New York,[g] has good Depth of Water for Sloops, and the Tide extended above Albany,[h] more than 180 Miles into the *Upland*. While all the Rivers, from thence South-westward, are navigable with Sea Vessels in the *Lower Flats* only, this opens Communications with the Inland Parts of the Continent, of the utmost Importance to the British Interest. The Communication between Albany and Montreal[i] is described below. A Route of no less Importance in the immediate Affairs of the English opens from Albany westward into the Heart of the Continent, and is performed commonly in the light flat-bottomed Boats.[2] To avoid a great Cataract of 75 Feet,[3] in the Mohocks [Mohawk] River,[k] they carry all the Goods, destined for the Inland Trade,[4] 16 Miles over Land to Skenèctady [Schenectady][l] in Waggons. There they embark on the Mohocks [Mohawk] River, which in general is pretty rapid and shallow, and proceed to the Long Fall,[m][5] where they are obliged to carry their

g F e
h D c
Hudson's river navigable with Sloops to Albany
i Page 19 Evans' *Analysis* inland Navigation from Albany to Oswego
k D c
l D c
m C d

[1]At present Four Counties: Kings, Queens, Nassau, and Suffolk.
[2]Small batteaux known as three handed and four handed boats. Jeptha R. Simms, *History of Schoharie County and Border Wars of New York* . . . (Albany, Munsell & Tanner, 1845), p. 139.
[3]Cohoes Falls.
[4][Pownall's note] The soil of the Land through which this Road goes is Sand for the first Seven Miles, the Timber nothing but Pitch Pine, the Underwood Fern in great Quantities, some Shumack and Dwarf Oak, Four Miles more the same; a wet Bottom crosses the Land here of about a Mile; the Wood Birch, Aspin, Chestnut, Oak; the remaining Five Miles much the same again as before. I observed in the Woods many Flowers, as the Heart's-ease, the Blue Lupin, the Convolvolies; and in the swampy Bottoms, the Orange Lilly, and the Iris.
[5]Known as the Little Falls in comparison with the great Cohoes Falls. This was the first carrying place on the Mohawk west of Schenectady. Simms, *op. cit.*, pp. 138-39. Present site of Little Falls, N.Y.

Boats and Goods a Mile over Land. The same River conducts them again to the Great Carrying-place,[n][1] where, according as the Season is wet or dry, they are obliged to carry over Land Four or Eight Miles to Wood Creek.[2] This Creek is very gentle and crooked, and together with Onoyda [Oneida] Lake and Onondaga River,[o][3] furnishes an easy passage to the Seneca River; which at 12 Miles above Oswego[p] has a Fall,[4] where they carry their Boats about 100 Feet, and Goods liable to damage by wet near a Mile and a Half; besides Three very bad Rifts, and several small ones in other Places. The Whole is performed in a Week.

n The Dragplat C d

o C e

p C e

"But if you intend to go to the Onondágas or Cayúgas Country,[5] you turn up the Seneca River, and in Half a Mile come to a little gentle Rippling, where the River may be forded on Horseback:[q] From hence upwards it is very deep, and so gentle as scarce to discover which Way it runs."[6]

The Passage up Seneca River q A Ford C e

The Tackonaëg [Taconic] Mountains, hereafter mentioned in the Description of the Eastern Division, run nearly parallel to Hudson's [Hudson] River at the Distance of 16 Miles one Place with another; the Land between these Mountains and the River is hilly, stony, and but indifferent Soil; the Timber White and Black Oak on the Hills, Hickory in the Valleys, with Swamps of Ash.

"Hudson's [Hudson] River has no Branches navigable with Ships or Shalops; for it is truly but a single Channel extended into the Land, where the Country East and West of it afford those Two Series already mentioned."[7]

The northern Part of this peculiar Division of the Country is formed by a Succession of Drowned Lands and Lakes,[8] lying in deep Chasms, that have the same Direction North and South.

Between the northern Part of the Hudson's [Hudson] River and the southern Parts of the Lakes and Drowned Land is the Height of the

---

[1]Site of Fort Stanwix, *N.Y.C.D.*, VII, 985. Present site of Rome, N.Y.

[2]Wood Creek in the vicinity of Rome, N.Y. Not to be confused with the Great Carrying Place (Fort Edward) and Wood Creek east of Lake George.

[3]Oneida River.

[4]Oswego Falls. On present maps that part of the Seneca River from Onondaga Lake to Oswego on Lake Ontario is called Oswego River.

[5]The Iroquois' lands extended from the Hudson River west along the Mohawk, and connecting waterways to Lake Erie. The five original tribes in the league were the Mohawks who lived in the east, the Oneidas and the Onondagas, who occupied the central portion, the Cayugas, in the Finger Lakes region, and the Senecas whose land bordered on Lake Erie. Lewis M. Morgan, *League of the Ho-Da'-no-Sau-nee, or Iroquois.* (Rochester, Sage & Brother, 1851), pp. 42-43. For location on map see: John Mitchell, *A Map of the British and French Dominions in North America . . .* London Published by the Author Feb[ry] 13th 1755, according to Act of Parliament.

[6]Quoted from Evans' *Analysis*, p. 20; reprinted in Gipson's *Lewis Evans*, p. 164.

[7]*Ibid.*

[8]Lake George and Lake Champlain region.

Land of about 12 or 14 Miles Breadth, whence the Waters run different Ways, Part to the South, Part to the North; over this Portage to Lake George is a Waggon Road about 13 Miles.[1]

Vide Appendix Van Schaik's Journal

The Country Between the Drowned Lands and Lake George, as the Journals of the European Scouts both French and English describe it, also according to the Information which the Indians give of it, is a very impracticable Country. The Mountains are high, steep, and abrupt; and the Vales filled with deep Lakes and Ponds. The deep narrow Vale through which the Wood Creek creeps, is a Mixture between Lake and Swamp. The great western Vale or rather Chasm is an intire Lake, the Lake George, deep, narrow, and bounded on both Sides to the Water's Edge with exceeding high Mountains. Kankusker Bay[2] indeed runs up into a swampy Cove between Two Ridges. The Navigation which this Lake affords is obstructed at its northern Embouchure by a Ridge or Ledge of Rocks over which the surplus Issue of its Waters falls. Here is a Portage, I mean the old Indian Hunters and Traders Portage, over a high Hill on the South East Side to Tiëonderôga [Ticonderoga]. The Course which our Troops took was generally to land on Sabbath-day Point, whence a Road, by a Mill which stood on a small Rivulet, leads

Ticonderoga

to Fort Carillon[3] at Chëonderôga [Ticonderoga] or Trois Rivieres. This word denotes the Fork of a River or the confluence of two branches which go off in one united Stream. This the French always translate *Trois-rivieres* The Dutch who first improved this rout, using the letters *tie* to express the sound, *che* as we do yᵉ letters *tion* to express *çhon* wrote the word Tiëonderôga, and the letter *e* in the correspondencies being mistaken for *c* this place gott the name of Ticonderoga. Custom has adopted this original mistake, And the using the real name in its true orthography looks so like affectation That I cannot but think this Explanation, by way of Apology at least has become necessary. The Situation on yᵉ Ohio, on which Fort de Quesne, afterwards called *Fort Pitt* was built, was by the Indians called Chëonderôga, & accordingly by the French called *Trois-rivieres*. It is recorded by that name in the famous *Leaden Plate*,[4] which was buried there as a Memorial of their

---

[1]See "A Map of the Site of the Battle of Lake George, September 8th, 1755." William Johnson, *Papers . . . , op. cit.*, II, map opposite 2.

[2]North Arm of Lake George. A high ridge of Tongue Mountain rises between this bay and Lake George proper.

[3]Fort Carillon (1756-1759). This fort was abandoned and burned by the French.

[4]According to the "Official Statement" of Celeron there was on the third of August, 1749 a leaden plate buried "upon the southern bank of the Ohio at four leagues distance below the River aux Boeufs, directly opposite a naked mountain, and near an immense stone upon which certain figures are rudely enough carved." This plate was buried on the Allegheny 115 miles above Pittsburgh. Charles

Possession. Untill I had occasion to explain this it was always a matter of Puzzle to our Ministers what Place in those Quarters the French meant to design by Trois-rivieres. Here follows an exact copy of that plate.

L'an 1749 Du Regne de Louis XV Roy de France Nous Celeron Commandant d'un detachment Envoie par Monsieur Le Mis de la Gallisoniere Commandant General De la Nouvelle France pour retablir la tranquillite dans quelques Villages Sauvages de ces cantons avons enterré Cette Plaque A. [3[1] rivieres dessous la riviere au beouf ce 3 Aoust] pres de la Riviere Oyo autrement belle Riviere pour Monument de Renouvellement de la Possession que nous avons pris de la ditte Riviere Oyo & de toutes celles qui y tombnt[2] & toutes les Terres des deux Cotes jusque aux Sources des dittes Rivieres ainsi qu'en ont jovy ou du jovir les precedent Roy de France et qu'ils s'y sont maintenûs par les Armes & par les Traites speciallement par ceux de Reswick du Trecht & d'Aix la Chapelle.

on ye Back is

Paul Labrosse Fecit

[Endorsed on back of Manuscript] Copy of the Leaden Plate Buried at the Forks of Monongahela & Ohio by Mon^{sr} Celeron by way of taking Possession & as a memorial & Testimony thereof 1753 or 2.

The Navigation from hence[3] to Crown Point and Fort Frederick[4] is uninterrupted through a River; the Narrows between these Points, which form the Entrance into Lake Champlain, the Indians call Teck-ya-dough Nigarêgé.[5] The Point on which Fort Frederick stands is not, as has been vulgarly imagined, Crown Point; it is the opposite Point, so

---

B. Galbreath, ed., *Expedition of Celeron to the Ohio Country in 1749.* (Columbus, Ohio, The F. J. Heer Printing Co., 1921), pp. 26, 64. Mr. Pownall has interpreted *3 rivieres,* scratched on the plate, to be *Trois Rivieres.* Probably the inscription was intended to connote the third stream below Riviere au Beouf. The *Proces Verbal* and inscription on the plate was not, in every case, identical.

[1][Pownall's note for revised and enlarged edition] This is only scratch'd with ye point of a knife & scarce legible in a space which was left blank to be fill'd up when buried.

[2][Pownall's note for revised and enlarged edition] It is so written in the Plate.

[3]Ticonderoga.

[4]French fort (1731-1759). For routes from Albany see "Trails, Military Roads and Forts from Albany to Crown Point." Johnson, *Papers, op. cit.,* I, map opp. p. 896.

[5]Johnson, *Papers, op. cit.,* II, map opp. 422, *note* 22.

called, by the Dutch Crun [Crûm P^t] Punt,[1] by the French, Pointe à la Chevelure,[2] from a remarkable Action of Scalping committed there: The Point on which the Fort stands, a long Point, and low in Comparison of the Mountains which surround it, runs into the Lake, having the River to the East and a narrow Bay, which runs up South, to the West of it; at the South Head of this Bay was a Carrying-place to the River, much used in order to avoid passing by the Fort, by the French Indians and Traders in their smuggling Intercourse with the People of Albany.

Lake Champlain, as the French call it; Corlaer, as the Dutch call it; but according to its Indian Name, Caniaderi Guarunté [Caniadere'-guaront'], signifying the Gate or Mouth of the Country,[3] lies in a deep narrow Chasm of the Land, bounded up to the Water's Edge with steep Mountains on the western Shore, which continue thus to bound it as far as Cumberland Bay; the Ranges of the Mountains then trend off North West, and the Shore is low and in many Parts swampy. Many Streams, some which at Times issue an Abundance of Waters, fall into this Lake on the West Side, but they cannot be called Rivers; they are mere Cataracts, and so barred with Rocks and Sand there is no Entrance to them.

The eastern Shores are formed by a low swampy Tract of Land; the Mountains keep off at the Distance of about 12 Miles.[b] The Soundings of the Lake are very deep in general, in many Places 60, 70, and 80, and in some Parts 100 Fathom. There are Three or Four considerable Streams fall into the Lake on the East Side. Otter Creek is the most considerable; an Account of which you have in Captain Hobbs's Journal in the Appendix.

Although these Lakes, Swamps, and Drowned Lands consist of such a Multitude of Waters, yet the Issue of their Surplus by the Sorel River is very small, and bears no Proportion to the Mass which seems to require an abundant Torrent. This is no singular Phaenomenon, it would have been singular were it otherwise than it is. The Issue of no River bears any Proportion to the Mass of Water which seems to flow in all the Parts of it.

Before I proceed to the Description of the Two principal Divisions of the Country, I must just passing (rather to mark my Ignorance than

b
Vide Capt.
Hobbs' and
Van Schaik's
Journals
Appendix
B b

B c d

---

[1]Johnson, *Papers, op. cit.*, II, map opp. 422, *note* 22. [2]Peter Palmer, *History of Lake Champlain . . .* (Albany, J. Munsell, 1866), p. 3.
[3]Johnson, *Papers, op. cit.*, II, map opp. 422, *note* 22.

presuming to give Information) observe, that the Country, lying to the West of these Lakes, bounded on the North West by Canada River,[1] and on the South by the Mohawks [Mohawk] River, called by the Indians Couxsachrâgé, which signifies the Dismal Wilderness or Habitation of Winter, is a triangular, high mountainous Tract, very little known to the Europeans; and although a hunting Ground of the Indians, yet either not much known to them, or, if known, very wisely by them kept from the Knowledge of the Europeans. It is said to be a broken unpracticable Tract; I own I could never learn any Thing about it.

[1]St. Lawrence River.

SECT. III.

Eastern Division

FROM a Review of this Division, collected from a thousand Particulars, we may here begin by saying, that the great Portion of this Country which lies East of Hudson's [Hudson] River and Lake Champlain, lies in the Form of a Lunet or the Quarter of a Circle. The range of the Land of this First Part, beginning at Long Island Sound, runs nearly North and South, and then in about North Lat. 45, curves away Eastward to the Gulf of St. Lawrence. It consists of a high, hilly, and in some Part mountainous, Tract of Land, running in Ranges which follow the general Course of the main Land, and in general keep nearly parallel to each other; it is from 180 to 200 Miles across: It is divided into several principal or main Ranges, each consisting of a Multitude of parallel Ridges, each also having many Spurs and Branches deviating from the Course of the general Range, which Branches are sometimes broken into irregular hilly Land.

The highest Part of this Tract of Mountains may be defined by a Line drawn North westerly from the White Hills (which will be hereafter described) to the 45th Parallel of North Lat.

A a l

Beginning from this Point in Lat. 45, and tracing this Tract to Long Island Sound, it is found to be divided into Two Parts by a great Vale through which Connecticut, or Long River (as its Indian Name signifies) flows; this Vale is from 12 to 20 Miles, in some Parts, broad. One of the main Ranges runs between Hudson's [Hudson] River, Wood Creek, Lake Champlain, and Connecticut River: Between Wood Creek, Lake Champlain, and Connecticut River it trends North North East, and afterwards North East. It consists of One high Range[1] only with hilly Lands, and not Ridges on each Side, suited for very fine Settlements.° This is The Tract of Country now settled & called *Vermont*.

c
Vide Capt. Hobbs' Journal in the Appendix

Capt. Holland has since the War run a Line from Connecticut River to the Mouth of St. Francis River, 90 Miles. The Topography of his Survey gives the same Account. On each Side of this great long Vale, at the Distance of about 100 Miles from Long Island Sound, the Two main

[1]Green Mountains, Vermont.

Ranges which form its Boundaries are again sub-divided into Two Parts, each by a Vale of near 100 Miles long; that on the West by the Vale through which the Hoosatonick [Housatonic] or Westonhoek River runs, passing to Sea by Milford, bounded on the West by the Taconick [Taconic], and on the East by Hoosatonick [Housatonic] Mountains, which also make the western Bound on the Vale of Connecticut. The most eastern Ridge of this main Range ends in a Bluff-head at Meridon [Meriden]: A Second ends in like Manner at Walingford [Wallingford]: A Third at New Haven: Where these Ridges terminate, the Face of the Country breaks into irregular hilly Ground. The Range of hills on the eastern Side of this Vale is subdivided by the Vale, beginning near the South of the great Ouätchuset [Wachusett], through which the River that hath acquired the Name of the Thames runs, passing to Sea by New London. This Vale is bordered on the West by a Range of the Chicabé [Chicopee] Mountains,[1] these terminate a little below East Hadham [Haddam], and the Face of the Country spreads in like Manner into hilly Land (These form the East Boundary of the Vale of Connecticut) and on the East by One of the Ranges of the Ouätchuset [Wachusett] Mountain continuing South to Stonington. Going from the same Line in Lat. 45, of the greatest Height of these Range of Mountains, and following them to the East northerly: They all seem to range as united until again divided by the Bay of Chaleurs [Chaleur], an Arm of the Gulf of St. Lawrence.

All the Rivers which have their Sources amidst the northern Ridges of this great Range fall into Canada or St. Lawrence River, as the St. Francis, Chaudiere, and many others. All which have their Sources amidst the southern Ridges fall into the Bay of Fundé [Fundy] or into the main Ocean; their Rise are almost universally from Lakes and Ponds, great Part of their first Courses lie in the Valleys amidst the mountainous Ridges in the Forms of drowned swampy Lands, or a Succession of Ponds, and while they do so their Courses are generally, I might say universally, from West to East: Whenever through Gaps or Intersections they can get away Southward they do so, tumbling over almost continued Falls across the Ranges. If they happen to find a Course along the Side of any Spur or Branch which runs South, it is otherwise, and their Courses are free. But the other Circumstance being that which forms in general their characteristic Nature; these Rivers in general are very little capable of Marine Navigation to any Length of Course within the Country; St. John's River in Nova Scotia excepted.

[1]Only the river retains this name. See p. 60 this work.

CONNECTICUT RIVER. This River rises in North Lat. 45°10′, at the Height of the Land, in Long. 4, East of the Meridian of Philadelphia. It hath its Birth in a swampy Cove at the Height of the Land; after having slept for Eight or 10 Miles in this State of Infancy, it leaves the Place of its Birth by tumbling over Four separate Falls; it then turns to the West, and keeps close under the Hills which form the northern Boundary of the Vale in which it runs; and in 10 Miles further Course runs under the Little Monadnaëg [Monadnock] Mountains for about Four Miles, at the End it turns round a high sharp Point, and for about a Mile runs North West, till coming under a high Hill it turns again to the South West; at Two Miles and a Half Distance from hence a little River called Leack's [Leech's] Stream[1] falls into it, coming down a Valley from the North West. This Stream[2] interlocks with some of Heads of St. Francis's Waters, and has been formerly an Indian Road. From hence, running under the Hills of the western Boundary of the Vale, it comes in Six or Seven Miles Course to the Grand Monadnaëg [Monadnock] Mountains on the West; as it runs Eight or 10 Miles further Course, it approrches the Mountains on the East Side of the Vale, and runs under rocky Mountains on the East. Almost opposite to this, in a flat swampy Interval on the West Shore, there is a Mineral Spring.[3] About Eight Miles below this is the Beginning of a new Settlement,[4] the First in the Course of this River; about Four Miles lower, opposite to Amanuseag [Ammonoosuc][5] River, which falls into it from the East, are Two more Settlements. Three Miles lower there is a Fall in the River. Here, once for all, let me observe, that these Ledges of Rocks over which the Rivers fall, serve in Nature the same Purposes which our Locks, that Art erects across our Rivers, are meant to serve: They hold up the Waters, and aid also the Navigation by causing Still Water above them. Three Miles below this Fall there is a very con-

[1]Probably the small unnamed stream which flows into the Upper Connecticut River at Stewartstown. For location on contemporary plan see *A Plan of a Survey Made to explore the Country for a Road between Connecticut River & St. Francis, op. cit.*

[2][Pownall's note] Here the Rout by Land from St. Francis's River, not 30 Miles, comes into the Connecticut River according to the Survey given to me by Capt. Holland Jan. 1776, which confirms what I had above noted.

[3]Near North Stratford, N.H. *A Map of the Province of New York, Reduc'd from the large Drawings of that Province, compiled from Actual Surveys*

by order of His Excellency William Tryon Esqʳ .... By Claude Sauthier . . . Engraved by William Faden, 1776. London, Wm. Faden, 1776. Reprinted by the United States Constitution Sesquicentennial Convention under the title, *New York at the time of the ratification of the Constitution from 1776 and 1787 originals in the Library of Congress at Washington.* Hereafter cited as Sauthier's *Map . . . 1776.*

[4][Pownall's note for revised and enlarged edition] This was transcribed in the year 1774.

[5]Upper Ammonoosuc River. Present Ammonoosuc River flows into the Connecticut south of Israel River.

siderable Settlement begun by ———— Burnside,[1] Esq; Five Miles below this Settlement Capt. Page's[2] Settlements lie on the Intervals amidst the Windings of the River, under a high Hill on the West; on the East Israel's [Israel] River comes in, and Two Miles lower are several Settlements on the Intervals called Cahass [Cohass], the Upper or Lesser Cahass [Cohass]: The River keeps its Course South westerly, and then quitting the Hills on the East, and the Vale in which it hath hitherto ran, crosses the western Range, and tumbles with a Course South West for 15 Miles together over Rifts and Ledges of Rocks[3] till it meets the high Lands on the West Side; and then, under the Foot of these, resumes its old Course South-westerly, in a Second Vale, or rather Second Stage of the same Vale. Here again on the Interval Lands are several new Settlements begun. In about Two Miles further Course the River gets again under the Hills on the eastern Side where comes in Hurd's River,[4] and running under them for about Two Miles falls Four Feet over a Ledge of Rocks which run across its Bed. Four Miles below this it passes a Strait betwixt Two Rocks. After this the New Settlements are found pretty thick upon the Meadows and Intervals of the Lower or Great Cohass. Townships are settling very fast on the Banks on both Sides. Running along the Township of Lebanon, under high steep Hills, on the West, called Cunney Mountain,[5] the River tumbles over several Falls. In Plainfield Township a Ledge of Rocks about Three Feet high crosses its Course: in Eight Miles further Course it runs close under the Ascutney Mountains which rise high on the West Side the Vale; it next runs under the Casowetchawêgé[6] Mountains on the same Side, close under the South Point of which a Road[7] goes off West to Crown Point. About Eight Miles further with a still deep Course the River passes by Charles Town [Charlestown], late a Garrison Number

Vide Capt. Hobbs' Journal Appendix

[1]Thomas Burnside, one of Roger's Rangers. Jeanette R. Thompson, *History of the Town of Stratford, New Hampshire, 1773-1925* (Concord, N.H., Rumford Pub. Co. 1925), p. 31.

[2]David Page. *Ibid.*, p. 31.

[3]Fifteen Miles Falls above Barnet, Vermont. Walter Hard, *The Connecticut* ... (N.Y., Rinehart & Co., c. 1947), pp. 9, 168.

[4]Not located. Probably a stream flowing into the Connecticut in the vicinity of Hards Island Falls in Lyman township, New Hampshire.

[5]Probably Sawyers Mountains. See "A Map of the Most Inhabited part of New England Containing the Provinces of Massachusets Bay and New Hamp-shire with the Colonies of Conecticut and Rhode Island.". . . November 29th, 1774. Published according to Act by Tho[s] Jefferys. Jefferys, *American Atlas, op. cit.*, nos. 15 and 16.

[6]Near the junction of Williams and Connecticut Rivers. Sauthier's *Map ... 1776, op. cit.*

[7]Crown Point Road, an old military road from Amherst, Mass. to Crown Point, N.Y. This road has been marked by a granite marker set up near Charlestown, N.H. Federal Writers' Project, New Hampshire, *New Hampshire, a guide to the Granite State* (Boston, Houghton, Mifflin, Co., 1938), pp. 366-367.

4,[1] a little above which comes in Black River from the North West. About Seven or Eight Miles below this the River runs under a very high Mountain,[2] rising on the East Shore opposite to Rockingham Township: Here are the great Falls,[3] in passing which the River shoots with great Rapidity between Two Rocks scarce 30 Feet asunder, and then extends itself into a wide Bason. The River continuing to run nearly the same Course in the same Kind of Vale amidst the like new Settlements for Two or Three Miles, then runs under the West River Mountains,[4] so called being opposite to a considerable River called West River, which runs from the North West; these Mountains are on the East Side the Vale. In these Mountains there is the Appearance of there having been some Eruption or Volcano. In 11 Miles more making a great Bend directly South West, and short back again North East. The River comes to the Boundary Line between the Provinces Massachuset's Bay [Massachusetts] and New York; a little to the North of which Line the Ashewelot [Ashuelot] River coming from the East falls into it; its Course then through Northfield Township is for Two-thirds of its South-Easterly, for the remaining Third South westerly; it continues winding in the same Course through Part of Deerfield, till it comes to where Miller's [Miller] River falls into it from the East; the River then turns short to the West, and in a sinuous Course comes to a Fall, which from a Battle fought with the Indians there, is called *The Fighting Falls*;[5] it hence turns South-westerly and tumbles over Deerfield Falls,[6] which Falls are impassable for Navigation. Above these Falls the River is wide and the Current slow. A little below these Falls Deerfield River coming from the West and making a Turn Northward falls into Connecticut from the South. Hence running in a broad and still Current between Deerfield and Sunderland Townships it passes just above Sunderland Meeting-house between Two Peaks of Mountains, Mount Toby on the East, and the Sugar Loaves[7] on the West: It then runs South through Hatfield and Hadley Townships, and just opposite to Hadley Meeting-house makes a great western Bend, returning to the East it then runs

---

[1] No. 4, as it was called, was a famous military post throughout the French and Indian War.

[2] Great Falls Mountain. Sauthier's *Map . . . 1776, op. cit.*

[3] At Bellows Falls, Vermont. Hard, *op. cit.*, pp. 21, 168-69.

[4] Not located on contemporary or modern maps. Probably the Northfield Mountains on "A Map of the Most Inhabited Part of New England Containing the Provinces of Massachusets Bay and New Hampshire with the Colonies of Conecticut and Rhode Island". . . November 29th, 1774. Published According to Act by Tho[s] Jefferys. Jefferys, *American Atlas, op. cit.*, nos. 15 and 16.

[5] Fighting Falls as mentioned by Pownall may be part of Deerfield Falls. The Fall fight, an Indian battle, took place at Deerfield Falls in May 1676. Samuel G. Drake, ed., *The Old Indian Chronicle . . .* (Boston, Samuel A. Drake, 1867), pp. 259-62.

[6] Now Turner's Falls. *Ibid.*, p. 260n.

[7] Mt. Sugarloaf.

South-westerly along under a high Ridge of Mountains called the Holy Oaks [Holyoke], which are on the East Side of the Vale, and making, just below Hampton Meeting-house, a great Bend to the West, returns again East directly against the Foot of these Mountains, and passes between that and a high Peak called Mount Tom, over a very bad Rift; hence it runs South, and then taking a South-eastern Course tumbles over Two Falls, the one called Hampton Upper Falls, the Lower one called the Fishing Falls, both these are passable. These Falls[1] are about a Mile and Half asunder, and the River between is broad and deep. Two or Three Miles below, the Chicabee [Chicopee] River, so called as coming from the Chicabee Ridge[2] of Mountains which form here the East Boundary of the Vale, a pretty large Stream runs into it on the East Side. There is another Rift[3] lower down the River just above Enfield Meeting-house, but passable. The River runs hence by Suffeild [Suffield], Simsbury, and Windsor in a strait South Course, with an easy though pretty quick Current, 12 Miles to Hertford [Hartford]. The Tide flows up very near, but not quite to Hertford [Hartford] Town. The River, where it is a Tide River, is said to be filled up from the Soil which is brought down by the Freshes mixing with the Silt which is rolled up by the Tide. But this I apprehend not to be the true Cause, because this Case being common to all Tide Rivers it must equally operate in all, which is not so. The River here ceases to run through a sloping decided Valley. The Land of the Bed of the Valley rises here in broken hilly Ground, and the River ceasing to have the same Slope as above, runs more upon a Level and more crooked: Wherever this happens, the Soil which was before kept suspended by the swifter Current always begins first to subside where the Current is first checked. Hence for 35 or 36 Miles running by Weathersfield [Wethersfield], Kensington, Middleton [Middletown], Haddam, and Durham on its West Banks; Glassenbury [Glastonbury] and Windham on its East Banks, it passes between Seabrook [Saybrook] and Lyme[4] to Sea that is, into Long Island Sound.

It will give some Idea of this delightfull Country & Vale, If one pursues the Account of ye Road through it, as I find it in my Journal. Going From New York into New England one leaves the Dutch towns & the little French Settlement of New Rochell [Rochelle], & Comes to Towns assuming the appearance of English Market Towns. The Spired Churches & Square Townhouses & Porched Houses give ye striking

[1]South Hadley Falls. Hard, *op. cit.*, p. 23.   [3]Enfield Falls. Hard, *ibid.*, p. 23.
[2]See p. 60 this work.   [4]Old Lyme, Connecticut.

Features of this likeness. The Road after Passing over a Bridge across Byram River which divides New York from New England & by Horsneck,[1] Coscal [Cos Cob], Stamford, Middleton [Middlesex],[2] Norwalk, Fairfeild [Fairfield], Stratfeild[3] & Pembroke,[4] rises up a very high hill called Stoney brook hill from whence The Traveller has a very fine View of the Country every way. On one side He views the Sound with all its Islands, bounded by the hilly shores of Long Island. In another Stratford Stratfeild[5] & ye sweet vales in which their Lands lye in every ye most pleasing Groupes of Habitancy Culture Woods & Water. The Road then runs through Stratford & over Stratford River[6] by a Ferry to Milford, hence 10 miles to Newhaven. Newhaven lyes at the NW end of the Harbour or Bay so Called in a Charming Vale, surrounded from the NW round to ye NE with high Cliffs of hills. The Vale is full of Culture in alternate Tillage & Meadows about two miles broad on each side the River. Just as the Road descends at about two miles from Newhaven, The Traveller has from the hills an enchanting view of the Vale & the Town; a Town of Trading, & ye Harbour full of Vessels. The Town is built on a regular designed Plan. Is a Square, has a Place or Square in the Middle, from the Angles of which go off in right lines eight Streets. The Houses are all built in the English Fashion. In the Center of the Square is a fine Meeting house with its Spire like our English Churches. On the East side is another like Meeting: at the South east corner of this Square is an English Church & on ye south side of this Square is a Third Meeting. The College, Called Yale College takes up the west side of the Square. It consists of Two buildings each of three Story besides the Garret. The Old one[7] has three Stair Cases like the sides of our Colleges. The New One[8] has two Staircases. The Old Building is a Framed Wooden Building. The New One is of Brick. From New-haven to Wallingford the road goes up north along ye same Vale[9] in which Newhaven stands. It is 8½ miles to North Haven & 6 to Wallingford. The Road continues in the same Vale four miles beyond

---

[1]Near the New York state line. Christopher Colles. *A Survey of the Roads of United States of America, 1789.* [New York, 1789] Sheet 4. Not indicated on present maps.

[2]Darien, Connecticut, post office. Connecticut (State) *Register and Manual, 1939,* (Hartford, the State, 1939), p. 374.

[3]Bridgeport, Connecticut. *Ibid.,* p. 390.

[4]Danbury, Connecticut post office. *Ibid.,* p. 392.

[5]Bridgeport.

[6]Housatonic.

[7]This building, erected in 1717, stood, in part, until 1782. All except the kitchen and dining room were razed in 1775. Yale University, *Historical Register . . . 1701-1937* (New Haven, Conn., Yale University, 1939), p. 9.

[8]Connecticut Hall (1750) later known as South Middle College. J. W. Barber, *History and Antiquities of New Haven, (Conn.)* . . . (New Haven, J. W. Barber, 1831), p. 21.

[9]Quinnipiac Valley.

Wallingford then crosses north east several ridges & comes into a second Vale called Great Swamp or Kensington. From Wallingford to Meridon [Meriden] 8 miles to Kensington 7. This is a rich well cultivated Vale thickly settled & swarming with People. From Kensington to Weatherfield [Wethersfield] 10 miles. At seven miles of this way, as it runns N East it crosses yᵉ ridges. From yᵉ last ridge three miles from Weathersfield [Wethersfield] The Traveller has a view of the Great Vale of Connecticut up the River, a Landschape picturesque in every assemblage of beautifull Objects that gives a View of a rich populous Inhabitancy of the Human Race enjoying in peace & Liberty every happiness that a *Heaven upon earth* can give. The Vale is from 12 to 8 miles broad, bounded on both sides with high blue hills in parts mountainous. The River runs through the middle of it & Go which you will on each side of it, It is as though you were still travelling along one continued town for 70 or 80 miles on end. At 6, 8, or 10 miles distance you come to yᵉ Body of a Large regular built town,[1] but yᵉ View of the Vale itself in the whole Like a most noble amphitheatre will at first possess the Eye & Mind. Strait, as Milton says, the Eye catches new pleasure when it fixes in detail on yᵉ Multitude of Towns the innumerable farms & settlements, The Groups of Woods & rivulets, amidst cleared & cultured lands teeming with abundance. How other People may be made I don't know and what the Reader may think of me I don't care, but I declare I could never view this scene of happiness nor do I now write yᵉ account of it without an overflowing of heart that putts a tear in My Eye, which Tear that was Sweet is now become a bitter one when I reflect that that Happiness has been destroyed; And most likely can never exist there again in the same degree.[2] From Weathersfeil [Wethersfield] the Road runs 8½ miles to Hertford [Hartford], To Windsor 10 miles coming down from hilly Land upon Windsor another Charming Prospect. To Southfeild[3] 10 miles: To Springfeild 10 miles.[4] Here the Road that goes to Boston goes away East. The Traveller crosses the River by a Ferry boat, and Leaves this charming Vale.

To describe now the Ranges of this Eastern Division, which lie between Connecticut Vale and the Ocean, one may in general state it as an Opinion formed from a Multitude of collected Facts, that this Tract, which is from 50 to 60 Miles broad consists of Three principal Ranges; the First is that which with its many subordinate Ridges forms the

---

[1]Hartford, Connecticut.
[2]Pownall here refers to the Revolutionary War crisis.
[3]Not indicated on present maps.
[4]Springfield, Massachusetts.

eastern Boundary of the Vale of Connecticut, running generally North and sometimes to the Eastward of North from East Hadham [East Haddam] in Connecticut Colony to the Head of the Vale: The Middle Range runs from Stonington in the same Colony along the great Ouätchuset [Wachusett] Mountains, and so away Northerly (as shall be particularly described) in a Direction nearly parallel to the former. The Third rising in the Townships of Hopkinton, Holliston, and Medford, in Massachuset's Province runs North in a like Direction by Watertown and Concord across the Merrimaeg [Merrimac] River and Pantookaëg [Pawtucket Falls][1] fall away to the White Hills [Mountains].

The First Ridge of the westernmost Range keeps in the Massachuset's Province about 10 or 12 Miles from Connecticut River; and the easternmost Ridge of the eastern Range runs in a Meridian about 11 Miles West of Boston, forming a Tract about 60 Miles across. These Ranges do not keep the same Height, but are in some Parts depressed and lowered greatly; in others again they run up into high Peaks of Mountains, or high mountainous Tracts. They are sometimes broken and discontinued, but take up again ranging in the same Direction. Within the Bounds of the Massachuset's Province the middle Range, by the high mountainous Tract called Great Watchusets [Wachusett], is the highest. In New Hampshire Province, about 20 Miles North of the Boundary Line, the western Range, by means of the high Peaks of Monadneag [Monadnock], is the highest. In Lat. 44, within the same Province, the eastern Range, by means of the *White Hills* [Mountains], is beyond all comparison the highest.

To give now some Description of each of these Ranges. The Western one, which as I said, begins in East Hadham [East Haddam], in the Colony of Connecticut, forms the East Boundary of Connecticut Vale; in this Colony, and in the Province of Massachuset[ts], it was called the Chicabee, though the River[2] which runs from and falls into Connecticut River at Springfield seems now to have appropriated that Name to itself alone; it is not very high while it ranges through these Provinces, but after it hath passed the Boundary Line between Massachuset[ts] and New Hampshire about 20 Miles, it runs up into a very high Peak called Monadneag,[3] the Ridge in which Monadneag [Monadnock] rises seems here to be discontinued, but the next West Ridge in the same Range keeps on, and in about Lat. 43° 20′ runs up into another

---

[1]At Lowell, Massachusetts. [2]Chicopee River.
[3]Grand Monadnock.

high Peak called Sunapee Mountains, on the West of which is Sunapee Pond [Lake]; it continues on, and in Lat. 44 rises again into a high Tract called Mooscoog [Moose] Mountain; beyond this my Information does not go.

The Middle Range may be taken as rising about Stonington, in the Colony of Connecticut, on the Sound; it ranges hence North-easterly, and in Rutland District, in the Province Massachuset[ts], runs up into a very high Tract of Land called the Great Watchuset [Wachusett]; this is the highest Land in all this Tract of Country: From the South Side of it springs the River which finally acquires the Name of the Thames; from the West Side the Chicabee [Chicopee]; from the North East Side the Nashaweag [Nashua] River, which runs away North East to Merrimac River; from the South East Side, the principal Branch of the River, afterward called Naraganset[1] River, which runs into Naraganset [Narragansett] Bay by Rhode Island. Ranging still North it rises again just at the Boundary Line into another high Mountain called Wadadeag;[2] keeping the same Course it lowers its Crest, and alternately rises again in Peaks Three or Four Times,[3] and at length in about the Lat. 43° 25' runs up into a high Peak called Cowesawaskoog:[4] Here my Information stops.

The Eastern Range begins by an humble lowly Birth about Hopkington, Holliston, or Medford; the eastern Ridge of this keeps a Course North by Concord, and runs across the River Merrimac at Pantookaëg [Pawtucket] Falls;[5] it begins to grow more considerable in the Province New Hampshire, and runs up into a high Ridge called Tower Hill;[6] it is depressed again, and again rises into rather a higher Ridge called Saddle-back Mountain:[7] It subsides, but soon again rises in what is called Packer's Hill,[8] it then ranges along the East of Winipissiocket [Winnipesaukee Lake] Pond, and at the North East Bay of that runs up into very high Mountains called Ossipee Hills; it continues then the same northern Course, and in Lat. 44 rises into the highest Mountains of this whole eastern Division called the White Hills, the Peak or

[1]Blackstone, named Providence River where it empties into Narragansett Bay.

[2]Watatic Mountain.

[3]From the south summit [Ragged Mt.] is a view of Mts. Kearsarge, Sunapee, Cardigan, and other peaks. Federal Writers' Project. New Hampshire, *op. cit.*, p. 452.

[4]Ragged Mountain is approximately in this latitude.

[5]At Lowell, Massachusetts.

[6]Not located on modern maps. Near Chester, Rockingham County, New Hampshire.

[7]Not located on modern maps. Probably Leavitts Hill, New Hampshire.

[8]Not located on modern maps. Probably mountains in Gilford Township, Belknap County, New Hampshire.

The White
Hills B a
Top of which being bare Rocks of a white Grit and Talk [Talc], and bleached by the eternal Beating of the Weather, has a very uncommon Appearance: These Hills; although more than 70 Miles within Land, are seen many Leagues off at Sea,[1] and always appear like an exceeding bright Cloud in the Horizon. A Ridge of the same Range, the next to the Westward, running on the West Side Winipissiocket [Winnipesaukee Lake] Pond, runs up at the North West Bay into a high Mountain of red shelly Land, and is called the Red Hill[2] or Mountain; this Range falls also in with the White Hills. A Range running hence crosses the East Boundary Line of New Hampshire in Lat. 44½, and trending North East forms the Height of the Land between Kenebaëg [Kennebec] and Chaudiere Rivers: Of the Nature and Course of this high Land in these Parts I am totally uninformed; and I have directed that the Map in these Parts should be so engraved as not to assume any great Authority.

All the Rivers in the Eastern Parts of New England, arising amidst the South and Southeastern Ridges of this high Range, generally spring from Lakes, great Ponds, or boggy Swamps in the Vales: While they run or rather creep along the Course of these Vales their Beds are broad and seem rather like a Succession of Ponds than the Channels of Rivers; but as the southern Ridges are much lower than the Northern ones, these Rivers get away South through the first Gap or Interlocking, or along the first Spur which sets off, and tumble across the several Strata in broken Currents over Rifts and Cataracts almost to their Mouths. They are from this Circumstance capable of admitting Marine Navigation but a very little Way within Land. It is generally stopt at about 20 or 30 Miles by Falls. The Projection of the Rivers in this Part of the Map may be depended upon, being laid down from actual Surveys. Of each of these Rivers and of the Coast I shall speak separately.

All the Rivers which arise amidst the northern Ridges fall into St. Lawrence River, the Heads of these Two Sets of Waters interlock with each other, and in the travelling this Country in its natural Wilderness State, which is conducted by means of and along these Waters, very short Portages over Land form the Communication.

BCDa
To speak of that Part of this high Tract in its northern Range through the Provinces Massachuset[ts] and New Hampshire, one finds

[1][Pownall's note] Nobody has been at the Summit of these Hills, the craggy Tops are perpendicular; some People impute this singular Appearance to their being always covered with Snow; but by what I learnt from Mr. Grant, who passed over Part of these Hills by a Passage through them, called THE NOTCH, I am induced to adopt the Opinion as above.

[2]East of Center Harbor, New Hampshire. Federal Writers' Project, New Hampshire, *op. cit.*, p. 416.

a numberless Multitude of Lakes and Ponds amidst the Ridges, whence spring a Multitude of Streams and Rivers, all interlocking in every Direction with each other; those of the western Side fall into the River Connecticut, those which run East into the Merrimac River.

Between this high mountainous Tract and the Ocean, both in its northern and in its eastern Range, there is a Piedmont of irregularly broken hilly Land. Of that in the eastern Parts of New England, especially East of Penbsceäg [Penobscot], I can say nothing with Accuracy, and will therefore say nothing at all. I have struck out of my Map most of the Hills which I found drawn in the Surveys whence I had the Rivers copied, as I suspected they were laid down too much *ad libitum*. I will not in these Parts vouch for even those which remain, except within the Line of my Scouting Parties from Penobscot to Kenebeäg [Kennebec], and on the Back of the Settlements of the Counties of York and Cumberland. Of the Piedmont which lies upon the western Division of the Massachuset[ts] Province I can speak with some Accuracy, from my own Knowledge, formed by collating the Observations of Dr. Douglas[1] and others on the Spot.

This Piedmont, which a Tartar[a] would call Mas-Tchudi, has been called by the Indians here Mais-Tchuseäg, which signifies the same Thing, namely, *The Country on this Side the Hills*. It doth not range in Ridges, but lies in irregular hilly, though not high Land. The Rivers within this Tract, which run in all Directions, mark this, if the Eye had not. First, Concord River,[3] which rises in One Branch from a Pond[4] in Framingham, and in Two others from amidst the eastern Ridges of the high Range about Marlborough [Marlboro], runs along the East Side at the Foot of the easternmost Ridge North to Merrimac River, a little below Pantucket [Pawtucket] Falls. Mystick and Medford[5] Rivers on the North of Boston Harbour run from the North to the South; across their Heads the Ipswich River, rising in Wilmington, in the County of Middlesex, runs East and then turns North East.

Charles River arises in Five or Six Sources[6] on the South East Side

Side notes (right margin):

Piedmont or Tract towards the Coast.

A B a 4

a
Vide
Van
Stralenberg's
Account of
Siberia,[2] &c

D a 1
Concord
River

D E a 2
Ipswich
River.

D E a 1
Charles
River

---

[1]Wm. Douglass. A Summary, Historical and Political . . . *op. cit.*

[2]John Philip von Strahlenberg. *An Historico-geographical description of the North and Eastern Parts of Europe and Asia; but More Particularly of Russia, Siberia and Great Tartary* . . . now faithfully translated into English (London, printed for W. Innis and R. Mansby, 1738), p. 42.

[3][Pownall's note] Sudbury River, a Branch of Concord River, rises in Westborough.

[4]Lake Cochituate.

[5]A stream, fed by ponds, flowing into the Mystic River at Medford, Massachusetts.

[6]Beaver Pond, Hoppin, Chicken, Mine and Shephard's Brooks, Mill River, and Archer's Pond. Nathaniel Shurtleff, *A Topographical and Historical Description of Boston* (3d ed., Boston, By Order of the Common Council 1891), p. 154.

of Hopkington and Holliston Ridge, all running South; the main Stream runs North East, then North round this Ridge, then North-easterly, and then in Natick Township, runs away with a sinuous Course East-northerly till it meets Mother Brook, in Dedham. The other Branch called Mother Brook, hath Three Sources, Two on each Side Mooshill,[1] Naponset [Neponset], and Mashapoog [Massapoag],[2] which runs North East; a Third[3] which springs from the high elevated Tract South the Blue Hills; these all join in the Branch above-named, and meet the western Branch or real Charles River, in Dedham. Hence, running West in Needham, it tumbles in Falls[4] across the South West End of Brooklin [Brookline] Hills, till it comes near Framingham Pond; it then runs away North East to Cambridge, where, winding round in a South West Course, it falls into Boston Harbour. The Hills of Roxbury and Dorchester are not Ridges, and are confined to the Northward of Mother Brook; the Part of this Piedmont, on the West and South West of Boston Bay, is divided by an elevated Tract of Land, whose general Direction may be described by a Line drawn from Squantum [Squantum's] Neck[5] to Mount Hope[6] at the Head of Naraganset [Narragansett] Bay. At the Back of Milton and Braintree it runs up into high Peaks of Hills called, by Sailors, the Blue Mountains.[7] The main Drain of the District on the East Side of this high Tract is Taunton River, which runs nearly a straight Course South West under the East Foot of it to Tiverton on Naraganset [Narragansett] Bay; all the Streams which fall into the North West Side of this River, come down South East from the High Land; not more than Two or Three, and those very small ones, falling into it from the South East.

The natural Vegitation of this Country, which I have been describing, is Pine of many Sorts, The White Masting Pine, and the Pitch Pine; Firs, Cedar, and Spruce; Oaks of many Sorts, Red, Black, and White; Beech, Birch, Maple, and Bass; Ash and Elm, both Black and White; Walnut, Hickory, Hornbeam, and Acacia. As these different Species of Wood predominate in each Place, the Soil may be pronounced to be of Mould, loomy and moist, stony or sandy, light or stiff.

In Tillage it produces Maize, Rye, Barley, Buck-wheat, and Pulse well; there is something in the Soil (at least as the New England Farmers

---

[1]Mouse Hill. Jefferys, *The American Atlas, op. cit.,* Map no. 16. Probably present Sharon Heights.

[2]Brook with Massapoag Pond as its source.

[3]Ponkapog with Ponkapog Pond as its source.

[4]Newton Upper and Newton Lower Falls.

[5]In 1855 Squantum's Neck was annexed to Quincy, Massachusetts. Shurtleff, *op. cit.,* p. 505.

[6]Bristol, R.I. Federal Writers' Project, *Rhode Island . . . Rhode Island . . .* (Boston, Houghton, Mifflin Co., 1937), pp. 183-84.

[7]Blue Hill Range near Milton, Massachusetts.

husband it) which does not well for Wheat; it is chiefly a grazing Country, and feeds many Sheep and immense Numbers of Oxen, and many Horses. Apples thrive in it to a great Degree, Peaches also, but not equal to what they do more to the Southward. Connecticut grows a great Quantity of Flax for Seed, which causes a considerable Export from thence.

The Fisheries on the Coast: The lesser Fisheries in those Rivers, amongst which are Shad, Sturgeon, and Salmon in the Season: The Ship Timber, the Masting, the Lumber, the Naval Stores, and of late Pot Ash, are its peculiar and native Staples. The eastern Parts of Massachuset[ts] Province, and the interior Parts of New Hampshire Province, being towards the Coast, of a strong moist Soil, did contain a Source of this Naval Supply, which might have been inexhaustible; but Plunder and Waste profiting of bad Regulations, have well nigh exhausted this Store near the Rivers.[1]

I shall here as I did through Connecticut Transcribe my Journal of yᵉ Road from Connecticut River to Boston as it appeared to me in 1754. From Springfield on Connecticut River to Day's[2] Tavern 10 miles sandy Land & Pine Woods: from Day's to Scott's[3] 5 miles; to Shaw's[4] 2 miles. At Scott's one crosses the Chicabee [Chicopee] River over a long Wooden bridge. Scotts' & Shaws both in a very pleasant Valley along which the Chicabee [Chicopee] runs winding from side to side. At the end ford the Chicabee [Chicopee] then over high & stoney mountains here & there pretty prospects of yᵉ valleys which are settled particularly coming down to Cutlers:[5] to Cutlers 8 miles. To Brookfield 6 miles. To Leicester 11 miles. This stage over hilly Country but not mountainous. To Worcester 9 miles, a Beautiful Clear New & Young looking Town in a pleasant broad Vale. This has been so settled about 23 Years. To Shrewsbery [Shrewsbury] 8 miles, about 6 miles of this over hills, the soil a white sand mixt with Isinglass, talck [talc] like that at New York in the Jerseys & Pensylvania [Pennsylvania]. This Country does not lye in steep hills & narrow vallies but in easy slopes & spacious bottoms. The Prospects charm the Travellers with their woody hills & with the Farms,

---

[1][Pownall's note] There are some few Furs; I have met with some black Fox Skins from the Parts about Ponobskaeg [Penobscot].

[2]Not identified.

[3]John, William, and William Scott Jr. were proprietors in the "Elbow Tract" which lay along the Chicopee River east of Springfield, Massachusetts. J. H. Temple, *History of the Town of Palmer, Mass., early known as The Elbow Tract* . . . (Palmer, Mass., published by the Town, 1889), p. 131; "Orig-

inal Elbow District, Mass., 1716 to 1752. Compiled by E. B. Gates." *Ibid.*, Map no. 1.

[4]Samuel, David, and Seth Shaw, names in "Petition of the Inhabitants of Elbow Tract," October, 1751. Massachusetts Archives, Manuscript Folio CXVI, 137. The Massachusetts Archives are housed in the Office of the Secretary of the Commonwealth, State House, Boston.

[5]Not identified.

Rivulets, little lakes, orchards & Feilds, in the bottoms. This cheifly a grazing Country. Of Sheep scarce any Flock above 40 or 50. But Multitudes of Oxen. To Marlborough [Marlboro] 7 miles; to Sudbury 11. The Vales here larger & wider rather swampy with extensive meadows. As the road advances from the interior & distant parts, The Farmers engage more in Tillage yet there is a great deal of Pine Land & Sandy Soil All the way intermixt. To Saltmarshe's[1] Tavern in Watertown 11 miles: The first six miles of this over ridges of Mountains; but the road is pretty easy & not steep, running through the Gaps; In this six miles little or no Tillage that I could observe. The other 5 miles across a spacious level plain of a mixt soil but good for tillage. Here Multitudes of Pretty Farms all with orchards round their Houses. To Boston 9½ miles. The Face of the Country in this Stage Hilly & rather Stony & of light soil: but better cultured than the rest.

Detailed and tedious as the Remarks above will seem and perhaps prove in the Reading, they always appeared to me necessary to be observed by any who wished, or whose Duty it was, to have a Knowledge of the Country. When I first went to America the Subject and the Object were both new to the Europeans; I thought the Situation in which I was employed required Attention to this Point; I never travelled without a Compass and a little Level, of my own Contrivance, for taking Elevations; besides that, from an Habit of Drawing from Nature, my Eye could mark an Angle with Exactness sufficient for Practice. I was very particular in observing and noting, not only from my own Observations but from Surveys, where such were projected with Care, the Ranges of the Hills and Mountains, I also marked the *Sections which their Out-lines formed*, also the Knobs or Bluff-endings, and the Peaks. I was particular in my Observations and Inquiries into the Courses and Nature of the Currents of the several Rivers, their Falls and Fords, wherever I had Opportunity. The Passes and Gaps in the Mountains, and especially the Places where Posts fixed might give a Command in the Country. The Reader may see a very early Use which I made of this Knowledge (such as it was) in the State of the Service,[2] which I drew up for the late Duke of Cumberland in the Year 1756; as also in the itinerary Observations[3] referred to by LEWIS EVANS, which gave some ad-

[1]Not identified.
[2]"A Memorial: Stating the Nature of the Service in North America, and proposing a General Plan of Operations, as founded thereon. Drawn up by Order of, and presented to, his Royal Highness the Duke of Cumberland, 1756." Thomas Pownall, *The Administration of the Colonies* (2d ed., London, Dodsley 1765), Appendix, pp. 2-49.
[3]See *note* 1, p. 3.

ditional Topographical Merit to the First Edition of this Map in 1755.

When I was afterwards in a Situation[1] to direct the Inquiries of others, I formed a Set of Instructions for directing the Observations and Remarks of such as were sent out to reconnoitre; and the Returns I received gave very sufficient Information as far as it could go. If the Plan, which I proposed and began, had been observed through the War, namely, that of obliging every Scout to keep a Journal with Topographical Remarks; and, upon the Returns of these, of copying into a Book (under a general Head, each within their respective District) all these Informations so returned; a very ample-Store of Topographical Knowledge of the Country might have been collected and classed, which is now dispersed and lost. I can speak from Experience of the Use of this; I experienced it in my own Province; such classed and posted Accounts would have proved a good Check on the Unfaithfulness of many an artificial Journal cooked up by the Scouting Parties; moreover the Habit of keeping such Journals, and making such Remarks, would have trained many a good Regimental Officer to become a real General. Without this Knowledge and practical Readiness in applying it, no Officer ought to be trusted with the Command of a Body of Men. It would be invidious, but it would be easy to show, how strongly this Truth was evinced in the Events of the last War in America. The Americans have been much used to this Habit. They will always have amongst their Officers good Partizans;[2] and I shall never be surprized to see Generals formed from these. I say this not to disparage but to excite the Emulation of the British Officers.

There are in many Parts of New England Mines of Iron Ore,[3] some of Copper; but I must suppose that either the Ore is not good, or that

[1]Governor of Massachusetts, 1757-60. Pownall's official title was "Captain-General and Commander-in-Chief of Massachusetts Bay in New England," Charles A. W. Pownall, *Thomas Pownall . . .* (London, Henry Stevens, son & Stiles, 1908), p. 71.

[2][Pownall's note] This remark was written in 1774.

[3][Pownall's note] Although what I have said above be the Fact as to New England in general, yet there are Iron Mines in some Parts of this main *Eastern Division;* I may instance those of Mr. Levington [Livingston] in particular: This famous Iron-work is at [b]Ancram, in the Manor of Levington [Livingston]; there are Two Beds of Ore which supply this Furnace, the One in the Tachonic [Taconic] Mountains near it, and the other by Salisbury Falls[c] in Connecticut, about 12 Miles off. The Tachonic [Taconic] Ore is

richer than that from the New England Bed. The Salisbury Ore costs 2s. 6d. per Ton raising, and 8s. per Ton carting to the Furnace: 2000 Tons of this Ore make 900 Tons of Pigs, and expend about 200 Tons of Limestone: 2700 Loads of Coals serve the Furnace to make 900 Tons of Pigs, and Three Fires in the Forge in the mean while. N.B. Small Coals that will not do for the Furnace serve the Forge. The Coals cost 12s. 6d. per Load, and 3s. Cartage from the River. A Load of Coals is 100 Bushels on the Bank. Mr. Levington [Livingston] pays 2s. per Cord for cutting the Wood, which is repaid to him by the Collier. The People employed, and their Wages are as followeth: The Founder has 5s. a Ton for his Pigs, and finds his Keeper, who is a second Hand to watch the Furnace while he sleeps. The

the Mines are not worth the Working, as most of the Iron which is forged in New England is brought from the southern Provinces in Pigs: And none of the Copper Mines are worked.

There is a great Quantity of Bog-Iron, which is used for Cast-metal, and is much esteemed.

I have been told, when I was in the Country, of a Mine or Bog in which Lumps of Native Steel were found; but I never saw Reason to remove the Doubt and Suspense of Opinion with which I always received the Account. There may be, for ought I know, a Species of Bog-Iron, which is peculiarly adapted to the Process by which Steel is formed from Iron, and which more readily receives that Temper. I always understood, however, that Steel is not Native but Artificial.

Having thus given a Description of the Interior of the Country, I shall now describe the Coasts and Rivers which run into the Ocean as far as falls within this Map.

B a 5 a 6 Pasamaquady Bay and Rivers St. Croix, a general Adjunct

The River Pasam-Aquâda [Passamaquoddy],[1] or Possam-Accâda, which runs into a Bay so called, is the supposed eastern Boundary of New England; To the East of this begins Aquâda [Acadia] or Nova Scotia; an incertain River St. Croix in the nominal Boundary. But as the French, according to their Mode of taking Possession, always fixed a Cross in every River they came to, almost every River on this Coast of Sagadahoc has in its Turn been deemed by them La Riviere de St. Croix. Under Equivocation of this general Appellative they have amused our

Jobber, whose Business it is to clear the Casting-room, has 3£ per Month. Two Mine Pounders, One Limestone Pounder, each 3£ 10s. per Month. Two Fillers at 4£ per Month. One Banksman at 3£ per Month. Two Coal-stockers 6d. a Load. Clerk 45£ per Ann. Carpenter 60£ per Ann. Blacksmith 40£ per Ann. One Ore-burner 3£ per Month. Two Men, Two Waggons, and Four Horses for fetching Lime-stone and Wood, and splitting Ditto.

The Furnace when in good Order makes 22 Tons of Pigs a Week, but generally on an Average 20 Tons.

The Forge; making Bar iron from the Pigs 4£ per Ton, or 2£ 5s. per Ton for making from the Pigs into Anchories, and 1£ 15s. from Anchories to Bars. They find the most profitable Way of working in the Forge is to keep Two Fires, One for refining, and One for Drawing. When the Forge is in Order and full Work, they can make 500 Weight of Anchories in a Day at each refining Fire, and 1000 Weight for Bar-iron. To make a Ton of Bar-iron it requires 2700 Weight of Pigs, and expends Four Load and an

Half of Coals. The Iron in Pigs sell in New York at 8£ Currency, and 6£ Sterling per Ton. Bar-Iron from 24£ to 26£ New York Currency per Ton.

N.B. These Observations were noted down in 1754, the Sums are in Currency, which was as 4 to 7 in its Proportion to Sterling.

Ancram Works. Philip Livingston erected Ancram Iron Works, consisting of a furnace and a forge. He used the rich ores from his newly discovered mines in Salisbury as well as New York ores. Ores were dis-covered on a tract of land granted by the Colony to Yale College. The tract was transferred in 1734 to Philip Livingston who built a blast furnace at Lime Rock. Arthur Cecil Bining, *British Regulations of the Colonial Iron Industry*. Ph. D. Thesis, University of Pennsylvania (Philadelphia, 1933), pp. 23-24.—Ed.

[1]Schoodic, named St. Croix River in the Treaties of 1783 and 1842. Read Israel Washburn's "The North Eastern Boundary," in the Maine Historical Society *Collections* (1st series, Portland, The Society, 1831-87), VIII, 3-106.

Negotiators on every Occasion. I am ashamed but surprised that I must here add to the foregoing remark that the adroitness of the Americans taking advantage of the ignorance of our Minister and Negotiators at the late treaty of peace,[1] was in a more special manner exemplified in the settling the boundary, in this part, between the British & the American Empires. By which The Massachusetts State has gained a large Tract of fine land bordering on Passam-aquaâda [Passamaquoddy] bay: as also the Bay, & the Island Grand Manan & several lesser Islands.[2]

The Source of Pasam-Aquâda [Passamaquoddy][3] River is formed by a Succession of Lakes[4] and Swamps running East 42 Miles; it then takes the Form of a River and runs East North East Eight Miles and an Half; then South and by East 12 Miles; then makes a Bend of about 10 Miles Course, running round by South, till it returns to the same Parallel at the Distance Five miles and an Half East; it turns then to the South, and here are the great Falls where Marine Navigation ends; hence it runs South East Six Miles, and then South and by East Six more to its Mouth.

In and off Pasam-Aquâda [Passamaquoddy] Bay are many fine Islands, as Grand Manán.

All the Land lying between Pasam-Aquâda [Passamaquoddy] and Penobskaëg [Penobscot] is White-Pine Land, a strong moist Soil, with some Mixture of Oaks, White Ash, Birch, and other Trees, and in the upper Inland Parts has almost generally Beech Ridges.

Mount Desert is a little Island of very high Land, which being B a 5 covered on the South with a String of little Islands forms a very fine and safe Harbour. The Entrance is from the Eastward; I went into it in my own Province 20 Gun Ship, the King George,[5] and found sufficient Depth; however there is a Middle Ground at the Entrance, of which the Navigator must take Cognizance.

[1]Definitive treaty of peace, signed at Paris, the third day of September, 1783.
[2]Massachusetts Second Charter, dated Oct. 7th, 1691 gave the colony "all islands and islets lying within 10 leagues directly opposite to the main land" within the boundaries set by the Charter. By the Treaty of Peace, Sept. 3rd, 1783 the United States gained all islands "within twenty leagues of any Part of the Shores of the United States." However the boundary line between British and American territory in North America was not set finally until the Webster-Ashburton Treaty, 1842. By the terms of this Treaty Great Britain gained over 571,570 acres of land in excess of the award by the Treaty of Ghent, 1814. For a full discussion on this subject read "The Webster-Ashburton Treaty," *U.S. Treaties, etc.* edited by Hunter Miller (Washington, U.S. Gov't. printing office, 1934), IV, Doc. 99.
[3]St. Croix River.
[4]North, Grand, and Chiputneticook Lakes.
[5]"The King George was a 20 Gun Ship fitted out at the Expense of my Province Massachusetts bay & Commissioned by me, Cap[t] Benj Hollowell Commander under my Commission." [Thomas Pownall]. This is a holograph note written on verso of pen sketch of Penobscot Bay by Thomas Pownall in 1769. See reproduction, frontispiece.

Behind this Island, which lies near the Shore, is a very large Opening that forms the Mouth or Bay[1] of Mount Desert River.[2]
To the East of this the Land advances South in Form of a Promontory, on the Front of which are Four large Islands and a Multitude of
little ones; the large ones are, Deer Island, the Two Foxes Islands,[3] and
Holt Island;[4] these, with the Promontory, form the East Side of Penôbskeäg [Penobscot] Bay.

Monhagon [Monhegan] Island, which lies between Three and Four
Leagues South South West from Duck Harbour,[5] may be said to form
the West Point of Penôbskeäg [Penobscot] Bay; Duck Harbour forms
the South Point of the West Side on the main Land; hence the Shore
trends North East Five Miles to Terrant's [Tenants] Harbour; the Land
a pretty high Ridge; hence North North East Four Miles, then rounding Four Miles more so as to make a North Course.

Here the Ridges of the Land rise higher and continue to range hence
about Three Miles and a Half to Owl's Head, so called from a Bluff
Point which the Sailors imagine to bear some Resemblance to an Owl's
Head; round this Point is Madom-bédeäg [Medomak] Bay, about Two
Miles and Half broad, lying at the Foot of Madom-bédeäg [Medomak]
Hill,[6] a high Ridge which goes off North: Behind this is another Ridge
running further North, called Magunticoog [Meduncook];[7] about here
begins the South Point of an Island, which lies Length-ways in the
Middle of the Bay, is about 12 Miles long, and is called Long Island:
The North Point, from the Shape in which it makes from Sea exactly
resembling a Turtle, we called Turtle Head.[8] If I had, as I once intended
annexed any Drawings to this Description, I should here have given
Sections of Out-lines of the Forms of all the Ranges and Heads as they
present themselves to the Eye out at Sea. From the North East Point of
Madombédeäg [Medomak] the Shore trends North East and by North,
about 15 Miles to Pasaôumkeäg (or Pumpking) Point, which forms the
West Point of the Mouth of Penôbskeäg [Penobscot] River, as Peguoit or
Cape Razier [Rosier] does the Eastern. The River at this Entrance is
about point blank Shot over.[9]

Passing between these Two Points, one finds the River opening on

[1]Present Union Bay.
[2]Present Union River.
[3]Present Vinalhaven. William D. Williamson. *The History of the State of Maine* ... (Hallowell, Maine, Glazier, Masters & Co., 1832), I, 72.
[4]Present Isle au Haut. *Ibid.*, I, 74.
[5]Probably present Port Clyde.
[6]Camden Mountains. Williamson, *op. cit.*, I, 95.
[7]Probably a ridge in the Camden Mountains.
[8]Not identified.
[9]Maine Historical Society, *op. cit.*, V, 380.

the West into a circular Bay; to the East is another Bay, called, by the French, Pentagoät or Pentooskeäg [Penobscot],[1] where I saw the Ruins of a French Settlement,[2] which from the Scite and Nature of the Houses, and the Remains of Fields and Orchards, had been once a pleasant Habitation; one's Heart felt Sorrow that it had ever been destroyed.

There is a large Island at the Entrance into the Channel of the River above this broad Part, called Bethune Island; the Land is pretty high on each Side the River. As one approaches to the Falls one sees on the North very high Hills, which, to distinguish from the Lesser ones, we call Mountains. At 35 Miles above the Mouth the River tumbles for near two Miles over Falls[3] which totally put a Stop to all Marine Navigation: About Two Miles North West above these are other Falls.

The Courses up the River from the Mouth to the Falls are as follow: From Peguoit N. 3 Miles, N. and by E. 2, N.W. and by N. 2, N.W. 8, N.N.E. 4½, N. 2, N.W. and by N. 1½, and N. by W. 12. Total 35.

In the Front of the Falls there runs across the River a Row of pointed Rocks,[4] which at Low Water appear like the Pickets across the River; I got over these at High Water in a large armed Sloop, the Massachuset[ts], and stuck upon a round smooth Rock in the Middle of the River while the Tide was running down Three Knots. Capt. HOLLOWELL,[5] who commanded the King George, and who went up the River with me, by running the Men from Side to Side of the Sloop, so as to give her a great Roll, rolled her off, and she tumbled off like a Seal into the Water. It was well that he was so quick in his Resource, and so ready in executing it, for soon after at Low Water this Rock stood more than a Fathom above the Water, the Tide running down Five Knots.

For Nine Miles above the Falls the River puts on the Appearance of a Lake Two Miles wide, lying North and South, and being full of Islands: The old Penôbsket Indian Town[6] stood at the Bottom of this, at the Head of the Falls. Here, and below on the western Banks of the River, were old worn-out clear Fields, extending Four or Five Miles.

[1]The French spelled Penobscot more than fifty different ways. Maine Historical Society, *ibid.*, VII, 3.

[2]The French settlement founded by Baron de St. Castine in 1677. Maine Historical Society, *ibid.*, p. 385 n. On the present site of Castine, Maine.

[3]Probably Treats Falls, Bangor, Maine. Federal Writers' Project. Maine, ... *Maine, a Guide 'Down East'* (Boston, Houghton, Mifflin Co., 1937), p. 130.

[4]Champlain's rocks, off the foot of Newbury Street, Bangor, Maine. Maine Historical Society, *op. cit.*, VII, 6.

[5]Captain Benjamin Hallowell (1725-1799), a landed proprietor of the Kennebec Region. As a loyalist he was banished in 1778, and his entire estate was confiscated. Massachusetts Historical Society, *Proceedings* ... (Boston, The Society, 1791-date), LXIII (October, 1929-June, 1932), 260.

[6]On the present site of Old Town, Maine.

Six Miles higher up North, where Passadâmkeäg [Passadumkeag] River comes in from the East, is Passadâmkeäg [Passadumkeag] Indian Town,[1] to which Site the Penôbskeägs [Penobscots] were removed. About Two Miles and Half above this One meets another Fork of Two Branches,[2] One comes South East about 11 Miles from Sebaëg [Sebec][3] Pond, the main One[4] from the North Two Miles. East North East Six Miles higher is Ma-âda-ôuamkeäg [Mattawamkeag] Indian Town, the River comes to this Place South East about 16 Miles from some Ponds whence it takes its Source.

This River and District of Penobskeäg [Penobscot] remained at the time of the last War in Possession of the Natives[5] who had put themselves and lived under the Patronage and Authority of the French, and were governed by a Jesuit as their Priest and Superintendant:[6] In the Year 1759 when we were in open War with the Indians as well as French, the Governor[7] of Massachuset[ts] took Possession of it by armed Force, which gives a title that the Indians distinctly understand & always acquiesce in: To maintain this Title & Possession He built a Fort, which the People of the Province were pleased to call FORT POWNALL,[8] and which, to all Purposes wanted, held command in it. This was the last River and District on the North American Coast unpossessed, and which thus taken completed the British Possession of that Coast.

St. George's River

At the Distance of about Two Leagues West-northerly is the Mouth of St. George's River, near a Mile wide at the Mouth; in going up to the Bason at the Forks, where stood Fort St. George,[9] it is a strait Course North East and by North about 16 Miles, the Land on each Side high; at Three Miles from the Mouth you pass the First Narrows, made so by

[1]On present site of Passadumkeag, Maine.

[2]At Howland, Maine, the Piscataquis River flows from the east into the Penobscot.

[3]The Sebec River, which has its source in Sebec Lake, flows into the Piscataquis.

[4]Pleasant River. Although the author states this is the main river of the forked branch of the Penobscot, modern maps show the Pleasant River is a small tributary of the Piscataquis.

[5]The Abnaki Indians were in sympathy with the French from early times to the end of French power in North America. This attachment was due chiefly to the influence of the French Missionaries. Frederick W. Hodge, ed., *Handbook of American Indians North of Mexico* (Washington, Government Printing Office, 1907), I, 2-5.

[6]Father Sebastian Ralé (Rasle) (1657-1724), massacred by the English at Norridgewock in 1724, was the missionary priest most hated by the English and best loved by the Abnaki Indians. Read Pierre F. X. de Charlevoix, *History and General Description of New France translated . . . by John Gilmary Shea* (New York, John Gilmary Shea, 1871), V, 272-282.

[7]Thomas Pownall, governor of Massachusetts, 1757-60.

[8]"In the present town of Prospect [Maine] at the mouth of Penobscot River." Maine Historical Society, *op. cit.*, V, 377n.

[9]Fort Georges, built in 1719-20 by the proprietors of the Waldo Patent and made a public garrison soon after this date. On the present site of Thomaston, Maine. Maine Historical Society, *op. cit.*, V, 367n.

the Points of the high Land running in; above this the River is wide again, and a Cove runs up on the Right Hand North East and by East Four Miles in Length, reckoned from the Narrows; from the Head of this Cove there is a Portage over the Neck to Terrant's [Tenants] Harbour; from the Lower Narrows to the Upper like Narrows is Seven Miles and an Half, from thence to the Bason Four Miles and an Half; from the Entrance of this up to the Fort One Mile. The Breadth of this Bason is nearly Two Miles, from hence there is an Indian Path and Portage of about a Mile to a little Creek which falls into Pen-ôb-skeäg [Penobscot] Bay. The Fort George[s] stands upon a Point of Land in the Forks between Two Branches of this River, the one coming from Two Ponds on Ma-adombedeäg [Medomak] Hill[1] about Six Miles, at a Mile and Three Quarters above the Fort is obstructed by the Falls; The other Branch at 10 Miles above the Fort hath Falls.

Five Miles West of [St.] George's River is Broad Bay; a Number of Islands lie in the Front of all this Coast, so that Sloops and small Vessels may sail within them as if in a covered Harbour. It would become tedious to give a List of all; the Principal beginning from the West Point of Pen-ôb-skeäg [Penobscot] Bay are, Metin-eäg [Metinic], Monhêgan, Duck Island, Planting Island, Crooked Sand, Leveret's Island; Ma-adom-côg off Point Pleasant, the West Point of [St.] George's River, Hatchet Island, Muscongus Island, Hog Island, and Oar Island; the Five last are in Broad Bay and in the Mouth of the Muscongus River.[2] Broad Bay
C a 4

Broad Bay runs up 10 Miles, and carries a Breadth from Two Miles to One Mile and a Half: Two Branches fall into it at the Head, the East one is stopped by a Fall at Two Miles and a Quarter, called Ma-adamëg[3] Falls: The other at Five Miles has Falls, called Cheôuanasäg.[4] C a 4

There are Three little Rivers betwixt Broad Bay and Kenebaëg [Kennebec] River, Pemequid [Pemaquid], Damariscotta, and Sheepscut [Sheepcot], all having Falls on them.

As the River KENEBAEG [Kennebec] has been now rendered famous as a Pass, by a March[5] of some Spirit and Enterprize made by the Americans, following its Course, across the Land to St. Lawrence or Canada River, I shall here give a more particular and detailed Description of it than I should otherwise have entered into. A B C a 3 Kenebaëg River

---

[1]Camden Mountains.

[2]Planting, Crooked Sand, Leveret's, Ma-adom-côg and Hatchet Islands are not indicated on modern maps or on *Topographic sheets* of the U.S. Geological Survey.

[3]Not identified.

[4]Not identified.

[5]Benedict Arnold's expedition against Quebec, 1775.

This River, in the Year 1754 and 1755, was talked of as a Rout by which an Army might pass, the best and shortest Way to attack Canada and Quebec. The Rout was supposed to be by an Indian Path and Carrying-place, which going off from Kenebaëg [Kennebec] about Eight or 10 Miles above Noridgewaëg [Norridgewock], in a North West Course of Six or Seven Miles, came to a Pond which issued into the River Chaudiere. Some such Information had been given to Government; it was of the utmost Importance that Government should not be misled. In the Year 1756, I had an Opportunity of inquiring into this Matter by scrutinizing a Journal[1] given to me, and signed by Capt. Hobbs[2] and Lieut. Kenedy,[3] and by examining the Journalists themselves as to the Authority of the Particulars. I found enough to be convinced that this supposed Pass was mere Conjecture, taken upon trust of BARTHOLEMON [Bartholemew][4] an Indian, who was found to be false and a Spy, and was in 1755 shot by our own People as he was attempting to desert. Government therefore was early cautioned against this Misinformation. When I was Governor of the Province of Massachuset's Bay, I had this Rout particularly investigated, by Ensign Howard[5] a Country Surveyor, under the Direction of Capt. Nicholls [Nickels][6] who commanded at Fort Frederick.[7]Instead of a short Pass of some Eight or 10 Miles of easy Portage, this Indian Path turned out to be a Rout, on a Line as the Bird flies, of near 50 Miles over Land, *impracticable to an Army that hath a Train of Artillery and heavy Baggage.* It appeared however that (although a difficult and very laborious Rout) it was practicable to any Body of Men who should go light armed, as a

---

[1]"Captain Hobbs and Lieut. Kennedy's Account of the River Kennebeck and Carrying Place to the River Chaudiere, Septemb[r] 17th 1756." Manuscript copy in Henry E. Huntington Library, LO 1824.

[2]Captain Humphrey Hobbs, the "Fighting Deacon" of Souhegan [Amherst], N.H., served in King George's War, in the Beauséjour campaign in Acadia in 1755, in John Winslow's expedition to the Kennebec River to build Fort Halifax in 1754; also as captain of a company of Rangers raised by Governor Shirley in 1756. Captain Hobbs died of smallpox early in 1757. Burt Garfield Loescher, *The History of Rogers Rangers . . .* , (San Francisco [the author] 1946), I, 101-03, 421.

[3]Lieutenant Samuel Kennedy, noted surveyor for Capt. John Winslow on the Kennebec in 1754 and lieutenant in Captain Thomas Speakman's regiment of Rangers. *Ibid.,* pp. 102-03. Lieutenant Kennedy was killed in the action near Ticonderoga January

21, 1757. Caleb Stark, *Memoir and Official Correspondence of General John Stark . . .* (Concord, G. Parker Lyon, 1860), p. 413.

[4]While acting as a guide to Governor Shirley on his trip to Oswego, this Indian, Bartholomew, attempted to desert and was shot. Capt. Hobbs and Lieut. Kennedy's Account . . . LO 1824, *op. cit.*

[5]Sergeant John Howard of Captain Humphrey Hobbs' Rangers was killed in the action near Ticonderoga January 21, 1757. Stark, *op. cit.,* p. 413.

[6]Capt. Alexander Nickels. A prominent man of New Castle and Pemaquid near Pemaquid Fort. Nickels was with Governor Pownall on his trip to Penobscot (1759) and afterwards commanded a company at Fort Pownall. William Otis Sawtelle, "Thomas Pownall," in Massachusetts Historical Society, *Proceedings, op. cit.,* LXIII, 254n, 268n, 274.

[7]On the east bank of the Pemaquid River. Also known as Fort William Henry and Fort George. Williamson, *op. cit.,* I, 57.

Scouting Party, either to reconnoitre or to break up Settlements. The
Sort of March which Arnold[1] and his People experienced, has confirmed
this Account given 17 or 18 Years ago. After taking Possession of the
Penobskaëg [Penobscot] Country, I had all the eastern Branches of this
River[2] traced to their Sources, and the Communications between them
and the Waters of Penobskaëg [Penobscot] scrutinized by constant
Scouting Parties. A general Map which I had plotted down from these
Routs and Journals, together with Surveys of the Rivers, is the Au-
thority to this Map in these Parts.

This River Kenebaëg [Kennebec], to begin from its principal
Branch,[3] may be described as rising on the Height of the Land in North
Lat. 45° 20', and in East Longitude, from Philadelphia, 5° 10' or there- A a 3
abouts; its Source is from a little Pond, and the first Courses of its
Birth a Succession of Ponds or drowned Lands, Swamps, and Falls. Its
first general Course is 30 Miles South East, it then makes a great Bow
whose String (lying East and by South and West and by North) is 12
Miles. It then runs North-easterly Nine Miles and an Half, and then
tumbling over Falls North East 10 Miles, joins the North Branch.[4] The
North Branch is said (I speak not here from the same Degree of Authority) to arise in and issue from a little Pond[5] about 16 Miles North
of this Crotch,[6] from whence (it is likewise said) there is a Carrying-
place of 13 or 14 Miles to an eastern Branch of the Chaudiere River.
This was represented to me as the shortest Rout to Canada, but I do not
find in my Journals that I have set this down as confirmed or sufficiently
authenticated. After these Two Branches join, they run South-easterly
about Three Miles, when a small River tumbling over Falls, and running
between high perpendicular rocky Banks for Seven Miles and an Half,
and issuing from a great Pond full of Islands, called Sebaïm [Sebec],[7] or
by some such Name, North East 12 Miles distant comes into the Kenebaëg [Kennebec]. This Stream is impracticable for any Navigation at
these Falls, but there is a Carrying-place on the East Side from a Cove
to the Head of the Falls. From the Junction of this Stream the River has
its Course South-westerly 12 Miles, when one comes to the Place whence
the Indian Path goes off to the North West, as shall be hereafter de-

[1]Benedict Arnold (1741-1801), see *note* 5, p. 73.
[2]The Chaudiere.
[3]Dead River. Williamson, *op. cit.*, I, 47.
[4]North Branch of the Kennebec. Williamson, *op.
cit.*, I, 47.
[5]Moosehead Lake.
[6]Mouth of Dead River known as The Forks.
Williamson, *op. cit.*, I, 13, 47.

[7][Pownall's note] From this Lake there is a Communication by a short Portage to the One of the
Sources of Penobskaeg, and I have been told with an
eastern Branch of Chaudiere also; but I do not give
this last as from Authority.

scribed. Hence with many Windings the River keeps its southern Course to Noridgewaëg [Norridgewock], where it has the Appearance of a Lake full of Islands. On the Banks of this was the Indian Dwelling of the Tribe of that Name. A little below are the Falls.[1] The River then runs in a winding Course Five Miles East, and at the Point[2] where it turns again South the River Wesseronsaëg [Wesserunsett][3] comes in from the North East. Keeping on the same Course 12 or 14 Miles more it comes to Tachonaëg [Ticonic] Falls,[4] below which Sebastoocoog [Sebasticook] comes into it, from a Pond[5] bearing North East, and distant about 25 Miles: In the Fork between these Two Streams Mr. Shirley[6] built Fort Halifax.[7] From hence the River runs in a Course South-westerly 17 Miles to Cushnoog;[8] here is a little Blockhouse called Fort Western.[9] The Fall at Cushnoog is the Head of Tide Water; Sloops of 90 Tons Burthen come up hither from Sea; which, if the River is reckoned to Small Point, is about 30 Miles distant. This River is in general narrow, and continued between high Banks, it runs through a ridgy rather than hilly Country; about Five or Six Miles below Cushnoog[10] the Stream Cobessiconti [Cobbessecontee] comes in from the West, running out of a Pond of the same Name, full of Islands, lying Five Miles West of Kenebaëg [Kennebec]. The River in the same Course, Distance about Eight or Nine Miles lower, comes to Swan Island; just above which, on a Point on the West Side of the River, is a Blockhouse called Richmond Fort;[11] from this Point to the North Point of Merry-meeting Bay is Four Miles.

This Bay, so called from some Event interesting to the First Adventurers, is formed by the Junction of the River Sagadahoc[12] (Ammerescoggin or Pejepschaëg) with the River Kenebaëg [Kennebec].

To describe next the River Kenebaëg [Kennebec] as a Rout[13] to Quebeck [Quebec], in the first Place the Reader has been told that Sloops of 90 Tons Burthen can go up to Cushnoog Falls, about 30 Miles from

[1]Norridgewock Falls just above the mouth of Sandy River, Maine. Williamson, *op. cit.*, I, 49.

[2]Skowhegan, Maine.

[3]Wesserunsett River flows through Cornville from the north into the Kennebec at Skowhegan. Williamson, *op. cit.*, I, 49.

[4]Ticonic, also spelled *Taconic*. At Waterville, Maine.

[5]Sebasticook Lake.

[6]William Shirley (1693-1771), Governor of Massachusetts from 1741 to 1757.

[7]Built in 1754 on the eastern bank of the Kennebec. Present site of Winslow, Maine, which is opposite the city of Waterville.

[8]Present site, Augusta, Maine. Williamson, *op. cit.*, II, 301.

[9]Built by the Plymouth Company in 1754. *Ibid.*, I, 50.

[10]Augusta.

[11]A very old fortification on the western side of the Kennebec nearly opposite the upper end of Swan Island. Williamson, *op. cit.*, I, 51.

[12]Androscoggin River.

[13]Here the author follows closely Arnold's march to Quebec in 1775. For a full account read William Allen's "Account of Arnold's Expedition," in Maine Historical Society, *op. cit.*, I, 499-532.

Small Point. From thence to Fort Hallifax [Halifax], at Tackonic [Ticonic] Falls, 17 Miles, is a Waggon Road.[1] Thence a certain Degree of Navigation for Bateaux takes Place, which is interrupted by Falls[2] and Rapids below Noridgewaëg [Norridgewock], at which Places all Baggage must be again carried over Land, where a Waggon Road might be made between the Hills and the River. Half a Mile above Noridgewaëg [Norridgewock] there is a long sharp Fall,[3] but that a good Waggon Road might be made quite up to the *Great Carrying-place*.[4] Hence the Indian Path goes off West from the River over Land about Four Miles and an Half to a Pond about Three Quarters of a Mile long; a good Waggon Road might be made here: This First Pond has been found to issue its Waters into the Kenebaëg [Kennebec]. Hence the Path runs over the like Grounds West-northerly about a Mile, and comes to a Second Pond, this has been found to issue its Waters into Sagadahoc[5] River. Hence over the like Land, and in the same Course about a Mile more, it comes to a Third Pond,[6] which issuing its Waters to the North, and falling into a River which runs North-easterly, gave rise to the Misinformation that here went the Rout to Canada by Chaudiere; but the River which this Pond empties itself into is found to be the Kenebaëg [Kennebec], which in this Place runs North-easterly; from this Pond the Path runs West-northerly near Four Miles, and strikes the southermost Bend of this main Branch of Kenebaëg [Kennebec]; up this Stream there may be an imperfect Navigation for Indians, and Traders, or Hunters, somewhat better in the Time of Freshes, but both the Navigation is bad and the travelling between high Ranges of Mountains, and in swampy boggy Vales very troublesome to Individuals, very arduous, and almost impracticable to Bodies of Men. When you get higher towards the Source of the River, you come to a Chain of Ponds which makes the Navigation better, but this is interrupted with Falls. From the Head of the River to a little Stream which falls into Agamuntaëg Pond,[7] is a Carrying-place of about Four Miles. That is the Indian Carrying-place, but I apprehend that if a Body of Men would transport any Baggage which requires a Depth of

[1] In 1754 Governor Shirley ordered a wagon road to be made from Fort Western (Augusta) to Fort Halifax. Williamson, *op. cit.*, II, 301.

[2] Skowhegan Falls. *Ibid.*, I, 49.

[3] Norridgewock Falls. Maine Historical Society, *op. cit.*, I, 459.

[4] This is a twelve mile portage from the Kennebec River above Cariotunk Falls to the Dead River. This portage was made in preference to ascending the Kennebec twenty miles to the mouth of the Dead River and then up the Dead River through shallows and rapids, a total distance over fifty miles. Maine Historical Society, *op. cit.*, I, 505.

[5] Androscoggin.

[6] [Pownall's note] The Pond, which was falsly said to be the Head of the River Chaudiere, and so set down in a Map published in 1754, has a Mark set upon it in this Map.

[7] Lake Megantic, the source of the Chaudiere River.

Water before it can be embarked, the Portage must be to, or near to, the Lake, about 10 Miles. This Lake[1] is the Head of Chaudiere River, and is about 40 Miles above the present Settlements of the Canadians.

Sagadahock
River
B a 2The River Sagadahock,[2] Ammerescoggin, or Pejepschaëg, which properly speaking is but the main western Branch of Kenebaëg [Kennebec], rises in Lat. 44° 50' North-easterly of the White Hills in New Hampshire, not far from the Head of Connecticut River; it has its Source in a Lake called Umbagoog [Umbagog]. Two or Three other lesser Streams[3] issuing from little Ponds to the East of this join it after it has run South about 26 Miles; it then turns East North East 60 Miles, and meets a Second main Source[4] rising from a Lake about 19 Miles West of Noridgewaëg [Norridgewock]. These Two Streams after the Western One has run about 86 Miles East South East, and the Eastern One about 34 Miles South join;[5] and hence the River runs South 40 Miles. In this Course it runs within Two Miles of the Sea Coast, but then turns short about North and runs over a Fall called Pejepskaëg [Pejepscot][6] into Merry-meeting Bay. In this Bay Kenebaëg [Kennebec] and this River unite, this loses its Name, and the River Kenebaëg [Kennebec] continues its South Course about Five or Six Miles to its Mouth, in which are two pretty large Islands, Arrôsaëg [Arrowsic] and Reskêgon.[7] If *Small-point* be reckoned to be the Mouth of the River, instead of Five or Six it is 16 or 17 Miles from Merry-meeting Bay to its Mouth. Round *Small-point* to the East is a deep Bay with a large Island in it called Sebasedâgon [Sebascodegan],[8] included between Long-reach and Merriconaëg Neck. This Neck is about 11 Miles long, and about Three Quarters of a Mile broad. It was in my Time incorporated into a District, and I named it *Harpswell*, from the Seat of my old Friend Mr. Wichcot of Lincolnshire, where I had spent many a happy Holiday when a School-boy. This became a very considerable Settlement last War; it had 84 taxable Polls in it, a Company of Militia, and paid besides Fifty Pounds per Ann. to the Province Tax.

C a 3
Casco BayCasco Bay: This Bay, if reckoned from Cape Elizabeth to Small Point, is 25 Miles wide, and about 14 deep; it is a most beautiful Bay, full of little Islands. Brunswick stands at the North East Cove of it,

---

[1]Lake Megantic.
[2]Androscoggin, Maine.
[3]Sunday, Bear, and Ellis Rivers, Maine.
[4]Swift River, Maine.
[5]At Rumford, Maine.
[6]Falls of the Androscoggin, Brunswick, Maine.

Federal Writers' Project. Maine, *op. cit.*, p. 144.
[7]Island of Georgetown formerly Parker's Island. Federal Writers' Project. Maine, *op. cit.*, p. 263. Parker's Island was originally Eraskohegan [Reskegon]. Williamson, *op. cit.*, I, 53.
[8]Great Island, known locally as East Harpswell. Federal Writers' Project. Maine, *op. cit.*, p. 257.

and Falmouth,[1] a sweet pretty Town, on a most delightful Scite, on a hilly Neck of Land at the South West End of it. As this is now no more, I will from my Journal describe what Falmouth was in 1759, when I was there: The Township consisted of 600 Families settled in Three Parishes, New Casco, Sapoodock, and Stroud Water: The Body of the Town sat elevated on a Neck of Land stretching out East from Stroud Water, and forming a kind of Mole to a little Cove within it. This Part consisted of a Church and Townhouse (this being a Country Town) and about 112 Houses. This Town was laid out in Lots forming Two Streets parallel to the Harbour, and Five at right Angles to them: Inhabitants were settling and building fast on these Lots. The Harbour is extremely fine, large, and commodious; Masts and Naval Stores were loaded here. There was much Trade carried from hence directly to the West Indies in Lumber, Boards, Staves, and Fish of the small Kind. Many Ships were also built here. Royal's [Royale's] River runs into the Bay at North Yarmouth, and the Presumskeag [Presumpscot] rising in Great Tobago [Sebago] Pond runs into it at New Casco. Stroud Water running East on the Back of the Scite of Falmouth, falls also into this Bay South of Falmouth. None of these Rivers are capable of marine Navigation to any Length, in most it is stopped by Falls.

Rounding Cape Elizabeth to the South West, and between that Point and the East Point of Winter Harbour,[2] is Scarborough Bay, into which Two or Three inconsiderable Streamlets run. C a 2

Rounding this last Point and Southak's Isles,[3] you come to Winter Harbour and Saco Bay, contained within this Point and Cape Porpoise.

The River Saco has Two principal Sources, one springs from the Ossipee Pond near Ossipee Hills, the other rises from the Notch amidst the White Hills; the one called Ossipee, the other Pigwaket River. These soon unite, and the River, keeping in general a South-eastern Course for about 60 or 70 Miles, runs between Scarborough and Biddiford Townships into Saco Bay by Winter Harbour: Marine Navigation is stopped in this River very near the Mouth of it by Saco Falls. Saco River

Rounding Cape Porpoise is Well's Bay, contained within this Cape and Cape Nedock [Neddick] or Bald-head [Cliffs]. Into this runs Kenebunk River, which has its Source in the Northernmost of Lovels [Lovewell's] Ponds in Lat. 43° 53'.

[1]Named Portland, July 4, 1786. Federal Writers' Project. Maine, *op. cit.*, p. 167.
[2]Biddiford Pool. Williamson, *op. cit.*, I, 26-27.
[3]Wood and Negro Islands. In 1808 a lighthouse was built on Wood Island. Williamson, *ibid.*, I, 27. *Wood Island Light* is in Biddiford Pool. Federal Writers' Project. Maine, *op. cit.*, p. 256.

Between Cape Nedock [Neddick] and Piscatua [Piscataqua] River is York Harbour.

Piscatua [Piscataqua] River being the Boundary between the eastern Division of the Massachuset[ts] and New Hampshire Province, I will here, before I proceed further, give such an Account as I am enabled to do with any Degree of Certainty, of the Ranges of the Hills in these Parts.

As I kept up, during the last War,[1] a constant Line of Scouting Parties on the Back of the Settlements in these Parts, and as I gave Instructions amongst other Points for their marking the Nature of the Land; and as these Scouts, after I took Possession of the Penobsceäg [Penobscot] Country, extended to that River, the Returns of the Officers did, in some small Degree, answer my Design as to this Point. I may state in general that the Parts towards the Coasts are White Pine Land. The upper or interior Parts Oak, with high Chesnut Ridges, having

Birch in the Vales; these Vales are almost intirely occupied by Swamps, Ponds, and little Lakes. There is a Communication between Penobsceäg [Penobscot] and Kenebek [Kennebec] Rivers, with very short Portages from Fort Pownall[2] to Fort Hallifax [Halifax], by a Succession of Ponds and by Sebastoocoog [Sebasticook] River. There is a like Communication of a still shorter Course between the Branches of these Rivers at their Heads. There is likewise a very easy Communication between the East Branches of Penobsceäg [Penobscot] and the Sources of Passamaquada[3] [Passamaquoddy] Rivers.

At the Back of York Township is a very high Peak called Agamanticoos [Agamenticus], from hence the Ridges of the Hills of these Parts range North East under various local Names.

The Ranges in York and Cumberland Counties trend to the Northward of North East, those in the County of Lincoln East of Kenebaëg [Kennebec] next the Coast do so likewise, but within Land they trend more and more to the East of North East. All the Heads of Kenebaëg [Kennebec], Penobskaëg [Penobscot], and Passam-aquâda [Passamaquoddy] River are on the Height of the Land running East North East.

Piscatua [Piscataqua] River is the only Port of the Province of New Hampshire; the Embouchure of this River for 10 Miles on one Course (reckoning this Course upwards as you enter it) North West, and then

---

[1]French and Indian War.
[2]Fort Pownall (1759-1775), built by Governor Pownall. For details read "Governor Pownall's Voyage from Boston to Penobscot River [1759]" in Maine Historical Society, *op. cit.*, V, 365-387. On the present site of Bangor, Maine.
[3]St. Croix River, Maine. See *note* 1, p. 68.

Five or Six Miles South into Little Bay and Exeter Bay,[1] has more the Appearance of a deep Bay than a River; there is in the Mouth of it the Island Newcastle, about a Mile and Half long and a Mile and Quarter broad. It is navigable up the First Course for Ships of any Burthen, for Nine Miles more up the West Branch to Exeter it is navigable for Sloops; and also up the East Branch or main River to the Falls. This River springs from the southernmost of Lovels [Lovewell's] Ponds, and tumbling over several Falls under the Name of Salmon [Falls] River, and running South and South-easterly falls into the broad Bay-like Part called Piscatua [Piscataqua]. A Line drawn North from the Head of this River till it meets the Boundary of the Province of Quebec, is the Boundary betwixt the Two Provinces of Massachuset[ts] and New Hampshire. In the Description which I gave of the Country at large, the Province of New Hampshire as well as the western Division of Massachuset[ts] was included. I therefore here pass on to Merrimaeg, commonly called Merrymack [Merrimac], River in Massachuset[t]'s Bay Province.

Continuing along the Coast South about 20 Miles, one comes to the Mouth of Merrimack [Merrimac] River, about a Quarter of a Mile broad; this River has Two principal Sources, the Western one is Squam Pond[2] in Lat. 43° 50′: The Branch which runs from this South bears the Indian Name Oûïïnaoûasset.[3] The eastern Branch springs in Oûinipissiocket [Winnepesaukee] or Richmond Lake; the Dimensions and Shape of this are accurately laid down in the Map, and need no further Explanation. Between these Two Ponds or Lakes run the Red Hills, so called from their apparent Soil being chiefly of the red shelly Land taken Notice of in other Parts of this Work. This Eastern or Merrimaeg [Merrimac] Branch runs out of the West or South-western Bay of this Lake. After Four or Five Miles tumbling over Falls it meets the western Branch which joins it. Its Course from hence to the Line which divides the South of New Hampshire, and the North of Massachuset[ts] is South according to the Course of the Ridges amidst which it runs. There are numberless Multitudes of Streams which run into it from the West, all which rise from little Ponds and Swamps in the Vales of the great middle Range. The first principal Stream which runs into it is the Conticoog [Contoocook] Branch from the West. Just below where this Stream enters, the River takes a turn East, and crosses through Pene-

D a 2
Merrimack
R'

---

[1]Great Bay, New Hampshire.
[2]Squam Lake, New Hampshire.

[3]Pemigewassett River, New Hampshire.

coog Ridge,[1] a little Stream called Sowcoog [Soucook] comes in from the North. About two Miles below this, coming also from the North, from a Pond[2] South of Oûinipissiocket [Winnepesaukee] Lake, comes in the Suncoog [Suncook]; below this the River runs through or across a Ridge of Hills, which range North East, called Amaiskaeg [Amoskeag], and here are the Amaiskaeg [Amoskeag] Falls.[3] Just above the Narrows where the Pitch of the Fall commences, the Waters of the River, pent up, spread to the Breadth of Half a Mile; at the Narrows the Channel is about 40 Rod across. The Stream after tumbling over Ledges of Rocks, at the Narrows shoots away in Three principal rocky Channels and over craggy Ledges, twisted round to the South West; the Fall is above 26 Feet in the Perpendicular. The Banks at the Narrows are steep Rocks, those on the East Side 10 Feet high. After this the River continues its Course uninterrupted to Pantucket [Pawtucket][4] or Pantoocoog great Falls.[5] About Three Miles before it crosses the Division Line, the Nashawaeg [Nashua] River, which I took Notice of before as arising on the Sides of the Watchuset [Wachusett] and Wadadeag [Watatic] Peaks, runs into it from the West. At these Falls the River turns East, and crosses a Ridge before noticed, ranging North; above the Falls the River is wide, at the Falls narrow; the rocky Ledge of the Falls is Slate; there are Two Pitches and the Stream shoots with an inconceivable Rapidity between the upper and lower Pitch or Falls. The upper Fall is 10 Feet perpendicular; the *Rapid*, between the Two Falls descends also 10 Feet in the Course of its Shot; the latter has 24 Feet Fall in 65 Rods Course. The Whole of these Falls is above 40 Feet.

A little below these Falls, the Concord River, running North along the East Foot of this Pentoocog Ridge,[6] comes into the Merrimaëg [Merrimac]. There are two lesser Falls[7] between this and Haverhill; that at Haverhill stops Marine Navigation.

Ca   The Country in which this River takes its Rise, as well as that through which it and its many attendant Waters run, is the great living Magazine of Masts and Naval Timber. These are floated down this River; but as very many fine Masts, and much valuable Timber, have

[1]Pawtuckaway Range. Federal Writers' Project. New Hampshire, *op. cit.*, p. 486.

[2]Suncook Pond.

[3]At Manchester, New Hampshire. Federal Writers' Project. New Hampshire, *op. cit.*, p. 54.

[4]At Lowell, Massachusetts.

[5][Pownall's note] Two large and principal Branches which come into the Merrimaeg [Merrimac] from the West (viz. The Piscatagnage [Piscataquog] and Sowhaeg or Sowhaegon [Souhegan] Rivers) are by an Oversight neglected to be inserted into the Text, which is supplied by their being mentioned in this Note. They run between Conticoog [Contoocook] and Nashawaeg [Nashua].

[6]Pawtuckaway Range.

[7]Mitchell's Falls. Massachusetts Historical Society, *Collections* . . . (2d series, Boston, John Eliot, 1814-23), IV, 121.

The Reason for which induced to repress the description of the Harbour & Town of Boston, in the last Edition, no
longer subsisting, I shall here insert it in this —
The Entrance into the Great Bay is between Cape Cod
& Cape Ann, an opening of the distance of between
about 40 or 50 miles: And from this opening the Bay
to the Entrance of Boston harbour by the Light-house is
about 30 miles. As you enter this Bay from
the East, Barnstable Bay is upon the left or south
-ward. This Bay is nearly circular, of a Diam: of
miles, with very large & increasing Populous Towns on its shores
on every side — besides Cape Cod Harbour there is
Province town on the southwest side within a safe
& convenient Harbour looking of the most pleasing
aspect from the multitude of Farms & settlements
on rising hills which form its sides. Its situated
the Town of Plymouth. This first settlement made
by the Adventurers, under the first New England
Charter, called the Plymouth Company of
the Seat of the Town is on y.e West side of a Cove
covered from the Bay by a Long Beach & is a
Place of no very inconsiderable business.

In advancing to the Harbour of Boston. Upon
the Starboard or right bow of the Ship lyes Nahant
Point, on the Larboard, or left, Point-alderton, at the
distance of about 7 or 8 miles from each other. These
are generally Reckoned the two points & possibly
of the Harbour; & are so taken to be, in as much as by the Entrance
of y.e 14.th of y.e Reign of George y.e 3.d enacted to disport the
Harbour of Boston, that is to disallow the Lading
or Landing of Goods or Merchandise at the
Town or within the Harbour of Boston. As Nahant
Nahant Bay is very if at all, used as an anchoring

been lost or at least spoiled in shooting the Falls, especially those of Amiskeag [Amoskeag][1] and Pentoocoog [Pawtucket],[2] I had, when I was Governor, several Projects and Proposals laid before me, for making Channels at those Falls, through which the Masts and Timber might be shot without Danger. Besides the Difficulty of the Measures proposed, and my Apprehension of the Damage which the River must sustain elsewhere by being drained off too low if the Measure did succeed, I had other Reasons for not entering into them. While I saw the almost invaluable Interest of this great Naval Magazine neglected and abandoned to every Waste and Rapine, for Want of common Attention to Regulations which had been repeatedly proposed to Ministers, and which would have cost nothing but Attention, I did not wish to propose a Jobb that would have expended Four or Five Thousand Pounds, and not have mended the Matter. From Haverhill the River runs winding along a pleasant rich Vale of Intervals, and passing between Newberry [port] and Salisbury runs to Sea.

Ipswich is the next River Southward on this Coast; that I have already taken Notice of.

Hence rounding Cape Ann to the West, one enters the Massachusett's Bay and so by the Harbours, Cape Ann, Salem, and Marblehead, between Nahant and Alderton [Allerton] Points, into Boston Harbour. It is sufficient here to say, that this Harbour is full of Islands, threading amidst which the Ship Channel runs.

The reason which induced me to repress the description of the Harbour & of the Town of Boston, in the last Edition, no longer subsisting, I shall here insert it in this. The Entrance into the Great Bay Massachusett[s] is Between Cape Cod & Cape Ann an opening of about 40 or 50 miles. And from a Line drawn across this opening to the Entrance of Boston harbour by y[e] Light house is about 30 miles.

In advancing to the Harbour of Boston upon the Starboard or right bow of the Ship lyes Nahant Point, on the Larboard, or left, Point Alderton [Allerton], at the distance of about 7 or 8 miles from each other. These are Generally Reckoned the two points of the Entrance of the Harbour; & are so taken to be, in a very silly Act of Parlt[3] of y[e] 14th of y[e] Reign of George y[e] 3[d] enacted to *Disport this Harbour* of Boston, that is to disallow the Lading or Landing of Goods or Merchandise at the Town or within the Harbour of Boston. As Nahant Bay is very little if at all, used as an Anchoring and Broad Sound on account of the

[1]At Manchester, New Hampshire.
[2]At Lowell, Massachusetts.

[3]Boston Port Bill, Mar. 25, 1774.

Danger from the Shoals & Sunken rocks very seldom Navigated but by small Vessels, I always Considered Shirley Point & Point Alderton [Allerton] as the points of the Entrance of the Harbour. These Points are nearly Five Miles Distance From Each other. In a Direct Line Between these Points beginning From Point Shirley lye Deer Island Lovels [Lovells] Island Gallops [Gallups] & George's Island. In the Front of Lovels [Lovells] & George's Islands advanced towards yᵉ Bay lye several Rocks & Rocky Small Islands called the Breakers[1] on one of which called Becon Island[2] is a Lighthouse. Deer Island is of high elevated Ground with a cliff towards Point Shirley & is about a mile long & somewhat better than a quarter of a Mile Broad. The other three are oval & from a Quarter to a half a mile Diameter. Between Deer Island & Shirley Point is an Entrance for small Craft, called the Gutt.[3] Between Deer Island & the other three is the Entrance by Broad Sound.[4] But Between George's Island Point Alderton [Allerton] & Hull Is the real Entrance & Ship Channel. Passing by Hull & Pettocks [Peddock] Island on the left & George's Island on the right through a Channel about a Mile broad, You advance into a kind of bay surrounded with Islands called Nantasket Road. Point Alderton [Allerton] is high land toward the Channel & slopes off from it to a Beach by which it is join'd to the Main Land. Nantasket (on which is Hull) in like Manner is high & Bluff toward yᵉ Channel but slopes off at yᵉ side to a beach by which joins Point Alderton [Allerton]. It slopes off also behind. Georges Island, is elevated but not so high as yᵉ last mentioned. Nantasket Road may be described as a Circular Bay enclosed by Long Island Gallop's [Gallups] George's Pettocks [Peddocks] & Sunken[5] behind which is Hangmans Island; with a very small Island in the Center called Rainsford Island. A Center being fixed on this Island a Radius of about a mile will sweep Long-Island Gallops [Gallups] George's Petticks [Peddocks] & yᵉ Sunken Island, with soundings from 3½ to 9 fathom all round. This road is out of & to the left of the Ships Channel which runs betwixt Georges & Gallops [Gallups] Island on one hand & Lovels [Lovells] on the other rounding to the left by an Island almost washed away to nothing & hence called Nix's Mate[6] through which passage called the narrows the Channel carries a Depth of 5, 6, & 7 fathom water. Hence

---

[1]"The Brewsters" named for William Brewster, elder of the first church of Plymouth, Shurtleff, *op. cit.*, pp. 435-36.

[2]Light House Island, sometimes called Little Brewster. *Ibid.*, p. 436.

[3]Shirley Gut. *Ibid.*, p. 437.

[4]Broad Channel. *Ibid.*

[5]Sunken ledge near Quarantine Rocks. Shurtleff *op. cit.*, p. 519.

[6]Marked by a monument in the Ships' Channel called the Narrows. *Ibid.*, pp. 538-39.

between the S point of Deer Island & N point of Long Island about three quarters of a mile distant from each other it runs by the North point of Spectacle Island for about a large league to Castle Island in a Channel rather confined by shoals on each side. There is a shoal called y⁰ Middle group to y⁰ right as you advance to Castle Island which is dry at low water. I take notice of this because on Castle Island, as part of y⁰ works of Castle William,[1] was a well placed Battery of heavy Cannon called Shirley's Battery which raked this Channel the whole way. Hence Passing Close under Castle Island on y⁰ left also between a middle ground to the right & the Shoals of Dorchester[2] again on y⁰ left & Governor's Island, Bird Island[3] & its shoals, & Noddles Island[4] on the right; The Channel leads up to the Town at three miles Distance.

As to the Nautical & Sailing Directions I should wish to referr to the Atlantick [Atlantic] Neptune[5] published by Mʳ Des Barres under the Directions of the Lords of the Admiralty & from Surveys made at a great expence paid by the publick, If I could settle which of the three several ones given to that work I could depend upon. They differr from each other in some bearings & distances And from y⁰ Printed Nautical Remarks and Directions in many instances. The second of Holland[6] mistakes the name of Spectacle Island calling it Hospital Island a name given, on account of a Lazarett or Pest house, to Rainsford's Island.

This Harbour is about 9 miles from the Light House at the Entrance to the Town & is from 3 & 4 & 5 miles wide in different parts from Point to point. It is rounded with several Points of Elevated Land that have the Appearance of Islands & has besides sett within it like a Clustered Jewell, 22 Islands most of them of elevated land with Bluff Points at their Ends & sloping sides. Some of them are a Mile, a Mile & ¾ a Mile & ½ by half a Mile in size, others a little round or oval ones of ¾ to ¼ of a mile diameter. These are all Cultivated as farms & some have very pretty Farmers Dwellings on them so as that any one of them would form a pleasing Landschape. Lett now the Reader prepare his mind to conceive what a most strikeing & even enchanting Picture The

---

[1]This was a fortification on Dorchester Neck, now South Boston. The fort was built between 1701 and 1703, burned by the British in 1776, repaired and renamed Fort Independence in 1797, converted into a prison in 1785, ceded to United States government in 1798, rebuilt 1801, and abandoned in 1880. Shurtleff, *op. cit.*, pp. 484-97; Federal Writers' Project. Massachusetts, . . . *Massachusetts; A Guide to its Places and People* . . . (Boston, Houghton Mifflin Co., 1937), p. 168 (Castle Island).

[2]South Boston.
[3]Bird Island has disappeared, only Bird Island Shoals remain. Shurtleff, *op. cit.*, pp. 442-43.
[4]East Boston. *Ibid.*, p. 443.
[5]*The Atlantic Neptune*, published for the use of the Royal Navy of Great Britain, by Joseph F. W. Des Barres . . . [London, 1774-1781] 3v.
[6]Samuel Holland. See *note* 4, p. 7.

Voyager sees as he Enters this Harbour & sails threading in amidst these beautifull Objects presenting themselves in perpetually varying shapes & varying groups releived by a thickly Inhabited Country on y[e] Sides of the Harbour. As He advances first up to Castle Island a high rising knol with its Fortress[1] on the Top & all its works on y[e] Sides forming a most Picturesque Foreground to the Town which Sitts on three hills[2] & therefore originally called Tremontane in all its pride of Populous Buisy Wealthy Inhabitancy at three miles distance. This Particular Scite of the Town Placed on a Peninsula a Group of three Hills forms with all its Shipping by its side & at its wharfs with all its Houses, Publick Buildings & Spired Churches grouped in sweeping lines around this hilly spott; a most peculiar & most pleasing view. I made Drawing of This View & M[r] Marlow[3] painted me a picture from it. It makes one of the most pleasing Landschapes I ever saw.

The Shape of the Town is somewhat like a Cross the triangular Space however between the stem & branches especially y[e] South end filled up with Buildings, the Head at y[e] North End rounded. The triangles between the head & branches are form'd to the East & SE by an indenture of y[e] Water into the Line of the Town & to the West & NW by the Common, a Cove of y[e] Harbour, & the Water called the Mill pond.[4] The Length is nearly from the South End to y[e] North Ferry one mile & three quarters. The breadth from Barton Point[5] to the south side of Fort Hill[6] one mile one furlong.

The Town was originally built as all our old English Towns were of Timber-framed Houses. And although one of the first Laws one meets with in their Law book directs that all Houses after the Passing of that Act in 1692[7] shall be built of Brick or Stone, Many of y[e] Houses under the pretext of repairing instead new building, are still of the same framed materials. The Principal Part & Body of the Town is of Brick as are most of the Public Places of Worship. The Church called the King's Chapel[8] is of Stone or at least cased with stone. There are 16 of these Places of Worship Ten Churches of the Congregationalist; Three of the Church of England, most of these are very spacious & Commodious:

---

[1]Castle William.

[2]North to east, namely: Copps, Beacon, and Fort Hill.

[3]Probably William Marlow (1740-1813), English landscape painter.

[4]Early in the 1800's Mill Pond, covering about 50 acres in the vicinity of present Haymarket Square, was filled in and made available for building sites. Shurtleff, *op. cit.*, pp. 108-10.

[5]At Barton Street near North Station. *Ibid.*, p. 107.

[6]Fort Hill Square, Oliver and High Streets.

[7]Massachusetts (Colony) Statutes. *Acts and laws, passed by the Great and General Court or Assembly of their Majesties Province of Massachusetts Bay . . .* (Boston, Benjamin Harris, 1692), p. 4.

[8]Present King's Chapel built in 1749 at School and Tremont Streets. Shurtleff, *op. cit.*, p. 195.

There are besides these an Anabaptist, a Friends or Quaker Meeting, & a Presbyterian Meeting. The Other Public Buildings are the State-House[1] in which are Council Chamber, Chamber of Representatives, Secretary's Office, And those of the Clerks of the Two Houses of Legislature & The Courts of yᵉ Assises. Fanueil Hall[2] is the Town Hall, a Place build for the assembling of yᵉ Town-meetings & other convocations of the People. There is a Public Granery[3] an Alms House[4] & Publick school.[5] The Province House[6] which is appropriated for the Governor's Residence is a very decent comfortable Dwelling. The House was that of a Private Merchant[7] & Bought for this purpose. It is a plain brick square building. There is a very neat elegant Building also called Concert hall at which the young People hold their Balls & Concerts. There is one Principal Street which runs direct from yᵉ South Entrance at yᵉ Neck to yᵉ State-house somewhat more than a mile in length and continues by one or two detours to the North End & Ferry in all 2 miles. It is spacious well built especially towards the Body of the Town, & well paved & makes a handsome Appearance. A Second Street strikes off north from this at about a Quarter of a mile from yᵉ South Entrance & then runs lateral to it for near three Quarters of a Mile whence it runs north to the Part called New Boston. The High Street[8] with the long wharf in one straight Line of half a mile in Length is a Spacious broad Street & really handsome as it approaches yᵉ State House at the upper end of it. The rest of the Town consists of various Cross Streets built without any regular design, many of which are narrow like those of our old English Market Towns. I remember that People use to reckon the Number of Houses & Buildings in Boston at 4,000. I cannot find amongst my papers the account which states the Number of Houses in my Time but as well as I can recollect I do not think that they exceeded 3,000. The Number of Inhabitants of this Town including the average of those birds of passage the sailors was stated at 22 or 23,000. If I were to State the Plenty & Abundance of the Market Supply in all Articles of Provisions Fish Flesh & Poultry & Game & add to this the common rates & prices of my time

[1]Built in 1712 at the head of State Street. *Ibid.*, p. 592.

[2]Original Fanueil Hall, completed in 1742, was destroyed by fire in 1762. It was rebuilt after the original plan and enlarged in 1805. The building still stands in Dock Square. Federal Writers' Project. Massachusetts, *op. cit.*, p. 157.

[3]Built in 1737 on Park Street. Shurtleff, *op. cit.*, p. 21.

[4]The old Almshouse stood on the corner of Beacon Street near the present City Hall Annex. Shurtleff, *ibid.*, pp. 309-10.

[5]Not identified.

[6]Built in 1679 for a private residence and acquired by the Province in 1716. On Washington Street opposite Old South Church. For history and description of the building read Shurtleff, *op. cit.*, pp. 596-604.

[7]Peter Sargeant. *Ibid.*

[8]King Street and Queen Street, now State Street.

as they stand in my house keeping books, People of these Times would Scarcely beleive me. Boston was originally the Principal almost the Sole Port & Mart of America, When Philadelphia had scarce any Trade & New York not above 7 or 8 Ships which came to Europe the major part of which too went to Holland, their fatherland, instead of coming to England. Since the amazing advance of Commerce in Rhode Island New York & Philadelphia, The Encrease of the prosperity Town of Boston has been checked. But another & Internal Reason has operated strongly in this event, but I deferr the discussion of that part where I shall speak of the Nature of the Inhabitancy of America.

Between the South Battery under Fort Hill & Hancock's Wharf[1] is the semicircular indenture of the Water into the Line of the town before mentioned the shores of this enclosed Water are lined with Quays, wharfs, & Docks of Private Property. The Long Wharf[2] a noble Publick Structure runs out across & nearly through the middle of this; into the main Harbour. It is projected for above a quarter of a Mile & runs into deep Water so that a Twenty Gun Ship of Warr can lye along side of it. It is so broad that there are Warehouses all on the north side of it the whole length with a road of sufficient breadth for Carts & Trucks to pass each other & not disturb y\ :e business of lading & unlading on y\ :e Quays as it going on at the same time. Hollowell's [Hallowell's] Ship & Dock Yard[3] with several other Quays of private property were to the South of this long Wharf & multitudes of others Along y\ :e Shore to the north of it. This whole water thus inclosed between Hancock's Wharf & the South Battery is fronted with a line of Isolated or Island Wharfs. There are also several Wharfs & Quays of Private Property in the south end part of the town.

There are three elevated points of Ground within the Town which commands all the rest. Fort Hill, Becon [Beacon] Hill & Cops [Copp's]-Hill. The Peninsula on which the Town stands is joined to the Continent by a low beach called the Neck about half a mile in length along which a good road, thrown up & shaped like the English turnpike roads, is made. This Neck & all the South-end parts of the Town is Commanded by the high grounds of Dorchester-Neck on a point which called Forsters [Fox] hill a Center being placed & a Circle with a radius of 5 furlong struck will over reach the neck & sweep y\ :e Southern Shores of y\ :e town.

---

[1]Hancock's Wharf was formerly Clark's Wharf, located at the eastern end of present Fleet Street. Shurtleff, *op. cit.*, p. 115; *The Town of Boston in New England.* By Capt. John Bonner (1722). Known as the Bonner *Map.*

[2]Built by Governor Jonathan Belcher.
[3]Near the foot of Milk Street. Shurtleff, *op. cit.*, p. 134.

Before I return '& quitt this Harbour I cannot but take notice of the Town of Cambridge which stands on the Charles River that runs into the Harbour & is about three miles to the NW of Boston. The River runs through a Salt Marsh or Meadow overflows with the tides about three Quarters of a mile broad opposite to the Town of Cambridge. There is a Bridge over the River; and an elevated Causeway made across yᵉ Marsh. On the Cambridge side at about a furlong & a half from yᵉ river, the Ground rises & on this rising ground upon a level spott is the Town of Cambridge situated. Its Platform is laied down on a regular Plan of a Parallelogram with its longest side to the River with the NW & SE Corners cutt off. It is near half a Mile in length & about Two thirds of that in breadth taking in the Common and Scite of the College[1] which is a detached part on the NE side. It is a most Charming little Town where numbers of Gentlemen of Fortune have fixt their abode of retirement. The Place called the Common is a very spacious Square in the Front of the College on all sides of which Houses are built & building.

The Structure of the College is a square of three sides built of Brick in the manner of our English Colleges; except that it is open at the Corners. The side to Common is open. The Side to the North E is called Harvard College, The Side to the S is Called Stoughton College & that to the SW Massachusetts College. On the outside of this Square is a very good Lodge for the President and Pretty modern built Chappel & a Printing House. There is a very good Library in the College furnished with several thousand of books encreasing by Donations every day.

To the Southward of Cape Ann, a long Hook of a Promontory called D a 3 CAPE COD, takes up again the Line of Coast. The Promontory itself is high Land & rises with steep upright cliffs on the east side to Seaward. The Long Low neck of land by which this is joined to the Main seems to have been formed by the Coil and Recoil of the Tides, rolling up Silt and Sand at the Thread of their least Force. In the Barb (if I may so express myself) of this Hook, is Cape-Cod Harbour. This Promontory forms One of the Counties of the Province now State Massachusetts, and is called *Barnstable County*.[2] It circumscribes Barnstable-Bay.[3] Many and various Alterations have been made, and are continually making on the East Coast at the Back of this Promontory: And a long Point of Sand has been formed into solid Marsh Land within these Forty Years, at the South Point of it. Let those who are curious in the Process

---

[1]Now Harvard University.

[2]Present Plymouth and Barnstable Counties, Massachusetts.
[3]Cape Cod Bay.

of the Operations of Nature, watch the Progress of George's Sand. From the Inquiries I made, and the Answers I got, I think that will in some Years, and perhaps not many hence, form into another Sable Island. Its southern Point is now at Low Water with a strong off Shore Wind visibly a Shoal.

Barnstable-bay[1] is nearly circular of a Diameter of 30 miles. Having thriving populous Towns, inhabited by numbers of Fishermen, on its Shores on every side. On the SW side is a convenient Harbour of the most pleasing aspect, from the number of farms & settlements on ye rising hills which surround it, is situated the Town of Plymouth. This was the First Settlement made by the Adventurers, under the New-England Charter, called the Plymouth Company. The Scite of the Town is on the West side of a Cove fenced off from the main bay by a long point of Land & is a Place of no inconsiderable share of Business. I have been told that it is a sweet pretty Town. It so happened that I never was at it which I have more than once regretted.

E a 3

Going round this Promontory South, and then West, the Islands NANTUCKETT [Nantucket] and MARTHA'S VINEYARD present themselves. The First is a Settlement of Whalers and Fishers, on a hilly, sandy, bare Island, which could give Subsistence to no other Species of Being. So improved, it swarms with Inhabitants; and is become so considerable in its Interest and Property, as to form One of the Counties of the Massachusetts, by the Name of *Nantuckett* [Nantucket] *County*.

E a 2

Martha's Vineyard is a very peculiar Spot of Ground, a triangular Plain of fine Meadow Land, hemmed in North West and North East by two hilly rocky Sides. This also swarms with Inhabitants, and is a Settlement of Consideration sufficient to have been formed into One of the Counties of the same State, by the Name of *Duke's County*.

E a 1

Hence rounding to the North, and passing by Elizabeth's Islands and Buzzard's Bay, on the North East, one comes to Naragenset [Narragansett] Bay and Rhode Island, the District of New England which forms the united Colony of RHODE ISLAND AND PROVIDENCE PLANTATION. The Land round this Bay is high and hilly; and through the Middle of Rhode-Island, from South to North, runs a hilly elevated Ridge.

[1]Cape Cod Bay.

SECT. IV.

Of the Western Division

The Western Series

"THE Land, South-westward of Hudson's River, may be considered as divided into a Number of Stages. The first Object worthy Regard, in this Part, is a Rief, or Vein of Rocks, of the Talky[1] or Isinglassy Kind, some Two or Three, or Half a Dozen Miles broad; rising generally some small Matter higher than the adjoining Land; and extending from New-York City, South-westerly by the Lower Falls of Delaware, Schuylkill, Susquehanna, Gun-Powder, Patapsco, Potomack [Potomac], Rapahannock [Rappahannock], James River, and Roanoak [Roanoke]. This was the antient maritime Boundary of America, and forms a very regular Curve. The Land between this Rief and the Sea, and from the Navesink Hills[a] South-westward as far as this Map Extends, and probably to the Extremity of Georgia, may be denominated the *Lower Plains*, and consists of Soil washed down from above, and Sand accumulated from the Ocean. Where these Plains are not penetrated by Rivers, they are a white Sea-Sand, about 20 Feet deep, and perfectly barren, as no Mixture of Soil helps to enrich them. But the Borders of the Rivers, which descend from the Uplands, are rendered fertile by the Soil washed down with the Floods, and mixed with the Sand gathered from the Sea. The Substratum of Sea Mud, Shells, and other foreign Subjects, is a perfect Confirmation of this Supposition. And hence it is, that for 40 or 50 Miles Inland, and all the Way from the Navesinks to Cape Florida, all is a perfect Barren, where the Wash from the Upland has not enriched the Borders of the Rivers; or some Ponds and Defiles have not furnished proper Support for the Growth of White Cedars."[2]

As I have now added to this Edition a Map of the Southern Colonies,[3] I shall in this topographical Description take a more extensive view of this Tract of Lands which lyes between y[e] Hills & the Sea-line. This Tract may be stiled (taking up the Name which the Dutch gave to those parts of it which they possessed) *New-Netherlands*. Or as it seems to

The Western Series

a

F c

First Stage, or Lower Plains

Description of the Lower Plains Continued

---

[1]Talc.
[2]Quoted from Evans' *Analysis*, pp. 6-7; reprinted in Gipson's *Lewis Evans*, pp. 150-51.

[3][Pownall's note for revised and enlarged edition] See [Map] at the End of the work.

have arisen above the Sea by Accretion of Soil both from Sea and Land, It may very well be a Name given under the Circumstances, be called *Zealand*. This Tract is in general very Sandy & like all other half-formed land full of Swamps & bogs. The Natural Vegetation of the Sandy Parts is most of the Species of Pines & Cedars. In the more Southern Parts, those of South Carolina & Georgia, The Palm Palmetta, Opuntia & a variety of other Shrubs. Where the Soil of the Hills or Mould, is become incorporated with the original sand as it is in the interval lands on the banks of Rivers, the vegetation is of live-oaks & Poplars white & yellow, Black walnut, Sycamore, Elm & Myrtle bushes & some sort of spiny grass. There are Swamps in which The Cedar Tree has for ages been growing and dyeing with perpetual Succession. The old ones lyeing as they fall, uncorrupted at y[e] bottom while the young ones Grow up between them. These The Inhabitants call Cedar Swamps. They are a kind of Mine of Timber, almost inexhaustible. I remember to have seen in New Jersey a pretty large park belonging to Col. Schyeler[1] with all its fences entirely formed with whole unsawed logs of this Swamp Cedar. In other swamps which are marshy no Tree or Shrub but Fresh-water Marsh Grass, wild oates & Southward, a Species of Cane, grow; these are said to be good food for Horses & Cattle. These latter Swamps when properly banked & slusced become Rice Lands. The Botanists, & particularly the ingenious M[r] William Gerard de Brahm[2] give long lists of the Trees & Shrubs which form the natural vegetation of these parts; but as I said before being myself no Botanist I must for these particulars referr to them.

On the sides of the Rivers which run through these Netherlands, the land lyes low. The Soil is generally of a very rich black mould with a Foundation of Clay. And in both its natural & cultured powers capable of every vegetation.

The very barren sands from New Jersey to Florida are capable by Culture of having a power of Vegetation given to them, as the Settlers, in different parts, by different culture suited to those parts, have found. These Netherlands are not intirely of this barren or unmixt Sandy Soil. There are Parts which Partake of Mould loam & clay & in these Parts the natural Vegetation is of Oak, Beech, Birch, Poplar, Black walnut &c. But there is a circumstance of Vegetation worth particular notice. This

---

[1]Peter Schuyler (1710-1762) younger son of Arent Schuyler who discovered and first operated the famous Schuyler copper mines. John O. Raum, *The History of New Jersey* (Phila., J. E. Potter, 1877), I, 237.

[2]In 1764 William Gerard de Brahm was appointed surveyor general for the Southern Department in North America.

is a kind of Moss[1] which is peculiar to the Trees of this Tract of Land. It grows upon & hangs down from the branches of the trees to a very great length, which I remember to have given occasion to a joke passed upon a credulous note-taking traveller under a ridiculous description of the Peruke tree which perhaps may sometime or other appear in some publication. Of the Circumstance & Thing itself take the Description of Mr de Brahm in his report[2] to the Lord of Trade. There seems to be a line which nature has drawn that marks this Zealand. "It spreads (says He) nearly parrallel with the Sea Coast as farr back in the Country as the Trees are hung with a kind of Moss.[3] This Moss grows to the length of three yards: When baked in ovens or when hanging long on the trees it assumes the likeness, & almost the nature, of long black horse hair; & is used to stuff saddles & mattrasses[4] by ye common inhabitants. As long as it is fresh on ye Trees in winter Horses & Cattle seem fond to feed on it. This Moss is no longer mett with in the Woods where the Air may be supposed to be impregnated with the Marine-exhalations. Through All ye Tract betwixt this Line & the Sea the Air may be called *Sea Air*, the Country within it Landwards may be said to have *fresh-Air*. Within this Line the Country begins to rise & becomes more particularly proper for European Culture."

To give some general Idea of the Shape of This Tract beginning from the point of Sandy-hoek [hook] at ye Mouth of Hudson's River & running back South westerly in an irregular Curve so as to include the Promontary of East Florida, it may be said to be of the Shape of a Harp.

The Country within or Interior to this Natural Demarkation begins to rise in hills. The first Ridge seems to be a Vein of Clay, "some Three or Four Miles wide; which is a coarse Fullers Earth, and excellently fitted, with a proper Portion of Loom, to make Bricks of."[5] Next with this is the vein of Isinglassy sand. This is not equally visible in all parts. {A Vein of Clay}

"From this Rief of Rocks, over which all the Rivers fall, to that Chain of broken Hills, called the South Mountain, there is a Distance of 50, 60, or 70 Miles of very uneven Ground, rising sensibly as you ad-

---

[1]Spanish moss.

[2]De Brahm spent 20 years, 1751-1771, collecting materials for his "Report of the General Survey in the Southern District of North America." This is a detailed account of the topography, towns, fortifications, inhabitants, flora and fauna of the Southern colonies. British Museum. King's Manuscripts, 210-11. Photostat in Library of Congress. Calendared in the Charles M. Andrews and Francis G. Davenport

Guide to the Manuscript Materials for the History of the United States to 1783, in the British Museum . . . (Washington, D.C., Carnegie Institution of Washington, 1908), p. 27.

[3]Spanish Moss.

[4]This moss is still used for this purpose and for other upholstering.

[5]Quoted from Evans' *Analysis* p. 7; reprinted in Gipson's *Lewis Evans*, p. 151.

94

Second Stage, or the Upland

vance further inland and may be denominated the *Upland*. This consists of Veins of different Kinds of Soil and Substrata, some Scores of Miles in Length; and in some Places overlaid with little Ridges and Chains of Hills."[1] There is a peculiar Stratum of Soil runs in the same Direction with the last through this Stage. The People of the Country call it *Red Shell Land*. It appears to me to be a Species of red Marl, although where it is dug up, or turned up with the Plough, it rises in slaty Kind of Lamina, and seems stony, yet it soon dissolves in the Air, and is excellent Wheat Land. When it has been tilled for many Years, so that it begins to fail in its Fertility, if the Husbandman sets his Plough a little deeper, so as to turn up a fresh Layer, this, mixed with the old worn Top, gives fresh Power of Vegetation to it.

The First Place in which this Stratum appears, as far as I have been able to learn, is in the Red Mountains,[2] West of Winnipissiocket [Winnepesaukee] Lake: As running in a Vein, the First Appearance of it is on the West Side of the Range of Mountains which run on the East Side of Connecticut River, and beginning at Hertford [Hartford], runs 10 Miles South West to Farmington, then Six Miles West to Penthorn,[3] then South West to the Mountains. It appears again in New Jersey, at Schuyler's Mines,[4] runs thence to Brunswick, and spreading goes across the Jerseys, over the high Ridge on which Prince-Town [Princeton] stands. I am told it continues in the same general Direction across Pennsylvania, but I had not the Means of pursuing it.

Lime Stone is found almost every where in the upper Parts of this Stage, and it is the general Dressing that the Husbandmen use.

There is found to the Northward of Newark in New-Jersey, an exceeding good Fire Stone, which stands well.

The Soap Stone is found about the Delaware River; and the Asbestos in many Parts of this Stage.

There are in New Jersey Two Copper Mines, One at Col. Schyler's[5] on the Passaick [Passaic] River, a very fruitful one of rich Ore; the Water obstructed the Working of it for some Time: a worse Perplexity about the Title since his Death hath stopped its being worked. It was said that there was Silver mixed in with this Ore,[6] it certainly sold as Ore

[1]Quoted from Evans' *Analysis*, p. 7; reprinted in Gipson's *Lewis Evans*, p. 151.
[2]East of Center Harbor, New Hampshire.
[3]Not identified.
[4]John Schuyler's Copper Mines in Bergen Co., New Jersey. John, fourth son of Arent Schuyler,

inherited these mines from his father. *N. J. Archives, op. cit.*, XII, 588.
[5]John Schuyler.
[6]"Four ounces of silver to each hundred weight of Cupreous Metal," J. L. Bishop, *History of American Manufacturers from 1608-1806*. (Phila., Edward Young & Co., 1864), I, 546.

at a great Price.[1] The other is at Mr. Stevens[2] on the upper Part of the Raritan. There is certainly now and then little Grains of native pure Gold found in this Ore, I have had some of it. This sold for 60£ and 62£ Sterling a Ton in 1754, Schyler's for above 70£ Sterling.

I have not heard of any Lead anywhere as yet found on the South or East Side the Mountains; there are several Appearances of it on the West Side. The French worked a Lead Mine in the Oïilinois [Illinois] Country.[3]

"The Declivity of the Whole gives Rapidity to the Streams; and our violent Gusts of Rain have washed it all into Gullies, and carried down the Soil to enrich the Borders of the Rivers in the *Lower Plains.* These Inequalities render Half the Country not easy capable of Culture, and impoverish it, where torn up with the Plough, by daily washing away the richer Mould that covers the Surface.

"The *South* Mountain[4] is not in Ridges like the *Endless* Mountains,[5] but in small, broken, steep, stony Hills; nor does it run with so much Regularity. In some Places it gradually degenerates to Nothing, not to appear again for some Miles, and in others spreads several Miles in Breadth."[6] It runs in more regular Ridges through Virginia under the Name of the Blue Ridge Pignut and South Mountain; after it has passed the Maryland, it spreads in more regular Hills, the North Ridges of which trending North for about 13 Miles approach near to the Kittatinny Ridge; but resuming again the main Course the Hills of this Mountain range along between Yellow Breeches and Conawegy [Conewaga] Creeks to the River Susquehanna opposite to the Mouth of Swataro [Swatara] Creek, and continue North East, under the Names of the Flying and Oley Hills,[7] through Pennsylvania to the Delaware: Its southern Ridge runs off East North East by Hanover to Susquehanna,

Third Stage, or Piemont

---

[1]Yield of copper was 80 percent and sold for £40 per ton. *Ibid.*

[2]John Stevens (1715?-1792). Stevens' Copper Mines were at Rocky Hill, Hunterdon County, New Jersey. New Jersey, *Archives, op. cit.,* XI, 526n. George Washington wrote his "Farewell Address to the American Army, Nov. 2, 1783" at Rocky Hill. George Washington, *Writings* . . . edited by John C. Fitzpatrick. (Washington, Gov't. Printing Office, 1931-44), XXVII, 222.

[3]Joseph Schlarman, *From Quebec to New Orleans* . . . (Belleville, Ill., Buechler Publishing Co., 1929), pp. 204-207.

[4][Pownall's note] This Mountain in its several Ridges as it crosses New Jersey, Pennsylvania, Maryland, and Virginia so abounds with Iron Ore

that it might not improperly be called the *Iron Mountain.*

[5]Allegheny Mountains. For description and extent read Lewis Evans' "Remarks on the Endless Mountain &c," printed on his *Map of Pennsylvania, New Jersey, New York and the Three Delaware Counties, 1749, op. cit.*

[6]Quoted from Evans' *Analysis,* p. 7; reprinted in Gipson's *Lewis Evans,* p. 151.

[7][Pownall's note] So called from the innumerable Flights of Turkeys on them.

"The Oley Hills are a continuation of the South Mountain and terminate at Reading." William Reichel, *Memorials of the Moravian Church* (Philadelphia, J. B. Lippincott & Co., 1870), p. 75.—Ed.

where Pequa [Pequea] Creek falls into it, and thence to Trenton. In New Jersey the northern Hills narrow and rise again into the Form of a Ridge, and it is called Mescapetcung [Musconetong]; and in New York the Highlands. Between this Range and the Kittatinny Mountains, as they run through Pennsylvania, lies the Vale of Talpahockin [Tulpehockin], One of the great rich Vales of Pennsylvania. In New Jersey and New York almost the whole Vale is a great Swamp or drowned Lands. Money alone has been wanting for the general Draining of these Lands. Whenever they are drained, this Tract will become One of the richest in America. The southern Part of this Tract as it passes through New Jersey is elevated Upland, but not Ranges of Hills. There are amongst the Hills into which this Mountain spreads itself, between the Susquehanna and Scuylkill [Schuylkill] Rivers, to a Breadth from 15 to 30 Miles, several Valleys. A Succession of such, divided from each other by little hilly Branchings of the main Hills, run from Wright's Ferry[1] on the Susquehanna to the Swedes Ford near Norriton [Norristown] on the Scuylkill [Schuylkill], some Two Miles broad, some more. The Lands are of a Limestone good farming Soil. Every Farmer has a Limekiln burnt for the dressing of his Land, and they raise a great deal of Wheat. The Sides of the Hills are covered with Woods: The Timber in general Oak, Chesnut, and Hickory. The First Valley which the Road from Philadelphia to Lancaster passes through runs from the Swedes Ford to the Middle Branch of Brandy-wine Creek, and is about Two Miles wide: Hence the Road runs slanting over Three Ascents and Three Rivulets about 13 Miles, and comes to a Second Valley which runs along the South Side of the Range called *Welsh Mountains* to Lancaster: Hence it continues in a Bosom of gently swelling Hills to Wright's Ferry[2] on the Susquehanna. These Successions of Valleys appeared to me as I rode along them the most charming of Landscapes. The Bottoms of the Vales were full of cultured Farms, with Houses, such as Yeomanry, not Tenants, live in: These were busked up with Gardens, and with Peach and Apple Orchards all round them, and with every convenience and Enjoyment that Property and Plenty could give to Peace and Liberty. My Heart felt an Overflowing of Benevolence at the Sight of so much and such real Happiness. "Between the South Mountain and the higher Chain of the Endless Mountains (often for Distinction called the North Mountain,[a] and in some Places the Kittatinni[b] [Kittatinny], and Pequil-

F f e

a H K   b C c

---

[1]John Wright, justice of the peace of Lancaster County and keeper of a ferry at present Columbia, Pennsylvania.   [2]*Ibid.*

p 20

Some Extracts from my Travelling Journal as I passed through the Jerseys and Pensylvania will give a kind of View of the Country — a view which in a Country that is by its progress of settlement & cultivation, changing every Day will become in this short space a matter of curiosity & antiquity rather a painting of what it was, than of what perhaps it is — The Topography however remaining the same.

In Going from New York to the Jerseys you pass in a Shallop across the bay to Staten Island & The Road, if you are going to Elizabeth Town, runs about six miles along the north side of this Island. At the End a Ferry conveys one over the sound to Elizabeth Town — A Township which knows no bounds & has been perpetually engaged in Law about them, The Scite of the Town is laid by Lotts running in strait lines so that Whatever Houses are built in consequence of this Plan the Streets, if they may be so called, for they have the appearance of wide Country Roads, are all in right lines. The Town Part is large The Houses Good & Handsome It looks more like a Collection of

out 12 miles.

engaged

Hitherto unpublished material in Pownall's own handwriting equals
a third of the work published in 1776.

in° [Pequea]) there is a Valley[1] of pretty even good Land, some Eight, c F e
10 or 20 Miles wide, which is the most considerable Quantity of valuable
Land the English are possessed of; and runs through New Jersey, Pennsylvania, Maryland, and Virginia. It has yet obtained no general Name,
but may properly enough be called *Piemont,* from its Situation. Besides
Conveniencies always attending good Land, this Valley is every where
enriched with Lime Stone."[2]

On the East Side of the Mountains, next the European Settlements,
there are some,[3] but very few, and those thin Beds of Coal: There are
some Brackish Licks or Springs, but no Salt Springs. On the West Side,
both these abound every where.

Some Extracts from my Travelling Journal[4] as I passed through the
Jerseys and Pensylvania will give a kind of View of the Country—A
View which in a Country whose Face is by its hasty advancing progress
of settlement & Cultivation changing everyday will become in this short
space a matter of curiosity & a record of antiquity rather painting what it
was, than what perhaps it is. The Topography however remains the same.

In Going from New York to the Jerseys You pass in a Shallop across
the bay[5] to Staten Island about 12 miles. The Road, if you are going to
Elizabeth Town, runs about six miles along the north side of the Island.
At the End a Ferry conveys one over the sound to Elizabeth Town—A
Township which knows no bounds & has been perpetually engaged in
Law about them.[6] The Scite of the Town is laid by Lotts ranging in
strait lines so that whatever Houses are built in consequence of this
Plan the Streets, if they may be so called, for they have yᵉ appearance of
wide Country Roads, are all in right line. The Town Part is large. The
Houses Good & Handsome. It looks more like a Collection of the Country Places of a rich & thriving Germany than a Town. It has the usual
Publick Edifices which are all large & Spacious. My First excursion into
the Jersies was to see Col. Schyelers[7] Copper Mine & Place, & the Pas-
saïck [Passaic] Falls. From [New] Brunswick to Newark a pleasant ride
of six Miles along a level way with picturesque hills on the left & an open
bay on the right. This is a neat Country Town of the same sort as the
last. There is an English Church & Congregation here. Col. Peter Schye-

[1]Cumberland or Great Valley. Henry F. Walling,
New Topographical Atlas of the State of Pennsylvania
. . . (Phila., Stedman, Brown & Lyon, 1782), p. 5.

[2]Quoted from Evans' *Analysis,* p. 7; reprinted in
Gipson's *Lewis Evans,* p. 151.

[3][Pownall's note] One at the Falls of James River.

[4]Pownall made this trip in 1754. See page 105
this work.

[5]New York Bay.

[6]For documents concerning boundary contro-
versies see New Jersey *Archives, op. cit.,* VI, 205-15;
XIX, 403-05.

[7]John Schuyler's copper mines in Bergen County,
New Jersey.

ler's Park is of 750 Acres of Land enclosed with fences made of Cedar Logs such are taken out of the Cedar Swamps which are frequent in this Province. Col. John Schyelers, at whose Place[1] the Copper Mines are, is 2 miles & quarter higher up the River. His Park contains 680 Acres & has in it three hundred head of Deer. Between the high Lands of Bergen a narrow Ridge which Forms the West side of N York bay & Hudson river & the East Side of Bergen bay to the rising hills west of Second River. The Bay & its salt marshes is a Flatt of about 5 miles long & 2 wide. These are not yet embanked. From yᵉ Top of the Fire Engine[2] at Schyeler's One has a view over all this Country of Staten Island & Part of Long Island an Extensive & Varied Prospect of Bays & Islands. I have mentioned the Mine & Copper before. The Settlements on this River being Dutch & what we English call towns, are there called Neighbourhoods. The Roads run along the Banks of the river which is a clear & smooth one up to the Rift at Aquacinock.[3] The Country being cleared only round the settlements has a natural Sylvan beauty which our Nobility & Gentry are at such great expence to procure by Planting & Dressing their Places. From Schyelers to Second-river[4] Neighbourhood 2 miles & a half: To Aquacinock[5] 6: Thence to Weisel[6] 6: Thence to the long bridge over the Passaick [Passaic] River 2: Thence to the Falls one.

A sloop drawing Ten feet of water can Navigate up the Passaick [Passaic] to a rift about 2 miles below Aquacinock Church.

When the Dutch satt down at New Amsteldam [Amsterdam] & Crossed yᵉ North River to penetrate into yᵉ Country not knowing the names given by Indians to the rivers which they Cross'd the Hackinsaeg [Hackinsack] being the first & parallel to the Passaik [Passaic] then They called these, The First & Second Rivers; names which they are still called by.

The Falls of Passaik [Passaic] are a very curious natural Phenomenon. The River running round the Back of a Rocky Cliff, which by

[1]Belleville, a suburb of Newark, New Jersey. John Raum, The History of New Jersey . . . op. cit., I, 241.

[2]Steam engine brought to Schuyler's copper mine from Europe by Josiah Hornblower on Sept. 9, 1753. New Jersey Archives, op. cit., XII, 535n.

[3]Acquackanonck, probably present Passaic River. Thomas Gordon, A Gazetteer of the State of New Jersey . . . (Trenton, Daniel Fenton, 1834), p. 92. Present 139-153 River Drive, Passaic, New Jersey, is the site of early Acquackanonk Landing. Federal Writers' Project, New Jersey, New Jersey, a Guide to its Present and Past (N.Y., The Viking Press, 1939), p. 348.

[4]Belleville, New Jersey.

[5]Present Passaic, New Jersey. Federal Writers' Project. New Jersey, op. cit., p. 346.

[6]Weasel, an early settlement extending nearly four miles along the right bank of the Passaic near Paterson, New Jersey. Thomas Gordon, op. cit., p. 262. Present Passaic, New Jersey. Federal Writers' Project. New Jersey, ibid., p. 346.

some Accident has been shattered & riven from Top to Bottom about 90 feet, turns short round & Tumbles head long with an Inconceivable force & Velocity down this horrid chasm foaming with its hoarse stunning roar at its base more like something combustible than Water. There is a lesser Chasm on the right side of this Through which a Column of Water shoots directly across the great fall & has a peculiar effect & appearance. The Rocks on the left hand of this great Chasm is a Steep Cliff the Rocks of which are riven in two Places from top to bottom. I measured their height with a pack thread & stone, &, as near as I could regulate my measure, they were 90 feet high. I jump'd across one of these Chasms to go to the Cliff: & when I had done it, my head so turned; my heart misgave me; and It required an effort of mind to go back again. I think of it now with dread. I made upon the Spott a drawing of this, from a coloured copy, which P. Sandby made of it an Engraving has been given to the Publick.[1]

The next journey which I shall transcribe, so far as it relates to the nature of the Country & its settlements is from Elizabeth Town to Easton on ye Delaware River & to Bethlehem on the Leigh [Lehigh] River, a Branch of the Delaware. From Elizabeth Town to Woodbridge 10 miles; from Woodbridge to [New] Brunswick 12. The road runs in many Parts through woods in several places not unlike Sherwood Forest. To about 4 miles beyond Woodbridge the road keeps on ye flatt ground & then begins to rise up the Hilly Country & the red Marly soil. From the Tops of these, one has a view of the Raritan River & of the Pine-land country beyond it.

[New] Brunswick stands on the SW side of the Raritan about 12 miles from the mouth of it. It consists of 134 Houses, an English Church,[2] a Dutch Church & a Presbyterian Church.

Its Navigation consists Cheifly of Boats sloop-riggd of about 40 Ton, & about 30 in number, which make each, once a week at least, a trip to New York with the produce of the Country, Also Two Schooners which go on ye same errand to Rhode-Island, a Snow & a large Schooner of 140 tons which go to West Indies. The Soil here a red Marl, hence to Mr Steven's Copper Mine.[3] The Mine is in a hill NE of his House. From the Top of this Hill there is a pleasing Prospect of a fine settled Vale

---

[1] "A View of the Falls on the Passaic or Second River in the Province of New Jersey . . . . Sketched on the Spot by His Excellency Governor Pownall. Painted and Engraved by Paul Sandby." Scenographia Americana, *op. cit.*

[2] Christ Protestant Episcopal Church, on Neilson Street in present New Brunswick, is on the site of the original eighteenth century church. Federal Writers' Project. New Jersey, *op. cit.*, p. 309.

[3] John Stevens' Copper Mine at Rocky Hill, Hunterdon County, New Jersey.

bounded by Mountains which at 5.7. & 10 Miles distance run round it.
It is a Vale in respect of these high mountains but lyes varied by lesser
vallies & ranges of gently swelling hills. From hence to the Forks of this
River Through the Woods all the Way Cheifly White oak & Walnut or
Hickory Some few Chestnuts. To Potterstown: hence to Allen's[1] &
Turners[2] Iron Workes. Hence five miles to the old Furnace called The
Union.[3] Crost the Raritan & Spruce run. The Country between this
Place & Mr. Stevens[4] lyes thru Ridges of Mountains & between them for
5, 8 or 10 miles a Vale-like Country of alternate rising hills & Vallies,
then again Ridges of Mountains & Alternate Vales of the like Sort but
mostly in Woods unclear'd & looks when one casts one's Eye down from
the high ground like a long rolling Sea of Woods.

We rode late in the Ev'ning from the New Furnace[5] to the Union.[6]
It growing dark & the road being but a mere track through the Woods,
we had much trouble to see our way & was on y[e] point of being benighted
& began to form our Ideas of sleeping in the Woods. At This Moment we
heard a Trio of French-Horns playing a pleasing meloncholly Tune. The
Reader may imagine this must have been pleasant under these circumstances, if it had not been good musick. It struck me then a Stranger in
y[e] Country like, & was really like, an Incident in a Romance. We followed
the Sound & our Horses found the way which led us to the Dwellings
about the Mines. As we approached We found our Concert was performed by an old German & his two Sons sitting at the Door of their
Cottage thus amusing themselves in peace & happiness at the close of
the Ev'ning after their day's labour. What pleasure must this Old Man,
escaped from the Sovereign Tyranny of his European Lords & while
here—placida â compôstus pace quiescit—feel in the Contrast: And yet
I thought the melancholly of the Musick had a retrospective regrett
of his Native Country. I asked him. He said No & yet I thought he felt
yes; so are we formed. We were most hospitably received & treated & I
never lay in a neater more cleanly comfortable bed in my Life.

From hence our rode led over large hills & vales to the
Hickory Tavern[7] 8 miles through the woods, oaks Hickory & some

---

[1]William Allen (1704-1780), prominent Phila-
delphian, mayor of the city and chief justice of the
Supreme Court of Pennsylvania.

[2]Joseph Turner of Philadelphia. New Jersey
Archives, VII, 560.

[3]Owned and operated by William Allen and
Joseph Turner. *Ibid.*

[4]John Stevens' Copper Mines were at Rocky Hill,
Hunterdon County, New Jersey.

[5]Not identified.

[6][Pownall's note for revised and enlarged edition]
These are the great Iron Works.

[7]On the road to Easton and the Moravian settle-
ments. In 1759 Hickory Tavern was advertised
"To be Lett or sold by Colonel John Hackett at
Union Iron Works and Anthony White in New
Brunswick." New Jersey *Archives, op. cit.*, XX, 316.

Chestnut, on the banks of the runs in yᵉ vallies. Some very tall Poplars.

Hence to Johnson's Mill[1] through woods of the same kind, 5 miles. Passed by the beginnings of some settlements only three in yᵉ whole way. We ford the Rivulet at the head of the mill dam: thence West northerly three miles to the Pohatcung [Pohatcong] Creek, on which stands Kitchen's Mill[2] over a high level land. This Mill stands about 3 miles (up yᵉ river) from yᵉ Delaware river. The wood still the same.

The road led hence N & by W over the ends of Ridges of mountains, whose Wood was cheifly oak, 5 miles to a new-settled Town Called Philipsburg [Phillipsburg]. This Town Plott as laied out contained 100 acres & consisted (1754) of 14 Houses.

Hence Ferry over the Delaware at the Forks to another new settled Town called Easton. First began in 1752 under the Care of Mʳ Parson's[3] a very uncommonly ingenious Man. A Man having no views in life, but Quietude & Retirement, but engaged in this business of settling & running this Sweet Settlement.

The Scite of the Town is at the Point of the Forks of the River Delaware. Having that River in its front; The West branch or Leighy [Lehigh] River on its left; & a small rivulet on its right: It was a Flat Point of Land on pretty elevated banks surrounded on all sides with high hills.

The Plott of the town was that of a square laid out in strait Streets crossing each other at right angles: Four running directly east & west parallel to each a four like streets running north & south with an open Square in the Center. The Street running directly from the River was called Spring-garden Street, Northampton Street, Ferry Street, the name of the other I have forgotten.[4] The Cross Streets were Front street, Fermer[5] Street, Pomfret[6] street & Hamilton[7] Street. Alas! these great names, the relatives of the Penns, fixt as a mark of boasted honor on this property remain now only as objects of regret & humiliation. The side of each square of buildings crossed by these streets was 480 feet.[8] Each Lott was 60 feet front by 230 deep. The settlers paied for this seven shil-

[1]Samuel Johnston's Mills on the Musconetung River. New Jersey *Archives, op. cit.*, XXIV, 527-28; XXXV, 225.

[2]Samuel Kitchen's Mills in Amwell Township, Hunterdon County, New Jersey. New Jersey *Archives*, XXX, 285; XXXIV, 290.

[3]William Parsons (—d. 1757), Surveyor General for Pennsylvania and founder of Easton, Pennsylvania.

[4]Lehigh Street, Easton, Pennsylvania.

[5]Now Second Street.

[6]Now Third Street.

[7]Now Fourth Street.

[8][Pownall's note for revised and enlarged edition] There were already 36 houses built in 1754 when I was there.

lings sterling per annum quitt rent to the Proprietor Penn. The Whole contained about 100 acres.

I was politely, it now enough to say hospitably entertained & most comfortably lodged by M[r] Parsons at his new house, a pretty neat habitation very compleatly furnished.

I went from hence about five o'clock in the afternoon of the next day, rode along a pathway road under the shade of woods so that although it was a very hott day we were very little incommoded & arrived at Bethlehem about sunsett. Coming out from amidst a wilderness of woods through which I had been travelling some daies all at once at the top of a hill & viewing hence this cultivated populous settlement & its cluster of College like buildings large & spacious all of stone; with the grounds all around planted with orchards; & varied with tillage in all its forms of culture; & border'd on the banks of the river on which it lyes & of the rivulet which runns thro' it which rich & green meadows My Eye was struck with unexpected pleasure. The Place itself makes a delightfull landskip but found, & thus seen in the center of a wilderness, derives unusual beauty from the contrast & surprise with which it presents itself. I made here a Sketch[1] of it after a drawing from which an engraving has been made & published.

The Distance of Bethlehem from Easton is 12 miles the ground between hilly all y[e] way but fine land. At about four miles from Easton I observed we were riding through a wood of Young Saplings, resembling a young planted wood rising near some of our fine new-made places in England. This was the first time that this circumstance in the Course of vegitation had mett my Observation: and I was totally at a loss to account for it. I state my doubts to M[r] Parsons,[2] who accompanied me to Bethlehem. He could not but look down upon my ignorance but with great good breeding said He did wonder to find that this circumstance was new to a person, who was born, & had always lived, in a world clear'd of its woods. He should have been more surprised at my inattention, if this circumstance had escaped my observation. As I could never have had in the old world an opportunity of examining this matter as to its fact, it was natural that I should be at a loss in reasoning about the State of the fact. He that had spent his life in the woods & had been conversant with the nature of their existence, had studied their vegitable life. He observed that every soil produced its natural race of vegitable

[1]"A View of Bethlehem, the great Moravian Settlement in the Province of Pennsylvania. Sketched on the Spot by his Excellency Gov. Pownall, Painted and Engraved by Paul Sandby." In *Scenographia Americana, op. cit.*
[2]William Parsons.

inhabitants; that each individual tree had & went through all the periods
of life from youth through adultness & sunk by old age to death as men
do: that their life was liable to defects in health & to disease which went
to loss of life, that this was not only so in the individual but that the
woods were liable to epidemical endemial maladies like the race of man;
that such when they happened would lay waste whole tracts of country,
that when this happened, if any change of circumstances made any
change of the nature of the soil either for the better or the worse Quite
a different race of Trees would spring up, if no change was made then
Trees of the same sort would spring in succession to those which had
dyed there as was the case in the present instance. But that an instance
of the former case had occurred to him some years prior to ye present
when he was surveying in the Valley beyond the Kittatiny Mountains.
He found a whole tract of Country full of Loggs of Pine trees lyeing
along the ground so as almost to Cover it the boles of trees which once
grown on it, but were now dead. That a young Wood was growing
amongst these, a young vegitation of quite a different Race; that to the
former inhabitants the Pines, Oakes & Hickory were coming up in succession. That in many parts, of America, in the as yet uncultured parts,
especially on the banks of rivers, where a new soil had accumulated many
feet above the old, & what one may call the original soil,—Trees of a very
different species were growing from those which by digging were found
lyeing on a different stratum of soil beneath the present face of the earth.

The next Day in the morning I waited on Bishop Spanenberg[1]
[Spangenberg], Superintendant general of the Outward & Inward, the
Temporal & Spiritual Oeconomy of the Moravians throughout all
America. He received me with that address & politeness which is peculiar
only to Men of the first fashion in the great world and treated me while I
staid in these settlements, with attentions that could only derive to me
who had no right to them from a benevolence that could alone exceed
his politeness.

These Settlements, which I will describe both as to the Farms as
also as to the peculiar Community which occupied them consisted of
about 10,000 acres of Good Land.

The Community settled on them was of those People, who stile
themselves the *Unitas Fratrum*,[2] & who being Emigrants from Moravia

[1]Augustus Gottlieb Spangenberg (1704-1792),
bishop in the Moravian Church at Bethlehem,
Pennsylvania, 1744 to 1750, when he was replaced
by Bishop John Nitschmann.

[2]From the original Bohemian name meaning
Brethren's Church. Joseph Levering, *A History of
Bethlehem, Pennsylvania, 1741-1892* (Bethlehem,
Pa., Times Publishing Co., 1903), p. 7, 8n.

are called Moravians, but named in their original settlement under Count Zinzendorf[1] Hereen-huters.[2] They are a Society of Christians, obeying, rather than what can be stiled governed by, an Episcopalian Hierarchy both as to their Temporal as well as Spiritual Interests. They hold that their Episcopacy hath preserved its succession pure & uninterrupted from the first ages of Christianity preserving the faith also pure incorrupted without mixture or connection with the Government or the Doctrines of the Church of Rome. They cannot therefore as they do not call themselves, be called Protestants or a reformed Church. They hold however pretty much in a catholick spirit, the same principles as the reformed Churches. The Church & Legislature of England have acknowledged them as being what they profess themselves to be in their Episcopalian Succession.

They have adopted in the litteral sense some expressions of the Holy Scriptures; and have adopted the idea of a Society found'd on a Community of Property & Labour;[3] without attending to that distribution of property & the paying taxes there from which Christ referred to when he saied render unto Caesar the things which are Caesars & unto God the things which are Gods. Be their Opinions on this point what they may; be they right or wrong, I am rather apt to think from what little I understand that the *Model of their Community* will be rather sooner found in Plato's Republick than in the Gospel of Christ or the Doctrines of his Apostles.

However such is their Doctrine & such is their Actual Establishment. Under This *Oconomy* (here I use their own peculiar term) they possess & Cultivate near 10,000 Acres of Land comprised in six Farms. viz Bethlehem,[4] Nazareth,[5] Gnadenhüt,[6] Christian-sprung,[7] Gnadenthall,[8] and Vriedenthall.[9] The Title to which is vested in David Nitchman

[1]Nicolaus Ludwig, Count von Zinzendorf (1700-1760).

[2]From village of Herrnhüt, Germany, first place of worship for the six leaders in the Moravian Church (1724). Levering, *op. cit.*, p. 22.

[3]The co-operative plan was not a part of the religious belief of the Moravians in America, but was adopted as an expedient in order to build a self-sustaining mission in Pennsylvania. By 1761 the mission had reached its goal and the cooperative plan was abolished. Information given to the editor by Dr. S. H. Gapp, Archivist, Archives of the Moravian Church, Bethlehem, Pennsylvania. However, it was not until 1814 that the oil mill, the tobacco factory, and the slaughterhouse, all run as

community enterprises were given up; the grist mill continued to be used by the community until 1825; and it was not until 1837 that the remaining business enterprises conducted by the Moravian Church in Bethlehem were sold. Warren N. Nonnemaker, "The Moravian Church in the United States during the Middle Period, 1812-1860" (Master's Thesis, Lehigh University, 1935), pp. 9, 13, and 16. For many years, Mr. Nonnemaker was principal of the Moravian Preparatory School in Bethlehem.

[4]Bethlehem. The deed for land on "The Allen Tract" was dated Apr. 2, 1741. On Christmas Eve, Dec. 24, 1741, the community was named Bethlehem by mutual consent of the religious congregation. Levering, *op. cit.*, p. 61, 79.

[Nitschmann][1] in trust for the use of the Unitas Fratrum. Writing from my Journal I speak of it as it was when I was there in the year 1754, & as it had long subsisted, I think about 14 years.[2]

The Principle which they hold out as the spirit which animates & unites them into one body in Christian Love to each other & to the United Community, the Unitas Fratrum, as members & the Body of Christ of which Body Christ is the Head. The Spirit which actuates the Oconomy is an Authority, rather than power, founded in an opinion that the Bishops, Deacons, Ministers, Spiritual Labourers, & Superintendants who administer the Spiritual & Direct the Temporal Matters of the Society are the visible Deputies being the Successors on Earth of the Apostles & Disciples of Christ.

The Model of the *Unitas Fratrum* as raised on this Basis was called their Oconomy and as the animal Oconomy of Man consists of an Union of Soul & Body each having their respective powers form & operation; so here The Oconomy of this *Unitas* had a Spiritual & Temporal Form. Bishop Spanenberg [Spangenberg] was the Intendant general throughout all America both of the Spiritual & Temporal Oconomy. He had under him two other Bishops—M[r] Beler[3] [Boehler] & M[r] Hale[4] [Heyl]. Under these were Ministers to administer the ordinances & to preach. They were sent out itinerant into various parts to preach as the Bishops & Synod should direct. There were also Deacons who preached who Baptised who were the Spiritual Labourers. There were also Schoolmasters & Catechists. Their Church Service was conducted by an established Liturgy. Their Psalmody & Hymns were accompanied with Musick of every sort. The Temporal Oconomy was superintended by Temporal Oconomists Temporal Deacons & their Assistants. The Deacons managed the whole of their Property & Revenue. They directed

---

[5]Nazareth (Ten miles north of Bethlehem). Deeded to Count Zinzendorf, May 11, 1740, by Wm. Allen. *Ibid.*, p. 44.

[6]Gnadenhütten (Habitation of Grace). On the Lehigh at the mouth of Mahoning Creek. The first 15 settlers left Bethlehem, June 13, 1746 to found this new Moravian settlement. *Ibid.*, p. 193.

[7]Christian Sprung (Christian's Spring). Was known as Albrecht's Brunn but officially named Christian's Brunn, Aug. 4, 1749. *Ibid.*, p. 190.

[8]Gnadenthal (Grace Dale). Settlement began Jan. 13, 1745. *Ibid.*, p. 190.

[9]Friedensthal (Vale of Peace). The mill was built in 1750, but the dwelling was not occupied until April 27, 1751. On that date the community was given its official name—Friedensthal. William C. Reichel, *Friedensthal and its stockaded mill . . . 1749-1767* (Nazareth, Pa., Whitfield House, 1877), pp. 7, 8.

[1]Bishop David Nitschmann, Sr. (1696-1772), first bishop of the Unitas Fratrum in America and the official founder of its first American Settlement.

[2]Founded in 1741.

[3]Peter Boehler (1712-1775), was consecrated bishop in the Moravian Church in 1748 and was acting superintendent of the Moravian Church in America, 1742-44.

[4]Matthew Gottfried Heyl (1705-1787), bishop of the Moravian Church for 30 years. Moravian Historical Society. *Transactions of . . .* (Nazareth, Pa., Whitfield House, 1876-date), VII, 243, no. 110.

the Supply & Consumption & Had the Care of all the personalty & Stock. Mr Lawatsch[1] was, under Bishop Spanenberg [Spangenberg], first Deacon & Superintendant for Temporal affairs; Treasurer & Auditor. The Persons who were members of this Society & composed this settlement were, in 1754, 910 individuals. They were considered & considered themselves as one Family. This family was divided into seperate classes, which were called *Choirs*. These choirs were not only thus distinguished for orders sake but lived seperately from each other & never mett but at Chapel. They had each Choir—seperate houses, even the Children were seperated from the parents & were nursed in their own choir, at first at Bethlehem & afterwards at Nazareth. These Choirs were: 1. The Choir of Infants who had Nurses & every other necessary attendant appointed to the care of them. 2. The Choirs of Children, that is of Boys & of Girls, in two seperate choirs. These had proper persons appointed to attend their nurture & Education. 3. The Choir of single men. 4. The Choir of Single Women and 5. The Choir of Married People. They had four Distinct Houses for these at Bethlehem & a fifth at Nazareth. These Houses were all Spacious large buildings of Stone plain but neat & handsome. The House for the Choir of single men was a long Building of four stories high, beside the base story. The first was assigned to the offices, the second was the Refrectory, one very long room the whole length of the building. The next, the Dormitory another long room of the same kind. The highest story another long room of the same sort which was the Vestiary for here their Cloathing was deposited. Each individual had two suits one for summer & one other for Winter annually. They all wore the same habit without distinction. The Apartments for the single Women were in a quadrangle open on one side to the South. The East & West sides were appropriated for the appartments, the North side was the Chapell. The Infants were in a House by themselves with their nurses. And the Married Couples had seperate lodgings in another House by themselves each in seperate lodgings, & accommodated to that state of life. The two Houses of the Single Men & Single Women had each a Garden & Orchard seperate & distinct, also each a laundry seperate. For none of these individuals were ever sufferrd to meet unless such as the Bishops & Ministers had destined for marriage with each other.

[1]Rev. Andrew Anthony Lawatsch, a principal elder in the Moravian Church in Bethlehem, was ordained in the Moravian Church in Marienborn, Germany, in 1745 and came to America in 1752. "Clergy of the American province of the Unitas Fratrum," I, 67. Manuscript in Moravian Archives, Bethlehem, Pennsylvania.

As the Property & its Produce was, as I have marked above Common to the whole Community & governed by the oconomy as above described: so was the Labor. The Deacons & their Assistants distributed & directed the individual each to that branch of buisness or that line of labour for which he was best calculated, or best understood. The Produce of which Common Labor, in each branch, was carried to the common Stock. Besides the Farm labourers in which both women as well men worked, There were, when I was there the Following Trades carried on by the Fratres at this Settlement. Saddle-tree maker, Sadler, Glover, Shoemaker, Stocking-weavers, 4 frames going, Button maker Taylor & Women Taylor, Hatter, Ribband-weavers, Linnen-weavers, 6 looms in work, Woollen-weavers, three looms at work, Wool-comber, Dyer, Fuller, Dresser, Tanner, Currier, Skinner, Butcher, Miller, Chandler, Oil-maker, Baker, Cooper, Joiner, Carpenter, Mason, Glazier, Brick maker Stone Cutter Turner Potter Stovemaker Wheelwright Blacksmith, Gunsmith Nail-Maker Lock-smith, Pewterer, Tinman Silver-smith, Clockmaker Harnes-maker, Hemp dresser, Boat-builder, Surgeon, Apothecary. These Artificers & Manufacturers had each seperate appartments & shops to themselves. Although this Community of Property Labour Supply & Consumption thus took place in general: Yet those of the Brethern who chose to live seperate & to keep their property & Labor distinct & to themselves were at liberty to do so. Those who partook of the Common supply, were bound to contribute their common labour to the raising & making of it, & è contra those who gave their labor to the common stock partook in all things of the Common Supply under the direction & distribution of the common Oconomy. Many however who were members of the Spiritual Oeconomy & of the Church; as to outward matter & Oconomy held possessed & actuated their own private property & oconomy distinct within themselves & to themselves of which were many, cheifly of the married People.

About ten miles N. of Bethlehem the Society had another noble Farm of 6000 acres of land called Nazareth, at which all the Children who were brought up as the Children of the Family, were nursed and educated from 18 months old to three Years. It was worked in the ordinary labour of the Farm by 30 couple of the married Choir. The Hay & Corn harvest was gotten in by Labourers sent from the other Choirs for the time under the superintendence & direction of the Deacons or Assistants. They had a little Farm of 60 Acres called Gnaden-hüt[ten] at an Indian town about 28 miles off Bethlehem where they had a Grist & Saw Mill. They told me they had Baptised 100 Indians at this place.[1]

They had another most noble farm & Settlement begun in 1748 Called Christian-sprung of — acres worked by 40 Brethern sent from the Single Mens choir & two couples from the Married Choir. The Familys Brewhouse Distillery, Dairy & Saw Mills were. Here first I saw some trout that would come to the edge of ye water & take bread out of one's hand, here first also I saw that sort of dairy called a spring-house.

There was another fine farm adjoining to this called Gnadenthall, begun in 1746, & worked by 14 couple sent from the married Choir.

About two miles from Nazareth there was another little Farm of about 300 acres purchased in 1749 & settled in 1750 & in great forwardness of Culture. This was worked by 6 Couple of the married Choir. This was called Vriedenthall. I dined here & was entertained at Dinner by a very good Harper. I thought a fine one. I'm sure 'twas pleasant & novel such thus removed from ye cultured world. One of finest Grist-Mills at this place that I ever saw in America, the mill at Trentown [Trenton][2] excepted. Every one of these Farms had large houses & round them Peach & Apple orchard planted with the best of Fruit as also gardens.

I forgott to mention The Grist Mills, Fulling mills, Oil-mills, & other mills which performed various operations at Bethlehem.

As this Curious Settlement was an instance existing in fact & actuating the plan of Plato's Utopeia, I could not in the description of this New World, which is rising intirely on an experimental System, avoid describing it. But apart the singlarity of its System of Community, The Fineness of its Settlements & Farms did of themselves deserve a special notice. I Confine myself to the description of ye Facts & enter not into reasoning about the System.

My Tour led me hence back to Easton & thence between 40 & 50 miles through the woods & over one ridge of mountains, & over to Trenton a Pretty good Town in the Jerseys on the banks of the river Delaware just below the falls.[3] It consisted at this time of 100 Houses & one of the finest mills working 4 pair of Horses, that I ever saw. It is the

[1]In 1754 the mission at Gnadenhütten numbered 137 Indians. Reichel, *Memorials . . . op. cit.*, p. 34n.
[2]The William Trent Mill, a two story stone structure built in 1690 on the site of the Mahlon Stacy Mill (1680). The building stood until carried away by flood waters in 1843. John Raum, *History of the city of Trenton, New Jersey . . .* (Trenton, N. J., W. T. Nicholson & Co., 1871), p. 234.

[3]At Trenton, New Jersey. "Known from earliest settlement as the Falls." Federal Writers' Project, New Jersey, *op. cit.*, p. 398.

Barcadore of the upper Country produce which goes down hence upon the Delaware to Philadelphia. The Articles sent from hence are, Wheat flour, Pipe-staves, Iron, Flax, Hemp &c. There were 8 schallops belonging to this town which plyed & were constantly employed in the navigation between this town & Philadelphia. There was a Plating mill here.[1] There are here an English Church[2] a Presbyterian[3] and a Quaker meeting.[4] The Majority of the Inhabitants are Quakers.

Before I quitt this town on my Way to Philadelphia I will mark the course of the road between [New] Brunswick & Trentown [Trenton] & the nature of the land & Country of Jersey in the settled Parts. A little to the East of [New] Brunswick that is, between that & Woodbridge begins the red marly stratum. Going west from [New] Brunswick the road rises up a country of swelling hills but at about 7 miles from [New] Brunswick begins to mount the ridge of the high lands of the Jerseys & runs along that ridge to Kingstown [Kingston], Prince [Princeton] & Maidenhead. As the road runs along this high ridge, one looks over to the left the low flatt Country of New Jersey. At the foot of this high ridge hilly ground which forms the foreground of a pleasing landskip, spangled thick which Gentleman's Houses & rich Farmers Places seen amongst the woods as if standing at the upper end of long spacious avenues of clear'd & cultured ground consisting of orchards of Peaches & Apples Growing in regular rows as also Cherry holly Wheat land, Flax & Hemp lands Pasture & Meadows below & beyond this foreground one looks over the great extensive level flatt of Sandy Pine land interspersed with Cedars away to the *Navesink*. The road was all the way from [New] Brunswick to Trenton through a continued succession of Plantations so that one is never out of sight of a House, except when the road runs through the little woods & Coppices which make part of each Plantation. A Farm or Plantation consists of a Good neat House, &, if it stands on a convenient run of water, of a mill also; it is generally busked upon each side or behind with an Apple & a Peach orchard. It hath generally a farm yard joining to it with a good barn, a hay rick, a Cyder press & mill a Corn Shed Hogsties & Cow-yard, with fields of English Grass, Indian Corn, Wheat, Buckwheat mostly belted round with woods. One rides thus through a kind of Garden the whole way.

[1]The only plating mill in New Jersey. Located at west end of Trenton and owned by Benjamin Yard of Hunterdon County. New Jersey *Archives, op. cit.,* VII, 558; X, 31.

[2]On the present site of St. Michael's Protestant Episcopal Church, 140 N. Warren St., Trenton.

Federal Writers' Project, New Jersey, *op. cit.,* p. 409.

[3]On the present site of the First Presbyterian Church, 114 E. State Street. *Ibid.*

[4]The Old Friends Meeting House, corner of E. Hanover and Montgomery Sts., Trenton. This Meeting House, built in 1739, is still standing. *Ibid.*

A very large & well built College has been erected at Princetown [Princeton] the highest & most healthy tract of Land in this rout.

On September 3 I left Trenton cross over the Delaware by a ferry[1] about a furlong broad into Pennsylvania. Thence through woods all the way 10 miles to Bristol. Bristol stands upon the west side, northerly, of a pretty circular bason near ¾ of a mile broad, & a mile & ¼ long. Opposite to this bearing South easterly sitts Burlington on the Banks on the Jersey side, Bristol had then 60 houses, three bake-houses for biscuit, a Meeting. Employ'd in its intercourse with Philadelphia, a Sloop & two Shallops. Burlington has 130 houses a Church & a Quaker Meeting, has one Biscuit Baking-house employs a shallop & two passage boats has a very pretty street right up from the river. Two neat Market-houses, & Court house being a Market Town. From Bristol through woods still, to a Ferry over a Creek,[2] from hence 4 miles to another Creek[3] & Ferry, where is a good tavern called Widow Amos's:[4] Hence 4 miles through pretty good settlements the land along most of this latter way the Isinglas soil. Hence 8 miles to Frankfort; & 5 to Philadelphia.

Fourth Stage, or the Endless Mountains

"The *Endless Mountains*,[5] so called from a Translation of the Indian Name bearing that Signification, come next in Order. They are not confusedly scattered, and in lofty Peaks over-topping one another, but stretch in long uniform Ridges, scarce Half a Mile perpendicular in any Place above the intermediate Vallies. Their Name is expressive of their Extent, though, no Doubt, not in a literal Sense. In some Places,

d J k

as the Head of Ronoak[d] [Roanoke], one would be induced to imagine he had found their End, but let him look a little on, and he will find them again spread in new Branches, of no less Extent than what first

Allegheny Mountains
e F h

presented themselves. The *further* Chain, or Allegeny Ridge of Mountains,[e] keeps mostly on a Parallel with the *Isinglassy* Rief, and terminates in a rough stony Piece of Ground at the Head of Ronoak [Roanoke]

f D c

and New River.[f] The more Easterly Chains, as they run further Southward, trend also more and more Westerly; which is the Reason that the *Upland* and *Piemont* Valley are so much wider in Virginia than farther Northward. This South-westerly Trending of the hither Chains brings them to meet the Allegeny Mountain, and in several Places to intersect

[1]Thomas Hooton was keeper of Trenton Ferry in 1750. New Jersey *Archives, op. cit.,* XII, 679-80.
[2]Mill Creek. See "Wm. Scull's Map of Pennsylvania . . . 1770," *op. cit.* Not shown on modern maps.
[3]Neshaminy Creek. *Ibid.*
[4]On Neshaminy Creek. *Ibid.*
[5]Read Lewis Evans' description of the Endless Mountains, printed on his *Map* of 1749.

it, and form new Series of Mountains; as is the Case I believe, of the
Ouasioto."[g][1]

g J a

They certainly do end to the Northward and North East, at the
[h]Kaats Kill [Catskill] Mountains, and at the [i]Brimston [Brimstone] and h C d
Oneida Ridge, which lie South of Mohawks River. The Triangular i B d e
Mountainous Tract of [k]Couchsackrage, [Couxsachrage] lying between k D e
the Mohawks and St. Lawrence Rivers and Lake Champlain, [Cham-
plain] and the Range of Mountains on the East Side Hudson River, are
distinct and different Ranges of Country.

"There are many Chains of the Endless Mountains, which, had
they come to my Knowledge, might have filled several Places which lie
vacant in the Map."[2] [Several of these are inserted in the present
Edition.] "But so far as we are acquainted with them, we observe that
each Chain consists of a particular Kind of Stone, and each different
from the rest; and these Differences continue for their whole Extent, as
far as I can learn. When I crossed them I was not apprehensive of this,
and omitted enumerating their Species. Some of the Chains are single
narrow Ridges, as the Kittatinni [Kittatinny]; some spread Two or
Three Miles broad on the Top; some steep on one Side, and extending
with a long Slope on the other; and the steeper they are, the more
rocky; but they are every where woody where there is Soil proper and
sufficient to supporr the Trees. Towards the further Chains North-
eastward, the Mountains consist of rich Land, and in some Places are
but as large broad Banks, which take Two or Three Miles to cross."[3]

Many of these Chains consist of several Ridges, one main Ridge,
and a Number of lesser ones, and sometimes with irregular Hills at their
Foot in the Vale. Where any of those Chains so spread, they meet and
sometimes cross each other; sometimes lesser Branches or Spurs shoot
out from the main Ridges, and these also generally end by irregular Hills.

"In the Way to Ohio, by Franks Town,[4] after you are past the E h
Allegeny [Allegheny] Mountain, the Ground is rough in many Places, and
continues, so to the River. Hereabouts the Lawrel [Laurel] Hill springs
from the Mountain, and continues though not large, in a very regular

---

[1]Renamed Cumberland Mountains in honor of the
Duke of Cumberland, by Dr. Thomas Walker of
Virginia in 1748. J. G. M. Ramsey, *Annals of
Tennessee* . . . (Kingsport, Tenn., Kingsport Press,
1926), pp. 65-66. This quotation is from Evans'
Analysis, pp. 7-8; reprinted in Gipson's *Lewis Evans*,
pp. 151-52.

[2]Quoted from Evans' *Analysis*, p. 8; reprinted in
Gipson's *Lewis Evans*, p. 152.

[3]*Ibid.*

[4]The Old Delaware and Shawnee Town (1731)
Assunepachla. Named Frank's Town by early
Indian Traders. Charles A. Hanna, *The Wilderness
Trail* . . . (N.Y., G. P. Putnam's Sons, 1911), I, 259.
Near present site of Hollidaysburg, Blair Co.,
Pennsylvania.

Chain, I believe, to the Ouasioto Mountain.[1] For though the Allegeny [Allegheny] Mountain is the most Westerly, on the West Branch of Susquehanna,[k] it is far from being so, back of Virginia.

Land
among the
Mountains

"Except the further Ridges, as just now mentioned, there is but little good Land in the Mountains; to be sure not one Tenth Part is capable of Culture; and what small Matter is so, consists of extreme rich Soil, in Lawns, on the River Edges, being so much rich Mud subsided there; and commonly gathered above Falls, formerly in drowned Land, and now drained by the Rivers wearing Channels through the Rocks,[2] which, like Dams, held up the Waters at each respective Fall."

The Cherokee or Apalachian [Appalachian] Mountain on the Back of the Carolinas & Northwestern parts of Georgia, although in like manner rocky & gravelly are yet well cloathed with Forest Trees & Shrubs. The Bay Cypress Cedar & Laurel, The Oak, Chestnut, Mulberry, Maple, Hickory, Acasia [Acacia], Walnut, Plumbtree [Plum] & vine both the Cluster & fox-grape. The vallies have a soil rich to a degree beyond what manure can produce on poorer cultured lands: the sides of ye ridges of the Mountains are bare the tops, where not clear'd of their natural Vegetation, are yet covered with a good coating of Soil. The Ridges in many parts are four or five hundred feet high & almost impracticably steep & not more than from six to twelve feet wide; in some places they are so narrow that two horses loaded cannot pass each other & yet it is necessary in most places to continue the road along these ridges untill a proper descent offerrs itself. But bad are ye best: And in general These descents are not only difficult almost to impracticability for Pack-horses but in many instances attended with imminent risque & danger. The Vallies here also, as has been observed of other Parts of these Mountains, are very deep & narrow in general, & liable to Flood: Yet in their Climate the most delightfull & beneficial Settlements may be established in them.

Amidst the Detail of these dry Descriptions, it may perhaps relieve and amuse the Reader to insert some Observations and Opinions which I found in and extracted from Mr. Evans's Journal.[3]

a E f

"The Stones in all Parts of these Mountains are full of Sea Shells: It is not in the loose Stones scattered through the Vales that these Shells abound only, but they are found at the Tops of the Mountains also. I saw some mixed with the rocky Base of a high Mountain; in [a] Wishoôchon

[1]Cumberland Mountain.
[2]Here ends this quotation from Evans' *Analysis*, pp. 8-9; reprinted in Gipson's *Lewis Evans*, pp 152-53.
[3]From the *Journal* of 1743, part of which is printed in *Appendix* of this work. Gipson, *op. cit.*, p. 3.

[Wissahickon] Creek I found a soft Stone Five or Six Feet long, as full of all Sorts of Shells as if they were kneaded into a lump of brown Clay: There was all the Variety that could be imagined, and many that had never before come under my Observation, many that I could not imagine to exist in Nature as the Shells of any Animal, particularly a large Escolop with Corbels, as fine as those of Cockles. I was almost disposed to pronounce this a Lusus Naturae, but I have since found that Sort of Shell, and many other of the Sorts which I saw here, in a Bed of Soil more than 30 Feet under Ground in Virginia. The Observations also which I had an Opportunity of making at Moor's Mill[1] near London Town,[2] in Maryland, shewed me how ill imagined any such Idea was. This Place is not far from the Sea Side, the Earth had been dug from an adjoining Bank for a Mill-dam; at the Top I found the Shells mixed with a loose Sand; at Three or Four Feet deep they were inclosed in a sandy Clay; and at Four or Five Feet deeper, the Clay was gradually hardened into a loose Kind of Stone, in which were mixed Shells, many resembling the Specimens which we had before observed in the Mountains. This Instance of the Soil hardening by Degrees from a loose Sand to an indifferent Stone in the Space of Eight or 10 Feet, where there could be no Doubt but that the Shells were genuine, and where the Shells were actually of the same Sort as those which I had observed in the Mountains, convinced me that those Shells of the Mountains were real, and had been mixed with and finally incrusted in the Stones where they were found, by the same Process as here appeared in its several Gradations.

"Various Systems and Theories of the present Earth have been devised in order to account for this Phaenomenon. One System supposes that the Whole of this Continent, the highest Mountains themselves, as they now appear, were formerly but one large Plain, inclining with a considerable Slant towards the Sea; that this has been worn into its present Appearance of Ridges, with Vales between them, by the Rains of the Heavens and Waters of the Earth washing away the Soil from the upper Parts, and carrying it down to Seawards. That the Soil thus carried down and lodged in various Places hath in a Series of Ages

[1] Dr. George Walker and Jonathan Hanson built two water-mills ca. 1711 and 1733 respectively. These mills were later called Moore's Mills. *Maryland Historical Magazine* (Baltimore, 1906-date), XVI, (1921), 216n. They were located near Jones Falls. See Warner & Hanna's *Plan of the City and Environs of Baltimore respectfully dedicated to the Mayor City Council, & Citizens thereof, by the Pro-prietors, 1801.* [Baltimore, 1801.]

[2] London Town was on the south bank of the South River, about four miles from Annapolis. In 1923 one brick mansion used as Anne Arundel County home was all that remained to mark the site of this once thriving town. *Maryland Historical Magazine, ibid.*, XVIII (1923), 254.

formed the lower Plains of the Jerseys, Pennsylvania, Maryland, Virginia, and the Carolinas. The most material Arguments to support this Hypothesis are, that the very Tops of the Mountains on the western Side, though much higher than those bordering on the English Pale, consist yet of extraordinary rich Land, but that towards our Side the Soil of the very Vales as well as of the Mountains is thin and stony, and the Rock almost bare as if the Earth had been swept away off from them. The Downfall of Waters from the Melting of the Snow, the Rains, and the swollen Springs is such amongst the Mountains, and the Discharge from thence so great, that the Freshes on the Susquehanna River, where it is a Mile broad, rise 20 Feet, though they are discharged with a violent and precipitate Current. These Freshes carry down with them immense Quantities of Soil which they begin to drop as the Velocity of their Course slackens in gliding over the lower Plains, and which they finally lodge in Bars and Islands at the Mouths of the Rivers where they meet the Sea.[1] Thus have been many very extensive Countries formed at the Mouths of all the great Rivers in the World, and thus at the several Mouths of the many great Rivers ranging so near one another along this Coast may that long continued Range of flat Country, which is herein before called the *Lower Plains*, be formed. And if we suppose this Operation to have begun immediately at the carrying off of the Waters of the Deluge when the Earth was in a State of Fluidity, and to have continued in Operation ever since, the Effects will not appear more than natural. This Hypothesis accounts for all the Appearances which are observed, and all the Peculiarities which are found on the lower Plains of America, such as the Nature of the difference Layers of Strata of which they consist, for the Sea Shells and Fish Bones being found at 30 and 40 Feet deep, and probably deeper, if examined for the various Logs, and especially for the Caedar Swamps and Pine Bogs, which are perfect Mines of Timber.

"But we must have recourse to some other Explanation in order to account for the Situation of the Shells on the Tops of the Mountains.

"It is easy to shew the Earth and Sea *may* assume one another's Places, but positively to assert *how that hath actually happened* in Times past, is hazardous; we know what an immense Body of Water is contained in the great Lakes at the Top of the Country, and that this is

[1][Pownall's note] I will here transcribe an Extract from a Letter of Monsieur Vaudreuil, the Governor of Louisiana, dated September 28, 1752. There is infinite Difficulty, says he, in settling towards the Mouth of the River Mississippi, on account of the immense Expence in Banking against the Inundations of the Sea and Land-floods. I am against settling it as yet; and for waiting until the Ground be more and more raised by the Accretion of Soil, as it hath been *Three Feet* in the Space of 15 Years.

damm'd and held up by Ridges of Rocks: Let us suppose these Ridges broken down by any natural Accident, or that in a long Course of Ages a Passage may be worn through them, the Space occupied by the Water would be drained: This Part of America, disburthened of such a Load of Waters, would of course rise, as the immediate Effect of the shifting of the Center of Gravity in the Globe at once or by Degrees, much or little, accordingly as the Operation of such Event had Effect on that Center. The directly opposite Part of the Earth would, as Part of the same Effect, sink and become depressed, and liable to be deluged without any apparent Reason discoverable in those Parts for such a Change. There is no Doubt but that many such Accidents have happened in the World before it became settled in its present Condition and State. That there have happened some such Accidents, by which the general Body of the Land of America hath been raised, we have Reason to collect from the Chinese Chorography, called Quang-yn-ki,[1] which describes Tshaossanas in Corea [Korea], which is now divided from it by the Gulf Leao Tong, where the Sea has encroached so much that the Mountain Kiesheshang, which was formerly Part of the Continent, is now near 500 Leagues off at Sea. If the Land of China became thus much depressed by the Change of the Center of Gravity of the Earth, those Parts of America which lie nearly in an opposite Meridian would be equally raised. No doubt many partial Deluges have happened from such Causes, the Reason of which, for want of Knowledge is what had passed on the opposite Side of the Globe, could never be explained. Some such Changes may have come gradually and advanced by such slow Degrees, as that in a Period of a few Ages would not be perceptible; History therefore could take no Notice of them.

"We know from Observation how much higher the Atlantic Ocean is than the Pacific, and how it is piled up against the American Coast on the western Shore of the Gulf of Mexico, driven thither by the Trade Winds and Attraction of the Moon and Sun. Let us suppose it possible that a Passage might be forced through the Isthmus of Darien[2] or some other Part of America between the Tropics; these Waters then would pour down from this Height and be discharged through this Passage, instead of running back through the Gulf of Florida; the Height of the Atlantic would be lower between the Tropics, and the Level of the Pacific Ocean would rise; the Center of Gravity of the Earth would

---

[1] "Kuang-yü chī, is a geography of the Empire in 24 books, written by Lŭh Ying-yâng about the commencement of the 17th century." Alexander Wylie, *Notes on Chinese Literature* . . . (Shanghai, Presbyterian Mission Press, 1922), p. 59.
[2] Panama.

shift, and there would be few Places on the Earth but what would perceive the Effect, although none would be able to conceive the Cause, that did not know the particular Event of this Passage being opened." Suppose now that the Bahama and Caribbee Islands were once (which they certainly appear to be) an Isthmus (like that of Darien) the Continuation of the Apalachian [Appalachian] Mountains and the Al-a-Bah'ma[1] Country; that what is now the Gulph of Mexico was a most extensive Plain, and that some such Accident as is above supposed did actually happen by the Breaking of the Sea through this Chain of Land into this Plain now the Great Gulf, that Part of the Globe actually becoming depressed, the opposite Point would be raised. "I have mentioned, says Evans, these different Systems as they occurr'd to me on viewing the various Phaenomena which meet our Eye in the Mountains; for the Information of those who are curious in enquiring into the System of our World; but I have neither pursued the Investigation with that Attention, nor explained them with that Closeness of Reasoning which I might have done had I been interested about them; I shall therefore beg the Reader to make Choice of that Hypothesis which he likes best and thinks most probable; for my own Part I can conclude on neither singly." The Editor[2] here will take up this Subject where Lewis Evans hath left it, and add One more Hypothesis or Theory to the many with which the Learned have been amused.

Mons' Buffon Modestly as a first step introduces his Theory of ye Formation of the Planets by the name of *Simple Conjectures*[3] but adds as ye next step that shall give it a much greater degree of probability that anyone of all the Theories which have been formed on the same subject can assume.

A mere Globe of Mud wherein all ye Parts remained in an indigested state of Fluidity which yet could not properly be called Water. I sufferr not my imagination to conceive by any theory What that Process of Nature was which first collected into a Globe these concentring particles because there is nothing even in analogy much less in experience to give ye least grounds to such Theory: But from analogy of what is now passing in the region of Worlds I can suppose this Chaotic Globe (as well as the rest of the Planets) to have been in every circumstance Just what the Comets now are. These Comets impressed with a pro-

---

[1] The Appalachian range terminates in the Al-a-Bah-ma or northern Alabama. The terrain slopes gradually to the Gulf of Mexico.

[2] Thomas Pownall.

[3] Georges Louis Leclerc, comte de Buffon (1707-1788), *Natural history, general and particular . . .* Translated into English . . . (3d ed., London, A. Strahan, 1791), I, 59-96.

jectile motion & in the progress of that motion coming with the Sphere of attraction of some those Immense bodies which at rest or nearly so acquire a parabolic & by degrees an elliptic course, in extremly excentric Orbits. Many of these may be supposed as Sr Isaac Newton thinks,[1] to accede nearer & nearer in a spiral Orbit to ye Center of their courses & so finally to fall into those Suns or Globes of Fire which first Attracted them. He states some appearance which seem to favor this Idea And then suggests that these Wandering Chaotick Globes do thus become a supply or alimentary fuel to ye Burning Globes or Suns. But although He supposes that this may be the Case with some of these Comets yet he supposes, & even shows by calculating the trajectory of their Course that being first attracted into parabolic, they do finally revolve in Elliptick Orbits round their respective Suns or rather round ye Center of Gravity of the System into which they have fallen. In General They make their Revolutions in extreme excentric Orbits, in all Directions, & all plains of courses. Had the Use, or final cause, which Sr Isaac Newton ascribes[2] to them is that with their vapours (raised from them by the heat of the Sun & dispersed through the System) they supply & replenish the Planets with moisture & Spirit, which is continually through Vegetation & Putrefaction consuming & growing deficient in the Planets.

Those who in their Perihelia approach nearly to ye sun must be so vitrifyed beyond all remaining Capacity of Vegetation may be supposed to be in ye first class who became fuel to ye Suns. The other whose orbits are more remote from that Center & who scarce descend nearer than ye Orbit of Jupiter is or of ye second of Chaotick Globes of Mud. While in the state of Cometts they are not unusefull to ye System into which they have been attracted & may finally by a concurrence of Positions & a Combination of different lines of Attraction becomes planets of the Secondary kind that is Sattellites at least. Perhaps the Primary Planets where at first something of the kind, receiving these Globes of Sulpher mediately by some second cause unknown to our limited Capacities a simple projectile Force such we see with that thus moving forward &

---

[1][Pownall's note for revised and enlarged edition] "Cometa qui anno 1680 apparuit, minus distabat a Sole in Perihelio suo quam parte sexta diametri Solis; & propter summam velocitatem in vicinia illa, & densitatem aliquam Atmosphaerae Solis, resistentiam nonnullam sentire debuit, & aliquantulum retardari & propius ad Solem accedere: & Singulus revolutionibus accedendo ad Solem, incidet is tandem in corpus Solis." Isaac Newton, *Philosophiae Naturalis Principia Mathematica*, Book III, Prop., 42, Prob., 22.

[2][Pownall's note for revised and enlarged edition] "ex quorum exhalationibus & vaporibus condensatis, quicquid liquoris per vegetationem & putrefactionem consumitur & in terram aridam convertitur, continuo suppleri & refici possit . . . Porro suspicor Spiritum illum, qui Aeris nostri pars minima est sed subtilissima & optima, & ad rerum omnium vitam requiritur, ex Cometis praecipue venire." Newton *op. cit.*, Prop., 41, Prob., 21.

what we call the shooting Starrs shoot forward Coming within the Sphere of attraction of some Starr or Sun acquired first a parabolic & by degrees an elliptic course round that Sun as the Center of its motion.

Viewing this Earth as it is, not as learned Theorists suppose it should have been, or was, at first made: Examining with attentive Investigation of Facts, the actual State & progress of its Existence: Analysing the Operations which Heat and Moisture, Vegetation, Corruption, and a continued Process of Exsiccation have on it, in its ordinary Course of Existence: Viewing the Effects of Earthquakes and Volcanoes, I am led, by a Combination of all the Ideas which these Objects offer, up to that State of this Globe which I conceive to have been *its original State*, and from thence I can, as I persuade myself, trace it through every Progress of its changing Existence. From the Manner in which the Land hath been continually encreasing upon the Waters of the Globe from its first Appearance, I traced back my Ideas to the Viewing This Planet in the First Stage of its Existence as *a mere Globe of Mud:* that as the earthy Parts subsided and began to concrete into Sand, or Clay, or Stone; this Globe, then became *an aqueous Planet*, & was the proper Habitation for the Inhabitants of that Element only: that in Time as the Planet, in the natural and ordinary Operations of the Power of Nature, directed by the great Creator, dried, the Land appeared; and was seperated from the Waters: As soon as it was thus emerged above the Face of the Waters, It began to vegetate. That such Animals then, as the advancing Vegetation became a proper Habition for, were created and came into Being; the Fowls of the Air first, and every creeping Thing, and the Beasts of the Field in the next Progress. That when this Earth had advanced so forward in the Melioration of Being as to become a proper Seat and Habitation for Man, then in this last State of the Planet, the Human Race was brought into Being; at first, *a mere Sylvan Animal* of the Woods. Having thus pursued this Theory (for I call it no other) by the Analysis and Combination of my philosophic Ideas, I proceed to examine it by the actual Account which our Holy Scripture give us of it.

I find therein that the First State of this Globe is there described just as my Ideas led me to conceive of it: There was a Firmament in the Midst of the Waters, which divided the Waters from the Waters, *those which were under the Firmament*, and those which were above it; the Latter were called the Heavens, the Former were this Planet. The next Progress of Creation was the Exsiccation of this aqueous Planet, so that dry Land appeared, and was called Earth. The next is, that the Earth began to vegetate Grass first, Shrubs next, and Trees next, whose Seed were in themselves. As these Waters and this Earth were prepared for Reception and Sustenance of their respective Inhabitants, the Waters brought forth abundantly the moving Creature that hath Life; the Fowl also multiplied, and every creeping Thing on the Earth; the Beast next after his Kind. The last Stage of this Process the Divine Creator allotted to the Production of Man, to whom he gave *every Herb bearing Seed*, and *every Tree in which is Fruit, to be to him for Meat*. He dwelt in a Paradise, and did not work the Land; nor gain his Food by the Sweat of his Brow. That was (as we are taught) a Curse which he afterward entailed upon himself, through an Ambition of being wise above what was ordained for him. Thus say the Indians, speaking to The European Land-workers You take a deal of Pains to spoil a good World.

That the literal Style of the Apologue describes the Process of the advancing Existence of this Planet and its Inhabitants by a Series of *Days*,[1] and that my Idea must suppose a Series of Ages makes no Difference; the Process is the same, a Myriad of Years in the Sight of God are but as one Day. As according to this Idea of mine, the Waters must naturally, and, as according to the Account in our Holy Scripture, they did actually cover the Whole of the Globe before the Earth appeared, and as its Appearance was gradually by a natural Separation, I never was surprized or thought it any extraordinary Circumstance which required the Supposition of some extraordinary Cause to account for it, that Shells and Marine Skeletons should be found on the highest Mountains, I should think it extraordinary and rather be surprized if they were not. If you will trust Nature or believe the Scriptures you will find that they have been from the Creation, and are a Proof, *not of the Deluge*, but of the Truth of the philosophic Account of the Creation given in the Book of Genesis.

But to return, from this Digression of Amusement and Speculation, to Business, the Analysis proceeds to describe the Fifth or Upper Stage which lies North West on the Back of the western Division. The northern Part of this may be considered as one great LEVEL PLAIN continuing as yet in its original State. Although it is the most elevated Tract at the Top of all this Country, yet it is occupied by a Mass of Waters which lies on its Face in Five great Lakes;[2] the Lands and Country bordering on these Lakes slope gently towards, and many Streams run hence into, them.[3]

Vide Memoire presented to the D. of Cumberland, Appendix to Administration of the Colonies

---

[1][Pownall's note] I am told that the Word used in the Original signifies not Days but Periods.

[2]The Great Lakes.

[3][Pownall's note] These Parts of the Map here

Lake Ontario C f g h j	"Ontario or Cataraqui, or *The beautiful Lake*, is a Mass of fresh Water, very deep, and has a moderate steep Bank and gravelly Shore along the South Side: The Rivers which fall into it are apt to be sometimes barred at the Entrances. This, like the Mediterranean, the Caspian, and other large invasated Waters, has a small Rising and Fall-
Its Tides	ing of the Water like Tides, some 12 or 18 Inches perpendicular[1] occa-

sioned by the Changes in the State of the Atmosphere; rising higher, as the Weight of the incumbent Air is less, and falling, as it becomes greater. This Lake is best fitted for the Passage of Batteaux and Canoes, along the South Side, the other having several Rocks near the Surface of the Water; but the Middle is every where safe for Shipping. The Snow is deeper on the South Side of this Lake than any other Place in these Parts, but the Lake does not freeze in the severest Winter out of Sight of

The Streight
of Niágara
a C D j
Portage

Land. The Streight of Oghniágara[a] [Niagara], between the Lake Ontario and Erie, is easily passable some Five or Six Miles with any Ships, or 10 Miles in all with Canoes; then you are obliged to make a Portage up Three pretty sharp Hills about Eight Miles, where there is now cut a pretty good Cartway. This Portage is made to avoid that stupendous

Falls

Fall of Oghniágara [Niagara][2] which in one Place precipitates headlong 25 or 26 Fathoms, and continues for Six or Seven Miles more to tumble in little Falls, and run with inconceivable Rapidity. And indeed the Streight for a Mile or Two is so rapid above the Fall, that it is not safe venturing near it. They embark again at the Fishing Battery,[3] and thence to Lake Erie it is 18 Miles, and the Stream so swift, that the stiffest Gale is scarce sufficient to stem it in a Ship; but it is easily passed in Canoes, where the Current here, as in all other Places, is less rapid along the Shore.

Lake Erie
b D E j K l
m n o

"Lake *Erie*[b] has a sandy Shore on the North Side, and in many Places such on the other, especially towards the South East Part. The Weather and Climate of this is far more moderate than that of Ontario." On account of the Sands the Navigation running amidst crooked Channels is perplex'd and difficult.

Streight of
St. Clair
c C D o

"The Streight St. Clair,[c4] as far as Fort Pontchartrain,[5] is passable

---

described are not pretended to be laid down accu-
rately. Future Discoveries will give local Precision.
We here only mean to exhibit a Sketch not a Plan.
    [1][Pownall's note] Partially also as the Wind setts.
    [2][Pownall's note] Vide Peter Calm's Account of it,
published at the End of Bartram's Journal.
Bartram, *op. cit.*, pp. 79-94.—Ed.
    [3]Fishing or Fisher's Battery, the site of Fort
Schlosser on the Niagara, was located at the Carry-

ing Place about a mile above the Falls. *N.Y.C.D.*,
VI, 608; X, 731n; Orsamus Marshall, *The Niagara
Frontier; Embracing Sketches of its Early History* ...
(Buffalo, printed for private circulation by Joseph
Warren & Co., 1865), p. 22.
    [4]St. Clair River.
    [5]French fort, built in 1701 on Lake St. Clair by
Antoine de la Mothe Cadillac. Present site Detroit,
Mich. *N.Y.C.D.*, *op. cit.*, IX, 671n.

in a Ship with a pretty moderate Gale, but from the upper Side of the Little Lake[1] to Lake Huron on the Channel is intricate, but deep enough, and the Stream to be stemm'd with a stiff Gale.

"The Lake Huron communicates with Lake Michigan or Illinois by a Streight[d2] that is wide, and the Current running sometimes in, and sometimes out, by reason of the small Runs which fall into this latter Lake, scarce supplying what is dissipated in Exhalations. Lake Huron
d Missilima-
kinack

"Mineami [Maumee] River,[e] *Sandusky*,[f] *Cayahóga*[g] [Cuyahoga], and *Cherâge*,[h3] fine Rivers, navigable a good Way with Shallops, fall into the South Side of Lake Erie. Though the Bank on this Side is about Eight or Ten Feet high, and dry enough in most Places; the Land a little Way back is generally wet and swampy, by reason of these Rivers wanting sufficient Descent, or better Channels made to drain it. e E n
f E m
g E l
h E k
Rivers on the
South Side of
Lake Erie.

"The Great and Little *Sèneca* Rivers[i] are the most considerable Waters that fall into the South Side of Lake Ontario, but neither navigable with Shallops, save about Half a Mile in the former, and Two or Three Miles in the latter. Their Falls over the Edge of the elevated Plains, are the Causes of these Obstructions. But after you are gone up the Little Seneca River above the Three Falls, and the Great Seneca River, about Half a Mile above the Mouth of Onondaga River, they are both very slow and deep. The latter is best laid down in the Map, for I have had an Opportunity of viewing it myself from Onondaga downwards, and thence upwards I have been favoured with the Observations of Mr. Bleecker."[4] On the South
of Lake
Ontario
i C e
C g

This Ocean of Waters, has but one Embouchure through the Canada River,[5] and the Issue of it is a Stream which bears no Proportion to the immeasurable Mass of Waters. These Lakes are found to have retired from Parts which seem to have been their former Shores, and decrease. There may be, in the Course of Nature, Accidents which may lay some of these Lakes quite dry, when they would become great Plains.

The southern Parts of this upper Stage lie as one extensive broad Bosom of a Vale more than 1500 Miles long, containing a Wilderness of Waters, which all fall into and drain through the Channel of the River Messachibee [Mississippi], which signifies *the Father of Rivers*, into the Messasiippi
River

---

[1] Lake St. Clair.
[2] Mackinac Straits.
[3] Cherage or Racoon River, later known as the Grand River. Hanna, *op. cit.*, I, 336.
The Grand River empties into Lake Erie at Painesville, Ohio.

[4] John Rutger Bleeker. This quotation is from Evans' *Analysis*, pp. 17-18; reprinted in Gipson's *Lewis Evans*, pp. 161-62.
[5] St. Lawrence River.

Gulf of Mexico; the East Side of this great Vale descends from the End-less Mountains[1] in gently swelling Hills: The Parts of this Country to the North East of the Kiskamenitas [Kiskiminetas] Creek were, when the First Edition of this Map was published, very little known; nor can I learn that they are much more at present unless to some Land-jobbers,[2] whose Interest it is to keep their Knowledge secret. I have however an Opportunity of giving the Reader a pretty accurate Account of that Part of it which is contained between the Ohio River and the Allegehenny [Allegheny] Mountains on the North West and South East, and the Monongahela and Great Kanawa [Kanawha] Rivers North East and South West. I extract it from the Journal of a second Tour made by Mr. Gist in 1761,[3] for the express Purpose of examining those Lands.

G i
G h

To begin with the Youghiogeny [Youghiogheny] and its Branches: The Valleys on the Branches or Springs which form the Middle Forks,[4] are but narrow at its Head; but there are about 2000 Acres of good farm-ing Land on the Hills about the largest Branch. As one approaches Lawrel-hill [Laurel],[5] the Undergrowth towards and over this Hill is so abundant in Lawrel Thickets that the Traveller must cut his Way through them: The Lands of the Country through which the Youghio-geny [Youghiogheny] runs are broken and stony, but rich and well timbered; in some Parts, as on a Creek called Lawrel [Laurel] Creek, rocky and mountainous.

From the Mountains[6] to Monongahêla, about 15 Miles in the Line of Gist's Rout, the first Five Miles are good level farming Land with fine Meadows; the Timber White Oak and Hickory. The same Kind of Land holds South to the upper Branches[7] or Forks of this River 10 Miles, and about the same Distance North to where the Youghiogeny [Youghio-gheny] falls into it;[8] the Lands for about Eight Miles along the same Course of the River on each Side, though hilly, are richer and better timbered; the Growth Walnuts, Locust, Poplars, the Sugar Trees or Sweet Maple. The Bottoms or Intervals by the River Side are about One Mile wide, in some Places Two Miles. For several Miles more down the River on the East Side the Intervals are very rich, and a Mile wide:

[1]Allegheny Mountains.
[2]Probably refers to the Ohio Company of Virginia.
[3]1751. Christopher Gist, in the employ of the Ohio Company of Virginia, began this second journey July 26, 1751. The *Journal* of his second journey was first published in 1893. Christopher Gist. *Journals of* . . . [ed.] by William M. Darlington.

(Pittsburgh, J. R. Weldin & Co., 1893), pp. 67-79.
[4]Castleman's River. Gist (Darlington edition), *op. cit.*, p. 138.
[5]A ridge of the Allegheny Mountains.
[6]Laurel Ridge, a ridge of the Alleghenies.
[7]Monongahela and Cheat Rivers unite in southern Pennsylvania near the Maryland border.
[8]At McKeesport, Pennsylvania.

The Upland, which he examined for Eight or 10 Miles East, extraordinary rich and well timbered. The Intervals on the West Side are not above 100 Yards wide; the Upland on this Side the River, both up and down it, rich Soil and full of the Sugar Tree.

He next examined the Lands in several Courses forming, to speak G k generally, a South West Course, first up by some Branches of the and Monongahêla, and then across the Heads of several Rivers[1] which run H 1 into the Ohio till he struck the great Kanâwa [Kanawha] River: He found the Land in general hilly but rich, rocky in some Places yet not poor; the Timber Walnut, Ash, and Sugar Trees. The Intervals on the Borders of the Creeks in some Places 200 Yards, in others a Quarter of a Mile broad. When he came within about 21 Miles of the Kanâwa [Kanawha], he crossed over a high Ridge of Pine Land which was but poor Soil, but descending thence the Land became pretty much the same as before.

The Kanâwa [Kanawha] 79 Poles wide; the Intervals on its Borders a Mile wide and very rich; further up the River a Mile and Half wide, and full of lofty Timber.

He went from the Kanâwa [Kanawha] on a West North West Course or thereabout[2] to the Ohio, and returned up the South East Side of that River by a North East Course by Le Fort's [Torts] Creek,[3] Little Kanâwa [Kanawha], or Buffalo Creek; Fishing or Nawmissippi [Naumissippia] Creek;[4] Weeling [Wheeling] Creek; and the Two Upper Creeks,[5] and thence East and South East to his old Camp on the Monongahêla. The Borders or Intervals on the Ohio a Mile, and in some Places a Mile and Half wide; the Land rich and good, but the Upland in general broken hilly Land: He met with Coal in some Places. He examined the Land up the Creeks as these, which we should think great Rivers, are called, and found the Face of the Country the same, rich

---

[1]Shurtees, Fishing or Little Conhaway, and Lawawlaconin Creeks. Manuscript map showing Christopher Gist's first and second tours to the Ohio. Great Britain Public Records Office. Colonial Office. *Maps, Virginia,* no. 13. Photostat, courtesy of Howard N. Eavenson, Pittsburgh, Pennsylvania. On modern maps: Shurtees (Chartiers), Fishing (Little Kanawha), and Lawawlaconin (Pond Creek, Wood County, W. Va.). Gist (Darlington edition), *op. cit.,* p. 145.

[2]"N 45 W 4 M W 7 M, to a high hill [Kanawha Ridge] from whence We could see the River Ohio." Gist (Darlington edition), *op. cit.,* pp. 75, 144.

[3]A creek which flows from the east and empties into the Ohio a short distance above the mouth of the Great Kanawha. Manuscript map showing Christopher Gist's *First and Second Journey, 1750-52.* Great Britain Public Records Office. Colonial Office. *Maps, Virginia,* no. 13, courtesy of Howard N. Eavenson.

[4]Apparently Mr. Pownall has confused names of creeks mentioned by Christopher Gist. Little Kanawha, Naumissippia, and Fishing Creek are one and the same. Gist (Darlington edition), *op. cit.,* pp. 76, 145.

[5]Buffalo Creek and Cross Creek, Ohio County, West Virginia. Gist (Darlington edition), *op. cit.,* p. 146.

Intervals and good farming Land on the Uplands. This whole Country abounds with Game, as Bear, Elk, Deer, Turkeys, and in one Place he killed a black Fox.[1]

This Country is now settling fast, and will soon be better known. The Triangular Tract of Land at the Head of this great Vale, and between the Mississippi, the Ohio, and Lake Erie (as that Lake is vulgarly called) the Country of the Ilinois [Illinois], is the finest Spot of Earth upon the Globe, swelling with moderate Hills, but no Mountains, watered by the finest Rivers, and of the most delightful Climate; the Soil, as appears from the Woods with which it is cloathed, is of the most abundant Fruitfulness in Vegetation. It abounds with Coal; and there are Multitudes of Salt Springs in all Parts of it. There are Mines of Iron, Copper, and Lead. Wild Rye grows here also spontaneously.[2]

Parts executed without actual Surveys appear less accurate in the Map.

"The Map in the *Ohio*, and its Branches, as well as the Passes through the Mountains Westward, is laid down by the Information of Traders, and others who have resided there, and travelled them for many Years together. Hitherto[3] there have not been any Surveys made of them, except the Road[4] which goes from Shippensburg round Parnel's Knob[5] and by Ray's Town, over the Allegeny [Allegheny] Mountains. For this Reason I have particularly endeavoured to give these Parts, which are done from Computations, another Appearance than those among the Settlements, where I had actual Surveys to assist me; lest the Reader be deceived by an Appearance of Accuracy, where it was impossible to attain it."[6]

In the present Edition[7] of this Map 1776, I have, by peck'd Lines, drawn a supposed Course of these lower Parts of the River Ohio, so as to

[1]Here ends the account taken from Christopher Gist's *Second Journal*.

[2]Information from George Mercer. See page 26 this work.

[3]Before 1755, the date of Lewis Evans' *Analysis*.

[4]This road, laid out in 1755 by George Croghan and his assistants, was requested by General Braddock, in preparation for his campaign against Fort Duquesne in 1755. The road began south of Shippensburg and followed an old Indian trail and traders' path. Albert Volwiler, *George Croghan and the Westward Movement, 1741-1782* (Cleveland, Ohio, Arthur H. Clark Co., 1926), pp. 91-92.

[5]Parnell's Knob is near the foot of the Tuscarora Valley. Uriah J. Jones, *History of the Early Settlement of the Juniata Valley* . . . (Phila., Henry B. Ashmead, 1856), I, 154.

[6]Quoted from Evans' *Analysis*, p. 10; reprinted in Gipson's *Lewis Evans*, p. 154.

[7][Pownall's note] None of the Parts of the Map West or North West of the Ohio are presumed to be other than such a Sketch as shall give a general Idea. Every new Map may correct the last before it, and yet be no more than a Sketch at best. We must wait for Observations and Surveys in our future Knowledge of this Country, in order to give an actual Map. There is none such yet: nor are there any Materials as yet from which any such Map can be compiled, whatever may be pretended. In Justice to Mr. Lewis Evans's Industry, I will venture to say none as yet can give a better Idea of those Parts than this Map has done, not even those done by the French while they had Possession and commanded in these Parts.

coincide in general with the Courses of Gist's Journal,[1] and the Observations of Latitude found in Capt. Gordon's Journal.[2]

"The Pass through the Mountains from Pennsylvania, by Shamokin[3] to Onondaga[4] and Oswego, is from my own Observations, and well deserves Regard; because I had a pretty good Instrument for observing the Latitude, and minutely noted all our Courses, and am well accustomed to form a Judgment of travelling Distance. Mr. William Franklin's Journal to Ohio[5] has been my principal Help in ascertaining the Longitude of the Fork[6] of Ohio and Monaungáhela [Monongahela]; but however I must not omit mentioning that the Latitude of this Fork is laid down from the Observation[7] of Colonel Fry, and is at least 10 Miles more Northerly than I would otherwise have thought it was. The River from hence downward is agreed by all who have gone down it, to be in general pretty strait, nor can its Curves be indeed considerable where it is confined in a Manner by a Chain of little Hills, from the last-mentioned Fork[8] to 10 Miles below the Falls.[9] Mr. Joseph Dobson[10] gave me an Account of the Distances from Creek to Creek as they fall in, and of the Islands, Rifts, and Falls all the Way from the Fork to Sioto [Scioto]; and Mr. Alexander Maginty [McGinty][11] and Mr. Alexander Lowry [Lowrey][12] gave me the rest to the Falls, as well as confirmed the others. The River from the Fork upwards is mostly from Mr. John Davison;[13] but that Part from Canaway [Conewango]

The Author's Route to Oswego

Latitude of Fort du Quesne

Ohio not very crooked.

[1]Christopher Gist's *Journal*. See pages 171-200 this work.

[2]Captain Harry Gordon, British army officer and chief engineer of the Western Department in 1766. His *Journal* is an account of his journey "down the Ohio to the Illinois, down the Mississippi to New Orleans, and from thence to Mobile and Pensacola," undertaken under official orders in 1766. The *Journal* is printed in Newton Mereness, ed., *Travels in the American Colonies* . . . (New York, Macmillan, 1916), pp. 457-58.

[3]Since it was the residence of Allummapees, the "king" of the Delawares, and Shikellamy, deputy of Iroquois, Shamokin was regarded as the Indian capital of Pennsylvania. Present site of Sunbury, Pennsylvania.

[4]Onondaga, chief village of the Onondagas, and capital of the League of the Iroquois or Six Nations. On present site of Syracuse, New York. In 1743 Lewis Evans accompanied John Bartram on his trip from Philadelphia to Onondago, Oswego, and Lake Ontario. Bartram, *op. cit.*, p. 9.

[5]Unfortunately Wm. Franklin's "Journal" is not extant. Gipson, *op. cit.*, p. 57.

[6]At present Pittsburgh, Pennsylvania.

[7]Col. Fry's "Observation of Latitude from Shannopin's Town, June 16, 1752" was communicated to Pennsylvania Provincial Council by William West. Printed in *Colonial Records of Pennsylvania*, V, 761.

[8]At present Pittsburgh, Pennsylvania.

[9]At Louisville, Kentucky, a limestone ledge extends across the Ohio River and forms rapids of about three miles. In this distance the river falls 26 feet. In 1825-1830 locks were built so that boats could proceed uninterrupted down the river. Writers' program, Kentucky. *Louisville, a Guide to the Falls City* . . . (N.Y., M. Barrows and Company, 1940), p. 9.

[10]Factor at Fort Pitt for the Philadelphia firm, Baynton, Wharton, and Morgan. Hanna, *op. cit.*, II, 234-235.

[11]Licensed Indian trader on the Ohio taken captive by the French January 26, 1753. Hanna, *op. cit.*, II, 253.

[12]Alexander Lowrey (1723-1805). A trader on the Ohio after 1744. Hanna, *op. cit.*, II, 335.

[13]Pennsylvania Indian trader. Interpreter for

General
Situations to the Head is entirely by guess, for I have no other Information of it, than that it heads with the Cayúga Branch of Susquehanna. The Routs across the Country, as well as the Situation of Indian Villages, trading Places, the Creeks that fall into Lake Erie, and other Affairs relating to Ohio and its Branches, are from a great Number of Informations of Traders and others, and especially of a very intelligent Indian called *The Eagle*,[1] who had a good Notion of Distances, Bearings, and Delineating." Indeed all the Indians have this Knowledge to a very great Degree of practical Purpose. They are very attentive to the Positions of the Sun and Stars, and on the Lakes can steer their Course by them. The different Aspects which the Hills exhibit on the North Side, from that which the South has impressed on their Eyes, suggest, habitually, at the Moment, in every Spot, an almost intuitive Knowledge of the Quarters of the Heavens which we, mechanically, mark by the Compass. This, at the first Blush, may appear incredible to some; but it may be explained even to the most incredulous. Can any, the most inattentive Observer, be at a Loss to pronounce, in a Moment, which is the North or South Side of any Building in the Country. The same Difference between the South or North Aspect of a Mountain or a Hill, or even a Tree, is equally striking to the Attention of an Indian; and is much more strongly marked by that Accuracy with which he views these Objects; he sees it instantly, and has, from Habit, this Impression continually on his Mind's Eye, and will mark his Courses as he runs, more readily than most Travellers who steer by the Compass. The Ranges of the Mountains, the Courses of the Rivers, the Bearings of the Peaks, the Knobs and Gaps in the Mountains, are all Land Marks, and picture the Face of the Country on his Mind. The Habit of travelling mark to him the Distances, and he will express accurately from these distinct Impressions, by drawing on the Sand a Map which would shame many a Thing called a Survey. When I have been among them at Albany, and enquiring of them about the Country, I have sat and Detroit seen them draw such. "The Situation of *Detroit* is chiefly determined by the Computation of its Distance from Fort Niagara by Mr. Maginty,[2] and its Bearing and Distance from the Mouth of Sandusky.

"I must not omit my Acknowledgment to Mr. William West[3] for

George Washington at Venango in 1753, and at Logstown Conference in 1754. Hanna, *op. cit.*, II, 330.

[1]Not identified.

[2]Alexander McGinty, who was captured by the French in 1753, was taken to Montreal via Detroit and Niagara. Hanna, *op. cit.*, II, 255-56.

[3]An Indian trader on the Ohio in 1753 and Pennsylvania Commissioner at the Lancaster Conference with the Indians in 1756. *Colonial Records of Pennsylvania*, V, 761; VII, 96.

several valuable Notes about Potomack [Potomac], the Forks of Ohio, Assistance
given the
Author and Parts adjacent; nor to Richard Peters,[1] Esq; for the great Chearfulness he assisted me with in this Composition. As for the Branches of Ohio, which head in the New Virginia,[2] I am particularly obliged to Dr. Thomas Walker,[3] for the Intelligence of what Names they bear, and what Rivers they fall into Northward and Westward; but this Gentleman being on a Journey[4] when I happened to see him, had not his Notes, whereby he might otherwise have rendered those Parts more perfect. But the Particulars of these and many other Articles relating to the Situation of Places, I must defer till I deliver an Account of the several Rivers and Creeks, their Navigation, Portages, and Lands thereon."[5]

A brief Description of the most considerable RIVERS, *in*

the WESTERN DIVISION

"The Face of the Country, as already represented, determines the All the
Rivers and
Creeks navi-
gable in the
Lower Plains. Nature of the Rivers. The flat Country (or *Lower Plains*) which lies between the Falls and the Sea, is every where interwoven with the most beautiful Bays, Rivers, and Creeks, navigable for all Sorts of Vessels; and is the Reason of so many fine Creeks spreading on every Side, from the Bays of Chesopeak [Chesapeake] and Delaware. For, as the Land has no Declivity, the Flux and Reflux of the Sea contribute to so wide extended Navigation. All the Creeks on Delaware, the Verges of the Sounds, which extend along the Sea-coast, and some Creeks in Virginia, and towards the Head of Chesopeak [Chesapeake] on the West Side, are bordered with Salt Marshes, some a Mile or Two wide. The First Salt Marshes Settlers of America, for the Sake of the Grass for the Winter Support of their Cattle, fixing their Habitations along these Places, being infested

---

[1]Richard Peters (1704-1776), prominent Pennsylvanian, secretary of the Land Office, rector of Christ (Episcopal) Church, Philadelphia, and secretary of the Provincial Council of Pennsylvania, 1743-1762.

[2][Pownall's note] So called for Distinction-sake, that Part of Virginia South East of the Ouasioto [Cumberland] Mountains, and on the Branches of Green Briar, New River, and Holston River.

[3]Thomas Walker (1715-1794). *Journal of an Exploration in the Spring of the Year 1750 . . . with a*

Preface by William Cabell Rives. (Boston, Little, Brown, and Company, 1888). About one-half of this book consists of a biography of Dr. Walker.

[4]Dr. Walker, while serving as commissary to the Virginia troops in Braddock's army, visited Philadelphia early in the year 1755. *Ibid.*, p. 16. Lewis Evans, a resident of Philadelphia, may have conferred with him at that time.—Ed.

[5]Quoted from Evans' *Analysis*, pp. 10-11; reprinted in Gipson's *Lewis Evans*, pp. 154-55.

with Muskitoes and Intermitting Fevers, gave the Foundation for supposing America unhealthy. The Rest of Chesopeak [Chesapeake] Bay, and its Branches, is almost all a clean, gravelly, steep, dry Bank; and, were it not for the Scarcity of Fresh Water in some Parts of the Eastern Shore, would be as pleasant a Country as Imagination could well represent.

"The Isinglass Vein already described,[1] though broken at New-York, to let the Tide through into Hudson's [Hudson] River, to a far greater Distance than any other River on this Coast, continues still North-eastward, but with less Uniformity, over the West End of Long-Island and the Connecticut Shore, appearing but here and there, by reason of its being overlaid with the Ridges which terminate here.[2]

Delaware
River
a D d E d

b B d F d

c F e

d E d

Leghei-
wachsein
E d

"Delaware River,[3] from the Head to Cushietunk,[a4] though not obstructed with Falls, has not been improved to any Inland Navigation, by reason of the Thinness of the Settlements that Way. From Cushietunk to Trenton Falls,[b5] are Fourteen considerable Rifts, yet all passable in the long flat Boats[6] used in the Navigation of these Parts; some carrying 500 or 600 Bushels of Wheat. The greatest Number of the Rifts are from Easton[c] downward. And those Fourteen Miles above Easton, another just below Well's Ferry,[7] and that at Trenton, are the worst. The Boats seldom come down but with Freshes, especially from the Minnesinks:[d8] The Freight thence to Philadelphia is 8d. a Bushel for Wheat, and 3s. a Barrel for Flour. From the Forks, and other Places below, 20s. a Ton for Pig Iron, 7d. a Bushel for Wheat, 2s. 6d. a Barrel for Flour. This River, above Trenton, has no Branches worth mentioning for Conveniency of Navigation; *Legheiwacsein*[e] [Lackawaxen] has not a Hundredth Part so much Water as Delaware has at the Mouth of it. This Creek takes the general Course laid down in the Map. But as

[1]Pages 93, 94 this work.

[2]Quoted from Evans' *Analysis*, pp. 16-17; reprinted in Gipson's *Lewis Evans*, pp. 160-61.

[3][Pownall's note] Called by the Natives *Petuxat;* and by the Dutch *South River*, correlative to that at New York called *North River*.

[4]A mountain range north and parallel to the Tuscarora Mountains in northeastern Pennsylvania shown on Pownall's map. Cushichtun Mountain. *W. Scull's, Map of Pennsylvania, op. cit.*

[5]At Trenton, New Jersey.

[6][Pownall's note] These Boats are made like Troughs, square above, the Heads and Sterns sloping a little fore and aft; generally 40 or 50 Feet long, Six or Seven Feet wide, and Two Feet Nine Inches

or Three Feet deep, and draw 20 or 22 Inches Water, when loaden.

These boats known as Durham boats were developed to carry bulk products over the rifts in the Delaware River. They followed the pattern of Indian canoes and could be rowed, poled, or sailed. *Steelways* (N.Y. American Iron and Steel Institute), I (1947), no. 13, p. 28.—Ed.

[7]Near Raven Rock, Bucks County, Pennsylvania.

[8]The Minisink lands, formerly the home of the Minisink, a clan of the Delaware tribe, are on both sides of the Delaware at the Water Gap. The eastern townships in Monroe and Pike Counties, Pennsylvania. Hanna, *op. cit.*, I, 91.

Mr. Edward Scull,[1] to whom I am obliged for many Observations in the Course of my Map, has lately laid out some great Tracts of Land on this Creek, and given me an Account of it, since the Engraving of that Part, I shall here deliver a few Particulars, to avert some public Disputes that have been about it. From the Mouth to the Fork the Course is S. 70° W. about Twelve Miles in a strait Line, the Creek crooked and rapid. There the Two Branches are nearly of a Bigness, the Southern one rather the largest. Half a Mile above the Fork, the South Branch, or Wallanpaupack [Wallenpaupack], tumbles about Thirty Feet perpendicularly; and a little Way higher are Two other Falls, not quite so large. From the Fork to the Proprietaries Tract,[2] it is S 60 W. Four or Five Miles, the Channel pretty strait. Thence for Ten Miles taken in a strait Line, the Course is S. 56 W. by Compass, the Stream crooked and very gentle. By the Range of the Hills, this Branch continues much the same Direction to its Source. The Northern Branch of Legheiwacsein [Lackawaxen] divides again into Two Branches, at about a Mile and a Quarter above the Mouth, where each is about large enough to turn an under-shot Grist Mill. Three Quarters of a Mile higher is a great Pine Swamp, through which both Branches come. Mr. Scull[3] thinks that these Branches, whose general Course is about N.W. do not at most extend above Fifteen Miles; and that all the Waters this Way are confined to the lower Side of the great Chains of Mountains, which extend from about the Station Point[4] to Susquehanna about Whioming [Wyoming].[5]

"The *West* Branch[f6] of Delaware is but inconsiderable, compared with the North-eastern Branch, into which it falls at Easton. Above the Tuscarora Hills at Gnadenhutten it is divided into little Creeks, and no Part goes North-westward of the Cushietunk Mountains. Delaware has no other Branches on the West Side between the Station Point and Easton worth the mentioning; the Country being drained by little Runs and Creeks.

"Schuylkill is a fine Branch, up which the Tide runs Five Miles

Margin notes:
Its Fork

The Southern Branch Three great Falls

The Northern Branch forks again

f The West Branch F e

---

[1]In 1749 Edward Scull was commissioned by the Proprietaries of Pennsylvania to survey the lands on the Lackawaxen, which had been sold to them by the Five Nations in 1748. *Colonial Records of Pennsylvania*, V, 489-90.

[2]See "Map of the Indian Walking Purchase, 1737, by Lewis Evans," frontispiece in Gipson, *op. cit.*

[3]Edward Scull.

[4]The Station fixed as the terminating point on the branch of the Delaware farthest north in 41° 40' north latitude. New Jersey *Archives, op. cit.*, VIII, 20-22.

[5]A section of the Susquehanna Valley about 100 miles due west of New York City. This valley extends about 20 miles from Lackawanna Gap to Nanticoke Gap. First important Indian territory and later the scene of the Connecticut-Pennsylvania land controversy. In the vicinity of the present city of Wilkesbarre, Pennsylvania. See also Pownall's *note* 4, p. 130.

[6]Lehigh River.

Schuykill
Philadelphia

above Philadelphia, where there is an impassable Fall; and Three Miles higher another not much better. Thence to Reading is a fine gliding Current easy set against, as the Bottom is gravelly and even; and at Seasons not very dry, would furnish 15 or 16 inches Water all the Way."[1]

A Conversation passing one day in 1755 at Mr Allen's[2] The Cheif-Justice of Pensylvania [Pennsylvania], on the uncommon Event of such a Town as Philadelphia arising, amidst a wilderness, in so short a time, & becoming so fine & populous a City as we all saw it. I addressed myself on the subject to his Mother then at table. The Old Lady told me that she who now lived to see this great Town with near Thirty thousand inhabitants in it, enjoying every comfort & elegance & even luxury that the first town in Europe could offerr, had seen the beginning of it; & what was more rememberd well when she lived with her Parents in New-Jersey, & when this Country now Pensylvania [Pennsylvania] was a Wilderness, to have heard them mention the period that to her it was merely talked of *as a Report*, That a Society of the Friends (so the people called Quakers are properly denominated) at the head of which Friend Penn was, did intend to transport themselves to America, & to make an Establishment somewhere about the Swedes upper settlements. That any Person should live to see any Object brought forward from speculation & realized in so extraordinary a manner is so singular an Anecdote in the History of Man, that I dare say my inserting it here will to whomsoever reads it, as it did to me who heard it, suggest matter & Views of curious disquisition into the powers of man, & the operations of Human Society, when founded in *natural* & established on *true* principles; & when conducted in the spirit of peace by the vigour of Liberty.

Susquehanna
River, its
upper Parts
navigable.
g G d p F f
i F f
k F f

"Susquehanna River is navigable with Canoes, quite from the Lakes at the Head^g to the Falls at Conewega [Conewago];^p[3] nor is there any Fall till that Three Miles below Whioming [Wyoming].^i[4] A Quarter of a Mile below Nescopeki [Nescopek]^k is another; both passable up or

---

[1]Quoted from Evans' *Analysis*, pp. 20-22; reprinted in Gipson's *Lewis Evans*, pp. 164-66.

[2]William Allen.

[3]The Conewago comes into the Susquehanna near York Haven, Pennsylvania.

[4][Pownall's note] This Place and the District is now settled by a populous Colony, which swarmed and came forth from Connecticut. The People of Connecticut say, that their Charter and the Grant of Lands under it was prior to that of Pennsylvania; that the Grant of Lands to them extended within the Latitudes of their Grant (except where possessed by other Powers at that Time) to the South Seas. They allow New York and New Jersey to have been so possessed at the Time of their Grant, but say, that their Right emerges again at the West Boundary of those Provinces. Mr. Penn, and the People of Pennsylvania who have taken Grants under him say, that this District is in the very Heart of the Province Pennsylvania. On this State of Claims the Two Colonies are in *actual War*, which they have not even remitted against each other here, although united in Arms against Great Britain 1775. See also *note 5*, p. 129.

down with Safety. The Water thence to Samokin [Shamokin][11] is generally pretty gentle. Thence to Conewega [Conewago] are several troublesome Falls, but all passable downward with Safety in Freshes. Conewega [Conewago] is the only Fall which tumbles headlong in this River. Below this are Three or Four others, which are passable only with Freshes. By reason of so many bad Falls this River has not yet any Inland Navigation; nor is it indeed capable of any from Conewega [Conewago] downwards. Its considerable Branches are, Owege,[m] Tohiccon or Cayuga,[2] Senaghse, or West Branch, Juniata, Swatara, Conewega [Conewago], Codorus,[3] Constoga [Conestoga]. *Tohiccon*[n] promises well for a good Navigation with Canoes to the Head of Ohio River, as it is a fine large Branch, and the Stream pretty moderate. The *West* Branch[o] is shallow and rapid, and has scarce a Fall worth the mentioning, and not one impassable. It is passable only when the Rains raise it; and then to the Path[p4] leading from Franks Town to Ohio, where a Portage of Forty Miles makes this Way a Communication with that River. Juniata,[q] as it is obstructed with short Falls, is gentle and pretty deep in the intermediate Places, and may be improved for the Carriage of Goods almost to Franks Town.[5] Swatara,[r] Conewega [Conewago], Codorus,[6] and Conestoga, some Centuries hence will, no Doubt, be improved to good Account.

"Chesopeak [Chesapeake] may be justly esteemed the Bay of Susquehanna; and as such we may reckon all the Creeks and Rivers from Potomack [Potomac] upwards, as so many Branches of it. The many Portages from the Creeks of this Bay to those of Delaware, are become already very useful, and in future Ages will be more so. Several are pointed out in the Map: And it may also be observed here, that the Road at each is extremely level and good; and Vessels of different Magnitude come up to the Portages.

"Large Sloops can come up to Snow Hill on *Pokomoke* [Pocomoke], the Portage is Five Miles from thence to Senepuxen Sound,[7] where Ships may come. If the Marylanders ever intend a direct Passage through their own Colony to the Sea, here an Attempt would be most likely to succeed.

Marginal notes:
l F f Conewega the only impassable Falls
m E e
n Tohiccon E f Its considerable Branches.
o West Branch F f
p F h
q Juniata F f
r Swatara &c F f
Chesopeak Bay Many Portages between its Creeks and those of Delaware
Portages from Pokomoke H e

[1]On present site of Sunbury, Pennsylvania.

[2]Chemung River, New York. Paul A. W. Wallace, *Conrad Weiser . . . Friend of Colonist and Mohawk* (Philadelphia, University of Pennsylvania Press, 1945), p. 157.

[3]Codorus Creek flows into Creitz Creek at York, Pennsylvania. Creitz Creek empties into the Susquehanna near Columbia.

[4]For full description of the Frankstown Path read Hanna, *op. cit.*, I, 247-273.

[5]Near present Hollidaysburg, Pennsylvania.

[6]A tributary of Creitz Creek in the vicinity of York, Pennsylvania.

[7]Sinepuxent Bay.

u From
Nanticoke
H e

"Shallops may go up *Nanticoke* River, near Twenty Miles into Delaware Colony;[u] the Portage from this River to Indian River is Thirteen Miles, and to Broad[1] Creek Twelve.

w From
Choptank
G e

"Choptank[w] is navigable with Shallops to the Bridge, about Six or Seven Miles within Delaware Colony; and the Portage thence to Motherkill[2] is Fifteen Miles.

x From
Chester and
Sassefras
Rivers.

"From *Chester* River[x] to Salisbury[3] on Duck Creek,[4] the Portage is Thirteen Miles. And from Sassefras[5] there is another Portage to the same Place Thirteen Miles also.

From
Frederick
& Bohemia to
Apoquinimy
G e

"From *Frederick*[6] on Sassefras, where good Ships can come, there is a Portage to Cantwell's Bridge[7] on Apoquinimy [Appoquinimink] Fourteen Miles.

"From *Bohemia*,[8] where large Flats or small Shallops can come, there is a Portage[9] of Eight Miles to Cantwell's Bridge. This is the most frequented of any between the Waters of Delaware and Chesopeak [Chesapeake]. All these Creeks which lead into Delaware will receive large Shallops, but no larger Vessels.

From Elk to
Christeen
Bridge. G e

"From the *Head of Elk*, where Shallops can come, the Portage is Twelve Miles to Christeen Bridge.[10] And it is about the same Distance to Omelanden Point,[11] a fast Landing on Delaware River, Three or Four Miles below Newcastle. This latter Portage has not been occupied since these Parts came last under the Dominion of the English.

Potomack
H f

"Potomack [Potomac] is navigable with large Shipping to Alexandria, and for Shallops Fourteen Miles more to the Falls; the Portage thence is Six Miles by a good Waggon Road. Boats[12] shaped like those of Delaware, and of something less Dimensions, may go up to the North Mountain without Obstruction, save at the Rift, or Falls, in the South Mountain,[y] which however is passable. The River runs through the

y G g

[1]Broadkill Creek, Delaware.
[2]Murderkill River, Delaware. Federal Writers' Project. Delaware, *op. cit.*, pp. 345-46.
[3]Duck Creek Village, Delaware. *Ibid.*, p. 376.
[4]Present Smyrna River. *Ibid.*, p. 477.
[5]Sassafras River, Delaware.
[6]On northern bank of Sassafras River opposite Georgetown, Delaware. Herman Böyë. *A Map of the State of Virginia Constructed in Conformity to Law from the late Surveys authorized by the Legislature ... 1825. Corrected by order of the Executive 1859.* [1859]. Not located on modern maps.
[7]Present Odessa, Delaware. *Ibid.*, pp. 340-41.

[8]Probably at the junction of Great and Little Bohemia Creeks. In the latter part of the seventeenth century Caspar and Ephriam Herman lived here on Bohemian Manor. *Ibid.*, p. 475.
[9]This portage or road from the Herman estate to Cantwell's Bridge, near Odessa, was in use as early as 1679. *Ibid.*
[10]Present Christiana, Delaware. Federal Writers' Project. Delaware. *Ibid.*, pp. 483-84.
[11]Probably at present Leipsic, Delaware. The first village, founded in 1723, was called *Fast Landing*. *Ibid.*, pp. 477-78.
[12]Durham boats.

North Mountain without any Fall; and from thence to Will's Creek,[z1] z G h
there are Three or Four Rifts passable with Canoes or Batteaux, when
the Water is not very low. The Inland Navigation by this River is
scarce begun; but one may foresee that it will become in Time the most
important in America, as it is likely to be the sole Passage from Ohio to
the Ocean. The North Branch is scarce passable with Canoes beyond
the Shawane Fields,[2] some Three or Four Miles above Will's Creek. The Portage from
Portage from this Branch to Ohio is yet unsettled, by reason of the bad Will's Creek
Roads and Hills. But as at this Time, it may be an Object of Enquiry, Youghiogani
some Account of the Ground will not be unacceptable. From Will's Creek
the Ground is very stony for the greater Part of the Allegeny [Allegheny]
Mountain;[a] but not so much so from the Shawane Fields.[3] The Moun- a G·h
tain, though pretty stony, may have a good Waggon Road made over it.
On the North West Side of this Chain of Hills there is all along a great
Deal of swampy Ground, which is a considerable Obstruction to a
direct Passage; but yet manageable by taking some little Compass round.
From this Westward you cross Two Branches[4] of Youghiogani [Youghio-
gheny]: the greater,[5] which is the most Westerly, at Three Miles above
the Joining of the Three Forks, or Turkey Foot.[b6] And the Three Forks b G j
are Three Miles above the Lawrel [Laurel] Hill, through which Youghio- Ohiopyle
gani [Youghiogheny] precipitates by a great Fall[7] of near Thirty Feet, Falls.
and continues to run with great Rapidity for Two or Three Miles
further. At this Time to go from the Crossing[8] to Youghiogani [Youghio-
gheny] below the Falls, they are obliged to go by the Meadows,[9] there
cross Lawrel [Laurel] Hill, and return again Northward, and by that
Means take near Thirty Miles to reach the navigable Water of this
River; whereas if a Road could be made near the Fall, Fifteen or Twenty
Miles might be saved in the Way to Fort du Quesne.[10] There is a good
Ford through Youghiogani [Youghiogheny], and the Ground all the Way

---

[1]At Cumberland, Maryland.

[2]Shawnee Fields on the Potomac on the flat lands
now in part occupied by the west side of the city of
Cumberland. Hanna, *op. cit.*, I, 157.

[3]*Ibid.*

[4]The two branches, Main, or south branch (i.e.
Youghiogheny River proper) and Castlemans River
rise in Virginia and Maryland respectively.

[5]Main or south branch.

[6]Present Confluence, Somerset County, Pennsyl-
vania. Here the third or Pennsylvania branch,
Laurel Hill Creek which rises in Somerset County,
Pennsylvania, meets the other two branches of the
Youghiogheny.

[7]Ohiopyle Falls in Fayette County, Pennsylvania.

[8]Great Crossing. An historic marker marks this
site, a bridge near Addison, Pennsylvania, on high-
way U.S. Route 40.

[9]Great Meadows, the site of Fort Necessity. A
Virginia fort was built and commanded by George
Washington in 1754. The reconstructed Fort, and
State Historical Museum are at Great Meadows near
Uniontown, Pennsylvania.

[10]Fort Duquesne (1754-58). French fort built at
the confluence of the Allegheny and Monongahela
Rivers. On present site of Pittsburgh, Pennsylvania.

Lawrel Hill
G j
good and sound; and a Road may easily be made along it. Lawrel [Laurel] Hill, though small, is a Ridge very hard to cross, by reason of its Steepness; but at the Meadows is the best Pass we know of yet towards Virginia; there a Waggon, which would require four Horses to travel with, may be drawn up by Six. Probably a Pass may also be found for Wheel Carriages to the North of the Falls; and if there should, it would much improve the Portage between Potomack [Potomac] and

Youghiogani Navigable to Falls

Youghiogani [Youghiogheny], and reduce it to Fifty Miles, whereas it is now but little short of Seventy. If we have the good Fortune of being Masters of Ohio, the Navigation of Youghiogani [Youghiogheny] will be of Importance, since it is passable with flat bottomed Boats, capable of carrying Four or Five Tons, from the Mouth to the Foot of the Rift below the Falls. A Horse Path may be conducted in Six or Seven Miles, without much Expence, from the great Crossing[1] to the Head of navigable Water. From this to Fort du Quesne[2] you may go down in a Day, but it requires at least Three to return up the Stream."[3]

The following very curious and very interesting Account of the Communications betwixt the Waters of the European present Settlements and the Waters of Ohio, I received from Lieutenant Governor Mercer,[4] which I give to the Reader in his own Words:

"During the last War[5] on the Ohio most of the heavy and bulky Commodities were landed at George Town[6] on Potomack [Potomac] River, and conveyed thence in Waggons to Conogochieg [Conecocheague],[7] where they were embarked on Batteaux and Canoes, and were landed at Fort Cumberland;[8] from Fort Cumberland they were conveyed in Waggons to the Monongahela at the Mouth of Red Stone Creek,[9] and there put on board Batteaux, which conveyed them to Pitsburg [Pittsburgh]; the Distance from Fort Cumberland to the Mouth of Red Stone Creek is 73 Miles, and was generally performed in Three Days; each Waggon with Four Horses carried 22 Cwt. and were allowed 9s. Sterling per Day; but it was afterwards known that a good Waggon Road might be made from Fort Cumberland on the North Branch of the Potomack [Potomac] to a Branch of the Youghiog[h]eny,

---

[1]Near present Addison, Pennsylvania.
[2]On present site of Pittsburgh, Pennsylvania.
[3]Quoted from Evans' *Analysis*, pp. 22-24; reprinted in Gipson's *Lewis Evans*, pp. 166-68.
[4]George Mercer.
[5][Pownall's note for revised and enlarged edition] The Warr of 1755.

[6]Georgetown, District of Columbia, is the head of navigation on the Potomac River.
[7]On present site of Williamsport, Maryland.
[8]Fort Cumberland, built in 1754 as Fort Mt. Pleasant, by Colonel James Innes, and renamed Fort Cumberland, in 1755. William H. Lowdermilk. *History of Cumberland*, (*Maryland*) . . . (Washington, D.C., James Anglim, 1878), pp. 89-94.
[9]Present Brownsville, Pennsylvania.

which would not exceed 40 Miles. The Troops left in Garrison at Pitsburg [Pittsburgh] after the Conclusion of the Indian War received very large Supplies of Provision, &c. from the Inhabitants of the South Branch of Potomack [Potomac] in Virginia, who cleared a Waggon Road and found a good Pass through the Mountains to Cheat River, a Branch of the Hj Monongahela, about 50 Miles above the Mouth of Red Stone Creek, and found a good and speedy Conveyance thence by Water to Pitsburg [Pittsburgh]. The Distance from the Waters of the South Branch of the Potomack [Potomac] to Cheat River is only 20 Miles, and Col. Wilson[1] has erected good Grist and Saw Mills on Cheat River: These Circumstances are known to all the Officers who served in that Quarter last War. And since the War some Persons in Virginia, in particular Mr. John Balleneine [Ballendine],[2] who is a good Mechanick, has explored these Waters and the several natural Advantages they offer; and is of Opinion, nay has proved, that for less than 40,000£. Locks,[3] &c. might be formed at the Falls both of Potomack [Potomac] and James Rivers, which would render those Rivers navigable at all Seasons of the Year for the largest Barges now used on the Thames, nay even of Barges of 200 Tons, as from his general Observations of those Rivers, particularly of Potomack [Potomac], at the Falls of which he has remarkable fine Mills and a Forge,[4] and was also Proprietor of a Furnace[5] for Iron Ore near the Mouth of the Shannandoah [Shenandoah] for many Years, that they never would have less than Four Feet Water in the driest Seasons; and from an actual Survey[6] he assures me that the Waters of James River and of those of the Kenhawa [Kanawha] are no more than Four Miles distant, and that the Waters of the Kenhawa [Kanawha] are also navigable, and together with those of the South Branch might be made completely so for the Expence above mentioned.

"Though in Search of the *Head of Potomac*, the King's and Lord Fairfax's Commissioners determined the *North* to be the main Branch; South Branch yet it is very well known, that the *South* Branch is navigable 40 Miles of Potomac up with Batteaux. And as it was not clear to me that the true Head of Potomac was at the Place those Gentlemen determined it, I have

---

[1]Not identified.

[2]John Ballendine—(d. 1785?), owner of iron furnaces in colonial Virginia.

[3]The *James River Company*, incorporated for the purpose of improving navigation of the James River was probably an outgrowth of the Ballendine interests. Virginia Laws, statutes, etc. *The Statutes at Large . . . of Virginia . . .* published by William W.

Hening. (Richmond, printed for the editor by George Cochran, 1823), XI, 450-62.

[4]John Ballendine's mills and forge were at Westham, near Richmond, Virginia. Virginia *Calendar of Virginia State Papers . . .* , edited by Wm. P. Palmer, (Richmond, R. F. Walker, 1875), I, 364.

[5]Probably Buckingham forge. *Ibid.*

[6]Not located.

not laid down the western Side of Maryland, which should be a Meridian drawn from the Head of Potomac to the Pennsylvania Line. If the Affair is candidly examined, it will probably be determined, that the South Branch is the most considerable. If so, the Head of the North Branch will not be the western Extremity of Maryland, though it now is of Lord Fairfax's Grant.[1] Very hilly and swampy Ground prevents a Portage by any tolerable Road from the South Branch to Monaungáhela [Monongahela].[a] As this latter River is fine and gentle some Use may in future Times be made of it, either in a Communication with Green Briar [Greenbrier] or Potomac; for it is passable with Flats a great Way above Red Stone Creek, and interrupted with one impassable Fall only.[2]

"Shanedore [Shenandoah] is a fine Branch of Potomac, but its Inland Navigation is yet inconsiderable; but, in future Time, it will no doubt be improved to a good Account.

"Rapahannock[b] [Rappahannock], *York River*,[b] *Matapany*[b] [Mattapony], and *Pamúnky*[b] [Pamunkey] though of excellent Marine Navigation, are but inconsiderable above the *Lower Plains;* their Branches being confined below the South Mountain, and impassable with the slightest Inland Craft.

"James River is scarce inferior to any in excellent Navigation for Marine as well as Inland Craft. The Tide runs up to the foot of the Falls,[3] a distance if measured in right line about 110 Miles, 140 & more as the Water winds. Marine Vessels of great Burthen go up to these Falls, or near them. At Jamestown the river is about 2½ Miles broad, at Richmond which is on the banks of the River a little below the falls it is about half a Mile broad. Its lower Falls being near Six Miles long, and tumbling in little short Cascades, are intirely impassable. The River thence upward to an impassable Fall[4] in the South Mountain is excellently fitted for large Boats[5] like those already described in Delaware.

Marginal notes: a Monaunga-hela G j / Shanedore G g / b Rapa-hannock York River, Matapany and Pamunky J f J g

[1]In 1733 Lord Fairfax petitioned the Crown to have the bounds of his grant in Virginia finally settled. The survey was made in 1736 and a map was made in duplicate to show the bounds of the Northern Neck of Virginia, Lord Fairfax's grant. Read "Proceedings of the Commissioners to Lay out the Bounds of the Northern Neck," in William Byrd's *History of the Dividing Line and Other Tracts . . .* (Richmond, Va., 1866), II, 83-139. One copy of the map is now in the Public Records Office, London, and the other* is in possession of the Darlington Memorial Library, University of Pitts-

burgh. *A Map of the Northern Neck in Virginia; The Territory of the Right Honourable Lord Fairfax; Situate between the Rivers Potomack and Rappahanock, according to a late Survey; Drawn in the Year 1737 by Wm. Mayo.
[2]In this paragraph Pownall's quotation from Evans' *Analysis* is almost paraphrase.
[3]At Richmond, Virginia.
[4]Balcony Falls. Blair Niles, The James, from Iron Gate to the Sea (N.Y., Farrar & Rinehart, [c1945]), p. 6. Near Glasgow, Virginia.
[5][Pownall's note] Generally 30 or 40 Feet Long,

And it is passable with lighter Craft much further, and would not require above 40 or 50 Miles Portage to the Branches of Kanhawa [Kanawha] River. But this however is not improveable to Ohio; for Kanhawa [Kanawha] has an impassable Fall[1] in a Ridge, which is impassable for Man or Beast by Land. But its opening a Passage to the New Virginia[2] is a very great Advantage.

"Roanoak [Roanoke], which falls into Albemarle Sound, beyond the Bounds of this Map, is barred at the Entrance, so as not to receive such large Ships as it would otherwise bear. It is passable with Shallops to the Falls.[c3] From thence upwards it is generally placid and wide, and in some Places interrupted with little Rifts and Falls, none of which, that I have heard of, impassable. It is liable to very great Freshes, and has not been yet improved to any Inland Navigation; for the People on its Branches, Holstein [Holston][4] River,[d] Yadkin,[e5] and New River,[f6] turn hitherto all their Commerce into James River. There is no River more likely to be of Importance in the future Navigation of the Inland Parts this Way than Roanoak [Roanoke], because it hath good Depth of Water, and extends right into the Country.

"There are many other Creeks and Rivers in the Settlements that are obscured by the superior Excellence of these already described, which would well deserve Description, if I were to give a Detail of any particular Colony.

"The little Acquaintance that the Public has had with the River OHIO, will be a sufficient Apology for my entering into a more minute Detail of it and its Branches than of any other already described.

"From the Head,[g] which interlocks with the Cayuga Branch[7] of Susquehanna to Canaway,[h8] I have little Knowledge, but suppose, from the Evenness of the Land, that it may afford good Inland Navigation in future Ages. From Canawagy[9] to Chartier's Old Town,[i10] the

Margin notes:
Kanhawa River

Roanoak River

c K k

d K l
e K g
f J k

Ohio

From the Head to Canawagúng
g E j h E g
Thence to Chartier's
i F j

Three or Four Feet broad, and drawing empty 10 to 12 Inches Water, and when loaded about 18 Inches. Durham boats.

[1]Kanawha Falls, about two miles below the junction of the New and Gauley Rivers, which forms the Great Kanawha River. George W. Atkinson, *History of Kanawha County* ... (Charleston, printed at the office of the West Virginia Journal, 1876), p. 10. In Fayette County, West Virginia.

[2]Kentucky.

[3]Roanoke Rapids.

[4]Holston is a tributary of the Tennessee River.

[5]Yadkin is a tributary of the Peedee River.

[6]New River is a tributary of the Great Kanawha River.

[7]Chemung River, N.Y.

[8]Conewango or Connewango, a Seneca Indian town that stood on the site of present Warren, Pennsylvania. This Indian town was destroyed by Colonel Brodhead in 1781. Hodge, *op. cit.*, I, 338.

[9]Present site, Warren, Pennsylvania.

[10]A Shawnee town on the Allegheny near the present site of Tarentum, Pennsylvania. The town was named for Peter Chartier, the French-Shawnee Indian trader. Hanna, *op. cit.*, I, 269, 307.

River is all along sufficiently moderate, and always deep enough for Canoes and Batteaux, which do not draw above 15 Inches Water; nor is it obstructed with any remarkable Rifts or Falls, save at a sharp Bent[1] some Miles below Licking Creek,[2] where the Water rushes on a Rock with great Violence;[k] and at Toby's Falls,[13] which is a Rift passable with Safety on the West Side. In this Part of the River are several Fording-places, but they are more rare as you come lower down. That at Chartier's Old Town[m4] is the best; which, as soon as the Rock appears above Water, is passable close above it. At Shanoppens[n5] [Shanoppin's] is another in very dry Times, and the lowest down the River. This Part, which is very crooked, has seldom been navigated by our People, because the great Number of Horses necessary to carry their Goods to Ohio, serve also to carry them there from Place to Place; and the little Game that Way makes it but little frequented.

"The Navigation from Chartier's Old Town,[o6] all the Way down to the Falls,[p7] has been hitherto performed in very large wooden Canoes,[8] which they make of great Length better fitted to steer against a rapid stream; they are navigated down by Two Men, and upwards by Four at least. From Chartier's to the Lower Shawane Town,[9] they are in the Spring about Four Days in going down with the Freshes; for then they let the Canoe drive in the Night; but towards the End of Summer, when the Water is low, and less swift, they usually spend 10 or 12 Days; but at moderate Seasons the Passage is performed in Six or Eight. In returning, they take often 30 or 40 Days, though double handed, and seldom less than 20. Supposing we go down the River from Chartier's, the Water is pretty moderate till you come to Sweep Chimney Island,[10]

A Sharp Bent below Licking Creek k E j
l F j
Fords

m
at Chartier's Old Town F j
n at Shanoppens. F j

Navigation from Chartier's Old Town to the Falls o F j
p J r

Small Rifts

[1]Probably Brady's Bend, Armstrong County, Pennsylvania.

[2]Present East Sandy Creek which flows into the Allegheny River five miles south of Franklin, Pennsylvania. Howard N. Eavenson, *The First Century and a Quarter of American Coal Industry.* (Pittsburgh, Pa., Privately printed, Koppers Building, 1942), p. 21.

[3]Toby Creek, present Clarion River. Hanna, *op. cit.*, I, 213-14. Probably near Parker's Landing on the Allegheny River at the mouth of the Clarion River.

[4]See *note* 10, page 137.

[5]A Delaware town on the Allegheny River about two miles above its junction with the Monongahela, at present Pittsburgh, Pennsylvania. Since this town, the home of Chief Shanopin, was on the path from the east to the Ohio country, it was much frequented by traders. Hodge, *op. cit.*, II, 526-27.

[6]Near present site of Tarentum, Pennsylvania.

[7]Louisville, Kentucky.

[8][Pownall's note] Generally 30 or 40 Feet long, Three or Four Feet broad, and drawing empty 10 or 12 Inches Water, and when loaded about 18 inches.

[9]This Shawnee town was just below the mouth of the Scioto until about 1750 when it was carried off by a flood and rebuilt on the opposite side of the river near the present site of Portsmouth, Ohio. Hodge, *op. cit.*, I, 777.

[10]Probably Nine Mile Island. E. L. Babbitt, *The Allegheny Pilot . . .* (Freeport, Pa., E. L. Babbitt, 1855), p. 53.

between Dick's[1] and Pine Creek,[2] where it is very rapid. It generally happens that where the River is confined to narrower Bounds by Islands it is more rapid, yet not so but Canoes may be easily set against it. At Fort du Quesne, at Paul's Island,[3] Five Miles lower, and at a Flat between that and Logs Town, the Water is pretty rapid; as it is also at a small Island[4] between that and Beaver Creek. These are, however, inconsiderable; nor are those Places just below Beaver Creek and at a Flat a little above the upper End of the Pipe Hills[5] much more worthy Regard. At *Hart's Rock*[q6] the River makes a quick Bend round a rocky Point, and a very sharp Rippling, where the Boatmen are obliged to wade and haul up near the Rock, the South East Side being full of Quicksands. At Weeling [Wheeling] Island,[r7] Muskingum Island[s8] (a little Way above a fine Branch of that Name) and at Beaty's Island,[9] the Current is pretty rapid. At Three or Four Miles above the big Bent[10] is a considerable Rift called *Le Tart's Falls*,[b11] where the Water is so rapid that they are obliged to haul the Canoes with Ropes in coming up for near a Furlong along the South East Side. From this to the Lower Shawane Town,[12] at the Mouth of Sioto [Scioto], is no Obstruction worth mentioning."[13] The Ohio, as I learn from Capt. Gordon's Journal of 1766,[14] from 50 Miles above Muskingum to the North of Sioto [Scioto], is most beautiful, and interspersed with Numbers of Islands covered with the most stately Timber, with several long straight Reaches, one of which is 16 Miles and an Half long. "And the Stream thence downward to the Falls is still more gentle, and better fitted for Vessels drawing

q Hart's Rock F k

r F k   s G l

Le Tart's Fall b H m

[1]Probably Deer Creek, which flows into the Allegheny River near Oakmont, Pennsylvania. Not located on modern maps.

[2]Pine Creek flows into the Allegheny River at Etna, a suburb of Pittsburgh, Pennsylvania.

[3][Pownall's note] Here are some Places mentioned, too inconsiderable to be laid down in this Map.

Paul's Island may be present Neville's Island, about six miles below Pittsburgh.—Ed.

[4]Crow's Island, 24 miles below Pittsburgh, is between Logstown and Big Beaver Creek. *The Navigator* . . . [by Zadok Cramer] (10th ed., Pittsburgh, Cramer & Spear, 1818), p. 70.

[5]Lewis Evans' *Map* of 1755 indicated that Pipe Hills are on both banks of the Ohio River above the mouth of Wheeling Creek. Pipe Hill is about 6 miles below Wheeling. "Fourth Rout down the Ohio." In William Smith, *Historical Account of Bouquet's Expedition Against the Ohio Indians* (Cincinnati, O., Robert Clarke & Co., 1868), p. 151.

[6]Present site of Smith's Ferry, Beaver County, Pennsylvania. Hanna, *op. cit.*, I, 207.

[7][Pownall's note] Above this there are Two remarkable Creeks, called, by the Traders, the Two Upper Creeks, which like Twins run about 30 Miles parallel to each other, and within Three Miles Distance, with a very rich Mesopatamia between them.

[8]Muskingum Island is three miles below the mouth of the Muskingum River. *Cramer's Navigator* (1818), *op. cit.*, p. 85.

[9]Not identified.

[10]The Great Bend in the Ohio.

[11]Also written Le Tort's Falls.

[12]Near present site of Portsmouth, Ohio.

[13]Quoted from Evans' *Analysis*, pp. 24-26; reprinted in Gipson's *Lewis Evans*, pp. 168-70.

[14]Extracts from Captain Harry Gordon's *Journal* are printed in Appendix IV of this book.

greater Depth of Water."[1] These Falls don't deserve that Name, as I am taught by Capt. Gordon's Journal, as the Stream on the North Side has no sudden Pitch, but only runs rapid over the Ledge of a Flat Limestone Rock; several Boats passed it in the driest Season of the Year, unloading One-third of their Freight, they passed on the North Side, where the Carrying-place is Three Quarters of a Mile long. On the South East Side it is about Half that Distance, and is reckoned the safest Passage for those who are unacquainted, but it is the most tedious, as during Part of the Summer and Fall they drag their Boats over the flat Rock. "The Fall is about Half a Mile rapid Water,[e] which however is passable, by wading and dragging the Canoe against the Stream, when lowest; and with still greater Ease when the Water is raised a little.

c The Falls of
Ohio J r

Great Floods

"Ohio, as the Winter Snows are thawed, by the Warmth or Rains in the Spring, rises in vast Floods, in some Places exceeding 20 Feet in Height, but scarce any where over-flowing its high and upright Banks. These Floods continue of some Height for at least a Month or Two, being guided in the Time by the late or early Breaking up of the Winter. The Stream is then too rapid to be stemmed upwards by Sailing or Rowing, and too deep for Setting,[2] but excellently fitted for large Vessels going down. Then Ships of 100 or 200 Tons may go from Fort du Quesne to the Sea with Safety; these Floods reducing the Falls, Rifts, and Shallows to an entire Equality with the rest of the River.

"Ohio carries a great Uniformity of Breadth, gradually increasing from Two or Three Furlongs at the Forks[d] to near a Mile, as you go lower down; and spreading to Two Miles or more, where damm'd by the Rief of Rocks, which make the Falls.[e] Thence to Mississippi its Breadth, Depth, and easy Current, equalling any River in Europe, except the Danube, affording there the finest Navigation for large sailing Vessels; but however in great Freshes it is full rapid to stem, without a good Breeze. And there is scarce any Gale stiff enough to stem the Falls, when deep enough to pass in Freshes. Upon the Whole, the Navigation of this River may be divided into Four Parts: 1. From Canawagy [Conewango] to Chartier's Old Town,[3] in Batteaux, capable of carrying about Three or Four Tons, and drawing 12 Inches Water.

d F j

e J r
Navigation
below the
Falls

Navigation
to Chartier's
F j

---

[1]Quoted from Evans' *Analysis*, p. 26; reprinted in Gipson's *Lewis Evans*, p. 170.

[2][Pownall's note] By the known Laws of Mechanics, a Man Setting a Boat over a firm hard Bottom has twice the Advantage of the like Strength employed in Rowing. In Rowing, the Water being moveable, receives Half the Motion; While in Setting, the Boat receives the Whole.

[3]From present Warren to Tarentum, Pennsylvania.

2. From Chartier's to the Pig Bent,[1] in Flats, like those used in Delaware,[2] or larger; bearing 18 or 20 Tons. These Two Parts must be performed in long flat-bottomed Boats, as better fitted for Setting in shallow Water and rapid Streams. 3. From the Big Bent [Great Bend] to the Falls, in Shallops or Schooners of 10 or 15 Tons. As these are made for sailing and working to Windward, they must have sharp Bottoms and deep Keels; and though made broader than the Flats, they will not admit such great Lengths, and therefore not capable of so large Burdens. 4. From the Falls[3] to Mississippi thence to the Sea is only fitted for light Canoes or Batteaux against the Stream; but for any Vessels downwards, when the Floods are not so high as to overflow the adjoining wide extended Flats. Hence, in Process of Time, large Ships may be built upon Ohio, and sent off to Sea with the heavy Produce of the Country, and sold with the Cargoes. To the Big Bent H m
To the Falls

To the Mississippi; thence to the Sea

"OHIO has a great many *Branches*, which furnish good Navigation to the adjacent Parts; the most remarkable I intend to enumerate.

"Canawagy[b] [Conewango], when raised with Freshes, is passable with Bark Canoes, or little Batteaux, to a little Lake at its Head; from which there is a Portage of 20 Miles to Lake Erie, at the Mouth of a little Creek called Jadághque.[4] This Portage is but little frequented, because Canawagy [Conewango] is too shallow in the Summer for the lightest Craft. b Canawagy. E j Portage to Lake Erie

"Bughaloons[c5] is not navigable, and noted only for large Meadows, as the Word signifies in the Delaware Indian Language. c Bughaloons. E j

"Toranadaghkoa, French Creek, or Riviere le Bieuf,[d] is noted for its furnishing the nearest Passage to Lake Erie. It is navigable with Canoes to the French Fort by a very crooked Channel; the Portage thence to another Fort on Lake Erie called *Presqu' Isle*,[6] from an adjoining Peninsula, is 15 Miles; this Way the French come from Canada to Ohio. *Licking Creek*[7] and *Lacomick*[8] have no Navigation; but the former has Plenty of Coals. d Riviere le Bieuf. E j
Portage to Lake Erie. Licking Creek, &c. E j

"Toby's Creek[9] is passable with Bark Canoes a good Way up Toby's Creek E j

---

[1]From present Tarentum to the Great Bend in the Ohio, the vicinity of Le Tort's Falls.

[2]See *note* 6, p. 128.

[3]At Louisville, Kentucky.

[4]Probably Lake Chautauqua and Chautauqua Creek.

[5]Present Brokenstraw Creek. M. H. Deardorff, "Zeisberger's Allegheny River Indian Towns: 1767-1770." In *Pennsylvania Archaeologist* (Phila., Society for Pennsylvania Archaeology, 1930-), XVI (1946), no. 1, p. 18.

[6]French fort built in 1753. On present site of Erie, Pennsylvania.

[7]East Sandy Creek.

[8]Sandy Creek which flows from the west into the Allegheny River at the Indian Bend, Venango County, Pennsylvania.

[9]Clarion River. Hanna, *op. cit.*, I, 214.

towards the West Branch of Susquehanna; and a pretty short Portage may probably be found between them.

_{Moghul-
bughkitum
F j} "Moghulbughkitum[1] is passable also a good Way towards the same Branch, and will probably furnish a good Portage also.

_{Kish-
keminetas
F j} "Kishkeminetas [Kiskiminetas] is passable with Canoes 40 or 50 Miles, and good Portages will probably be found between it and Juniata and Potomac. It has Coal and Salt.

_{Monaunga-
hela F j} "Monaungahela [Monongahela] is a very large Branch, at whose Junction with Ohio stands Fort du Quesne. It is deep and gentle, and passable with large Batteaux beyond Redstone Creek, and still farther with lighter Craft. At Six Miles from the Mouth it divides into Two _{Youghigani
F j} Branches; the Northernmost Youghiogani [Youghiogheny], passable with good Batteaux to the Foot of the Rift at Lawrel [Laurel] Hill. The Portage from this to Potamac has been already mentioned.

_{Sorts of Land
on Ohio
above Fort
du Quesne.} "The *Soil* along these Parts of Ohio and its eastern Branches, though but little broken with high Mountains, is none of the best; consisting in general of low dry Ridges of White Oak and Chesnut Land, with very rich interval low Meadow Ground. Here and there are Spots of fine White Pines, and in many Places great Extents of poor Pitch Pines. The Land from the back Part of the Endless Mountains, Westward to Ohio, and from Fort du Quesne upward, is of these Sorts. The same little broken Chain of Hills, which borders it here, near the River Side, continues South-westerly, till it ends at 10 Miles below the Falls; keeping at some 10 or 15 Miles from the general Course of the River all the Way down."

Capt. Gordon's Journal gives the following a Description of this Part of the Country: From the Falls to about 155 Miles and Three Quarters it is very hilly, the Course of the River very winding and narrow, and but very few Spots of level Land on the Sides of the River. The Hills are mostly stony and steep, but from the great Herds of Buffaloes which we saw on the Beaches of the River, and on the Islands into which they came, there must be good Pasture. After this the ridgy Ground ends, the Country then grows flat, and the River, whose Bed widens, is divided by Islands. The Navigation is good from the Falls, but where the flat Country begins Boats must keep the principal Channel, which is on the Right Hand going down.

_{e Beaver
Creek F K} "Beaver Creek[e] is navigable with Canoes only. At Kishkuskes[2]

[1]Probably Mahoning Creek.
[2]An Indian village of mixed Delaware and Iro- quois, which from 1753 to 1770 was on the banks of Beaver Creek near New Castle, Lawrence County, Pennsylvania. Hodge, *op. cit.*, I, 737.

[Kuskuskies], about 16 Miles up, Two Branches[1] spread opposite Ways; one interlocks with French Creek and Cherâge,[2] the other Westward with Muskingum and Cayahôga [Cuyahoga]; on this are many Salt Springs, about 35 Miles above the Forks; it is canoable about 20 Miles farther. The eastern Branch is less considerable, and both are very slow, spreading through a very rich level Country, full of Swamps and Ponds, which prevent a good Portage that might otherwise be made to Cayahóga [Cuyahoga]; but will, no doubt, in future Ages, be fit to open a Canal between the Waters of Ohio and Lake Erie.

"Muskingum[f] is a fine gentle River, confined within high Banks that prevent its Floods from damaging the surrounding Land." It is 250 Yards wide at its Confluence with the Ohio. "It is passable with large Batteaux to the Three Logs [Legs],[3] and with small Ones to a little Lake at its Head, without any Obstruction from Falls or Rifts. From hence to Cayahoga [Cuyahoga] is a Portage[a] a Mile long. *Cayhahoga* [Cuyahoga], the Creek that leads from this Portage to Lake Erie, is muddy and middling swift, but no where obstructed with Falls or Rifts. As this has fine Land, wide extended Meadows, lofty Timber, Oak and Mulberry fitted for Shipbuilding, Walnut, Chesnut, and Poplar for domestic Services, and furnishes the shortest and best Portage between Ohio and Lake Erie; and its Mouth is sufficient to receive good Sloops from the Lake: It will in Time become a Place of Consequence. *Muskingum*, though so wide extended in its Branches, spreads all in most excellent Land, abounding in good Springs and Conveniencies, particularly adapted for Settlements remote from Marine Navigation, as Coal, Clay, and Freestone. In 1748 a Coal Mine, opposite Lamenshikola[4] Mouth, took Fire, and kept burning above a Twelve-month, where great Quantities are still left. Near the same Place is excellent Whetstone; and about Eight Miles higher up the River is Plenty of white and blue Clay for Glass Works and Pottery. Though the Quantity of good Land on Ohio, and its Branches, is vastly great, and the Conveniencies attending it so likewise; we may esteem that on Muskingum the Flower of it all.

"Hockhocking[a5] is passable with Batteaux Seventy or Eighty

f Muskingum
G l

a Portage to Cayahoga
F f
Cayahoga
E m
Its consequence
Muskingum

a Hockhocking
G m

[1]Shenango Creek interlocks with French Creek and the Grand River, the Mahoning with Muskingum and Cuyahoga Rivers. Hanna, *op. cit.*, I, 342.
[2]Grand River in Ohio. *Ibid.*
[3][Pownall's note] The Forks at which the Tuscaroras dwelt should have been placed 15 Miles North of the Three Logs [Legs].
Three Legs, an Indian town, abandoned before

1764, was located at the mouth of Big Stillwater Creek. Hanna, *op. cit.*, II, 188. Stillwater River is a tributary of the Tuscarawa River.—Ed.
[4]Probably Sandy Creek, Stark County, Ohio. Not located on contemporary (excepting Evans' *Map*) or modern maps.
[5]Also spelled *Hocking*.

Miles up; it has fine rich Land, and vast grassy Meadows, high Banks, and seldom overflows. It has Coals about Fifteen Miles up, and some Knowls of Freestone.

b
Big Canhawa
H m

"Big Canhawa[b] [Kanawha] falls into Ohio on the South East Side, and is so considerable a Branch, that it may, by Persons coming up Ohio on that Side, be mistaken for the main River. It is slow for Ten Miles, to the little broken Hills, and the Land very rich; as it is for about the same Breadth along Ohio, all the Way from the Pipe Hills[1] to the Falls.[2] After Ten Miles up Canhawa [Kanawha], the Land is hilly, the Water pretty rapid, for Fifty or Sixty Miles further to the Falls, to

Its Falls
impassible
H m

which Boats may go. This is a very remarkable Fall, not for its great Height, but for coming through a Mountain now thought impassable for Man or Beast, and is itself impassable. But no Doubt Foot or Horse Paths will be found when a greater Number of People make the Search, and under less Inconveniencies than our Travellers are at present. By reason of the Difficulty of passing the Ouasioto Mountains,[3] I thought them a very natural Boundary between Virginia and Ohio in these Parts; and for that Reason made them the Bounds of the Colours (in the coloured Maps) not that there is any Difference of Right between one

Its branches

Side and the other. *Louisa, New River*, and *Green Briar* [Greenbrier] are fine large Branches of Canhawa [Kanawha]; which in future Times will be of Service for the Inland Navigation of New Virginia,[4] as they interlock with Monaungahela [Monongahela], Potomack [Potomac], James River, Ronoak [Roanoke] and the Cuttawa River.[5]

c Totteroy
H n

"Totteroy[c6] falls into Ohio on the same Side, and is passable with Boats to the Mountains. It is long, and has not many Branches, inter-

d J n

locks with Red Creek, or Clinch's [Clinch] River[d] (a Branch of Cuttawa).[7] It has below the Mountains, especially for Fifteen Miles from the Mouth, very good Land. And here is a visible Effect of the Difference of Climate from the upper Parts of Ohio. Here the large Reed, or Carolina Cane, grows in Plenty, even upon the Upland, and the Severity of the Winter does not kill them; so that Travellers this Way are not obliged to provide any Winter Support for their Horses. And the same holds all the

e J r

Way down Ohio, especially on the South East Side to the Falls,[e8] and thence on both Sides.

[1]On both sides of the Ohio River above Wheeling Creek.
[2]At Louisville, Kentucky.
[3]Cumberland Mountains.
[4]Kentucky.

[5]Tennessee River. Donald Davidson, *The Tennessee*, (N.Y. Rinehart & Company, Inc., [1946-48]), I, 39.
[6]Big Sandy River, Kentucky.
[7]Tennessee River.
[8]At Louisville, Kentucky.

"Great Salt Lick Creek[f1] is remarkable for fine Land. Plenty of Buffaloes, Salt Springs, White Clay, and Limestone. Canoes may come up to the Crossing of the War Path, or something higher, without a Fall. The Salt Springs hurt its Water for Drinking, but the Number of fresh Springs near it make sufficient Amends.

"Kentucke[g] [Kentucky] is larger than the foregoing, has high Clay Banks, abounds in Cane and Buffaloes, and has also some very large Salt Springs. It has no Limestone yet discovered, but some other fit for building. Its Navigation is interrupted with Shoals, but passable with Canoes to the Gap,[2] where the War Path[3] goes through the Ouasioto[4] Mountain. This Gap[k] I point out in the Map, as a very important Pass, and it is truly so, by reason of its being the only Way passable with Horses, from Ohio Southward, for 300 or 400 Miles Extent. And if the Government has a Mind to preserve the Country back of Carolina, is should be looked to in Time.

"As we go further down Ohio, the Distance from the Ouasioto Mountains[5] to the River becomes more considerable. The Land, from the little broken Hills to the Mountains, is of a middling Kind, and consists of different Veins and Stratas; and though everywhere as good as any Part of the English Settlements, falls far short of that on the other Side of Ohio, or between the little Hills and the River. These Hills[b] are small, and seem only the Brink of a rising Stage of Land, and dividing the rich Plains of Ohio from the Upland, bordering on the Ouasioto Mountains. They terminate at Ten Miles below the Falls; indeed a little Spur extended from their Side is that Limestone Reach that Ohio ripples over at the Falls.

"Now to return to the other Side of Ohio. *Sioto* [Scioto] is a large gentle River, bordered with rich Flats, which it overflows in the Spring; spreading then above Half a Mile in Breadth, though when confined to its Banks it is scarce a Furlong wide.[6] If it floods early, it scarce retires within its Banks in a Month, or is fordable in a Month or Two more. The Land is so level, that in the Freshes of Ohio the Back-water runs Eight Miles up. Opposite the Mouth of this River is the Lower Shawane Town,[17] removed from the other Side, which was One of the most noted

f Great Salt Lick Creek H p

g Kentucke J p

k An important Pass thro' Ouasioto Mountain J o

b The little Hills South of Ohio J q to F j

Sioto H o

i Lower Shawane Town. H o

[1]Probably Licking River which flows into the Ohio at Newport, Kentucky.

[2]Cumberland Gap.

[3]Catawba or Great Warriors' Trail. Hanna, *op. cit.*, II, 119.

[4]Cumberland Mountains.

[5]*Ibid.*

[6][Pownall's note] The Latitude of its Mouth 38° 22'. I have marked the Error of its being placed too high in the Map. Muskingum is in Evans's Map placed in its general Run much too far to the West; I have in some Measure corrected it in this Edition.

[7]Site of present Portsmouth, Ohio.

Places of English Trade with the Indians. This River, besides vast Extents of good Land, is furnished with Salt on an Eastern Branch, and Red Bole on Necunsia Skeintat. The Stream is very gentle, and passable with large Batteaux a great Way up, and with Canoes near 200 Miles to a Portage near the Head, where you carry over good Ground Four Miles to Sanduski [Sandusky]. *Sanduski*[k] [Sandusky] is a considerable River, abounding in level rich Land, its Stream gentle all the Way to the Mouth, where it will receive considerable Sloops. This River is an important Pass, and the French have secured it as such; the Northern Indians cross the Lake here from Island to Island,[1] land at Sanduski [Sandusky], and go by a direct Path[1] to the Lower Shawane Town, and thence to the Gap of Ouasioto,[2] in their Way to the Cuttawas [Catawba] Country. This will, no Doubt, be the Way that the French will take from *Detroit* to *Moville* [Mobile],[3] unless the English will be advised to secure it, now that it is in their Power.

"Little Mineami [Miami] River[m] is too small to be gone far with Canoes. It has much fine Land, and some Salt Springs; its high Banks, and middling Current, prevent its overflowing much the surrounding Land.

"Great Mineami [Miami] River, Assereniet, or Rocky River,[n] has a very stony Channel, a swift Stream, but no Falls. It has several large Branches, passable with Canoes a great Way; one[o4] extending Westward towards the Quiaaghtena River;[5] another[6] towards a Branch of Mineami [Maumee] River (which runs into Lake Erie) to which there is a Portage, and a Third[7] has a Portage to the West Branch of Sanduski [Sandusky]; besides Mad Creek, where the French have lately established themselves. A Vein of elevated Land, here and there a little stony, which begins in the Northern Part of the Peninsula, between the Lakes Erie, Huron, and Michigan, extends across the Lake Mineami [Maumee] River, below the Fork, and Southward along the Rocky River,[8] to Ohio; and is the Reason of this River's being stony, and the Grounds rising a little higher than the adjacent Plains. It is, like all the Land on this River, very rich, and would scarce have been perceived, had not the River worn the Channel down to the Rocks which lie beneath.

"Quiaaghtena River, called by the French *Ouabach* [Wabash],

k Sanduski, F n, an Important Place

E n

m Little Mineami River H p

n Rocky River G p o H q

Quiaaghtena River. G r

[1]Catawba or Great Warriors' Path.
[2]Cumberland Gap.
[3]Founded by the French in 1702. Schlarman, *op. cit.*, p. 118.
[4]Whitewater River.
[5]Wabash River.
[6]Loramic Creek which flows into the Miami River near Lockington, Shelby County, Ohio.
[7]Great Miami River proper.
[8]Great Miami River.

though that is truly the Name of its South-Eastern Branch, is very large, and furnishes a fine Navigation; but whether interrupted with Rifts or Falls, I am not informed, but probably it is not, as the Lands round are fine level Flats, of vast Extent. The *Western League of Indians*,[1] known to themselves by the general Name of WELINIS, corruptly called by the French *Ilinois* [Illinois] (frequently distinguished by us, according to the several Tribes[2] or Nations that it consists of; as the Piancashas [Piankashaws], Wawiaghtas [Weas], Piques [Picts], Tawightawis [Twightwees], and Mineamis [Miamis]) are seated from this River to Sioto [Scioto]; and were permitted, about Sixteen Years ago, to settle there by the express Leave of the Confederates. Present State of the Welinis

"Into the Western End of Lake Erie falls Mineami [Maumee] River, a considerable Stream, navigable with Canoes to the Portages, which lead to the Quiaaghtena[3] and Rocky River,[4] interrupted with Three considerable Rifts below the Forks: But however it is an important River, because of the Portages it furnishes South-Westward."[5] Mineami River E o

I shall close this Account of the natural State of the Country with some Considerations on the Nature of its Climate.

The principal Circumstances on which singly and combined the Nature of the Climate of any Country depends, are, 1st. the Aspect of the given Horizon, as constituted and situated to *receive*, and 2dly The Nature of the Soil as constituted to *retain* the heat of the Sun: a Third is the Nature of the Atmosphere which is in the longest Continuance of Contact with this Horizon.

1st. If this Globe of Earth had One uniform plain Surface, the nearer Approach to, or greater Elongation from the Equator which any Country had (*caeteris paribus*) the greater or lesser Degree of Heat its Climate would partake of, because the more directly, or more obliquely that the Rays of the Sun strike any Surface, the greater or the lesser must the Reverberation of Heat be, as the Angle of Reflection is more acute or more obtuse: The more or less also will the Atmosphere in Contact with this Land be heated by this Reverberation; but as this is

[1]"A confederacy of Algonquin tribes, occupying S. Wisconsin, N. Illinois, and sections of Iowa and Missouri, comprising the Cahokia, Kaskaskia, Michigamea, the Moingwena, Peoria, and Tamaroa." Hodge, *op. cit.*, I, 597.

[2]The Piankashaw and Wea were subtribes of the Miami, but later became separate people. In 1854 the remnants of these tribes joined the Illinois which at that time were known as the Peoria or Kaskaskia. Hodge, *op. cit.*, II, 240, 925. Miamis and Twight-wees were considered one and the same. The English usually designated the Miamis as Twightwees. *Ibid.*, I, 852-53. Of the Picts little is known excepting that they lived in the vicinity of the Miami village, Pickawillany (present Piqua, Ohio). *Ibid.*, II, 242.

[3]Wabash River.

[4]Great Miami River.

[5]Quoted from Evans' *Analysis*, pp. 26-31; reprinted in Gipson's *Lewis Evans*, pp. 170-75.

not the Case of the Surface of the Earth, a thousand other collateral Circumstances interfere with and break this Rule. As the Surface of the Earth is broken with numberless Irregularities, wherever the Inclination of the given Horizon lies different from the general Horizon of the Globe, it counteracts this general Effect: If on the North of the Equator it slopes Southward, or on the South of the Equator slopes Northward, so as to extend its general Plain nearer at right Angles with the Rays of the Sun than the spherick Plain of its Latitude would have been, it will receive and retain more heat in proportion than belongs to that Latitude. Hence the intense Heat of the southern Parts of Persia, and of those Parts which we call the East Indies. Hence also, principally, though other Circumstances may concur in the Cause, is the Climate of North America hotter than in the same Latitudes in Europe. Hence also, in Part it happens, that the Regions in North America, in the upper Stages, are not so liable to Heat as those in the lower Plains, though in the same Latitude. If on the contrary the given Horizon slopes from the Sun's Place, the Heat in the lower Latitudes will be more moderate, which is the Case of France and Germany compared with the Countries of the same Latitude in America, and in the higher Latitudes the Country will suffer more rigorous Cold. This latter is the Case of Siberia, the Plain of whose Horizon being in a high North Latitude slopes from the high Tartar Plains Northward; hence the more than natural Rigour of the Climate; hence the unfruitful and inhospitable Nature of its Soil.

2. Some Surfaces and some Soils (other Circumstances remaining alike) are more formed to create a Reverberation of Heat and to retain it. A sandy Soil soon heats, and also retains its Heats. A Surface uneven and irregular Hills and deep Vales, and even that which is broken with Mountains (if those be not too high, as explained below) reflecting the Rays of the Sun a thousand Ways, and occasioning them to cross each other constantly in all Directions, creates a stronger Reverberation of local Heat than is found in any extended Plain. A Country cloathed with Woods, which shade the Earth from the Action of the Sun, will always (taking in the whole Region) be colder than a Country cleared of those Woods; and the Air which lies in Contact with it, or passes over it, will be always colder. As these Regions become cleared of these Woods, are dried and cultured, that Part of the Climate which depends on this Circumstance always meliorates in Proportion. This has been found to be the Case with Gaul and Germany. This Effect was sensibly felt, and very early observed, by some of the First Settlers in North

America; some of the very earliest written Accounts which I have seen relate this Circumstance very particularly, and Men of Observation in that Country have in every successive Age marked the Progress of this Melioration.

There is another Circumstance, which indeed does not much enter into the Case of the Climate of North America, but is amongst these general Propositions worth Notice. It is this:

The longer the Portion is of any given Period of Time, in which the Sun shines in any Horizon, the hotter in that Season will the Region of that Horizon be. Hence the intense Heat of the latter End of Summer in Russia.

3. The Air or Atmosphere can be acted upon by the Reverberation of the Sun's Rays, and be heated only in Proportion to its greater Density near the Earth, and in Proportion to the Continuity of Contact which it hath with the heated Parts of the Earth. The Earth also in Proportion to this more continued Contact amongst its Parts, in the general Level of the Surface, receives and retains more Heat than it does in the higher mountainous discontinued Parts above that Level. From these Two Circumstances combined it arises, that in the very high Mountains, even under the Equator, the Cold is intense; and at a certain Elevation above the general Level of the Globe, so rigorous and intense as to put a Stop to all Vegetation.

The Atmosphere will also be heated or chilled according to the Nature of the Particles which attracted by it are mixed and suspended in it, whether they be aqueous, or whether nitrous or sulphureous Salts, and according to the Fixation, Fermentation, or Precipitation of these Particles.

The Regions covered with great Lakes of fresh Water, but more especially the Region of the main Ocean, the component Parts of whose Mass are in perpetual Motion, are in general warmer than, although in hot Seasons and Climates never so hot as, the Body of the Land: It retains however a more equable Heat while the Heat of the Land changes from one Degree of Heat to an opposite one of Cold.

The general Currents of the Air, and the Nature of the Vapours which may be mixed with them, must depend greatly on the Position which these different Portions of the Globe have in respect of each other in any Region. In Summer, and in other Seasons when the Land is heated, the Winds which blow from Sea must prevail; in Winter, when the Land is chilled, and while the Sea retains its usual Warmth, the Wind will blow from Land to Sea, and more or less violent in Proportion to the Contrast. The Position of these Regions in respect to the general Currents of the Atmosphere and of the Ocean operate greatly in forming the Courses of the Seasons, and the Nature of the Climate.

These Principles, thus laid down and explained, I will proceed to state the Facts. The Climate of the Continent at large, or rather of that Portion of North America which is contained within the Limits of this Map, may be thus stated.

Its Seasons are *Summer*, Autumn, or what the Americans more expressively call *The Fall*, and *Winter*. The Transition from the Locking up of all Vegetation in Winter to the sudden Burst of it again to Life at the Beginning of the Summer, excludes that progressive Season which in the more moderate Climate of Europe we call Spring.

The Season begins to break soon after the Fall of the Leaf, and temporary cold Rains and Sleets of Snow fall in November, the North West Winds begin, and towards Christmas Winter in all its Rigour sets in; the Ground is covered with Snow, the Frost is settled, the Sky becomes clear and one continued Expanse of Azure, with constant Sunshine; temporary Blasts and Storms are at Intervals Exceptions to this. Towards April the Currents of the Air begin to change to North, and round to North East, and the Season of hazy, foggy, and rainy Squalls from North East begin towards the latter End of April in some Parts, towards the Beginning of May in others. The Frost breaks up, the Snow melts, and within a Week or 10 Days after, the Woods and the Orchards are in the full Glow of Bloom. About the Middle of September the Mornings and Evenings begin to grow cool, and from that Time to the Beginning of the Winter Season it is the Climate of Paradise.

To give a Description of the Climate of New England, which Part is now first published and added to this Map, I shall transcribe that Account which Dr. Douglas[1] gives, as he, during a long Residence therein, did, with a peculiar scientific Attention observe it. "In New England generally the falling Weather is from North East to South East in Winter: If the Wind is North of East, Snow; if South of East, Rain. The North East Storms are of the greatest Continuance; the South East are the most violent. A North West freezing Wind backing to the South West, if reverberated, proves the most intense cold Weather. Our great Rains are in August about Two Months after the Summer Solstice; and our great Snows about Two Months after the Winter Solstice. In falling Weather the further the Wind is from the East the finer and drier is the Snow; the further South from the East the more humid and fleaky. When

---

[1] Dr. William Douglass.

the Wind gets South of South East it turns to Rain. The Winds from West South West to North North West are dry Winds, fit for dry curing of Salt-fish; further North they are damp and soft, as coming from the Ocean; further South are from the hot Latitudes, and Sun-burn the Fish. Our intense hot Days are with the Wind from South to West South West; from North to East North East our most chilly Weather. The dry Winds are from West to North North West, all other Winds carry more or less. From the Middle of October begin, and about the Middle of April leave off, Chamber Fires. Our Seasons as to Temper of the Weather may be reckoned as follows: Winter, from the Winter Solstice to the Spring Equinox: Spring, from said Equinox to Summer Solstice. Summer, from said Summer Solstice to Winter Equinox; and Autumn from thence to Winter Solstice." I have as above ventured to differ from this Division of the Doctor's[1] having divided the Seasons into Winter, Summer, and Fall; in his next Paragraph he seems to be sensible of this Division: "At the End of August the Symptoms of approaching Winter begin to appear, we call it the *Fall* of the Year," as the Leaves begin to fall.

Lewis Evans, in a Map of Pennsylvania, New Jersey, and New York, which he published in 1749, says, "That at Philadelphia, by many Years Observations, the Extremes of the Barometer were 28 59 and 30 78. And that by One Year's Observation, which was not remarkable either for Heat or Cold, Farenheit's Pocket Thermometer was from 14 to 84."

The Courses and the Nature of the Winds are in this Region exactly what from the above Principles one might pronounce them to be. In Winter generally, and taking the Year through for near Half the Period, the Land Winds blow, that is, the Course of the Air is from the colder Region of a shaded uncultivated Land, to the milder Region of the Sea: These Land Winds are the West and North West Winds. These Winds are always dry, and in the Winter Season intensely cold. These Land Winds in very dry Weather are endued with a strong Power of Attraction, and absorb the Vapours of the Inland Waters of the Country, and create, as they approach towards the lower Plains, very thick Fogs, which intercept the direct Rays of Light, so that the luminous Object of the Sun appears as red as Blood; there are various other Phaenomena attendant on this State of Refraction. These Vapours are greatly heated by the Sun, and greatly heat the Air; in consequence of this, when these Fogs are dissipated, the most intense Heat succeeds them. If they last

[1]Dr. William Douglass.

till Evening before they are dissipated, they are frequently followed by Thunder Gusts. As the West and North West Winds are steady and equable, the South West are unsettled and squally. The North Winds are the Carriers of Sleet, both Snow and Rain. The North East when it takes to blow, as it does at the Season between the Breaking-up of Winter and the Commencement of Summer, is settled Cold, and blows hard, with continued Rains; and to the Northward, as for Example, on the Coasts of Nova Scotia, and often on the Coast of New England, when it does not bring Rain, it drives in thick and fixed Fogs before it. The East Winds are warm, but not settled under a fixed Characteristic as to wet or dry. The South East are warm and wet.

I cannot close these Observations without transcribing from Lewis Evans's Map of Pennsylvania, New York, and New Jersey, printed at Philadelphia 1749, the following curious, at that Time novel and very curious, philosophic Propositions; not only as they point to very ingenious Experiments, but as they shew what Progress *He* had made in that singular Branch of Philosophy, *Electricity*, at a Period when even the first Philosophers were but Empirics in it.

"All our Storms, says he, begin to Leeward; thus a North East Storm will be a Day sooner in Virginia than in Boston.

"Thunder never happens but by the Meeting of Sea and Land Clouds, the Sea Clouds coming, *freighted with Electricity*, meeting and others less so, the Equilibrium is restored by *Snaps of Lightening;* and the more opposite the Winds and the larger and compacter the Clouds, the more dreadful are these Shocks: The Sea Clouds thus suddenly bereft of that universal Element of Repellancy, contract, and their Waters gush down in Torrents."

His Philosophy here is not perfectly just, though it contains very shrewd leading Theorems, of which, with a true and painful philosophic Course of Experiments, Dr. Franklin[1] elicited the real Truth.

I did intend to have continued this Paper with a Description of the ORIGINAL INDIGENOUS INHABITANTS,

> Haec Nemora Indigenae fauni Nymphaeque tenebant
> Gensque Virûm truncis et duro robore Nati
> Queîs nec *Mos nec Cultus* erat, nec jungere Tauros
> Aut Componere Opes nôrant, aut parcere parto,
> Sed Rami atque asper victu *Venatus* alebat.

I should have inserted a List of the Tribes or Nations both in the northern and southern District marking their Dwellings. This Part

---

[1] Benjamin Franklin (1706-1790).

would contain a Description of their Nature, their System of Life, and Mode of Subsistence; of the Progress they have made, and of the Point in which they are found as to Society, Communion, and Government; as to their Manners in the Individual, the Family, the Tribe; as to the general Spirit by which they regulate themselves when considered as a Nation. But although I have many Materials, and these nearly arranged, yet I cannot at present find either Leisure or Spirits to undertake this Part. On this Head therefore I will take the Liberty at present to refer the Reader, who may be desirous of seeing something on this Subject, to those Parts of*c* *the Administration of the Colonies*[1] where these Matters c Vol. 1 are treated of, so far as respects the general Subject of that Treatise. Ch 7

I had also proposed to have given an Account of this Country IN ITS SETTLED AND CULTIVATED STATE, containing an Account of the Mode[2] of Settling, and a Detail of the Nature, Progress, and Completion of these Settlements; of the Produce of this cultivated Continent in the Three different Regions into which the Nature of this Produce divides it; of the internal forensic, and external commercial Value of these Products; of the Nature of the Inhabitancy of the Country, and of the great Towns; of the Spirit and Character in Religion, Manners, and Government of each Province and Colony: And finally, from my Journals, a portrayed Description of the Country as one sees it in travelling through it. The wretched State of Confusion and Ruin into which it has fallen, compared with the happy State in which I saw it, is, I own, a View that my Eye and Heart turn away from; nor can I bear the Retrospect, which the very reading over my Journals opens to me. If I live, and have Leisure, when I may see their happier Days of Peace and good Government return again, most likely I shall insert these Matters in some future Edition of this Work.

[1]By Thomas Pownall. *Op. cit.*

[2][Pownall's note for revised and enlarged edition] Nullas Germanorum populis urbes habitari, satis notum est: ne pati quidem inter se junctas sedes. Colunt discreti ac diversi, ut fons, ut campus, ut nemus placuit. Tacitus De Germania, xvi.

APPENDIX

NUMBER I.

The Account[1] *of* CAPT. ANTHONY VAN SCHAICK[2] *of the Ground between the Entrance of Lake Champlain at Crown Point, and the Mouth of Otter Creek.*

I WAS commmissioned by Lieutenant Governor Phipps,[3] of the Massachuset's [Massachusetts] Bay, to go to Canada to exchange and procure the redemption of prisoners. I set out from Albany on the 28th of January, 1752. I have been at Crown Point six several Times. I have heard people talk with one another from Fort Saint Frederick to the opposite shore, without any difficulty of making each other hear, and I do think it is at most 700 yards across. The bay on the west side of Fort St. Frederick does at the upper end trend to the eastward, so that from the head of it to *the drowned lands*, there is a short carryingplace, over which the Indians carry when they come from Canada with smuggled beaver. From Fort Saint Frederick I went over the ice (it being froze) across the lake, to a point about two miles on the east side of the lake, there I landed on the banks, thence due east about threefourths of a mile, and struck a meadow of about 150 yards across which trended in the same direction as the lake to the mouth of Otter Creek. I followed this Meadow, which, as it approached to Otter Creek, become *drowned land* more and more flooded, till, as it approached the Creek, it became all water, and a river: that the mouth of Otter Creek, where it empties itself, is a large bay.[4] To the east of this drowned land is a ridge of high land, that comes down to this bay, but sloped away before it comes to the water; for at the banks there is low land for about 60 yards. As near as I can guess from hence, that is to say, this point, to the opposite side of this bay, or mouth of Otter Creek, is near a mile. The land on the opposite side all low marshy land.

ANTHONY VAN SCHAICK.

[1]The original manuscript of this account is in the Henry E. Huntingdon Library. LO 432.

[2]Captain of a company of New York militia, who was taken prisoner by the French before October, 1748 and was not exchanged until June 26, 1750. For the next few years he acted as interpreter and officer appointed to exchange and redeem prisoners held in New France. In 1756 he was commissioned as Captain of a company of Rangers. *N.Y.C.D.*, VI, 492, 495; X, 211-15.

[3]Spencer Phips (1685-1757), member of the Council of Massachusetts and Lieutenant Governor of the colony from 1732 to 1757. Shirley, *op. cit.*, I, 489n.

[4]Baye des Vasseaux. "William Brassier. A Survey

NUMBER II.

CAPTAIN ANTHONY VAN SCHAICK'S JOURNAL.[1] 1756.

I LEFT Fort Edward August 18th, about 12 o'clock; travelled north three miles; came to the falls on Hudson's River; steered N.N.E. pine woods; the soil indifferent; travelled about two miles; there halted; very good road; continued the same course two miles more; came to the head of the brook which empties itself at Ford Edward; the soil very good; the woods, oak, maple, beech, and hemlock; the country full of coves and ridges, but easy to be avoided; there encamped.

19th, set off about seven o'clock; travelled one mile and a half N.E. by E. the soil rich, the country level; the woods beech in general; turned E. about four miles more; came to Fort Ann; there encamped; Wood Creek being very low, not above 15 inches of water, but its banks pleasant, about 10 feet high, about 20 or 25 feet across, goosebury bushes on the banks.

20th, Left Fort Ann early in the morning; travelled one mile; came to Fork's Creek,[2] about half a mile from the mouth thereof; travelled down to the mouth, where its course is E. by N. for about half a mile, then turns N. is about 30 feet wide; the country level; the soil exceeding rich; the wood, maple, beech, bass wood; this kind of land about a mile wide, one place with another, on each side; its banks about 10 feet perpendicular; steered straight north about four miles; came to the foot of a mountain which ranges due north; strove to go round it to the westward, but the men seemed discouraged, ascended the mountain, then travelled due north about six miles; discovered two more ridges of mountains ranging the same course, with two intervals between them which seemed to be pretty level at the bottom; it being near four miles from top to top; but the eastmost mountain running farthest north; there encamped near the top of the mountain, by a pleasant spring.

---

of Lake Champlain including Lake George, Crown Point and St. John . . ." In Jeffery's *American Atlas*, *op. cit.*, map no. 18.

Now Kellogg Bay, Lake Champlain.

[1]On August 13, 1756, Captain Anthony Van Schaick received his commission from Lord Loudoun to organize a Company of Rangers. Manuscript in the Henry E. Huntingdon Library. LO 1400.

Although the Company was never completed this *Journal* is an account of a scouting trip made under the Warrant. The original manuscript of this account is in the Henry E. Huntingdon Library. LO 1663.

[2]Located and named on Brassier, *A Survey of Lake Champlain, op. cit.* Located but not named on modern maps.

The first
Narrows,
vide fig. 11
in the map.

21st, Set off due east about two miles and a half; came to Wood Creek; travelled about one mile and a half along Wood Creek; there was about 20 feet water in the Creek; and it was about 50 feet wide; travelled along the Creek about a quarter of a Mile; here a spur of the mountain runs quite close to the Creek side, and forms the banks; but by cutting 30 yards through this, a road may be made, if thought more convenient. This part of Wood Creek is a very good situation for a bridge, having good footing for the heads of a bridge, and being not more than 40 or 50 feet across, and it being good travelling on the east side, which leads to the place noticed below, the general course being N.E. by N. about three miles: fell in with Col. Fitch's[1] Tracks, coming from the south west end of South Bay, continued our course along Wood Creek five miles more, the passage of the river being stopped up with trees for about a quarter of a mile, felled down by the French last War,[2] forms a kind of dam, which must be cut before any canoes or batteaux can pass; came to Montour's[3] river, which stands into Wood Creek out of E. by N. travelled about two miles more; encamped.

The 22d, Set off; travelled about two miles and a half, came to the Falls which run N.N.E. where there is a good place for a fort, followed the river for near a mile, then turned west to the top of a mountain, between Wood Creek and South Bay, which mountain terminates in a perpendicular at its north point, beneath which there is a triangle of flat hemlock woods, of about half a mile wide, at the north point of which there is a triangle of reeds and water weeds of about four acres, then the channel of Wood Creek and South Bay meet. This is the seventh time I have been at South Bay by different ways, and have endeavoured to find a way by which a carriage, or at least a horse might go, but could never find any such.

ANTHONY VAN SCHAICK.

[1]Lieutenant-colonel Eliezer Fitch of the first regiment, Connecticut Provincials. This regiment was raised to serve under the general command of John Winslow in his expedition against Crown Point in 1756. Connecticut (Colony), *Public Records of* . . . . Edited by Charles J. Hoadly (Hartford, Case, Lockwood & Brainard Co., [etc.], 1850-90), X, 470-71.

[2]Terminated by the Treaty of Aix la Chapelle, Oct. 7, 1748.

[3]Probably East Creek, present Poultney River.

NUMBER III.

CAPTAIN HOBBS'S ACCOUNT[1] OF THE WAY FROM NO. 4, D b IN NEW HAMPSHIRE, TO THE MOUTH OF OTTER CREEK.

FROM No. 4,[2] up the river,[3] on the east side about a mile, to avoid crossing Black River; then cross the river, deep still water, good landing on the banks, to the northward of north west to the foot of a mountain called Ascoudne [Ascutney] about two miles, the land white oak and pine, sandy and of course full of gullies, at the foot of the mountain, struck into the Indian road, which followed to Otter Creek: left the mountain to the northward; the land much the same but more inclined to oak and beech, tolerable level, steered about W.N.W. four days and came to Otter Creek, the land pretty much the same till I came towards Otter Creek, when it inclined more to beech, and the sugar-maple tree: called it then 60 miles, but do not think it is so much, thence down the river, on each side of which interval, land about a mile wide, and continued after this sort to the Great Falls.[4] I am very confident a good waggon road may be made hitherto. I crossed below the Falls, the water about knee deep: from the Falls down the west side, to the mouth two days. Rough land, no sharp hills, or pitches nor rocky. The road I kept was between the interval land on Otter Creek, and the swamp meadow that runs down the east side of Lake Champlain, upon the up land, which is a ridge, that runs between these quite down the lake; the interval land below the Falls being wet rushy drowned lands. The second time I went down this river, just before I came to the Falls I turned away east, and left a big mountain on the left hand to the west, followed an Indian path, till I struck a river that falls into Otter Creek, then went on the east side. Rough bad travelling.

A little fortified post on Connecticut River, so numbered and called.

HUMPHREY HOBBS.

Albany, *Sept.* 18*th*, 1756.

[1]The manuscript of this account is in the Henry E. Huntingdon Library. LO 1839.
[2]Present Charlestown, New Hampshire.
[3]The Connecticut River.
[4]Unidentified. Four separate falls are indicated on Brassier, *A Survey of Lake Champlain, op. cit.*

NUMBER IV.

EXTRACTS FROM THE JOURNAL OF CAPTAIN HARRY GORDON, CHIEF ENGINEER IN THE WESTERN DEPARTMENT IN NORTH AMERICA, WHO WAS SENT FROM FORT PITT ON THE RIVER OHIO, DOWN THE SAID RIVER, &c. TO ILINOIS, IN 1766.[1]

Now
Pitsburg
F j

JUNE the 18th, 1766, embarked at Fort Pitt,[2] on the River Ohio, and arrived at the Mingo[3] Town, 71 miles, on the 19th. The country between these two Places is broken, with many high ridges or hills; the vallies narrow, and the course of the river plunged from many high grounds which compose its banks. When the water is high, you go with moderate rowing from six to seven miles an hour.

G 1

The 23d, arrived at the mouth of Muskingum River, in latitude 39° 19'. Muskingum is 250 yards wide, at its confluence with the Ohio, and navigable for batteauxs 150 up: it runs through a very pleasant and extremely fertile country. Killed several buffaloes between the Mingo Town and Muskingum; but the first we met with were about 100 miles below Fort Pitt, which is distant from Muskingum 161 miles.

H n

The 29th, arrived at the mouth[4] of the Scioto 366 miles; navigation good at all seasons without the least obstruction from the Mingo Town, 71 miles and a half from Fort Pitt, and indeed very little from the mouth[5] of Big Beaver Creek, which is 29 miles and a quarter from Fort Pitt. The Ohio River from 50 miles above Muskingum to Scioto is most beautiful, and interspersed with numbers of islands of different sizes, covered with the most stately timber; with several long reaches, one of which is 16 miles and a half, inclosed with the finest trees of various verdures, which afford a noble and inchanting prospect. A glorious vista found on one of these islands, is terminated by two small hills, shaped like sugar-loaves, of very easy ascent, from whence you may see all this magnificient variety.

[1] Captain Harry Gordon's "Journal" (1766) is printed in Clarence W. Alvord, ed., *The New Regime*, 1765-1767 (Springfield, Illinois State Historical Library, 1916), pp. 290-311; Newton Mereness, ed., *op. cit.*, pp. 464-89. Extracts and abridged versions are printed in various other places.

[2] Fort Pitt (1758-91) an English fort built at the forks of the Ohio. Present site of Pittsburgh, Pennsylvania.

[3] Present site of Mingo [Junction], Jefferson Co., Ohio. Hanna, *op. cit.*, II, 141.

[4] Present site of Portsmouth, Ohio.

[5] Near present Beaver, Pennsylvania.

The rivers Hockhocking [Hocking] and Canhawa [Kanawha],[1] fall G m & H n
into the Ohio in this space, beside many others of a smaller size. Up the
Big Cahawa [Great Kanawha], the western Indians penetrate into the
Cherokee country.[2] It is a fine large river, and navigable by report,
100 miles towards the southward. The country on the Ohio, &c. is every
where pleasant, with large level spots of the richest land, remarkably
healthy. One general remark of this nature may serve for the whole
tract of the globe, comprehended between the western skirts of the
Allegany [Allegheny] Mountains, beginning at Fort Ligonier,[3] thence F h
bearing south westerly to the distance of 500 miles opposite the Ohio
Falls,[4] then crossing them northerly to the heads of the rivers that empty
themselves into the Ohio; thence east along the ridge[5] that separates the
lakes and Ohio's streams to French Creek,[6] which is opposite to the
above-mentioned Fort Ligonier northerly. This country may, from a
proper knowledge, be affirmed to be the most healthy (as no sort of
chronic disorder ever prevailed in it) the most pleasant, the most
commodious, and most fertile spot of earth known to European people.

The latitude of Scioto is 38° 22'. Remained here till the 8th of July. J o

The 16th of July, encamped opposite to the Great Lick,[7] 390 miles;[8]
it is five miles distance south of the river. The extent of the muddy part
of the Lick is three-fourths of an acre.

The Ohio continues to be narrow from Fort Pitt to within 100
miles of the Falls; its breadth seldom exceeds 500 yards, and is confined
by rising grounds, which cause many windings, although the reaches are
sometimes from two to four miles long; the largest and most beautiful
(as has been already mentioned) is above the Scioto, and is 16 miles and
a half. The Ohio, 100 miles above the Falls, widens to 700 yards in

---

[1]Little Kanawha. Mereness, *op. cit.*, p. 465n.

[2]The Cherokees in early time held the whole
mountain region of the southern Alleghenies in southern West Virginia, western North & South Carolina,
northern Georgia, eastern Tennessee and north
eastern Alabama, and claimed the land as far north
as the Ohio River. Hodge, *op. cit.*, I, 245.

[3]In 1758 Captain Harry Gordon, in preparation
for General John Forbes' expedition against Fort
Duquesne, built Fort Ligonier at Loyalhanning.
Western Pennsylvania Historical Magazine (Pittsburgh, Historical Society of Western Pennsylvania,
1918-date), XVII (1934), 265. On present site of
Ligonier, Pennsylvania.

[4]At present Louisville, Kentucky.

[5]A ridge of high lands that determine the course

which the streams run from east to west across the
entire state. Benson J. Lossing, *A Pictorial Description of Ohio* . . . (New York, Ensings & Thayer,
1849), pp. 12-13. The ridge ranges E.N.E. from the
northern part of Darke to Trumbull County. Mereness, *op. cit.*, p. 466n.

[6]In northwestern Pennsylvania.

[7]Big Bone Lick in the valley of Bone Lick Creek
in Boone County, Kentucky, one and one-half miles
east of Hamilton on the Ohio River. Richard H.
Collins, *History of Kentucky* (Covington, Collins &
Co., 1874), II, 51.

[8]Here Mr. Pownall has confused the distance of
Big Bone Lick and Big Buffalo Lick. Captain
Gordon's *table of miles from Fort Pitt* gives 560¼
and 390 miles respectively.

many places, and contains a great number of islands. The grounds diminish generally in height, and the country is not so broken. Some of the banks are, at times, overflowed by freshes; and there is scarce any place from Fort Pitt to the Falls, where a good road may not be made along the banks of the river, and horses employed in drawing up bilanders against the stream, which is gentle, except in freshes. The height of the banks permit them every where to be settled; and they are not subject to crumble away.

H q

The little and big Mineami [Little and Great Miami] rivers fall in between the Scioto on the north side, and the Licking Creek and Kentucke [Kentucky] on the south side.

There are many good encampments on the islands, and one in particular very remarkable, and safe, opposite to the Big Lick.

H r

The waters at the Falls were low; it being the summer. They do not, however, deserve the name of Falls, as the stream on the north side has no sudden pitch, but only runs rapid over the ledge of a flat limestone rock, which the Author of Nature put here to keep up the waters of the higher Ohio, and to be the cause of that beautiful stillness of the river's course above.

This bed or dam is made almost flat and smooth to resist less the current, which would soon get the better of greater resistance; but as it is subject to wear, there is enough of it, being two miles wide, and its length in the country unknown.

Several boats passed it at the very driest season of the year, when the waters are at the lowest by unloading one-third of their freight. They passed on the north-side, where the carrying-place is three-fourths of a mile long; and on the south-east side it is about half that distance, and is reckoned the safest passage for these who are unacquainted, but it is the most tedious; as, during part of the summer, and fall, they must drag their *boats* over the flat rock.

The heat by day is by no means intense, and the coolness of the nights always required a blanket even in their tents. Notwithstanding the distance from Port Pitt is 682 miles, the latitude is not much southerly; the Falls being 38° 8'.

For all the remaining part of this journal the reader must refer to the little sketch on the west side of the map.

Westerly and south-west winds generally blow, and will greatly assist the navigation up the river Ohio.

The 23d July left the Falls, and encamped the 31st on a large island[1] opposite to the mouth of the Wabash, which is 317 miles and a half below the Falls, and 999 Miles and a half from Fort Pitt.

[1]Wabash Island.

From the Falls to about half this distance of 317 miles and a half, the country is very hilly; the course of the river very winding and narrow, and but very few spots of level land on the sides of the river. The hills are mostly stoney and steep; but from the great herds of buffalo, we observed on the beaches of the river and islands into which they come for air, and coolness in the heat of the day, there must be good pasturage.

The ridgy ground ends 837 miles below Fort Pitt; the country then grows flat, and the river, whose bed widens, is often divided by islands.

The navigation is good from the Falls; but where the flat country begins, boats must keep the *principal channel*, which is on the *right hand* going down.

The Wabash is marked by a large island,[1] round which boats may go most times of the year. The end of the fork of the two rivers,[2] the Ohio and Wabash, is narrow, and overflowed; a mile and a half upwards the ground is higher. Very large herds of buffaloes are frequently seen in this country.

The river Wabash, at its confluence with the Ohio, is 306 yards wide, and it discharges a great quantity of a muddy kind of water into the Ohio. It is navigable 300 or 400 miles upwards, but boats smaller than 33 feet long and seven feet wide, the size they then had, should be used on it, as there is no great depth of water in the summer and fall. Latitude of Wabash 37' 41°.[3] The country between the course of this river and the Missisippi is in general flat, open, and of a rich luxuriant soil; that on the banks of the Ohio is level, and in many places hereabouts overflows.

The 2d August, in the evening, left Wabash, stopped next morning near the Saline,[4] or Salt Run; of which any quantity of good salt may be made here.

From hence Indians were sent to the Ilinois [Illinois], to notify our intended visit to that place.

The 6th of August, halted at Port Massiac [Fort Massac],[5] formerly a French post, 120 miles below the mouth of the Wabash, and eleven

[1]Wabash Island.

[2]"Here ends the Indiana territory, and the Illinois Commences." Cramer, *op. cit.*, p. 117.

[3]That is 37° 41'.

[4]Saline River. Around the mouth of this river grew the chief pioneer trading center for salt on the lower Ohio. Thomas Hutchins, *The Courses of the Ohio River . . .* ed. by Beverly Bond (Cincinnati, Historical and Philosophical Society of Ohio, 1942), p. 68, *note* 37.

[5]Fort Ascension, renamed Fort Massac, was built in 1757, abandoned by the French in 1764, and rebuilt and occupied by a United States garrison during the 1794 campaign. Clarence Alvord and Clarence E. Carter, editors, *The Critical Period, 1763-1765* (Springfield, Ill., Illinois State Historical Library, 1915), p. 3n. On the present site of Metropolis, Illinois. Schlarman, *op. cit.*, p. 342.

miles below the mouth of the Cherokee river.[1] The country 25 miles from the Wabash begins again to be mountainous, being the north-west end of the Apalachian [Appalachian] mountains, which entirely terminate a small distance from the river northerly. They are here between 50 and 60 miles across, and are scarpt, rocky precipices, below them no more high lands to be seen to the westward as far as those that border on the Mexican provinces. The French fixed a post here,[2] to secure their traders against the Cherokees; and it would be proper for the English to have one on the same spot, to prevent an illicit trade being carried on up the Wabash.

Hunters from this fort, may get any quantity of buffaloes, and salt from the Saline, with very little trouble or expense.

The river Ohio is here,[3] that is, from the entrance[4] of the Cherokee river,[5] between 700 and 800 yards wide. There is no proper spot for a post nearer the Cherokee river above, or on the Missisippi [Mississippi] below, but this; as the grounds on the banks of the Ohio begin to be very low. The current of the river towards the Missisippi is very still, and may be easily ascended, if affairs are any ways doubtful at or near the Ilinois [Illinois].

The 7th, we arrived at the fork[6] of the Ohio, in latitude 36° 43'. The gentle Ohio is pushed back by the impetuous stream of the Missisippi [Mississippi], where the muddy white water of the latter, is to be seen above 200 yards up the former. Examined the ground for several miles within the fork: it is an aggregation of mud and dirt, interspersed with marsh, and some ponds of water, and is in high times of the Missisippi [Mississippi] overflowed, which is the case with the other sides of both the Ohio and it. The mouth of the Ohio is 1164 miles from Fort Pitt.

The 9th and 10th of August, stayed at the mouth of the Ohio. The 10th, began to ascend the Missisippi [Mississippi], whose rapid stream had broke through the country, and divided it every where with a number of islands. The low lands on each side continue eight leagues upwards, when it becomes broken, and small ridges appear the rest of the way to Kuskuskies [Kaskaskia]:[7] there are many islands in this distance, some of which are entirely rock.

---

[1]Tennessee River.
[2]Fort Massac.
[3]*Ibid.*
[4]Near Paducah, Kentucky.
[5]Tennessee River.
[6]At present Cairo, Illinois.

[7]Indian village, *Kaskaskia*, was located at the mouth of Kaskaskia River near the site of the present town of Kaskaskia, Randolph County, Illinois. The Kaskaskias, a tribe of the Illinois, lived here from about 1700 to 1832. This tribe with remnants of the Weas and Piankashaws are now known officially as the Peorias. Hodge, *op. cit.*, I, 662.

The island of La Tour[1] is six leagues below the Kuskuskies [Kaskaskia] river, which is 31 leagues from the fork of the Ohio.

The principal stream of the Missisippi [Mississippi] is from 500 to 700 yards wide, but it is scarcely ever to be seen together, and some small parts are above a mile distant from one another. The principal stream likewise often shifts, as well as the depth of the channel, which make the pilotage of the river difficult, and boats often get aground in ascending, when endeavouring to avoid the rapid current.

The 19th, in the morning, arrived at the small river of the Kuskuskies [Kaskaskia], 80 yards wide at its mouth; it is deep; carries five feet water up to the village, which is two leagues from the mouth of the river, and is said to be navigable 50 leagues further up. The high grounds before-mentioned skirt along the south side of the Kuskuskies [Kaskaskia] River, come opposite to the village, and continue along northerly, in a chain nearly parallel to the east branch of the Missisippi [Mississippi], at the distance of two or three miles from it. The space between is level, mostly open, and of the richest kind of soil, in which the inhabitants of the Ilinois [Illinois] raise their grain, &c.

The Kuskuskies [Kaskaskia] village is on the plain; it consists of 80 houses, well built, mostly of stone, with gardens, and large lots. The inhabitants generally live well, and have large stocks of cattle and hogs.

The road to Fort Chartres[2] is along the plain, passing in some places near the chain of rocky height above-mentioned. The distance to the front is 18 miles. The road passes through the Indian village of the Keskesquois [Kaskaskias],[3] of fifteen cabbins; also, through a French one, called Prairi de Roché [Prairie du Rocher],[4] in which are 14 families: this last is three miles from Fort Chartres; between which is the village

---

[1]Unidentified.

[2]The new Fort Chartres, built near the site of the first fort, was completed in 1755. By the terms of the Treaty of Peace of 1763 it came into British possession in 1765, and was renamed Fort Cavendish. The fort was abandoned and destroyed by the British in 1772. Lawrence H. Gipson, *The British Empire Before the American Revolution* (New York, Alfred A. Knopf, 1936-), IV, 145; Alvord, *The New Regime, op. cit.*, p. 123n. The foundation of Fort Chartres has been cleared and repaired and the powder magazine has been restored. These remains and exact reproductions of other parts of the fort may be viewed in the Illinois Fort Chartres State Park, located four miles from Prairie du Rocher,

Illinois. Federal Writers' Project. Illinois, *Illinois, A Descriptive and Historical Guide* . . . (Chicago, A. C. McClurg & Co., 1939), p. 496.

[3]It is interesting to note that in addition to the French and Indian village of Kaskaskia, there was also a small Indian village in this vicinity.

[4]Founded about 1725 on lands granted to Pierre Dugué Boisbriant, builder of the first Fort Chartres. Gipson, *The British Empire, op. cit.*, IV, 124. For location of Prairie de Roche and other French and Indian establishments in the Illinois Country see: "Plan des Differents Villages Francois dans le Pays des Illynois. . . ." *Op. cit.*, map opposite page 126. This early French village was on the present site of Prairie du Rocher, Randolph County, Illinois.

called l'Etablissement,[1] mostly deserted, and the inhabitants removed to Misaini [Misère],[2] on the west branch[3] of the river, a little higher up[4] the Kuskuskies [Kaskaskia].

The 20th of August, arrived at Fort Chartres, which is well imagined and finished. It has four bastions of stone masonry, designed defensible against musquetry. The barracks are also of masonry, commodious and elegant. The fort is large enough to contain 400 men, but may be defended by one third of that number against Indians.

Visited Kyashshie [Cahokia],[5] 45 miles distant from Fort Chartres, and is the uppermost settlement on our side. In this rout we pass l'petit village,[6] five miles from Fort Chartres, formerly inhabited by 12, but now by one family only. The abandoned houses are most of them well built, and are left in good order. The ground is excellent for grain, and a sufficiency cleared for 100 men.

At Kyaboshie [Cahokia] are 40 families of French, who live well, and so might three times the number, as there is a great quantity of clear land near it: there are likewise 20 cabbins of the Periorie [Peoris] Indians left here; the rest, and best part of them, are removed to the French side, two miles below Point Court [Pain Court].[7] Wheat thrives better here than at Kuskuskies [Kaskaskia], owing, probably, to its being more northerly by near a degree.

The village of Point Court [Pain Court] is pleasantly situated on a high bank, which forms the western bank of the Missisippi; it is three miles higher up than Kyaboskie [Cahokia], has already 50 families, chiefly supported from thence. At this place, found Mr. Le Clef,[8] the principal Indian trader, (he resides here) who takes such good measures, that the whole trade of the Missouri, that of the Missisippi [Mississippi] northward, and that of the nations near le Baye,[9] Lake Machigan

[1]Nouvelle Chartres, later called Cavendish, a village around Fort Chartres. Alvord, *The New Regime, op. cit.*, pp. 154n, 298.

[2]Ste. Genevieve, on the west bank of the Missisippi nearly opposite Kaskaskia. Gipson, *op. cit.*, map opposite page 126. This ancient village was situated, on what was once the river's bank, about three miles below the present town of Ste. Genevieve, Missouri. Writers' Program. Missouri, *Missouri, a Guide to the "Show Me" State* (New York, Duell, Sloan and Pearce (1941), p. 521.

[3]According to the official copy, "on the bank" not "on the west branch." Great Britain. Public Record Office, C. O. 5: 85/128.

[4]"than" not "up." *Ibid.*

[5]The Indian town on the present site of Cahokia,

near the southern limits of East St. Louis, Illinois. In 1721 this town was second in importance among the Illinois. Hodge, *op. cit.*, I, 185.

[6]St. Philippe, founded about 1725 on lands granted to Philippe Francois Renault. Gipson, *The British Empire, op. cit.*, IV, 124. This village was probably near the present site of Renault, Monroe County, Illinois.

[7]A French village or trading post founded early in 1764 by Pierre Laclede Liguest on the present site of St. Louis, Missouri. Pain Court was the nickname for Laclede's settlement.

[8]Pierre Laclede Liguest, the founder of St. Louis. Alvord, *The Critical Period, op. cit.*, p. 127n.

[9]Green Bay, Wisconsin. Alvord, *The New Regime, op. cit.*, index *Green Bay*.

[Michigan] and Saint Josepho [Joseph],[1] by the Ilinois [Illinois] River, is entirely brought to him. He is sensible and clever; has a good education; is very active, and will give us some trouble before we get the parts of this trade that belong to us into our hands. Our possession of the Ilinois [Illinois] is only useful to us at present in one respect; it shews the Indian nations our superiority over the French, to whom they can thence perceive we give law; this is dearly bought to us, by the expence and inconvenience of supporting it. The French carry on the trade all around us by land and water. First, up the Missisippi [Mississippi], and to the lakes by Ouisconsia [Wisconsin], Foxes,[2] Chicegou [Chicago] and Ilinois [Illinois] Rivers. Secondly, up the Ohio to the Wabash Indians; and even the small quantity of skins and furrs that the Kuskuskies [Kaskaskias] and Picarias [Peoris] (who are also on our side) get by hunting, is carried under our nose to Misere[3] and Pain Court.[4]

A garrison at the Ilinois [Illinois] River, and a post at le Baye,[5] will partly prevent the first; and one at Massiac [Massac] will, as has been said, stop their intercourse with the people on the Wabash, who consist of several nations.

Cooped up at Fort Chartres only, we make a foolish figure; hardly have the dominion of the country, or as much credit with the inhabitants as to induce them to give us any thing for money, while our neighbours have plenty on trust.

The French have large boats of 20 tons, rowed with 20 oars, which will go in *seventy odd days* from New Orleans to the Ilinois [Illinois]. These boats go to the Ilinois [Illinois] twice a year, and are not half loaded on their return: was there any produce worth sending to market, they could carry it at no great expence. They, however, carry lead, the produce of a mine[6] on the French side of the river, which yields but a small quantity, as they have not hands to work it. These boats, in times of the floods, which happen only in May and June, go down to New Orleans from the Ilinois [Illinois] in 14 and 16 days.

Distances from Fort Pitt in Latitude 40° 26' to the Mouth of the Ohio, in Latitude 36° 43', taken by Captain Harry Gordon, Chief Engineer in America, on his Passage down the River Ohio, undertaken by Order in 1766; together with the Latitude of some of the most remarkable Places which he took at the same Time, viz.

[1] Potawatomis lived on St. Joseph River near the south end of Lake Michigan. A French Mission was established there in 1688. The inhabitants were known as St. Joseph Indians. Hodge, *op. cit.*, II, 412.

[2] Fox River in Wisconsin and Fox River in Illinois.

[3] Ste. Genevieve.

[4] St. Louis.

[5] Green Bay, Wisconsin.

[6] Near Ste. Genevieve, Missouri. Alvord, *The Critical Period, op. cit.*, p. 210.

	Latitude	Miles	Miles
Logg's Town – – – – – – – – – – –		–	18½
Big Beaver Creek – – – – – – – –		10¾	29¼
Little Beaver Creek – – – – – – – –		12¾	42
Yellow Creek – – – – – – – – –		10½	52
Mingo Town – – – – – – – – – –		19¾	71½
Two Creeks – – – – – – – – – –		–	72¼
Long Reach – – – – – – – – – –		51	123¼
End of Long Reach – – – – – – –		14¾	138
Muskingum Run – – – – – – –	39° 16′	23	161
Little Kanhawa River – – – – – –		12¾	172¾
Hockhocking River – – – – – – –		13¼	126
Big Kanhawa River – – – – – – –		80¼	266¼
Big Guyandot – – – – – – – – –		41¾	308
Big Sandy Creek – – – – – – –		13	321
Scioto River – – – – – – – – –	38° 22′	45	366
Big Buffalo Lick, one mile eastward of the Ohio – – – – – – – – –		24	390
Large Island, divided by a gravelly beach – –		20½	410½
Little Mineami River – – – – – –		81¾	492¼
Licking Creek – – – – – – – –		8	500¼
Great Mineami River – – – – – –		26¾	527½
The place where the elephant's bones were found – – – – – – –		32¾	560¼
Kentucké River – – – – – – – –		44¼	604½
The Falls – – – – – – – – – –	38° 8′	77½	682
Where the Low Country begins – – – –		155¾	837¾
Beginning of the Five Islands – – – –		37¾	875¼
Large river on the east side – – – –		27	902¼
Very large island in the middle of the river – – – – – – – – – – –		58	690¼ [1]
Wabash River – – – – – – – –		38¾	999½
Big rock and cave on the west side – –		42¾	1042¼
Shawana River – – – – – – – –		52½	1094¾
Cherokee River – – – – – – – –		13	1107¾
Fort Massiac – – – – – – – – –		11	1118¾
The mouth of the Ohio River – – – –	36° 43′	46	1164

[1] 990¼

NUMBER V.

EXTRACT FROM MR. LEWIS EVAN'S JOURNAL. 1743.

OUR journey[1] from Philadelphia, for about seventy miles, was through the English and Dutch settlements to the Blue Mountains.[2] The way we took was up the Schuyl-kill River; and we crossed it to the west, about four miles above Monotawny [Manatawny] Creek. Then by a new road over the Flyeing-hills[3] into Tulpohoocking [Tulpehocken] Vale,[4] which is a very beautiful and healthy bottom, extending under different names from Hudson's River to Georgia, about two hundred miles short of Apalachy [Apalachicola] Bay. It is generally eight, ten, or twelve miles broad; bounded on the S.E. by the Flyeing-hills, on the N.W. by the Blue or Apalachian [Appalachian] Mountains. This south-eastern ridge is called in New York the Highlands; in New Jersey, Mascapetcunk [Musconetcong]; in Pennsylvania the Oley Hills and Flyeing-hills; in Virginia the Blue Ridge.

The reader, who is curious in the knowledge of this new country, may on this subject refer to J. Bartram's journal of the same journey, published by Whiston and White, London, 1751 F f

Tulpohoocking [Tulpehocken] is settled by High-Dutchers,[5] who have fine plantations; raise great quantity of wheat, and manufacture it into very fine flour, which they bring in the spring and fall seventy or eighty miles to Philadelphia.

About twenty-four miles west of the waggon-ford over Schuyllkill, is the passage[6] through the first ridge of the Kittocktinny [Kittatinny] Mountains: it is easily known by its lying west of the bluff head[7] of a mountain: it is also a mile of ascent, and as much descent and steep.

[1]Lewis Evans and John Bartram accompanied Conrad Weiser on his mission to the Six Nations at Onondaga for William Gooch, lieutenant governor of Virginia. The attack of Virginians upon Indians of the Six Nations who had penetrated into the Shenandoah Valley threatened to disturb the peace between the Six Nations and the Virginians. Conrad Weiser, the trusted Indian interpreter of Pennsylvania was sent to confer with the Iroquois and thus prevent the conflict. A conflict with Virginia would involve Pennsylvania as well. It was not the Six Nations but the Shawnee under French influence who were expected to use the ruse of loyalty to the Six Nations as an excuse to attack all white men. Wallace, *op. cit.*, pp. 145-54.

[2]A range of the Alleghenies called Kittatinny or Blue Mountains.

[3]A continuation of South Mountain which terminates at Reading, Pennsylvania.

[4]Tulpehocken or Lebanon Valley. Between Kittatinny and South Mountains. Reading is the eastern and Harrisburg the western entrance to the valley. Wallace, *op. cit.*, p. 36.

[5]Germans who emigrated, for the most part, from southern Germany. In contrast to Low German the dialect of the inhabitants of the Lowlands.

[6]Great Swatara Gap in Lebanon County. Reichel, *Memorials, op. cit.*, p. 80n.

[7]Named Thurnstein by Conrad Weiser. *Ibid.*, p. 82. Present Peters Mountain. *Pennsylvania Magazine of History and Biography, op. cit.*, II (1878), 426n.

From the top of this pass we have a view of a vale ten miles across, varied here and there with swelling hills, some of them appearing at a distance like clear land, but they are covered with dwarf oak, in about elbow or shoulder high: these oaks bear acorns, and the best gall nuts of any we have. Count Zinzindorff [Zinzendorf] gave this vale the name of *Saint Anthony's Wilderness;*[1] and designs, as Mr. Conrad Weisar [Weiser][2] tells me, to bring over some Germans to settle it. The soil is but poor and ordinary, except on the Swartaro [Swatara] Creek; and there is at present no practicable road over the mountain, by which it may communicate with the settled part of the province. The vegetation is at present chiefly of spruce fir, white oak, and some pine: the native wood grass grows here in great abundance, but this always dies with the first frost.

In this St. Anthony's Wilderness, we crossed the branches of the *Swartaro* [Swatara] Creek. At the conflux of two of these branches, is a small Indian settlement, of five Delaware families. The westernmost branch of the Swartaro [Swatara] comes through a ridge of the Kittock-tinny [Kittatinny] Mountains. Along the eastern banks of this creek, we passed through the first ridge of these mountains, and in one-third of a mile more we crost it to the left: we then passed upon a stony reach, and over two or three rugged barren mountains, covered with only hurtleberries, dwarf-oak, and a few pitch-pines; in six miles more, we went down a very stony deep descent to Lawrel [Laurel] Creek,[3] a rivulet, which falls into Kind Creek, about eight miles lower down. On the north sides of Lawrel [Laurel] and Kind Creeks, is a pleasant and fruitful valley two or three miles wide, varies here and there with most beautiful groves of white-pines and white oak. This would make a pretty settlement.

We came in fifteen miles travel, west along this valley, to the strait by which Kind Creek passes to the north, through one of the ridges of the mountains, into another little pleasant valley. We pass along the banks of this creek for four miles more; then leaving this creek on our left hand, the path led us through a narrow pass between two mountains, where grew the tallest white pines that I ever saw; I will not hazard my judgement to what height I guessed them to be, because it is

F f

[1]Location of St. Anthony's Wilderness. Wallace, *op. cit.*, map opposite p. 139.

[2]Conrad Weiser (1696-1760), Pennsylvania colonial Indian agent, interpreter, and official representative of the colony at many Indian conferences. In 1741 Mr. Weiser was named a justice of the peace for Lancaster County, and, in 1752 at the time of the erection of Berks County, he was made its first justice of the peace, and from 1752 to 1760 served as the first president judge of the county.

[3]Present Pine Creek. Wallace, *op. cit.*, p. 155.

so incredible. I going out, had time to measure them, and when I returned I had lost my triangle.

A mile beyond this gap we passed by a path, or Indian road, led N.W. directly over the mountains to *Shamokin*;[1] but this is little frequented, on account of the great steeps over which it leads. Passing thence three miles, along a continued slant of shrub and white-oak, we came to more ridges: our path led us up some of these, and along the tops of others for twelve miles; we then came to a creek which falls into the Susquahanna [Susquehanna] River, and has at its confluence an island in the mouth of it. This creek is called Moxenay [Mahanoy], and hath some old Indian fields on its banks, and near it.

It is now the Scite of Sunbury, the county town of Northumberland county, 1775

We crossed this creek, and came along a rich border, about two miles to the Susquahanna [Susquehanna] River. This river is here about a mile and a half wide, is full of islands, and glides with a bright and easy current over a stony and gravelly bottom, and may be easily forded. Passing up along the east side of this river, we came under a high peaked mountain, here we struck off to the right, and for twelve months[2] our path led us over several ordinary hills, and across several vales, not much better, to a hill just above Shamokin: in one of these we saw the appearance of an iron mine. Descending this hill, it was so steep, we were obliged to hold the horse which carried our baggage, both by the head and tail, to prevent his tumbling head-long: at the bottom we crossed the creek[3] on which Shamokin is, and came to the town.

This Indian town is a settlement or dwelling-place of Delaware Indians, situate on the confluence of two main branches of the Susquahanna [Susquehanna] River. Its latitude is 40° 45'. Here are about *** wigwaums,[4] or Indian huts, lying pretty near together, and many more scattered here and there, over a very fruitful spot of ground, of about seven or eight hundred acres. This is encompassed with the river on one side, and enclosed in by the mountains on the other. The freshes of the river, which run with great impetuosity, generally when they come down lay the land under water, although it lies 15 or 20 feet higher than the common surface of the river.

Ff

"*The observations and reflections which Lewis Evans made in his passage through these mountains,*[5] *called by the Indians by a name which imports Endless Mountains, to Goosberry-hill, the westernmost ridge of*

De

---

[1]Present site of Sunbury, Pennsylvania.
[2]Miles.
[3]Shamokin Creek.
[4]There were eight cabins in Shamokin at this time. Bartram, *op. cit.*, p. 14.

[5]The northerly continuation of the Allegheny Mountains terminates in Tioga County, New York. Franklin B. Hough, *Gazetteer of the State of New York* (Albany, N.Y., Andrew Boyd, 1872), p. 650.

them are either marked in the map or inserted in the analysis, where a general description of these mountains is given."

D e   From Goosberry-hill, travelling N.N.E. through a most beautiful and fruitful country about eight and forty miles, we reached the first town[1] of the Onondâga Indians. This country is varied with pleasant swelling knolls, brooks and little lakes. In its vegitation it abounds with sweet-maple, linden, birch, elm, white pines and spruce in some places; and with gooseberry under-woods on the north side of all the hills.

    At twenty-five miles we passed between a lake,[2] at the head of one of the lesser branches of *the Susquahanna* [Susquehanna], and a mountain called by the Indians *Onugareckny*.[3] From this lake canoes may go down the Susquahanna [Susquehanna] to the settlements of

D e Pennsylvania with a fresh. On this mountain the Indians, as their tradition says, first found Indian corn or maize, tobacco, squashes and pompions.

    In 18 miles further travel, we passed over a mountain, which we called Table Mountain.[4] This is the height of the land, for on the other side of it, the rivers run north and west, and fall into the lakes.

D e   In 10 miles further travel down this hill, we came to the great council-residence of the *Five Nation Confederacy* at Onondada [Onondaga].[5] This stands upon a creek to S.W. of a little lake of the same name. On the sides of this lake are salt springs, very strongly impregnated with that mineral, so that bushes on the margins hang glittering with the salt like splendid icicles.

    This lake,[6] which is about five miles long, and a mile and a half broad, falls at the N.W. into the Seneca River. This river having

C e received the waters of this lake, holds on its waters in a slow still stream for about ten miles northerly. The river which comes W. from the Oheyda [Oneida] Lake joins it, and they hold on in the same still way a little further, and then, with rapids and over-falls tumble into the great Lake Ontario by Oswêgo.

C e   Oswêgo is rather a collection of trading huts, built for the residence of the Indian traders during the mart, or trading season, than a fixt habitation of settlers. It consists of about seventy logg-houses, in two rows, forming a street, on the west shore of the river, at its mouth. The fort stood at the point next the Lake. The latitude of this place is 43° 22′.

---

[1]Cachiadachse. Wallace, *op. cit.*, p. 159.
[2]One of the Tully Lakes. Wallace, *op. cit.*, p. 158.
[3]Not identified.
[4]Onondaga West Hill. Joshua Clark, *Onondaga; or*
Reminiscences of Earlier and Later Times . . . (Syracuse, Stoddard and Babcock, 1849), I, 323.
[5]Present site of Syracuse, New York.
[6]Onondaga Lake.

NUMBER VI.

A JOURNAL.[1]

OF Christopher Gist's[2] journey, began from Col. Cresap's,[3] at the *old town*[4] *on Potomack* [Potomac] *river, Maryland*, October 31, Old town G h 1750, continued *down the Ohio*, within 15 *miles of the Falls*[5] *thereof;* and from thence to *Roanoak* [Roanoke] *river in North Carolina*, where he arrived May 19, 1751; undertaken on the account of the Ohio company,[6] and by the instructions of their committee.

Instructions given Mr. Christopher Gist by the committee of the Gist's instructions Ohio company, the 11th day of September 1750.

You are to go out as soon as possible to the westward of the great mountains, and carry with you such a number of men as you think necessary, in order to search out and discover the lands upon the *river Ohio* (and other adjoining branches of the *Missisippi* [Mississippi]) down as low as the *great Falls* thereof.

You are particularly to observe the ways and passes through all the mountains you cross, and take an exact account of the soil, quality, and product of the land; the width and depth of the rivers, and the several falls belonging to them; together with the courses and bearings of the rivers and mountains as near as you conveniently can: You are also to observe what nations of Indians inhabit there, their To discover the nations of Indians, strength and numbers, who they trade with, and in what commodities they deal. and their trade.

When you find a large quantity of good level land, such as you think trade. will suit the company, you are to measure the breadth of it, in three or four different places, and take the courses of the river and mountains on which it binds, in order to judge the quantity; you are to fix the beginning and bounds in such a manner, that they may be easily found again

---

[1]This *Journal* was edited by Wm. Darlington in 1893. Christopher Gist, "*Journals with Historical, Geographical, and Ethnological notes* . . . " by William M. Darlington (Pittsburgh, J. R. Weldin & Co., 1893).

[2]See *note* 2, p. 26.

[3]Thomas Cresap (1700?-1790?), Indian trader and agent, and member of the Ohio Company of Virginia. For biographical sketch read Kenneth Bailey, *The Ohio Company of Virginia* ... (Glendale,

California, The Arthur H. Clark Company, 1939), pp. 46-49.

[4]Located on the north bank of the Potomac opposite Green Spring, Maryland. Gist, *Journals* (Darlington ed.), *op. cit.*, p. 90; Scull's Map of Pennsylvania (1770), *op. cit.*

[5]Falls in the Ohio at Louisville, Kentucky.

[6]Ohio Company of Virginia. Christopher Gist was an agent for this company.

by your description; the nearer in the land lies the better, provided it be good and level, but we had rather go quite down the Missisippi [Mississippi] than take mean broken land. After finding a large body of good level land, you are not to stop, but proceed farther as low as the falls of the Ohio, that we may be informed of that navigation; and you are to take an exact account of all the large bodies of good level land in the same manner as above directed, that the company may the better judge where it will be most convenient for them to take theirs.

To examine the Naviga-
tion of the Ohio to the Falls.

You are to note all the bodies of good land as you go along, though there is not a sufficient quantity for the Company's grant; but you need not be so particular in the mensuration of that, as in the large bodies.

To note all the bodies of good land

You are to draw as good a plan as you can of the country you pass through, and take an exact and particular journal of all your proceedings, and make a true report thereof to the Ohio company.

To draw a plan of the country, and keep a journal

In compliance with my instructions from the committee of the Ohio company, bearing date the 11th day of September 1750.

Gist begins his journey

Wednesday, October 31, 1750. Set out from Col. Cresap's,[1] at the *Old Town on Potomack* [Potomac] *river, in Maryland,* and went along an old Indian path,[2] N. 30 d. E. about 11 miles.

Old town

Thursday, November 1. N. 1 m. N. 30 d. E. 3 m. Here I was taken sick and stayed all night.

G h

Friday 2. N. 30 d. E. 6 m. Here I was so bad that I was not able to proceed any farther that night, but grew better in the morning.

Saturday 3. N. 3 m.[3] to *Juniatta* [Juniata], a large branch of Susquahanna [Susquehanna], where I stayed all night.

Juniatta

Sunday 4th. Crossed *Juniatta* [Juniata] and went up it S. 55 d. W. about 16 min.[4]

Monday 5th. Continued the same course S. 55 d. W. 6 m. to the top of a *large mountain, called the Allegany* [Allegheny] *Mountain;* here our path turned, and we went N. 45 d. W. 6 m. and encamped.

Allegany Mountains

Tuesday 6, Wednesday 7, and Thursday 8, had snow, and such bad weather that we could not travel; but I killed a young bear, so that we had provision enough.

---

[1]Thomas Cresap.

[2]"Gist's route from Old Town lay by the Warrior's Path along the base of the Great Warrior Mountain now known as Tussey Mountain, on the eastern side, passing through the present district of Flintstone, Allegheny County, Maryland, and the townships of Southampton, Monroe, and Providence, in Bedford County, Pennsylvania, reaching the Juniata at the Warrior's Gap, near the village of Bloody Run [Everett], Pennsylvania, eight miles east of the present town of Bedford." Gist (Darlington edition), *op. cit.,* p. 90.

[3]Eight miles not three miles. *Ibid.,* p. 32.

[4]"Miles" not "minutes." Here Pownall has interpreted "M" to be minutes not miles.

Friday 9th. Set out N. 70 d. W. about 8 min.[1] Here I crossed a creek of *Susquahanna* [Susquehanna],[2] and it raining hard, I went into an old Indian cabbin,[3] where I stayed all night.

Saturday, November 10. Rain and snow all day, but cleared away in the evening.

Sunday 11th. Set out late in the morning, N. 70 d. W. 6 m. crossing F j two forks of a creek[4] of Susquahanna [Susquehanna]; here the way being bad, I encamped and killed a turkey.

Monday 12th. Set out N. 45 d. W. 8 m. and crossed a great *Laurel* Laurel *mountain.* Mountain

Tuesday 13th. Rain and snow.

Wednesday 14th. Set out N. 45 d. W. 6 m. to *Loylhannon*,[5] an old Loylhannon Indian town on a creek of the Ohio, called *Kiskeminetas* [Kiskiminetas], Kiskeminetas then N. 1 m. N.W. 1 m. to an Indian camp on the said creek. F j

Thursday 15. The weather being bad, and I unwell, stayed here all day. The Indian, to whom this camp belonged, spoke good English, and directed me the way to his town, which is called *Shanoppin*;[6] he said it was about sixty miles, and a pretty good way.

Friday 16th. Set out S. 70 d. W. 10 m.

Saturday 17th. The same course (S 70 d. W) 15 m. to an old Indian camp.[7]

Sunday 18th. I was very sick, and sweated myself according to the Indian custom, in a sweat-house, which gave me ease, and my fever abated.

Monday 19th. Set out early in the morning the same course, (S. 70 d. F j W.) travelled very hard about twenty miles to a small Indian town of Shannoppin's the Delawares, called *Shanoppin* [Shannopin], *on the S.E. side of the* Town *river Ohio*,[8] where we rested and got corn for our horses.

Tuesday 20th. I was unwell, and stayed in this town to recover myself. While I was here I took an opportunity to set my compass privately, and took the distance across the river; for I understood it was dangerous to let a compass be seen: *the Ohio is 76 poles wide here.* There Width of the Ohio

---

[1]"Miles" not "minutes."

[2]The path led across Stoney Creek near Stoyes-town, Somerset County, Pennsylvania. This creek is a tributary of the Allegheny not the Susquehanna River. Gist (Darlington edition), *op. cit.*, p. 91.

[3]Cabin of Kickeney Paulin, a Delaware minor chief. Hanna, *op. cit.*, I, 282.

[4]Quemahoning, a branch of Stoney Creek. Gist (Darlington edition), *op. cit.*, p. 91.

[5]Loyalhanna, on the present site of Ligioner, Pennsylvania. Hanna, *op. cit.*, I, 269.

[6]On the site of present twelfth ward, Pittsburgh, Pennsylvania.

[7]Cockey or Cock Eye's Cabin on Bushy Run, Westmoreland County, Pennsylvania. Gist (Darlington edition), p. 92.

[8]Allegheny River. In early time the French considered the Allegheny River the Ohio; the English often did likewise.

Land mean   are about twenty families in this town. *The land in general from Potomack* [Potomac] *to this place is mean, stony, and broken, with here and there good spots upon the creeks and branches, but no body of it.*

Land good   Saturday 24th. Set out from *Shanoppin* [Shannopin], and swam our horses across the *Ohio*, and went down the river S. 75 d. W. 4 m. N. 75 d. W. 7 m. W. 2 m. the land from Shanoppin [Shannopin] is good along the river, but the bottoms not broad: at a distance from the river good land for farming, covered with small white and red oaks, and tolerable level: fine runs for mills, *&c.*

F k   Sunday 25th. Down the river W. 3 m. N.W. 5 m. to *Loggs Town*
Logg's Town. [Logstown]:[1] the lands for these last eight miles very rich, the bottoms
Land very   above a mile wide, but on the S.E. side scarce a mile, the hills high and
rich.   steep. In the town I found scarce any body but a parcel of reprobate Indian traders, the chief of the Indians being out hunting; here I was informed, that George Croghan[2] and Andrew Montour,[3] who were sent upon an embassy[4] from Pennsylvania to the Indians, were passed about a week before me. The people here enquiring my business; and, because I did not readily inform them, began to suspect me, saying, I was come to settle the Indian lands, and that I should never go home again safe. I found this discourse was like to be of ill consequence, so pretended to speak very slightingly of what they had said, and enquired for [George] Croghan (who is a mere idol among his countrymen, the Irish traders) and Andrew Montour, the interpreter for Pennsylvania; and told them I had a message to deliver the Indians from the king, by order of the president of Virginia, and for that reason wanted to see Mr. Montour. This made them all pretty easy (being afraid to interrupt the king's message) and obtained me quiet and respect among them; otherwise, I doubt not, they would have contrived some evil against me. I immediately wrote to Mr. Croghan by one of the traders people.

F k   Monday 26th. Though I was unwell, I preferred the woods to such
Great Beaver company; and set out from Loggs Town [Logstown][5] down the river
Creek   N.W. 6 m. to *Great Beaver Creek*, where I met one Burny Curran,[6] a

[1]Logstown, on the north bank of the Ohio River about 18 miles below Pittsburgh and near the present site of Economy, Pennsylvania. Hanna, *op. cit.*, I, 289.

[2]George Croghan (—— d. 1782). Famous Indian trader, land speculator, and deputy Indian agent under Sir Wm. Johnson.

[3]Andrew Montour, noted Indian interpreter. For sketch of his life read Hanna, *op. cit.*, I, 223-46.

[4]George Croghan and Andrew Montour were sent

to the Ohio Country with a small present for the Twightwees; and to inform the Indians that a present prepared for them by the government of Pennsylvania would be distributed at Logstown in the spring of 1751. *Colonial Records of Pennsylvania, op. cit.*, V, 496-98, 517-24.

[5]See *note* 1, this page.

[6]Barnaby Curran, an Indian trader. Curran, at one time, was employed by Hugh Parker for the Ohio Company and was later a guide to George

trader for the Ohio company, and we continued together as far as Muskingum.[1] The bottoms upon the river below Loggs Town [Logstown] are very rich, but narrow; the high land pretty good, but not very rich; the land upon Beaver Creek of the same kind. From this place we left the Ohio to the S.E. and travelled across the country.

Tuesday 27th. Set out from the E. side of *Beaver Creek*, N.W. 6 m. W. 4 m. upon these two last courses very good high land, and not much broken, fit for farming. Land very good.

Wednesday 28th. Rained, and we could not travel.

Thursday 29th. W. 6 m. through good land; the same course continued 6 m. farther, through very broken land: here I found myself pretty well recovered, and being in want of provision, went out and killed a deer.

Friday 30. Set out S. 45 d. W. 12 m. crossed the last branch of *Beaver Creek*,[2] where one of Curran's[3] men and myself killed twelve turkeys.

Saturday, December 1st. N. 45 d. W. 10 m.[4] the land high and tolerable good.

Sunday 2d. N. 45 d. W. 8 m.[5] the same sort of land, but near the creeks bushy, and very full of thorns.

Monday 3d. Killed a deer, and stayed in our camp all day.

Tuesday 4th. Set out late S. 45 d. W. about 4 m. here I killed three fine fat deer; so that tho' we were eleven in company, we had great plenty of provisions.

Wednesday 5th. Set out down the side of a creek, called *Elk's Eye Creek*,[6] S. 70 d. W. 6 m. good land, but void of timber; meadows upon the creek, and fine runs for mills. F1 Elk's Eye Creek No timber.

Thursday 6th. Rained all day, so that we were obliged to continue in our camp.

Friday 7th. Set out S.W. 8 min.[7] crossing *Elk's Eye Creek* to a *town of the Ottawa's*,[8] a nation of French Indians; an old Frenchman, Ottawa's Town

Washington on his trip to Venango in 1753. Hanna, *op. cit.*, II, 330.

[1]Muskingum or Conchake, a Wyandot town at the forks of the Muskingum River. Near the present site of Coshocton, Ohio. *Ibid.*, II, 188, 268.

[2]West branch of Little Beaver Creek in southern Columbiana County, Ohio. Gist (Darlington edition), *op. cit.*, p. 103.

[3]Barnaby Curran.

[4]To a point near present Hanover, Columbiana

County, Ohio. Gist (Darlington edition), *ibid.*, p. 103.

[5]To a point near Bayard, Columbiana County, Ohio. *Ibid.*

[6]Big Sandy Creek, a tributary of the Tuscawaras River. *Ibid.*

[7]Miles.

[8]At the junction of the Big Sandy and Tuscawaras Rivers near the present town of Bolivar, Ohio. Fort Laurens, in Revolutionary times, was located here. Gist (Darlington edition), *op. cit.*, pp. 103-05.

named Mark Coonce,[1] who had married an Indian woman of the Six Nations, lived here. The Indians were all out hunting; the old man was civil to me; but after I was gone to my camp, upon his understanding I came from Virginia, he called me the Big Knife.[2] There are not above six or eight families belonging to this town.

Saturday 8th. Stayed in the town.

Sunday 9th. Set out down the *Elk's Eye Creek* S. 45 d. W. 6 m. to *Margaret's Creek*,[3] *a branch of Elk's Eye Creek*.

Margaret's Creek

Monday 10th. The same course S. 45 d. W. 2 m. to a large creek.

Tuesday 11th. The same course twelve miles; killed two deer.

Wednesday 12th. The same course eight miles; encamped by the side of *Elk's Eye Creek*.

Thursday 13. Rained all day.

F M
Muskingum
Lands broken
Wiandots
divided.

Friday 14th. Set out W. 5 m. to *Muskingum*,[4] a town of the Wiandots [Wyandots]. The land upon *Elk's Eye Creek* is in general very broken, the bottoms narrow. The Wiandots [Wyandots][5] or little Mingoes are divided between the French and English; one half of them adhere to the first; and the other half are firmly attached to the latter: the town of Muskingum consists of about one hundred families; when we came within sight of it, we perceived English colours hoisted on the king's house, and at George Croghan's,[6] upon enquiring the reason, I was informed, that the French had lately taken several English traders;[7] and that Mr. Croghan had ordered all the white men to come into this town,[8] and had sent expresses to the traders of the lower towns, and among the Picqualinees [Pickawillanys]; and the Indians had sent to their people to come to council about it.

Saturday 15, and Sunday 16. Nothing remarkable happened.

Monday 17. Two traders belonging to Mr. Croghan came into town,

[1]Probably Macoonce or Maconce, a French interpreter at Saguin's (Seguin's) trading house on the Cuyahoga River. Hanna, *op. cit.*, I, 333-34.

[2]Assarigoa, or Long Knife, was the Iroquois name for the Virginians.

[3]Present Sugar Creek which empties into the Tuscarawas River at Dover, Ohio. Gist (Darlington edition), *op. cit.*, p. 105.

[4]See *note* 1, p. 175.

[5]A dependent people who, in order to escape destruction by the Iroquois in 1639, gained refuge with the Huron Confederation. Hodge, *op. cit.*, I, 584.

[6]George Croghan had a trading post at Muskingum. Gist (Darlington edition), *op. cit.*, p. 108.

[7]The four English traders were Luke Irwin [Erwin] of Philadelphia, Joseph Fortiner [Faulkner] of New York, Thomas Bourke [Burk] of Lancaster, and George Pathon [John Pattin] of Wilmington. All were traders, licensed in Philadelphia. For full details read "Extract of the interrogatories of the four English traders, taken upon the territories of France." In *The Conduct of the Late Ministry, or A Memorial; Containing a Summary of Facts with their Vouchers, in Answer to The Observations, sent by the English Ministry, to the Courts of Europe...* (London, W. Bizet, 1757), pp. 92-106.

[8]Muskingum.

and informed us, that two[1] of his people were taken by forty Frenchmen, and twenty French Indians, who had carried them, with seven horse-loads of skins, to a new fort[2] that the French were building on one of the branches of Lake Erie.

Tuesday 18th. I acquainted Mr. Croghan and Andrew Montour with my business with the Indians, and talked much of a regulation of trade, with which they were pleased, and treated me very well.

Talk of a regulation in the trade.

Wednesday 19th to Monday 24th. Nothing remarkable.

Tuesday 25th. This being Christmas-day, I intended to read prayers; but after inviting some of the white men, they informed each other of my intentions; and being of several different persuasions, and few of them inclined to hear any good, they refused to come: but one Thomas Burney, a black-smith, who is settled there, went about and talked to them, and then several of them came; and Andrew Montour invited several of the well-disposed Indians who came freely. By this time the morning was spent, and I had given over all thoughts of them; but seeing them come, to oblige all and offend none, I stood up and said, Gentlemen, I have no design or intention to give offence to any particular sect or religion; but as our king indulges us all in a liberty of conscience, and hinders none of you in the exercise of your religious worship, so it would be unjust in you to endeavour to stop the propagation of his. The doctrine of salvation, faith and good works, is what I only propose to treat of, as I find it extracted from the homilies of the church of England, which I then read to them in the best manner I could; and after I had done, the interpreter told the Indians what I had read, and that it was the true faith which the great King, and his church, recommended to his children: the Indians seemed well pleased, and came up to me, and returned me their thanks, and then invited me to live among them, and gave me a name in their language, Annosannoah: the interpreter told me this was the name of a good man that had formerly lived among them, and their King said that must be always my name, for which I returned them thanks; but, as to living among them, I excused myself by saying, I did not know whether the governor would give me leave; and if he did, the French would come and carry me away, as they had done the English traders; to which they answered, I might bring great guns and make a fort, that they had now left the French, and

Christmas-day, Gist proposes to read prayers.

Indians attend

Gist reads prayers

Indians much pleased, give him an Indian name;

desire a fort to be built;

---

[1]Probably two of the four traders mentioned in note 7, p. 176.

[2]Probably "Fort Sandoski, which is a small Pallisadoed Fort, with about 20 Men lying on the South side of Lake Erie, and was built the latter end of the Year 1750." "A Journal or Account of the Capture of John Pattin." *Pennsylvania Magazine, op. cit.*, LXV (1941), 427.

were very desirous of being instructed in the principles of Christianity, that they liked me very well, and wanted me to marry them after the christian manner, and baptize their children; and then, they said, they would never desire to return to the French, or suffer them or their priests to come near them more; for they loved the English, but had seen little religion among them. Some of their great men came and wanted me to baptize their children, for as I had read to them, and appeared to talk about religion, they took me to be a minister of the gospel; upon which I desired Mr. Montour,[1] the interpreter, to tell them that no minister could venture to baptize any children, until those that were to be sureties for them, were well instructed in the faith themselves; and that was according to the great King's religion, in which he desired his children should be instructed, and we dare not do it in any other way than by law established; but I hoped, if I could not be admitted to live among them, that the great King would send them proper ministers to exercise that office among them, at which they seemed well pleased; and one of them went and brought me his book, which was a kind of almanack contrived for them by the French, in which the days of the week were so marked, that by moving a pin every morning, they kept a pretty exact account of the time, to shew me that he understood me, and that he and his family always observed the Sabbath day.

desire to be married, and have their children baptized

Wednesday 26th. This day a woman, who had been long a prisoner, and had deserted, being retaken, and brought into the town on Christmas Eve, was put to death in the following manner. They carried her without the town, and let her loose; and when she attempted to run away, the persons appointed for that purpose, pursued her, and struck her on the ear, on the right side of her head, which beat her flat on her face to the ground; they then stuck her several times through the back with a dart, to the heart, scalped her, and threw the scalp in the air, and another cut off her head. Thus the dismal spectacle lay till the evening, and then Barney [Barnaby] Curran desired leave to bury her, which he and his men, and some of the Indians did, just at dark.

A woman who was a prisoner put to death.

Thursday 27th to Thursday, January 3d, 1775 [1750-51]. Nothing remarkable happened in the town.

Friday 4th, one Taaf,[2] an Indian trader, came to town from near Lake Erie, and informed us that the Wiandots [Wyandots][3] had advised

---

[1] Andrew Montour.
[2] Michael Teaffe (Taffe) was associated in the Indian trade with William Trent, Robert Callendar, and George Croghan. Volwiler, *op. cit.*, p. 39.
[3] Wyandots or Hurons.

him to keep clear of the Outawais [Ottawas] (a nation of Indians firmly attached to the French, living near the lakes) and told him that the branches of the lakes were claimed by the French; but that all the branches of the Ohio belong to them, and their brothers the English; and that the French had no business there, and that it was expected that the other part of the Wiandots [Wyandots] would desert the French, and come over to the English interest, and join their brethren on Elk's Eye Creek, and build a strong fort and town there.

Saturday 5th. The weather still continuing bad, I stayed in the town to recruit my horses; and though corn was very dear among the Indians, I was obliged to feed them well, or run the risque of losing them, as I had a great way to travel.

Wednesday 9th. The wind southerly, and the weather something warmer: This day came into town two traders from among the Picqualinnees [Pickawillany] (a tribe of the Tawightwis [Twightwees]) and brought news that another English trader[1] was also taken prisoner by the French; and that three French soldiers had deserted and come over to the English, and surrendered themselves to some of the traders of the Pick town;[2] and that the Indians would have put them to death, to revenge their taking our traders, but as the French had surrendered themselves to the English, they would not let the Indians hurt them; but had ordered them to be sent under the care of three of our traders, and delivered at this town[3] to George Croghan. *Traders protect three French deserters from the Indians.*

Thursday, January the 10th. Wind still at South, and warm.

Friday 11th. This day came into town an Indian from near the lakes, and confirmed the news we had heard.

Saturday 12th. We sent away our people towards the lower town,[4] intending to follow them the next morning; and this evening we went into council in the Wiandot [Wyandot] king's house; The council had been put off a long time, expecting some of their great men in, but few of them came; and this evening some of the king's council being a little disordered with liquor, no business could be done, but we were desired to come next day.

Sunday 13th. No Business done.

Monday 14th. This day George Croghan, by the assistance of Andrew Montour, acquainted the king and council of this nation

---

[1]Probably John Pattin who was taken captive by the French in November, 1750.

[2]Picktown (Pickawillany), an important trading center on the Great Miami River near the present site of Piqua, Miami County, Ohio, Hodge, *op. cit.*, II, 242.

[3]Muskingum.

[4]An Indian town on White Woman's Creek.

Acquaints the Indians the king had sent them a present, and invites them to come down to receive it. Indians would not give an answer till a full council should assemble.

(presenting them four strings of wampum) that the great King over the water, their Roggony (father) had sent, under the care of the governor of Virginia, their brother, a large present of goods, which were now landed safe in Virginia; and that the governor had sent me to invite them to come and see him, and partake of their father's charity, to all his children on the branches of Ohio.

In answer to which one of the chiefs stood up and said, "That their king and all of them, thanked their brother the governor of Virginia, for his care, and me for bringing them the news; but they could not give an answer, until they had a full, or general council of the several nations of Indians, which could not be till next spring; and so the king and council shaking hands with us, we took our leave."

F m White Woman's Creek

Tuesday 15th. We left *Muskingum* and went W. 5 m. to the *White Woman's Creek*,[1] on which is a small town.[2] This white woman was taken away from New England, when she was not above ten years old, by the French Indians. She is now upwards of fifty, has an Indian husband and several children, her name is Mary Harris;[3] she still remembers they used to be very religious in New England, and wonders how the white men can be so wicked as she has seen them in these woods.

G m Licking Creek Land rich but broken Salt ponds.

Wednesday 16th. Set out S.W. 25 m. to *Licking Creek*,[4] the land from *Muskingum* to this place, rich but broken. *Upon the North side of Licking Creek, about six miles from the mouth, are several salt licks, or ponds, formed by little streams or drains of water, clear, but of a bluish colour, and salt taste. The traders and Indians boil their meat in this water, which if proper care be not taken, will sometimes make it too salt to eat.*

Thursday 17th. Set out W. 5 m. S.W. 15 m. to a great swamp.

Friday 18th. Set out from the great swamp S.W. 15 m.

G n Hockhocking Town

Saturday 19th. W. 15 m. to *Hochocking*,[5] a small town with only four or five Delaware families.[6]

G n Maguck Town

Sunday 20th. The snow began to grow thin, and the weather warmer. Set out from *Hockhocking* S. 5 m. then W. 5 m. then S.W. 5 m. to

[1]Walhonding River. Henry Howe, *Historical Collections of Ohio* . . . (Cincinnati, Derby, Bradley & Co., 1848), pp. 115-16.
[2]White Woman's Town.
[3]Mary Harris was taken captive at Deerfield, Massachusetts on February 29, 1704. John Williams, *The Redeemed Captive returning to Zion: or, A Faithful History of Remarkable Occurrences in the Captivity and Deliverance of Mr. John Williams* . . . (6th ed., Boston, Samuel Hall, 1795), p. 108.
[4]Present Licking River, Ohio.

[5]Hockhocking, on present site of Lancaster, Fairfield County, Ohio. Gist (Darlington edition), *op. cit.*, p. 116.
[6]Near the beginning of the eighteenth century the Delawares who occupied a greater part of New Jersey, Delaware, eastern Pennsylvania, and New York were subdued by the Iroquois. After this time they gradually moved westward and in 1751, a group was invited by the Hurons or Wyandots to settle on the Muskingum and other streams in eastern Ohio. Hodge, *op. cit.*, I, 385.

Maguck,[1] a little Delaware town of about ten families, by the north side of a plain, or clear field, about five miles in length, N.E. and S.W. and two miles broad, with a small rising in the middle, which gives a fine prospect over the whole plain, and a large creek on the north side of it, called *Sioto Creek* [Scioto River]; all the way from *Licking Creek*[2] to this place, is fine, rich, level land, with large meadows and fine clover bottoms, with spacious plains, covered with wild rye; the wood chiefly large walnuts and hiccories, here and there mixed with poplars, cherry-trees, and sugar-trees.

Monday 21st to Wednesday 23d. Stayed in the *Maguck town*.

Thursday 24th. Set out from *Maguck town*, S. about 15 m. through fine, rich, level land, to a small town called *Hurricane Tom's*,[3] consisting of about five or six Delaware Families, on the S.W. of *Sioto Creek* [Scioto River].

Friday 25th. The creek being very high, and full of ice, we could not ford, and were obliged to go down it on the S.E. side, S.E. 4 m. to the *Salt Lick Creek;*[4] *about a mile up this creek, on the south side is a very large salt lick, the streams which run into this lick are very salt, and, though clear, leave a bluish sediment: the Indians and traders make salt for their horses of this water, by boiling it; it has at first a bluish colour, and somewhat bitter taste, but upon being dissolved in fair water, and boiled the second time, it comes to tolerably pure salt.*

Saturday 26th. Set out S. 2 m. S.W. 14 m.

Sunday 27th. S. 12 m. to a small Delaware town,[5] of about twenty families, on the S.E. side of *Sioto Creek* [Scioto River]. We lodged at the house of an Indian, whose name was Windaughalah,[6] a great man, and chief of this town, and much in the English interest; he entertained us very kindly, and ordered a negro man that belonged to him, to feed our horses well: this night it snowed, and in the morning, *though the snow was six or seven inches deep, the wild rye*[7] *appeared very green and flourishing through it*, and our horses had very fine feeding.

Monday 28th. We went into council with the Indians of this town,

Margin notes:
Land very rich, with fine meadows and variety of fine timber

G n Hurricane Tom's Town

Land rich and level. H n Salt Lick Creek Salt springs Indians make salt.

Wild rye appears above the snow, which was 6 or 7 inches deep.

[1]Located between Scippo Creek and the Scioto River, about three and one-half miles south of present Circleville, Pickaway County, Ohio. *Ibid.* For "Map of the Ancient Shawanoese Towns, on the Pickaway Plain" see Howe, *op. cit.*, p. 402.

[2]Licking River.

[3]Harrickintom's Town located below the present Chillicothe, Ohio, and opposite the mouth of Paint Creek. Gist (Darlington edition), *op. cit.*, pp. 118-19.

[4]Present Salt Creek which flows into the Scioto River in southeastern Ross County, Ohio. Gist (Darlington edition), *op. cit.*, p. 119.

[5]Situated on the east branch of the Scioto in present Clay Township, Scioto County, Ohio. Gist (Darlington edition), *op. cit.*, p. 119.

[6]Windaughulah, or The Council Door, a celebrated Delaware chief who represented the Delawares and Wyandots at several conferences in Pennsylvania. *Ibid.*, pp. 119-20.

[7]See page 26, this work.

Message
from the
Governor of
Pennsylvania

Indians
promise to be
firm to the
English.

Delawares
500 fighting
men, not part
of the Six
Nations, but
have leave
to hunt on
their lands

H n
Shawane
town. Land
rich but
broken.
Shawane
town situ-
ated, contains
300 men.
Shawanes not
a part of the
Six Nations.

English
protected
them from
the fury of the
Six Nations

Messages
from the
governor of
Pennsylvania

and after the interpreter had informed them of his instructions[1] from the governor of Pennsylvania, and given them some cautions in regard to the French, they returned for answer as follows: The speaker, with four strings of wampum in his hand, stood up, and addressing himself to the governor of Pennsylvania, said, "Brothers, we the Delawares, return you our hearty thanks for the news you have sent us, and we assure you, we will not hear the voice of any other nation; for we are to be directed by you, our brothers, the English, and by none else; we shall be very glad to hear what our brothers have to say to us at the Logg's town [Logstown] in the spring; and do assure you of our hearty good will and love to our brothers, we present you with these four strings of wampum."

This is the last town of the Delawares to the westward. The Delaware Indians, by the best accounts I could gather, consist of about five hundred fighting men, all firmly attached to the English interest: they are not properly a part of the Six Nations, but are scattered about among most of the Indians upon the Ohio, and some of them among the Six Nations,[2] from whom they have leave to hunt upon their lands.

Tuesday 29th. Set out S.W. 5 m. to the mouth of *Sioto Creek* [Scioto River], opposite to the *Shawane town*;[3] here we fired our guns to alarm the traders, who soon answered, and came and ferried us over. The land, about the mouth of *Sioto Creek* [Scioto River], is rich, but broken, fine bottoms upon the river and creek. The *Shawane town* is situate on both sides of the Ohio, just below the mouth of *Sioto Creek* [Scioto River], and contains about three hundred men; there are about forty Houses on the south side of the river, and about a hundred on the north side, with a kind of state house of about ninety feet long, with a light cover of bark, in which they hold their councils: the Shawanes [Shawnee] are not a part of the Six Nations, but were formerly at variance with them, though now reconciled; they are great friends to the English, who once protected them from the fury of the Six Nations, which they gratefully remember.

Wednesday 30th. We were conducted into council, where George Croghan delivered sundry speeches from the government of Pennsylvania to the chiefs[4] of this nation; in which he informed them, "That two prisoners[5] who had been taken by the French, and had made their escape

---

[1]See *note* 4, p. 174.

[2]Iroquois Confederacy. Six Nations consisting of the tribes of the Cayugas, Mohawks, Oneidas, Onondagas, Senecas, and Tuscaroras. Known as the Five nations until the admission of the Tuscaroras in 1722.

[3]Lower Shawnee Town.

[4]Takentoa, Molsinoughkio, and Nynickenowea, Piankashaw and Wea chiefs. *Colonial Records of Pennsylvania, op. cit.*, V, 523.

[5]Morris Turner and Ralph Kilgore. *Ibid.*, 482-84.

from the French officer at Lake Erie, as he was carrying them toward Canada, brought news that the French offered a large sum of money to any who would bring to them the said Croghan, and Andrew Montour alive, or if dead, their scalps; and that the French also threatened those Indians and the Wiandots [Wyandots] with war in the spring. The same person farther said, that they had seen twenty French canoes, loaded with stores, for a new fort[1] they designed on the south side Lake Erie." Mr. Croghan also informed them, that several of our traders had been taken, and advised them to keep their warriors at home, until they could see what the French intended, which he doubted not would appear in the spring. Then Andrew Montour informed this nation, as he had done the Wiandots [Wyandots] and the Delawares, "That the King of Great Britain had sent them a large present of goods in company with the Six Nations, which was under the care of the governor of Virginia, who had sent me out to invite them to come and see him, and partake of their father's present next summer." To which we received this answer, Big Hanoahansa[2] their speaker, taking in his hand the several strings of wampum, which had been given by the English, said, "These are the speeches received by us from your great men. From the beginning of our friendship, all that our brothers the English have told us has been good and true, for which we return our hearty thanks; then taking up four other strings of wampum in his hand, he said; Brothers, I now speak the sentiments of all our people. When first our forefathers the English met our brothers, they found what our brothers the English told them to be true, and so have we; we are but a small people, but it is not to us only that you speak, but to all nations: we shall be glad to hear what our brothers will say to us at the Logg's town [Logstown] in the spring; and we hope that the friendship now subsisting between us and our brothers will last as long as the sun shines or the moon gives light. We hope that our children will hear and believe what our brothers say to them as we have always done; and to assure you of our hearty good-will towards you our brothers, we present you with these four strings of wampum." After the council was over, they had much talk about sending a guard with us to the Picqualinnee [Pickawillany] town (these are a tribe of the Tawightwis [Twightwees])[3] which was reckoned near 200 miles; but after a long consultation, their king being sick, they came to no determination about it.

Acquaints the Indians the king had sent them a present

Indians answer

---

[1]Probably Presqu' Isle. [3]Miamis.
[2]Big Hominy, a Shawnee Chief. Hanna, *op. cit.*, II, 139.

Appendix
page 185
Resolves to
go to the
Tawightwis

Thursday 31st, to Monday February 11th. Stayed in the *Shawane*[1] *town*. While I was here the Indians had a very extraordinary festival, at which I was present, and which I have exactly described at the end of my journal. As I had particular instructions from the president of Virginia to discover the strength and number of some Indian nations to the westward, who had lately revolted from the French, and had some messages to deliver them from him, I resolved to set out for the *Tawightwi town*.[2]

Tuesday 12th. Having left my boy to take care of my horses in the *Shawane town*, and supplied myself with a fresh horse to ride, I set out with my old company, viz. George Croghan, Andrew Montour, Robert Kallendar [Callendar], and a servant to carry our provision, &c. N.W. 10 m.

Wednesday 13th. The same course, N.W. about 35 m.

Thursday 14th. The same course about 30 m.

Friday 15th. The same course 15 m. we met with nine Shawane [Shawnee] Indians coming from one of the Picqualinnee [Pickawillany] towns, where they had been to council; they told us there were fifteen more of them behind at the Tawightwi [Twightwee] town, waiting for the arrival of the Wawiaghtas[3] (a tribe of the Tawightwis [Twightwees]) who were to bring with them a Shawane [Shawnee] woman and child to deliver to their men that were behind. This woman, they informed us, was taken prisoner last fall by some of the Wawiaghta warriors through a mistake, which was like to have engaged those nations in war.

G o
Little
Mineami
river.

Saturday 16th. Set out the same course, N.W. about 35 m. to the *little Mineami* [Miami] *river or creek*.[4]

G p
Big Mineami
river.
Tawightwi
town. Land
very rich,
with fine
meadows and
streams,
variety of
timber, and
abundance of
game. The
Ohio abounds
with fish.

Sunday 17th. Crossed the *little Mineami*[5] [Miami], and altered our course S.W. 25 m. to the *big Mineami* [Great Miami] *river*, opposite to the *Tawightwi* [Twightwee] town. All the land from the *Shawane* [Shawnee][6] *town* to this place (except the first twenty miles, which is broken) is fine rich level land, well timbered, with large walnut, ash, sugar-trees, cherry-trees, &c. well watered with a great number of little streams and rivulets; full of beautiful natural meadows, covered with wild rye, blue grass, and clover; and abounds with turkeys, deer, elks, and most sorts of game, particularly buffaloes, thirty or forty of which are frequently seen feeding in one meadow; in short, it wants nothing

[1]Lower Shawnee Town.
[2]Pickawillany.
[3]Wea, a subtribe of the Miami.

[4]Mad River not the Little Miami River. Gist (Darlington edition), *op. cit.*, p. 123.
[5]*Ibid.*
[6]Lower Shawnee Town.

but cultivation to make it a most delightful country. The Ohio and all the large branches are said to be full of fine fish of several kinds, particularly a sort of cat-fish[1] of a prodigious size; but as I was not there at a proper season, I had not an opportunity of seeing any of them. The traders had always reckoned it 200 miles from the *Shawane* [Shawnee] *town*[2] to the *Tawightwi* [Twightwee] *town;*[3] but by my computation, I could make it no more than 150. The *Mineami* [Miami] *river* being high, we were obliged to make a raft of logs to transport our goods and saddles, and swim our horses over: after firing a few guns and pistols, and smoak- ing in the warriors pipe, who came to invite us to the town, according to their custom of inviting and welcoming strangers, and great men, we entered the town with English colours before us, and were kindly re- ceived by their king, who invited us into his own house, and set our colours upon the top of it. The firing of the guns held about a quarter of an hour, and then all the white men and traders that were there came and welcomed us to the *Tawightwi* [Twightwee] *town. This town is situate on the N.W. side of the big Mineami* [Miami] *river, about 150 miles from the mouth thereof;* it consists of about four hundred families, and is daily increasing; it is accounted one of the strongest Indian towns upon this part of the continent. The Tawightwis [Twightwee] are a very numerous people, consisting of many different tribes, under the same form of government; each tribe has a particular chief, or king, one of which is chosen indifferently out of any tribe to rule the whole nation, and is vested with greater authorities than any of the others. They are accounted the most powerful nation to the westward of the English settlements, and much superior to the Six Nations with whom they are now in amity. Their strength and numbers are not thoroughly known, as they have but lately traded with the English, and indeed have very little trade among them; they deal in much the same commodities as the northern Indians: there are other nations or tribes still farther to the westward daily coming in to them; and it is thought their power and interest reaches to the westward of the Missisippi, if not across the continent; they are at present very well affected to the English, and seem fond of an alliance with them; they formerly lived on the farther side of the Wabash, and were in the French interest, who supplied them with some few trifles, at a most exorbitant price; they were called by the French Mineamis [Miamis], but they have now revolted from them, and

Margin notes:
Smoak the pipe of peace.

Is kindly received by the Tawightwi king

Remarks on the Tawightwi town and nation

---

[1][Pownall's note]. The editor has seen them of 60 pounds weight.

[2]Lower Shawnee Town.

[3]Pickawillany, near present site of Piqua, Ohio.

left their former habitations, for the sake of trading with the English, and notwithstanding all the artifices the French have used, they have not been able to recall them. After we had been some time in the king's house, Mr. Montour told him that we wanted to speak with him, and the chiefs of this nation this evening, upon which we were invited into the long house, and having taken our places, Mr. Montour began as follows.

Montour tells the king he had come on business to him. Montour speaks to the Tawightwis.

"Brothers the Tawightwis [Twightwees][1] as we have been hindered by the high waters, and some business with our other Indian brothers, no doubt our long stay has caused some trouble among our brothers here, therefore we now present you with two strings of wampum, to remove all the trouble of your hearts, and clear your eyes that you may see the sun shine clear, for we have a great deal to say to you; and would have you send for one of your friends that can speak the Mohickan [Mahican] or Mingo tongue[2] well, that we may understand each other thoroughly, as we have a great deal of business to do." The Mohickons [Machican][3] are a small tribe, who most of them speak English, and are also well acquainted with the language of the Tawightwis [Twightwee], and they with theirs. Mr. Montour then proceeded to deliver them a message from the Wiandots [Wyandots] and Delawares as follows.

Speech from the Wiandots and Delawares to the Tawightwis

"Brothers the Tawightwis [Twightwees], this comes by our brothers the English, who are coming with good news to you. We hope you will take care of them, and all our brothers, the English, who are trading among you. You made a road for our brothers the English to come and trade among you, but it is now very foul, great logs are fallen across it, and we would have you be strong, like men, and have one heart with us, and make the road clear, that our brothers the English may have free course and recourse between you and us. In the sincerity of our hearts we send you these four strings of wampum." To which they gave their usual Yo Ho. They then said they wanted some tobacco to smoak with us, and that to-morrow they would send for their interpreter.

Monday 18th. We walked about, and viewed the fort, which wanted some repairs, and the trader's men helped them to bring logs to line the inside.

Tuesday 19th. We gave their kings and great men some cloaths, paint, and shirts, and they were busy dressing and preparing themselves for the council. The weather grew warm, and the creeks began to lower very fast.

[1]Miamis.

[2]Refers to Algonquin language. Hodge, *op. cit.*, I, 786, 867.

[3]Mingoes.

Wednesday 20th. About twelve o'clock we were informed that some of the foreign tribes were coming, upon which proper persons were ordered to meet them, and conduct them to the town, and then we were invited into the long house: after we had been seated about a quarter of an hour, four Indians, two from each tribe, who had been sent before to bring the long pipe, and to inform us that the rest were coming, came in and informed us, that their friends had sent those pipes that we might smoak the calumet pipe of peace with them, and that they intended to do the same with us.

Thursday 21st. We were invited again into the long house (where Mr. Croghan made them) with the foreign tribes, a present to the value of one hundred pounds Pennsylvania money, and delivered all our speeches to them, at which they seemed well pleased, and said they would take time and consider well what we had said to them. Croghan delivers a present and messages.

Friday 22d. Nothing remarkable happened.

Saturday 23d. In the afternoon there was an alarm, which caused great confusion and running about among the Indians; upon enquiring the reason of this stir, they told us, it was occasioned by six Indians that came to war against them from the southward, three of them Cuttawas [Catawbas], and three Shawanes [Shawnee]; these were some of the Shawanes [Shawnee] who had formerly deserted from the other part of the nation, and now lived to the southward: towards night there was a report spread in town, that four Indians, and four hundred French, were on their march and just by the town, but soon after the messenger who brought the news said, there were only four French Indians coming to council, and that they bid him say so, only to see how the English would behave themselves, but as they had behaved themselves like men, he now told the truth.

Sunday, February 24th. This morning the four French Indians came into town and were kindly received by the town Indians. They marched in under French colours, and were conducted into the long house, and after they had been in about a quarter of an hour, the council sat, and we were sent for, that we might hear what the French had to say. The *Piankasha* [Piankeshaw] king,[1] who was at that time the principal man, and commander in chief of the *Tawightwis* [Twightwee], said he would have the English colours set up in this council, Four French Indians come in

---

[1]LaDemoiselle, or Old Briton, famous Miami chief who founded Pickawillany about 1748. This village was the center of English influence in this region, until 1752, when it was destroyed by Indians under French command. Chief Demoiselle was killed in battle and afterwards the enemy boiled his body and ate it. Gipson, *The British Regime, op. cit.*, IV, 177, 222-23.

as well as the French; to which we answered he might do as he thought fit; after we were seated opposite to the French ambassadors,

one of them said he had a present to make them, so a place was prepared, as they had before done for our present, between them and us, and then their speaker stood up and laid his hands upon two keggs of brandy that held about seven quarts each, and a roll of Tobacco of about ten pounds weight, then taking two strings of wampum in his hand, he said, "What he had to deliver them was from their father (meaning the French king) and he desired that they would hear what he was about to say." Then he laid the two strings of wampum upon the keggs, and taking up four other strings of black and white wampum, he said,

"That their father, remembering his children, had sent them two keggs of milk,[1] and some tobacco, and that he had now made a clear road for them, to come and see him and his officers, and pressed them very much to come and see him." Then he took another string of wampum in his hand, and said, "Their father would now forget all little differences that had been between them, and desired them not to be of two minds, but to let him know their minds freely, for he would send for them no

more." To which the *Piankasha* [Piankeshaw] king replied, it was true their father had sent for them several times, and said the road was clear, but he understood it was made foul and bloddy, and by them. We, said he, have cleared a road for our brothers the English, and your fathers have made it bad, and have taken some of our brothers prisoners, which we look upon as done to us," and he turned short about, and went out of council. After the French ambassador had delivered his message, he went into one of the private houses, and endeavoured much to prevail on some Indians there, and was seen to cry and lament, which was, as he said, for the loss of that nation.

Monday 25th. This day we received a speech from the *Wawiaghtas*[2] and *Piankashas* [Piankeshaws], two tribes of the *Tawightwis* [Twight-wees], one of the chiefs of the former spoke, "Brothers, we have heard what you have said to us by the interpreter, and we see you take pity upon our poor wives and children, and have taken us by the hand into the great chain of friendship, therefore we present you with these two bundles of skins, to make *shoes* for your people, and this pipe to smoak in, to assure you our hearts are good and true towards you our brothers, and we hope that we shall all continue in true love and friendship with one another, as people with one head and one heart ought to do. You

[1]Brandy.
[2]Weas, a subtribe of the Miamis.

have pitied us, as you always did the rest of our Indian brothers. We hope the pity you have always shewn, will remain as long as the sun gives light, and on our side you may depend upon sincere and true friendship towards you, as long as we have strength." This person stood up and spoke with the air and gesture of an orator.

Tuesday 26th. The *Tawightwis* [Twightwees] delivered the following answer to the four Indians sent by the French. The Captain of the warriors stood up, and taking some strings of black and white wampum in his hand, he spoke with a fierce tone, and very warlike air: "Brothers the *Owtawais* [Ottawas],[1] you are always differing with the French yourselves, and yet you listen to what they say, but we will let you know by these four strings of wampum that we will not hear any thing they say to us, or do any thing they bid us do." Then the same speaker, with six strouds, two matchcoats, and a string of black wampum (I understood the goods were in return for the milk[2] and tobacco) directed his speech to the French and said, "Fathers you desire that we will speak our minds from our hearts, which I am going to do. You have often desired we should go home to you, but I tell you it is not our home, for we have made a road as far as the sea, to the sun rising, and have been taken by the hand by our brothers, *the English, the Six Nations, the Delawares, Shawanes* [Shawnee], *and Wiandots* [Wyandots], and we assure you that is the road we will go; and as you threaten us with war in the spring,[3] we tell you if you are angry we are ready to receive you, and resolve to die here, before we will go to you, and that you may know this is our mind, we send you this string of black wampum." After a short pause the same speaker spoke again thus; "Brothers, the *Owtawais* [Ottawas] you hear what I say, tell that to your fathers the French, for that is our mind, and we speak it from our hearts."

Wednesday February 27th. This day they took down the French colours, and dismissed the four French Indians, so they took their leave of the town, and set off for the French fort.[4]

Thursday 28th. The cryer of the town, came by the king's order, and invited us to the long house, to see the *warriors feather-dance*.[5] it

Marginal notes:
Tawightwi's reply to the French speech

Refuse to go among the French, and say they have joined the English, &c.

Tell them they are ready for war.

Indian feather dance

---

[1] Friends and allies of the French. Hodge, *op. cit.*, II, 169.

[2] Brandy. See p. 188, this work.

[3] The Ottawa and Chippewa under the command of Langlade did attack and destroy Pickawillany in June, 1752. For a concise account of this attack read Gipson's *The British Empire, op. cit.*, IV, 222-23.

[4] French Fort Miami on the present site of Fort Wayne, Indiana. Gist (Darlington edition), *op. cit.*, p. 126.

[5] "Tcitahaia, popularly known as the 'feather dance' because the dancers have canes in their hands with feathers fastened at the ends. This is distinctly a peace dance." U. S. Bureau of Ethnology, *Annual Report of the Bureau of Ethnology to the Secretary of Smithsonian Institution*, 1924-25 (Washington, Government Printing Office, 1928), XLII, 609.

was performed by three dancing masters who were painted all over of various colours, with long sticks in their hands, upon the ends of which, are fastened long feathers of swans, and other birds, neatly woven in the shape of a fowl's wing; in this disguise they performed many antick tricks, waving their sticks and feathers about with great skill, to imitate the flying and fluttering of birds, keeping exact time with their musick; while they are dancing, some of the warriors strike a post, upon which the musick and dancers cease, and the warrior gives an account of his atchievements in war, and when he has done, throws down some goods as a recompence to the performers and musicians, after which they proceed in their dance as before, till another warrior strikes the post, and so on as long as they think fit.

Tawightwi's speech to the governor of Pennsylvania Friday, March 1st. We received the following speech from the *Tawightwis* [Twightwees]. The speaker stood up, and addressing himself as to the governor of Pennsylvania, with two strings of wampum in his hand, he said, "Brothers, our hearts are glad that you have taken notice of us; and surely, brothers, we hope, that you will order a smith to settle here to mend our guns and hatchets: your kindness makes us so bold as to ask this request. You told us our friendship should last as long, and be as the greatest mountain. We have considered well, and all our great kings and warriors are come to a resolution, never to give heed to what the French say to us, but always to hear and believe what you, our brothers, say to us. Brothers, we are obliged to you for your kind invitation to receive a present at the Logg's town [Logstown], but as our foreign tribes are not yet come, we must wait for them, but you may depend we will come as soon as our women have planted corn, to hear what our brothers will say to us. Brothers, we present you with this bundle of skins, as we are but poor, to be for shoes for you on the road, and we return you our hearty thanks for the cloaths which you have put upon our wives and children."

We then took our leaves of the kings and chiefs, and they ordered that a small party of Indians should go with us as far as *Hockhocking;* but as I had left my boy and horses at the *Lower Shawane town*, I was obliged to go by myself, or to go sixty or seventy miles out of my way, which I did not care to do; so we all came over the *Mineami* [Miami] *River* together this evening, but Mr. Croghan and Mr. Montour, went over again and lodged in the town, I stayed on this side at one Robert Smith's, a trader, where we had left our horses. Before the French Indians had come into town, we had drawn articles of peace and alliance between the

English and *Wawiaghtas*[1] and *Piankashas* [Piankashaws], the indentures were signed, sealed, and delivered on both sides, and as I drew them I took a copy. The land upon the great *Mineami* [Miami] *River* is very rich, level, and well timbered, some of the finest meadows that can be: the Indians and traders assure me that it holds as good, and, if possible better, to the westward as far as the *Wabash*, which is accounted 100 miles, and quite up to the head of the *Mineami* [Miami] *River*, which is sixty miles above the *Tawightwi* [Twightwee] *town*, and down the said river quite to the *Ohio*, which is reckoned 150 miles. The grass here grows to a great height in the clear fields, of which there are a great number, and the bottoms are full of white clover, wild rye, and blue grass.

Saturday 2d. George Croghan, and the rest of our company, came over the river; we got our horses, and travelled about 35 m. to *Mad Creek*, this is a place where some English traders had been taken prisoners[2] by the French.

Sunday 3d. We parted, they for *Hockhocking*, and I for the *Shawane* [Shawnee] *town*;[3] and as I was quite alone, and knew that the French Indians had threatened us, and would probably pursue, or lie in wait for us, I left the path, and went to the southwestward, down the little *Mineami* [Miami] *river* or *creek*, where I had fine travelling, through rich land and beautiful meadows, in which I could sometimes see forty or fifty buffaloes feeding at once. The little *Mineami* [Miami] *river* or *creek* continued to run through the middle of a fine meadow, about a mile wide, very clear, like an old field, and not a bush in it. I could see the buffaloes in it about two miles off. I travelled this day about thirty miles.

Monday 4th. This day I heard several guns, but was afraid to examine who fired them, lest they might be some of the French Indians; so I travelled through the woods about 30 m. just at night I killed a fine barren cow buffaloe, and took out her tongue, and a little of the best of her meat. The land still level, rich, and well timbered with oak, walnut, ash, locust, and sugar-trees.

Tuesday 5th. I travelled about 30 miles.

Wednesday 6th. I travelled about thirty miles and killed a fat bear.

Thursday 7th. Set out with my horse load of bear, and travelled about 30 m. This afternoon I met a young man, a trader, and we en-

---

[1]Weas, a subtribe of the Miamis.

[2]In 1750 Morris Turner and Ralph Kilgore were taken prisoners at this place which is about seven miles west of Springfield, Clarke County, Ohio. Gist (Darlington edition), *op. cit.*, pp. 126-27.

[3]Lower Shawnee Town, on the present site of Portsmouth, Ohio.

camped together that night; he happened to have some bread with him, and I had plenty of meat, so we fared very well.

Shawane town

Friday 8th. Travelled about 30 m. and arrived at night at the *Shawane* [Shawnee] *town*. All the Indians, as well as the white men, came out to welcome my return to their town, being very glad that all things were rightly settled in the *Mineami* [Miami] country; they fired upwards of 150 guns in the town, and made an entertainment on account of the peace with the western Indians. On my return from the *Tawightwi* [Twightwee], to the *Shawane* [Shawnee] *town*, I did not keep an exact account of course or distance, for as the land thereabout was much the same, and the situation of the country was sufficiently described in my journey to the *Tawightwi* [Twightwee] *town*, I thought it unnecessary, but have, notwithstanding, laid down my track pretty nearly in my plot.

Saturday 9th. In the *Shawane* [Shawnee] *town* I met with one of the Mingoe [Mingo] chiefs, who had been down at the falls of Ohio, so that we did not see him as we went up. I informed him of the king's present, and the invitation down to Virginia; he told me that there was a party of French Indians hunting at the falls, and if I went they would kill or carry me away prisoner to the French, for it was certain they would not let me pass; however as I had a great inclination to see the Falls, and the lands on the east side the Ohio, I resolved to venture as far as possible.

Sunday 10th. Stayed in the town and prepared for my departure.

Ohio at the Shawane town ¾ mile wide, very deep, and a gentle current.

Tuesday 12th. I got my horses over the river,[1] and after breakfast, my boy and I got ferried over. The Ohio is near three quarters of a mile wide at the Shawane [Shawnee] town, and is very deep and smooth.

Wednesday 13th. We set out S. 45d. W. down the river, on the S.E. side 8 m. then S. 10 m. here I met two men belonging to Robert Smith at whose house I lodged on this side the *Mineami* [Miami] *river*, and one Hugh Crawford;[2] the said Robert Smith had given me an order upon these men, for two of the teeth of a large beast,[3] which they were bringing from towards the Falls of Ohio, one of which I brought in and delivered to the Ohio company. Robert Smith informed me that about seven years ago, these teeth, and the bones of three large beasts, one of which was somewhat smaller than the other two, *were found in a salt lick*[4] *or spring, upon a small creek, which runs into the south side of the*

Three very large car-casses of beasts found on the Ohio

[1]Meaning Ohio River.

[2]Distinguished Indian trader and soldier. Gist (Darlington edition), *op. cit.*, pp. 128-29.

[3]The early explorers found bones, tusks, and teeth, remains of the mammoth that inhabited this region, in the valley of Big Bone Creek in Boone County, Kentucky. Collins, *op. cit.*, II, 51-52; Gist (Darlington edition), *op. cit.*, pp. 129-30.

[4]Big Bone Lick, Boone County, Kentucky.

Ohio, about fifteen miles below the mouth of the great Mineami river, and twenty above the Falls of Ohio; he assured me that the rib bones of the largest of those beasts, were eleven feet long, and the scull bone six feet across the forehead, and the other bones in proportion, and that there were several teeth there, some of which he called horns, and said they were upwards of five feet long, and as much as a man could well carry; that he had hid one in a branch at some distance from the place, lest the French Indians should carry it away. The tooth which I brought in, for the Ohio company, was a jaw tooth, of better than four pounds weight, it appeared to be the farthest tooth in the jaw, and looked like fine ivory, when the outside was scraped off. I also met with four *Shawane* [Shawnee] Indians coming up the river in their canoes, who informed me that there were about sixty French Indians encamped at the Falls.

Thursday 14th. I went down the river S. 15 m. the land upon this side the Ohio chiefly broken, and the bottoms but narrow.

Friday 15th. S. 5 m. S.W. 10 m. to a creek[1] that was so high that we could not get over that night.

Saturday 16th. S. 45d. W. about 35 m.

Sunday 17th. The same course 15 m. then N. 45 d. W. 5 m.

Monday 18th. N. 45 d. W. 5 m. then S.W. 20 m. to the *lower salt lick creek*,[2] which Robert Smith and the Indians told me was about 15 miles above the *Falls of Ohio;* the land still hilly, the salt lick here much the same with those before described. This day we heard several guns, which made me imagine the French Indians were not moved, but were still hunting and firing thereabouts; we also saw some traps newly set, and the footsteps of some Indians, plain on the ground, as if they had been there the day before. I was now much troubled that I could not comply with my instructions, and was once resolved to leave the boy and horses, and go privately on foot to view the Falls; but the boy being a poor hunter, was afraid he would starve if I was long from him, and there was also great danger lest the French Indians should come upon our horses tracks, or hear their bells, and as I had seen good land enough, I thought perhaps I might be blamed for venturing so far, in such dangerous times, so I concluded not to got to the Falls, but travelled away to the southward, till we were over the *little Cuttawa river.*[3] *The Falls of Ohio*, by the best information I could get, are not very

Marginal notes: Rib bones 11 feet Scull bone 6 feet across / Teeth 5 feet long / Tooth / Gist brought above 4 pounds in weight / Land broken, bottoms narrow / 10 / Lower salt lick 15 miles from the falls of the Ohio / J p / Afraid to go to the falls. / Little Cuttawa river / Falls of Ohio described

---

[1]"Probably the Licking River at the Lower Blue Licks," Gist (Darlington edition), *op. cit.*, p. 130. The Licking River flows into the Ohio at Newport, Kentucky.

[2]Salt River, Kentucky.

[3]Kentucky River. Gist crossed the Kentucky River near the present site of Frankfort, Kentucky. Gist (Darlington edition), *op. cit.*, pp. 130-31.

steep; on the S.E. side there is a bar of sand at some distance from the shore, the water between the bar and the shore, is not above three feet deep, and the stream moderately strong: the Indians frequently pass safely in their canoes, through this passage, but are obliged to take great care as they go down, lest the current, which is much the strongest on the N.W. side, should draw them that way, which would be very dangerous, as the water on that side runs with great rapidity, over several ledges of rocks. The waters below the Falls, as they say, is about six fathoms deep, and the river continues without any obstruction, till it empties itself into the Missisippi, which is accounted upwards of 400 miles. The Ohio, near the mouth, is said to be very wide, and the land upon both sides very rich, and in general very level all the way from the Falls. After I had determined not to go to the Falls, we turned from salt lick creek, to a ridge of mountains that made towards the [Little] *Cuttawa river*,[1] and from the top of the mountain, we saw a fine level country S.W. as far as our eyes could behold; and it was a very clear day. We then went down the mountain, and set out S. 20 d. W. about 5 m. through rich level land, covered with small walnut, sugar-trees, red-buds, &c.

Tuesday 19th. We set out south, and crossed several creeks, all running to the S.W. at about twelve miles came to the *little Cuttawa river*, we were obliged to go up it about a mile to an island which was the shoalest place we could find to cross[2] at: we then continued our course in all about thirty miles, through rich level land, except about two miles, which was broken and indifferent: this level is about thirty five miles broad, and as we came up the side of it along the branches of the *little Cuttawa*,[3] we found it about 150 miles long, and how far towards the S.W. we could not tell, but imagined it held as far as the *great Cuttawa river*,[4] which would be upwards of 100 miles more, and appeared much broader that way, than here, as I could discern from the tops of the mountains.

Wednesday 20th. We did not travel. I went up to the top of a mountain to view the country: To the S.E. it looked very broken, and mountainous, but to the eastward and S.W. it appeared very level.

Thursday 21st. Set out S. 45 d. E. 15 m. S. 5 m. here I found a place[5] where the stones shined like high coloured brass; the heat of the

Marginal notes:
400 miles from the falls to the Mississippi Ohio wide Lands very rich.

Lands on the Cuttawa river rich, and level, for a great distance. Great Cuttawa river.

Finds a kind of borax.

---

[1]Kentucky River.
[2]Gist crossed the Kentucky River in the vicinity of present Frankfort, Kentucky. Gist (Darlington edition), *op. cit.*, p. 130.
[3]Kentucky River.
[4]Tennessee River.
[5]On the Kentucky River near the mouth of the Red River. Gist (Darlington edition), *op. cit.*, p. 133.

sun drew out of them a kind of borax, or salt petre, only something sweeter, some of which I brought in to the Ohio Company, though I believe it was nothing but a sort of sulphur.

Friday 22d. S.E. 12 m. I killed a fat bear, and was taken sick that night.

Saturday 23d. I stayed here, and sweated after the Indian manner, which helped me.

Sunday 24th. Set out E. 2 m. N.E. 3 m. N. 1 m. E. 2 m. S.E. 5 m. E. 2 m. N. 2 m. S.E. 7 m. to a small creek,[1] where we encamped, in a place where we had but poor food for our horses, and both we and they were very much wearied. The reason of our making so many short courses was, we were driven by a branch of the *little Cuttawa river*,[2] whose banks were so exceeding steep, that it was impossible to ford it, into a ledge of rocky laurel mountains, which was almost impassable.

Monday 25th. Set out S.E. 12 m. N. 2 m. E. 1 m. S. 4 m. S.E. 2 m. we killed a buck elk here, and took out his tongue to carry with us.

Tuesday 26th. Set out S.E. 10 m. S.W. 1 m. S.E. 1 m. S.W. 1 m. S.E. 1 m. S.W. 1 m. S.E. 5 m. killed two buffaloes, and took out their tongues, and encamped. These two days we travelled through rocks and mountains, full of laurel thickets, which we could hardly creep through, without cutting our way.

Laurel thickets J o

Wednesday 27th. Our horses and selves were so tired, that we were obliged to stay this day to rest, for we were unable to travel: *On all the branches of the little Cuttawa river was great plenty of fine coal*, some of which I brought in to the Ohio company.

Plenty of fine coal on the Cuttawa J o

Thursday 28th. Set out S.E. 15 m. crossing several creeks of the *little Cuttawa river; the land still full of coal, and black slate.*

Coal and slate

Friday 29th. The same course S.E. about 12 m. the land still mountainous.

Saturday 30th. Stayed to rest our horses. I went on foot, and found a passage through the mountains, to another creek, or a fork of the same creek, that we were upon.

Sunday 31st. The same course S.E. 15 m. killed a buffaloe, and encamped.

Monday, April 1st. Set out the same course about 20 m. part of the way we went along a path up the side of a little creek, at the head of which, was a gap in the mountains,[3] then our path went down another

---

[1]North fork of the Kentucky River. Gist (Darlington edition), *op. cit.*, p. 133.

[2]Kentucky River.

[3]Pound or Stony Gap near Whitesburg, Letcher County, Kentucky. Gist (Darlington edition), *op. cit.*, p. 134.

Blocks of coal eight inches square, on the surface of the earth.

creek[1] to a lick, *where blocks of coal about eight or ten inches square lay upon the surface of the ground;* here we killed a bear, and encamped.

Tuesday 2d. Set out S. 2 m. S.E. 1 m. N.E. 3 m. killed a buffaloe.

Wednesday 3d. S. 1 m. S.W. 3 m. E. 3 m. S.E. 2 m. to a small creek,[2] on which was a large warrior's camp that would contain seventy or eighty warriors; their captain's name or title was the crane,[3] as I knew by his picture or arms painted on a tree.

Thursday 4th. I stayed here all day to rest our horses: I plotted down our courses, and found I had still near 200 miles home upon a straight line.

Friday 5th. Rained, and we staid at the warrior's camp.

Saturday 6th. We went along the warrior's road S. 1 m. S.E. 3 m. S. 2 m. S.E. 3 m. E. 3 m. killed a bear.

Sunday 7th. Set out E. 2 m. N.E. 1 m. S.E. 1 m. S. 1 m. W. 1 m. S.W. 1 m. S. 1 m. S.E. 2 m. S. 1 m.

Monday 8th. S. 1 m. S.E. 1 m. E. 3 m. S.E. 1 m. E. 3 m. N.E. 2 m. N. 1 m. E. 1 m. N. 1 m. E. 2 m. and encamped on a small laurel creek.

Country mountainous, with laurel thickets

Tuesday 9th, and Wednesday 10th. The weather being bad, we did not travel these two days, the country being still rocky, mountainous, and full of laurel thickets; the worst travelling[4] I ever saw.

Thursday 11th. We travelled several courses near 20 miles, but in the afternoon, as I could see from the top of a mountain the place we came from, I found we had not come upon a straight line more than N. 65 d. E. 10 m.

Friday 12th. Set out through very difficult ways E. 5 m. to a small creek.

Saturday 13th. The same course E. upon a straight line; though the way we were obliged to travel was near twenty miles: here we killed two bears, the way still rocky and mountainous.

Sunday 14th. As food was very scarce in these barren mountains, we were obliged to move for fresh feeding for our horses; in climbing up the clifts and rocks this day, two of our horses fell down, and were much

Paroquets on the Ohio

hurt, and a paroquet, which I had got from the Indians on the other side of the Ohio, where there are a great number, died of a bruise he got by the fall; though it was but a trifle, I was much concerned at losing him,

[1]Pound Creek fork of the Big Sandy River. *Ibid.*
[2]Indian Creek, the middle fork of Big Sandy River. Gist (Darlington edition), *op. cit.*, p. 134.
[3]This must have been a camp of the Miami tribe, for the crane is the totem of the Miamis. Hodge, *op. cit.*, I, 852.

[4]Gist was traveling through the country that has been called the Switzerland of Virginia. This territory in and around Tazewell County, Virginia has the appearance of a "tossed bed of mountains." Edward A. Pollard, *The Virginia Tourist . . .* (Philadelphia, J. B. Lippincott & Co., 1870), pp. 155-56.

as he was perfectly tame, and had been very brisk all the way, and I had still corn enough left to feed him. In the afternoon I left the horses, and went all the way down the creek, and found such a precipice, and such laurel thickets that we could not pass, and the horses were not able to go up the mountain, till they had rested a day or two.

Monday 15th. We cut a passage through the laurels better than two miles; as I was climbing up the rocks, I got a fall which hurt me much. This afternoon we wanted provision. I killed a bear. Cut a passage thro' a laurel thicket two miles.

Tuesday 16th. Thunder and rain, in the morning we set out N. 25 d. E. 3 m.

Wednesday 17th. This day I went to the top of a mountain to view the way, and found it so bad that I did not care to engage in it, but rather chose to go out of the way, and keep down along the side of a creek, till I could find a branch or run, on the other side to go up.

Thursday 18th. Set out down the creek's side, N. 3 m. then the creek, turning N.W. I was obliged to leave it, and go up a ridge N.E. 1 m. E. 2 m. S.E. 2 m. N.E. 1 m. to the fork of a river.

Friday 19th. Set out down the run N.E. 2 m. E. 2 m. S.E. 2 m. N. 20 d. E. 2 m. E. 2 m. up a large run.

Saturday 20th. Set out S.E. 10 m. E. 4 m. over a small creek. We had such bad travelling down this creek, that we had like to have lost one of our horses.

Sunday 21st. Stayed to rest our horses.

Monday 22d. Rained all day, we could not travel.

Tuesday 23d. Set out E. 8 m. along a ridge of mountains,[1] then S.E. 5 m. E. 3 m. S.E. 4 m. and encamped among very steep mountains.

Wednesday 24th. S.E. 4 m. through steep mountains and thickets, E. 6 m.

Thursday 25th. E. 5 m. S.E. 1 m. N.E. 2 m. S.E. 2 m. E. 1 m. then S. 2 m. E. 1 m. killed a bear.

Friday 26th. Set out S.E. 2 m. here it rained so hard we were obliged to stop.

Saturday 27th, to Monday 29th. These three days it continued rainy and bad weather, so that we could not travel. All the way from Salt Lick creek to this place,[2] the branches of the little Cuttawa were so high that we could not pass them, which obliged us to go over the heads

---

[1]Along the New Garden ridge dividing Buchanan and Russell Counties, Virginia. Gist (Darlington edition), *op. cit.*, p. 134.

[2]In Baptist Valley, Tazewell Co. Gist traveled the valley of the Clinch River, on the south side of the ridge dividing the heads of the Big Sandy from the Clinch River. Gist thought the Clinch River was the Kentucky. *Ibid.*

of them, through a continued ledge of almost inaccessible mountains, rocks, and laurel thickets.

Blue Stone river J 1

Tuesday 30th. Fair weather, set out E. 3 m. S.E. 8 m. E. 2 m. to a *little river or creek which falls into the Big Kanhawa* [Kanawha], *called Blue Stone*, where we encamped and had good feeding for our horses.

Remarkable rock J 1

Wednesday, May 1st. Set out N. 75 d. E. 10 m. and killed a buffaloe; then went up a very high mountain,[1] upon the top of which was a rock sixty or seventy feet high, and a cavity in the middle, into which I went, and found there was a passage through it, which gradually ascended to the top, with several holes in the rock, which let in the light; when I got to the top of this rock, I could see a prodigious distance, and could plainly discover where the Big Kanhawa [Kanawha] river broke through the next high mountain.[2] I then came down and continued my course N. 75 d. E. 6 m. farther, and encamped.

Thursday 2d, and Friday 3d. These two days it rained, and we staid at our camp, to take care of some provision we had killed.

Saturday 4th. This day our horses ran away, and it was late before we got them, so we could not travel far; we went N. 75 d. E. 4 m.

Sunday 5th. Rained all day.

Monday 6th. Set out through very bad ways E. 3 m. N.E. 6 m. over a bad laurel creek E. 4 m.

Big Kanhawa, or New River. J k

Tuesday 7th. Set out E. 10 m. to the *Big Kanhawa* [Kanawha] *or new river*, and got over half of it to a *large island*, where we lodged all night.

Kanhawa 200 yards wide, deep, with many falls. Bottoms rich but narrow: high land broken.

Wednesday 8th. We made a raft of logs, and crossed the other half of the river, and went up it S. 2 m. *The Kanhawa* [Kanawha] *or new river (by some called Wood's river)* where I crossed it, which was about eight miles above the mouth of the *Blue Stone river*, is better than 200 yards wide, and pretty deep, but full of rocks and falls. The bottoms upon it, and *Blue Stone river* are very rich, but narrow; the high land broken.

Thursday 9. Set out E. 13 m. to a large Indian warrior's camp, where we killed a bear, and staid all night.

Friday 10th. Set out E. 4 m. S.E. 3 m. S. 3 m. through mountains covered with ivy, and laurel thickets.

Saturday 11th. Set out S. 2 m. S.E. 5 m. to a creek, and a meadow where we let our horses feed, then S.E. 2 m. S. 1 m. S.E. 2 m. to a very

---

[1] A high peak in Mercer County, Virginia. Gist (Darlington edition), *op. cit.*, p. 135.

[2] The Big Kanawha River breaks through the mountains below the mouth of Greenbrier River, in Raleigh County, West Virginia.

high mountain, upon the top of which was a lake or pond[1] about three quarters of a mile long N.E. and S.W. and a quarter of a mile wide, the water fresh and clear, and a clean gravelly shore about ten yards wide with a fine meadow, and six fine springs in it; then S. about 4 m. to a branch of the Kanhawa called *Sinking Creek*.[2]

A lake on the top of a mountain

Sunday 12th. Stayed to rest our horses, and dry some meat we had killed.

Monday 13th. Set out S.E. 2 m. E. 1 m. S.E. 3 m. S. 12 m. to one Richard Hall's,[3] in Augusta county; this man is one of the farthest settlers to the westward up the new river.

R. Hall the farthest settler to the west of new river.

Tuesday 14th. Stayed at Richard Hall's, and wrote to the president of Virginia,[4] and the Ohio company, to let them know I should be with them by the 15th day of June.

Wednesday 15th. Set out from Richard Hall's S. 16 m.

Thursday 16th. The same course S. 22 m. and encamped at *Beaver Island Creek*,[5] *a branch of the Kanhawa* [Kanawha], opposite to the head of *Roanoak* [Roanoke].

K k
Beaver Island creek

Friday 17th. Set out S.W. 3 m. then S. 9 m. to the dividing line between Carolina and Virginia, where I stayed all night. The land from Richard Hall's to this place is broken.

Line between North Carolina and Virginia.

Saturday 18th. Set out S. 20 m. to my own house on the *Yadkin river;* when I came there, I found all my family gone, for the Indians had killed five people in the winter near that place, which frightened my wife and family away to *Roanoak* [Roanoke], about 35 miles nearer in among the inhabitants, which I was informed of by an old man I met near the place.

Gist arrives at his own house, on the Yadkin river.

Sunday 19th. Set out for *Roanoak* [Roanoke], and as we had now a path, we got there the same night, where I found all my family well.

CHRISTOPHER GIST.

[1]Salt Pond, a lake of pure fresh water located on top of Salt Pond Mountain, about 16 miles from Christianburg, Montgomery County, Virginia. Pollard, *op. cit.*, p. 146. At present this lake is called Mountain Lake.

[2]In Giles County, Virginia.

[3]Near Christianburg, Montgomery County, Virginia. Gist (Darlington edition), *op. cit.*, p. 136.

[4]Thomas Lee (1690-1751), member and later president of the Virginia Council, Virginia's commissioner to the Indian treaty at Lancaster in 1744, and member of the Ohio Company of Virginia.

[5]Now called Reed Island Creek in Carroll County, Virginia.

Shawane festival. Indian marriages dissolved.

An account of the Festival at the Shawane [Lower Shawnee] Town mentioned in my Journal, page 184. In the evening a proper officer made a public proclamation, that all the Indian marriages were dissolved, and a public feast was to be held for the three succeeding days after, in which the women (as their custom was) were again to choose their husbands.

The next morning early the Indians breakfasted, and after spent the day in dancing, till the evening, when a plentiful feast was prepared; after feasting, they spent the night in dancing.

The same way they passed the two next days till the evening, the men dancing by themselves, and then the women in turns round fires, and dancing in their manner in the form of the figure 8, about 60 or 70 of them at a time. The women, the whole time they danced, sung a song in their language, the chorus of which was,

> I am not afraid of my husband;
> I will choose what man I please.

Singing those lines alternately.

Indian women choose husbands.

The third day, in the evening, the men, being about 100 in number, danced in a long string, following one another, sometimes at length, at other times in a figure of 8 quite round the fort, and in and out of the long house, where they held their councils, the women standing together as the men danced by them; and as any of the women liked a man passing by, she stepped in, and joined in the dance, taking hold of the man's stroud, whom she chose, and then continued in the dance, till the rest of the women stepped in, and made their choice in the same manner; after which the dance ended, and they all retired to consummate.

N.B. This was given to me by colonel [George] Mercer,[1] agent to the Ohio Company, and now lieutenant-governor of North Carolina.

[1]See *note* 5, p. 26.

FINIS

BIBLIOGRAPHY

GENERAL REFERENCE WORKS
(Not cited in footnotes)

Dictionary of American Biography .... New York, C. Scribner's Sons, 1928-44. 21 vols.

Dictionary of National Biography .... London, Smith Elder & Co., 1885-1901. 66 vols.

The Encyclopaedia Americana .... New York, The Encyclopaedia Americana Corporation, 1924. 30 vols.

The Encyclopaedia Britannica. New York, 14th ed., Encyclopaedia Britannica, Inc., [c1929]. 24 vols.

Lippincott's Pronouncing Gazetteer. A Complete Pronouncing Gazetteer or Geographical Dictionary of the World. Philadelphia, J. B. Lippincott & Co., 1856. 2 vols.

Lossing, Benson J. ... *Harper's Encyclopaedia of United States History* .... New York, Harper & Brothers, [c1905]. 10 vols.

Rand McNally Commercial Atlas and Marketing Guide. Chicago, 56th ed., Rand McNally & Co., 1925.

U.S. Geological Survey. *Topographic Maps of the United States.*

BIBLIOGRAPHIES

MANUSCRIPT

Great Britain. Board of Trade and Plantations. "List of Maps, Plans, &c belonging to the Right Honble the Lords Commissioners for Trade and Plantations Under the Care of Francis Aegidius Assiotti, Draughtsman, 1780." Public Records Office. CO 326/15.

PRINTED

Andrews, Charles, comp. *Guide to the Manuscript Materials for the History of the United States to 1783, in the British Museum, in Minor London Archives, and in the Libraries of Oxford and Cambridge.* By Charles M. Andrews and Frances G. Davenport. Washington, The Carnegie Institution of Washington, 1908. (Carnegie Institution of Washington. *Publication* No. 90.)

Sabin, Joseph [and others]. *A Dictionary of Books Relating to America, From its Discovery to the Present Time.* New York, J. Sabin [etc.], 1868-1936. 29 vols.

U.S. Library of Congress. Division of Maps. *A List of Geographical Atlases in the Library of Congress, with Bibliographical Notes.* Compiled Under the Direction of Philip Lee Phillips. Washington, Government Printing Office, 1909-20. 4 vols.

────── *List of Maps of America in the Library of Congress, preceded by a List of Works Relating to Cartography.* By P. Lee Phillips. Washington, Government Printing Office, 1901.

Wylie, Alexander. *Notes on Chinese Literature.* Shanghai, Presbyterian Mission Press, 1922.

SOURCE MATERIAL

MANUSCRIPTS

"The Account of Captain Anthony Van Schaick, of the Ground between the Enterance of Lake Champlain at Crown Point & the Mouth of Otter Creek." Photostat from Henry E. Huntington Library and Art Gallery, San Marino, Calif. LO 432.

"Capt. Hobbs' and Lieut. Kennedy's Account of the River Kennebeck & the Carrying Place to the River Chaudiere. Septembr 17th 1756." Photostat from Henry E. Huntington Library and Art Gallery, San Marino, Calif. LO 1824.

"Capt. Hobbs' Account of the Way from No. 4, in New Hampshire, to the Mouth of Otter Creek. Sept. 18, 1756." Photostat from Henry E. Huntington Library and Art Gallery, San Marino, Calif. LO 1839.

"Clergy of the American Province of the Unitas Fratrum," I, 67. Manuscript in the Moravian Archives. These Archives are housed in the Moravian Archives Building, Bethlehem, Pa.

"Commission to Anthony Van Schaick from Lord Loudoun to organize a Company of Rangers." Photostat from Henry E. Huntington Library and Art Gallery, San Marino, Calif. LO 1400.

"Massachusetts Archives," CXVI, 17. The Massachusetts Archives are housed in the Secretary of State's Office, State House, Boston, Mass.

"Report of the General Survey in the Southern District of North America." British Museum. King's Manuscripts. Nos. 210-211. This report is in transcript and photostat form in the Library of Congress.

"To his Excellency the R^t Honble The Earl of Loudoun, Commander in Chief &c, &c, &c." Letter from Anthony Van Schaick to Lord Loudoun. Photostat from Henry E. Huntington Library and Art Gallery, San Marino, Calif. LO 1663.

PRINTED DOCUMENTS

American Archives: Fourth Series, Containing a Documentary History of the English Colonies in North America, from the King's Message to Parliament, of March 7, 1774, to the Declaration of Independence by the United States. Washington, Published by M. St. Clair Clarke and Peter Force, 1837-1846. 6 vols.

Connecticut (Colony). *The Public Records of the Colony of Connecticut [1636-1776].* . . . Transcribed and published, in accordance with a resolution of the General Assembly. Hartford, Press of the Case Lockwood & Brainard Company [etc.], 1850-90. 15 vols.

Documents Relating to the Colonial History of New Jersey. . . . v. p., v. pub., 1880-1929. 33 vols. (*Archives of the State of New Jersey, First series,* Vols. I-XXXIII.)

Documents Relative to the Colonial History of the State of New York. . . . Albany, Weed, Parsons and Company, printers, 1853-87. 15 vols.

Great Britain (1760-1820). George III. House of Commons. *Debates of the House of Commons in the Year 1774, of the Bill for Making More Effective Provision for the Government of the Province of Quebec.* Drawn from the Notes of Sir Henry Cavendish. With a Map of Canada, Copied from the Second Edition of Mitchell's Map of North America Referred to in the Debates. London, Ridgay, 1839.

Massachusetts (Colony) Statutes. *Acts and Laws, Passed by the Great and General Court or Assembly of Their Majesties Province of Massachusetts Bay in New England. Begun at Boston the Eighth Day of June, 1692. And Continued by Adjournment, Unto Wednesday the Twelfth Day of October Following.* . . . Boston, Benjamin Harris, 1692.

Pennsylvania (Colony). General Assembly. House of Representatives. *Votes and Proceedings of the House of Representatives of the Province of Pennsylvania . . . from 15th Day of October, 1774 to September 30, 1758.* Philadelphia, Henry Miller, 1774. Vol. IV. There are six volumes in this set, each published separately.

Pennsylvania (Colony). Provincial Council. *Minutes of the Provincial Council from its organization to the Termination of the Proprietary*

Government. Philadelphia [etc.], Jo[seph] Severns & Co. [etc.], 1852-54. 16 vols.

Pennsylvania Archives. First series. Philadelphia, Joseph Severns & Co., 1852-1856. 12 vols.

U.S. Treaties, etc. *Treaties and Other International Acts of the United States of America.* Hunter Miller, ed. . . . Washington, Government Printing Office, 1931-42. Vols. II-VII. 6 vols. Vol. I not published.

Virginia. *Calendar of Virginia State Papers and Other Manuscripts. . . . Preserved in the Capitol at Richmond.* Arranged and edited by William P. Palmer. Richmond, R. F. Walker [etc.], 1875-93. 11 vols.

Virginia. Laws, Statutes, etc. *The Statutes at Large; Being a Collection of All the Laws of Virginia from the First Session of the Legislature, in the Year 1619.* By William Waller Hening. v. p., v. pub., 1809-1823. 13 vols.

OTHER PRINTED SOURCES

Alvord, Clarence, ed. *The Critical Period, 1763-1765.* Edited with Introduction and Notes by Clarence Walworth Alvord and Clarence Edwin Carter. Springfield, Ill., The Trustees of the Illinois State Historical Library, 1915. (*Collections* of the Illinois State Historical Library. Vol. X, "British" series, Vol. I.)

———— *The New Regime, 1765-1767.* Edited with Introduction and Notes by Clarence Walworth Alvord and Clarence Edwin Carter. Springfield, Ill., Illinois State Historical Library, 1916. (*Collections* of the Illinois State Historical Library. Vol. XI, "British" series, Vol. II.)

American Philosophical Society, Philadelphia. *Transactions of. . . .* Philadelphia, William and Thomas Bradford, 1769-1809. First series. 6 vols.

Babbitt, E. L. *The Allegheny Pilot.* Freeport, Pa., E. L. Babbitt, 1855.

Bartram, John. *Observations on the Inhabitants, Climate, Soil, Rivers, Productions, Animals, and Other Matters Worthy of Notice . . . . To Which is Annex'd a Curious Account of the Cataracts at Niagara.* By Peter Kalm. London, Printed for J. Whiston and B. White, 1751.

Buffon, George Louis Leclerc, comte de. *Natural History, General and Particular. . . .* Translated into English . . . by William Smellis . . . . London, 3rd ed., A. Strahan [etc.], 1791. 9 vols.

Byrd, William. *History of the Dividing Line, and Other Tracts.* From the Papers of William Byrd, of Westover, in Virginia, Esquire. Richmond, Va., 1866. 2 vols. (*Historical Documents from the Old Dominion*, Nos. 2-3.)

Champlain, Samuel de. *The Works of.* . . . Reprinted, translated and annotated by Six Canadian Scholars Under the General Editorship of H. G. Biggar. . . . Toronto, The Champlain Society, 1922-36. 6 vols. (The *Publications* of the Champlain Society. New Series.)

Charlesvoix, Pierre Francois Xavier de. *History and General Description of New France.* By Rev. P. F. X. de Charlevoix. Translated with notes by John Gilmary Shea. . . . New York, J. G. Shea, 1866-72. 6 vols.

Colles, Christopher. *A Survey of the Roads of United States of America, 1789.* [New York, 1789.]

Conduct of the late Ministry: or, A Memorial: Containing a Summary of Facts with Their Vouchers, in Answer to the Observations, Sent by the English Ministry to the Courts of Europe. . . . London, W. Bizet, 1757.

Connecticut. Secretary of State. *Register and Manual of the State of Connecticut, 1939.* Hartford, The State, 1939.

Cramer, Zadok. *The Navigator.* . . . Pittsburgh, 10th ed., Cramer & Spear, 1818.

Douglass, William. *A Summary, Historical and Political of the First Planting Progressive Movements, and Present State of the British Settlements in North America; With Some Transient Accounts of the Bordering French and Spanish Settlements.* Boston, New England, printed: London, Reprinted for R. Baldwin, 1755. 2 vols.

Drake, Samuel Gardner, ed. *The Old Indian Chronicle; Being a Collection of Exceeding Rare Tracts Written and Published in the Time of King Philip's War, by Persons Residing in the Country; to Which are now Added an Introduction and Notes by Samuel G. Drake.* Boston, S. A. Drake, 1867.

Dwight, Timothy. *Travels in New England and New York.* London, Printed for W. Baynes and Son [etc.], 1823. 4 vols.

Evans, Lewis. *Geographical, Historical, Political, Philosophical and Mechanical Essays. The First, Containing an Analysis of a General Map of the Middle British Colonies in America.* . . . Philadelphia, B. Franklin, and D. Hall, 1755.

Evans, Lewis. *Geographical, Historical, Political, Philosophical and Mechanical Essays. Number II Containing a Letter Representing the Impropriety of Sending Forces to Virginia.* . . . *Published in the New York Mercury, No. 178, January 5, 1756, With an Answer to so*

Much Thereof as Concerns the Public. Philadelphia, Printed for the Author, 1756. Reprinted in Lawrence H. Gipson's *Lewis Evans*. . . . Philadelphia, Historical Society of Pennsylvania, 1939.

Gage, Thomas. *The Correspondence of General Thomas Gage*. . . . Compiled and Edited by Clarence Edwin Carter. . . . New Haven, Yale University Press; London, H. Milford, Oxford University Press, 1931-33. 2 vols. (*Yale Historical Publications. Manuscripts and Edited Texts*, Nos. 11-12.)

Galbreath, Charles B., ed. *Expeditions of Céloron to the Ohio Country in 1749*. . . . Columbus, Ohio, The F. J. Heer Printing Co., 1921. (Republished with additions from the *Ohio Archaeological and Historical Quarterly*, October, 1920.)

Gist, Christopher. *Christopher Gist's Journals with Historical, Geographical, and Ethnological Notes and Biographies of his Contemporaries, by William M. Darlington*. Pittsburgh, J. R. Weldin & Co. 1893.

Hutchins, Thomas. *The Courses of the Ohio River taken by Lt. T. Hutchins Anno 1766 and Two Accompanying Maps*. Beverly W. Bond, Jr., ed. Cincinnati, Historical and Philosophical Society of Ohio, 1942. (*Publications* of the Historical and Philosophical Society of Ohio.)

Johnson, Sir William. *The Papers of Sir William Johnson*. Prepared for Publication by the Division of Archives and History. . . . Albany, The University of the State of New York, 1921-39. 9 vols.

Kalm, Per. *Travels in North America*. . . . Translated into English by John Reinhold Forster. London, Printed for the Editor, 1770-71. 3 vols.

Le Page Du Pratz. *Histoire de la Louisiane, Contenant la Découverte de ce Vaste Pays; sa Description Géographique; un Voyage dans les Terres: l'Histoire Naturelle: les Moeurs, Coûtumes & Religion des Naturels, avec leurs Origines*. . . . Paris, De Bure, 1758. 3 vols.

Maine Historical Society. *Collections*. . . . First series. Portland, The Society, 1831-37. 10 vols.

Mereness, Newton D., ed. *Travels in the American Colonies*. New York, The Macmillan Company, 1916.

Moravian Historical Society. *Transactions*. . . . Nazareth, Whitfield House, 1876-date. Published irregularly.

Pownall, Thomas. *The Administration of the Colonies*. London, 2nd ed., R. Dodsley, 1765.

Royal Society of London. *Philosophical Transactions*. . . . First series. London, The Society, 1665-1885. Nos. 270-272 (1701); 385 (1724).

Shirley, William. *Correspondence of William Shirley, Governor of Massachusetts and Military Commander in America, 1731-1760.* Charles Henry Lincoln, ed. New York, The Macmillan Company, 1912. 2 vols.

Smith, William. *Historical Account of Bouquet's Expedition Against the Ohio Indians.* Cincinnati, Ohio, Robert Clarke & Co., 1868. "Ohio Valley Historical Series," No. 1.

Stark, Caleb. *Memoir and Official Correspondence of Gen. John Stark, With Notices of Several Other Officers of the Revolution. Also a Biography of Capt. Phineas Stevens and of Col. Robert Rogers, With Account of His Service in America during the "Seven Years War."* Concord [N.H.], G. P. Lyon, 1860.

Strahlenberg, John Philip von. *An Historico-geographical Description of the North and Eastern Parts of Europe and Asia; but More Particularly of Prussia, Siberia and Great Tartary....* Now Faithfully Translated into English. . . . London, Printed for Innys and R. Mansby, 1738.

Walker, Thomas. *Journal of an Exploration in the Spring of the Year 1750 . . . with a Preface by William Cabell Rives.* Boston, Little, Brown, and Company, 1888.

Washington, George. *The Writings of....* From the Original Manuscript Sources, *1745-1799.* Prepared under the direction of the U.S. George Washington Bicentennial Commission and published by authority of Congress; John C. Fitzpatrick, ed. Washington, Government Printing Office, [1931-44]. 39 vols.

Williams, John. *The Redeemed Captive Returning to Zion: or, A Faithful History of Remarkable Occurrences in the Captivity and Deliverance of Mr. John Williams....* The Sixth Edition. Boston, Samuel Hall, 1795.

ATLASES

SOURCE MATERIAL

The Atlantic Neptune, Published for the Use of the Royal Navy of Great Britain, by Joseph F. W. Des Barres.... Under the Directions of the Right Honble the Lords Commissioners of the Admiralty. [London, 1774-1781.] 3 vols.

Jefferys, Thomas, engr. *The American Atlas....* London, R. Sayer & J. Bennett, 1776.

Jefferys, Thomas, engr. *A General Topography of North America and the West Indies.* London, for R. Sayer & T. Jefferys, 1768.

Sayer, Robert and J. Bennett. *The American Military Pocket Atlas of the British Colonies; Especially Those Which Now Are, or Probably May Be the Theatre of War. Taken Principally From the Actual Surveys and Judicious Observations of Engineers De Brahm and Romans; Cook, Jackson and Collet; Maj. Holland, and Other Officers, Employed in His Majesty's Fleets and Armies.* London, for R. Sayer and J. Bennett, [1776].

SECONDARY MATERIAL

Walling, Henry F. *New Topographical Atlas of the State of Pennsylvania* .... By Henry F. Walling and A. W. Gray. Philadelphia, Stedman Brown & Lyon, 1872.

MAPS

SOURCE MATERIAL

1722   *The Town of Boston in New England by Cap*^t *John Bonner, 1722.* Engraven and Printed by Fra: Dewing, Boston N.E. 1722. Sold by Capt John Bonner and Willm Price against ye Town House. Reproduction in Shurtleff's. . . *Boston.*

1735   *To the Merchants of London Trading to Virginia & Maryland This Mapp of the Bay of Chesepeack, with the Rivers Potomack, Potapsco, North East, and Part of Chester.* London, W. Beitts and E. Baldwin, 1755. Photostat in New York Public Library.

1737   *Map of the Indian Walking Purchase, 1737, by Lewis Evans.* Frontispiece in Lawrence Gipson's *Lewis Evans.* . . .

1737   "A Map of the Northern Neck in Virginia; The Territory of the Right Honourable Thomas Lord Fairfax; Situate betwixt the Rivers Potomack and Rappahanock, According to a Late Survey; Drawn in the Year 1737 by Wm Mayo." Manuscript Map in the Darlington Memorial Library, University of Pittsburgh.

1739   *A Map of Part of the Province of Pennsylvania and of the Counties of New Castle, Kent and Sussex on Delaware: Showing the Temporary Limits of the Jurisdiction of Pennsylvania and Maryland, Fixed According to an Order of His Majesty in Coun-*

cil dated the 25th Day of May in the Year 1738. Surveyed in the Year 1739. Reproduction in *Pennsylvania Archives,* Vol. I.

1749   *A Map of Pensilvania, New Jersey, New York, and the Three Delaware Counties: by Lewis Evans, 1749.* L. Herbert, sculp. Philadelphia, L. Evans, 1749.

1750-   "Map of Albany County With the Country of the Five Nations."
1770?   By Jno R. Bleecker. Manuscript Map in the New York Historical Society, New York, N.Y.

1751   *A Map of the Most Inhabited Part of Virginia Containing the Whole Province of Maryland With Part of Pensilvania, New Jersey and North Carolina.* Drawn by Joshua Fry and Peter Jefferson in 1751. Printed for Robt. Sayer at No. 53 in Fleet Street & Thos. Jefferys at the Corner of St. Martins Lane, Charing Cross, London.

1752   *A Map of Pensilvania, New Jersey, New York and the Three Delaware Counties: By Lewis Evans,* 1749. The Second Edition. July 1752. Reproduction in Gipson's *Lewis Evans....*

1753   *Plan of the British Dominions of New England in North America Composed from Actual Surveys.* By Dr. William Douglas. Engraved by R. W. Seale, London, 1753.

1753?   *Map. Virginia.* [A sketch showing the Courses of Christopher Gist's First and Second Tours] MSS. Great Britain. Public Records Office, Colonial Office. Maps, Virginia, No. 13. (Photostat, courtesy of Howard N. Eavenson.)

1755   *A General Map of the Middle British Colonies, in America: ... By Lewis Evans. 1755.* Engraved by Ja⁸ Turner in Philadelphia. Published According to Act of Parliament, by Lewis Evans, June 23, 1755. And Sold by R. Dodsley, in Pall-Mall, London, & by the Author in Philadelphia.

1755   [Sir William] *Johnson's Map of Lake George and Vicinity.* Printed in Sir William Johnson's *Papers,* II, Map opposite p. 422.

1755   *A Map of the British and French Dominions in North America, with the Roads, Distances, Limits, and Extent of the Settlements. ...* By Jnᵒ Mitchell. London, Printed for Jefferys & Faden, Feb. 13th, 1755.

1758   *A General Map of the Middle British Colonies in America: viz. Virginia, Maryland, Delaware, Pensilvania. ... By Lewis Evans. Corrected and Improved in the Addition of the Line of Forts on the Back Settlements.* By Thomas Jefferys. [London], R. Sayer & T. Jefferys, 1758.

1759   *To the Honourable Thomas Penn and Richard Penn, this Map of the Improved Part of the Province of Pennsylvania is Humbly Dedicated by Nicholas Scull* . . . . Philadelphia, Engraved by J. Turner, and printed by J. Davis for the Author, 1759.

1762   *A Survey of Lake Champlain including Lake George, Crown Point and St. John. Surveyed by Order of His Excellency Major General S*^{r} *Jeffery Amherst* . . . . By William Brassier, Draughtsman, 1762. London; Printed for Robt Sayer & Jn° Bennett . . . , Aug. 5th 1776. In Jeffery's *American Atlas*, No. 18.

Before 1764   *Plan des Différents Villages François dans le Pays des Illynois avec une Partie de la Riviere Missisipi et des Confluents des Fleuves Missouri et Illinois.* Printed in Lawrence H. Gipson's *The British Empire* . . . , IV, Map opposite p. 126.

1768   *Map of the Frontiers of the Northern Colonies with the Boundary Line Established Between Them and the Indians at the Treaty Held by S*^{r} *Will Johnson at Fort Stanwix in Nov'r 1768. Corrected and Improved from Evans' Map.* By Guy Johnson, Agt. for Indian Affairs. Printed in Sir William Johnson's *Papers* . . . , VI, Map opposite p. 450.

1770   *A New and Accurate Map of Virginia Wherein Most of the Counties Are Laid Down From Actual Surveys. With a Concise Account of the Number of Inhabitants, the Trade, Soil, and Produce of that Province.* By John Henry. Engraved by Thomas Jefferys, Geographer to the King. London, February, 1770. Published According to Act of Parliament for the Author, by Thos Jefferys at the Corner of St. Martins Lane in the Strand. Reproduction in Abernethy's *Western Lands*. . . .

1770   *To the Honorable Thomas Penn and Richard Penn, esquires, True and Absolute Proprietors and Governors of the Province of Pennsylvania and the Territories Thereunto Belonging and to the Honorable John Penn, Esquire, Lieutenant Governor of the Same. This Map of the Province of Pennsylvania is Humbly Dedicated by Their Most Obedient Serv't W. Scull.* Henry Dawkins Sculp't. Philadelphia, James Nevil, for the Author, April 1st, 1770.

1770   *A Plan of the West Line or Parallel of Latitude Which is the Boundary Between the Provinces of Maryland and Pennsylvania.* Engraved by J. Smither, 1770. Title from: Great Britain. Board of Trade and Plantations, *List of Maps.* . . .

1773-1774?   "A Plan of a Survey made to Explore the Country for a Road Between Connecticut River and St. Francis." [By Hugh Finlay, anon.] MSS in Library of Congress. Division of Maps.

1774 *A Map of the Most Inhabited Part of New England Containing the Provinces of Massachusets Bay and New Hampshire With the Colonies of Conecticut and Rhode Island Divided into Counties and Townships.* [By J. Green, anon.] November 29th, 1774. Published According to Act by Thoˢ Jefferys. In Jefferys' *American Atlas . . .* , Nos. 15-16.

1776 *A General Map of the Southern British Colonies in America . . . .* By B. Romans. London, Printed for R. Sayer and J. Bennett, 15th Octʳ 1776.

1776 *A Map of the Province of New York, Reduc'd From the Large Scale Drawings of That Province, Compiled From Actual Surveys by Order of His Excellency William Tryon.* By Claude Joseph Sauthier . . . . Engraved by William Faden, 1776. London, Wᵐ Faden, 1776. Reprinted by U.S. Constitution Sesquicentennial Convention under the Title: *New York at the Time of the Ratification of the Constitution from 1776 and 1787 originals in the Library of Congress at Washington.*

1776 *To His Excellency Sir Henry Moore . . . This Plan of the City of New York and its Environs, Survey'd and Laid Down: Is Most Humbly Dedicated by His Excellency's Most obedt. Humble Servant, B. Ratzer, Lieut. in His Majesty's 60th or Royal American Regt. . . . Plan of the City of New York in North America: Surveyed in The Years 1766 & 1767.* London, W. Faden & Jefferys, 1776.

1777 *The Province of New Jersey, Divided Into East and West, Commonly Called the Jerseys. Drawn From the Survey Made in 1769 by Order of the Commissioners Appointed to Settle the Partition Line Between the Provinces of New York & New Jersey by Bernard Ratzer, and From Another Large Survey of the Northern Parts by Gerard Barker.* Engraved by Wᵐ Faden. London, W. Faden, Dec. 1, 1777. In William Faden's *North American Atlas . . .* , No. 22.

1779 *A Chorographical Map of the Province of New York, Divided Into Counties, Manors, etc. Compiled From Actual Surveys Deposited in the Patent Office at New York by Order of General William Tryon.* By Claude Joseph Sauthier. London, W. Faden. Jan. 1, 1779. In Jefferys' *American Atlas . . .* , No. 17½.

1784 *A Topographical Map of the Province of New Hampshire Surveyed by Mr. Thomas Wright and Others.* Author, S. Holland, London,

1784. Printed for William Faden, Mar. 1, 1784. Title from: Great Britain. Board of Trade and Plantations, *List of Maps* ....

1801 *Warner & Hanna's Plan of the City and Environs of Baltimore Respectfully Dedicated to the Mayor, City Council, and Citizens Thereof by the Proprietors, 1801.* [Baltimore, 1801.]

1859 *A Map of the State of Virginia. Constructed in Conformity to Law from the Late Surveys, Authorized by the Legislature.* By Herman Böyë. Corrected by Order of the Executive, 1859. n.p., n. pub., [1859].

SECONDARY MATERIAL

"A Map of the Site of the Battle of Lake George, September 8th, 1755. In Caldwell, Warren County, N.Y." From the *Fifth Annual Report of the Society for the Preservation of Scenic and Historic Places and Objects.* Albany: 1900. Reprinted in Sir William Johnson's *Papers*, II, Map opposite p. 2.

"Map of the Ancient Shawanoese Towns, on the Pickaway Plain." Howe's *Historical Collections of Ohio*, p. 402.

"Original Elbow District, Mass., 1716-1752." Compiled by E. B. Gates. Temple's *History of the Town of Palmer*, Map No. 1.

"Trails, Military Roads and Forts from Albany to Crown Point, 1750-1780." Prepared by R. J. Brown formerly Warren County engineer under supervision of James A. Holden. Sir William Johnson's *Papers*, I, opposite p. 896.

"Vandalia as Originally Plotted on Evans' Map." Abernethy's *Western Lands. . .* , Map opposite p. 39.

VIEWS

MANUSCRIPT

"A View of the Cohoes or Great Falls on the Mohawk River." Pen and Ink Sketch. Library of Congress. Division of Maps.

ENGRAVINGS

Scenographia Americana; or, A Collection of Views in North America and the West Indies. Neatly Engraved by Messrs. Sandby, Grignion, Rooker, Canot, Elliot, and Others; From Drawings On the Spot, by

Several Officers of the British Navy & Army.... London, Printed for John Bowles, Robert Sayer, Thomas Jefferys, Carington Bowles & Henry Packer, 1768. A List of engravings executed from Governor Pownall's sketches mentioned in this work is as follows:

"A View of Bethlehem, the Great Moravian Settlement in the Province of Pennsylvania. . . ."

"A View of Hudson's River at the Entrance of What is Called the Topan Sea. . . ."

"A View of Hudson's River of the Pakepsey and the Catts-kill Mountains from Sopos Island. . . ."

"A View of the Falls on the Passaic or Second River in the Province of New Jersey. . . ."

"A View of the Great Cohoes Falls on the Mohawk River; the Fall About Seventy Feet; the River Near a Quarter of a Mile Broad. . . ."

SECONDARY MATERIAL

Abernethy, Thomas Perkins. *Western Lands and the American Revolution.* New York, London, D. Appleton-Century Co., Inc., 1937. (University of Virginia, Institute for Research in the Social Sciences. *Institute Monograph,* No. 25.)

Atkinson, George. *History of Kanawha County, from its Organization in 1789 Until the Present Time....* Charleston, printed at the office of the West Virginia Journal, 1876.

Bailey, Kenneth P. *The Ohio Company of Virginia and the Westward Movement 1748-1792. . . .* Glendale, California, The Arthur H. Clark Company, 1939.

Baldwin, Leland D. *Pittsburgh, the Story of a City.* [Pittsburgh], University of Pittsburgh Press, 1939.

Barber, John Warner. *History and Antiquities of New Haven, Conn., from the Earliest Settlement to the Present Time....* New Haven, J. W. Barber, 1831.

Benton, Nathaniel S. *A History of Herkimer County, Including the Upper Mohawk Valley, from the Earliest Period to the Present Time.* Albany, J. Munsell, 1856.

Bining, Arthur Cecil. *British Regulation of the Colonial Iron Industry.* Philadelphia, Ph.D. Dissertation, University of Pennsylvania, 1933.

Bishop, John L. *A History of American Manufactures, from 1608 to 1860 . . . Comprising Annals of the Industry of the United States in*

Machinery, Manufactures and Useful Arts. Philadelphia, E. Young & Co.; London, S. Low, Son & Co., 1864. 2 vols.

Boynton, Edward C. *History of West Point*. London, Sampson Low, Son & Marston, 1864.

Carrier, Lyman. *The Beginnings of Agriculture in America*. New York, McGraw Hill, 1923.

Clark, Joshua V. H. *Onondaga; or, Reminiscences of Earlier and Later Times; Being a Series of Historical Sketches Relative to Onondaga*. . . . Syracuse, Stoddard and Babcock, 1849. 2 vols.

Collins, Lewis. *History of Kentucky. Revised, Enlarged . . . and Brought Down to the Year 1874*. . . . Covington, Ky., Collins & Co., 1874. 2 vols.

Davidson, Donald. *The Tennessee*. . . . New York, Toronto, Rinehart & Co., Inc., [1946-1948]. 2 vols. "Rivers of America" series.

Eavenson, Howard N. *The First Century and a Quarter of American Coal Industry*. Pittsburgh, Pa., Privately printed, 1942.

Federal Writers' Project. Delaware. *Delaware, a Guide to the First State*. New York, The Viking Press, 1938. "American Guide Series."

Federal Writers' Project. Illinois. *Illinois, a Descriptive and Historical Guide*. . . . Chicago, A. C. McClurg & Co., 1939. "American Guide Series."

Federal Writers' Project. Maine. *Maine, 'A Guide Down East.'* Boston, Houghton Mifflin Co., 1937. "American Guide Series."

Federal Writers' Project. Massachusetts. *Massachusetts: a Guide to Its Places and People*. Boston, Houghton Mifflin Co., 1937. "American Guide Series."

Federal Writers' Project. New Hampshire. *New Hampshire, a Guide to the Granite State*. Boston, Houghton Mifflin Co., 1938. "American Guide Series."

Federal Writers' Project. New Jersey. *New Jersey, a Guide to its Past and Present*. New York, The Viking Press, 1939. "American Guide Series."

Federal Writers' Project. Rhode Island. *Rhode Island, a Guide to the Smallest State*. Boston, Houghton Mifflin Co., 1937. "American Guide Series."

Gipson, Lawrence Henry. *The British Empire Before the American Revolution: Provincial Characteristics and Sectional Tendencies in the Era Preceding the American Crisis*. . . . Caldwell, Idaho, The Caxton Printers; New York, Alfred A. Knopf, 1936-date. 6 vols., all published to date.

Gipson, Lawrence Henry. *Lewis Evans, by Lawrence Henry Gipson: to Which is Added Evans' A Brief Account of Pennsylvania, Together with Facsimiles of His Geographical, Political, Philosophical and Mechanical Essays, Numbers I and II ... Also Facsimiles of Evans' Maps.* Philadelphia, The Historical Society of Pennsylvania, 1939.

Gordon, Thomas F. *A Gazetteer of the State of New Jersey.* Trenton, Daniel Fenton, 1834.

Hanna, Charles A. *The Wilderness Trail; or, The Ventures and Adventures of the Pennsylvania Traders on the Allegheny Path, with Some New Annals of the Old West, and the Records of Some Strong Men and Some Bad Ones.* New York, London, G. P. Putnam's Sons, 1911. 2 vols.

Hard, Walter. *The Connecticut.* New York, Rinehart & Co., [c1947]. "Rivers of America" series.

Hodge, Frederick, ed. *Handbook of American Indians North of Mexico.* Washington, Government Printing Office, 1907-10. 2 vols. (Smithsonian Institution. Bureau of Ethnology. *Bulletin* 30.)

Hough, Franklin B. *Gazetteer of the State of New York, Embracing a Comprehensive Account of the History and Statistics of the State. . . .* Albany, N.Y., A. Boyd, 1872.

Howe, Henry. *Historical Collections of Ohio.* Cincinnati, Derby, Bradley & Co., 1848.

Jones, Uriah. *History of the Early Settlement of the Juniata Valley.* Philadelphia, H. B. Ashmead, 1856.

Levering, Joseph M. *A History of Bethlehem, Pennsylvania, 1741-1892, With Some Account of Its Founders, and Their Early Activity in America. . . .* Bethlehem, Pa., Times Publishing Co., 1903.

Loescher, Burt Garfield. *The History of Rogers Rangers. . . .* San Francisco, [The Author], 1946-date. Vol. I, all published to date.

Lossing, Benson J., comp. *A Pictorial Description of Ohio.* New York, Ensigns & Thayer, 1849.

Lowdermilk, William H. *History of Cumberland (Maryland) From the Time of the Indian Town, Caiuctucuc, in 1728, up to the Present Day, Embracing an Account of Washington's First Campaign, and Battle of Fort Necessity, Together With a History of Braddock's Expedition.* Washington, D.C., J. Anglis, 1878.

Marshall, Orsamus. *The Niagara Frontier. Embracing Sketches of Its Early History, and Indian, French and English Local Names.* Read before the Buffalo Historical Society, February 27th, 1865. [Buffalo], 1881. (Buffalo Historical Society. *Publications.*)

Maryland Historical Magazine. Baltimore, The Society, 1906-date. 43 vols.

Massachusetts Historical Society. *Collections.* Second series, Boston, John Eliot, 1814-23. 10 vols.

———— *Proceedings.* Boston, The Society, 1791-date. 67 vols.

Morgan, Lewis H. *League of the Ho-dá-sau-nee, or Iroquois.* Rochester, Sage & Brothers, 1851.

Niles, Blair. *The James, from Iron Gate to the Sea.* New York, Farrar & Rinehart, [c1945]. "Rivers of America" series.

Nonnemaker, Warren N. "The Moravian Church in the United States during the Middle Period, 1812-1860." M. A. Thesis, Lehigh University, 1935.

Palmer, Peter S. *History of Lake Champlain, From Its First Exploration by the French in 1609, to the Close of the Year 1814.* Albany, J. Munsell, 1866.

Pennsylvania Archaeologist. Philadelphia, Society for Pennsylvania Archaeology, 1930-date. 18 vols.

Pennsylvania Magazine of History and Biography. Philadelphia, Publication Fund of the Historical Society of Pennsylvania, 1877-date. 47 vols.

Pollard, Edward A. *The Virginia Tourist.* Philadelphia, J. B. Lippincott & Co., 1870.

Pownall, Charles. *Thomas Pownall.... Governor of Massachusetts Bay, Author of the Letters of Junius, With a Supplement Comparing the Colonies of Kings George III and Edward VII....* London, H. Stevens, Son, & Stiles, [c1908].

Ramsey, J. G. M. *Annals of Tennessee....* [Kingsport, Tenn.], Kingsport Press, 1926.

Raum, John O. *History of the City of Trenton, New Jersey, Embracing a Period of Nearly Two Hundred Years....* Trenton, W. T. Nicholson & Co., 1871.

———— *The History of New Jersey, from its Earliest Settlement to the Present Time....* Philadelphia, J. E. Potter and Company, [1877]. 2 vols.

Reichel, William C. *Friedensthal and Its Stockaded Mill. A Moravian Chronicle, 1749-1767.* Nazareth, Pa., printed for the Society, 1877. (Moravian Historical Society. *Transactions,* Vol. II.)

Reichel, William C., ed. *Memorials of the Moravian Church.* Philadelphia, J. B. Lippincott & Co., 1870. Vol. I, all published.

Schlarman, Joseph. *From Quebec to New Orleans.* Belleville, Ill., Buechler Publishing Co., 1929.

Schuyler, George E. *Colonial New York; Philip Schuyler and His Family.* New York, C. Scribner's Sons, 1885. 2 vols.

Shurtleff, Nathaniel B. *A Topographical and Historical Description of Boston.* Boston, 3rd ed., Published by Order of the Common Council, 1891.

Simms, Jeptha. *History of Schoharie County, and Border Wars of New York.* Albany, Munsell & Tanner, 1845.

Steelways. New York, American Iron and Steel Institute, 1947-date. 2 vols.

Stevens, Henry N. *Lewis Evans, His Map of the Middle English Colonies in America.* London, 3rd ed., H. Stevens, Son & Stiles, 1924.

Temple, Josiah H. *History of the Town of Palmer, Massachusetts, Early Known as the Elbow Tract: Including Records of the Plantation, District and Town, 1716-1889.* [Springfield], published by the town of Palmer, 1889.

Thompson, Jeanette R. *History of the Town of Stratford, New Hampshire, 1773-1925.* ... Concord, N. H., The Rumford Press, 1925.

U.S. Bureau of American Ethnology. *Annual Reports of the Bureau of Ethnology to the Secretary of Smithsonian Institution.* Washington, U.S. Government Printing Office, 1879/80 - 1930/31. Forty-eight reports in 54 vols.

Valentine's Manual of Old New York, 1924. Edited by Henry Collins Brown. New York, Gracie Mansion, [c1923]. (Museum of the City of New York. *Yearbook.*)

Volwiler, Albert T. *George Croghan and the Westward Movement, 1741-1782.* Cleveland, The Arthur H. Clark Company, 1926. (Early Western Journals, No. 3.)

Wallace, Paul A. W. *Conrad Weiser, 1696-1760, Friend of Colonist and Mohawk.* Philadelphia; University of Pennsylvania Press, 1945.

Watson, John Fanning. *Annals of Philadelphia* .... Philadelphia, For Sale by Uriah Hunt, 1830.

Watson, John F. *Annals and Occurrences of New York City and State in the Olden Time.* Philadelphia, H. F. Anners, 1846.

Williamson, William D. *The History of the State of Maine; From its First Discovery, A.D. 1602, to the Separation, A.D. 1820, inclusive.* Hallowell, [Me.], Glazier, Masters & Co., 1832. 2 vols.

Western Pennsylvania Historical Magazine. Pittsburgh, Published by the Historical Society of Western Pennsylvania, 1918-date. 30 vols.

Writers' Program. Kentucky. *Louisville: a Guide to the Falls City.* .... New York, M. Barrows & Company, Inc., 1940. "American Guide Series."

Writers' Program. Missouri. *Missouri, a Guide to the "Show Me" State* . . . . New York, Duell, Sloan and Pearce, [c1941]. "American Guide Series."

Yale University. *Historical Register of Yale University, 1701-1937.* New Haven, Conn., Yale University, 1939.

INDEX

The additions and corrections listed in this index under the heading, Pownall, Thomas, *Topographical Descriptions* revised (1949), are new material, never before published.

AMERICA IN TWO CENTURIES:
An Inventory

An Arno Press Collection

American Association of Museums. **A Statistical Survey of Museums in the United States and Canada.** 1965

Andrews, Israel D. **On the Trade and Commerce of the British North American Colonies, and Upon the Trade of the Great Lakes and Rivers.** 1853

Audit Bureau of Circulations. **Scientific Space Selection.** 1921

Austin, E. L. and Odell Hauser. **The Sesqui-Centennial International Exposition.** 1929

Barnett, James H. **The American Christmas.** 1954

Barton, L[eslie] M. **A Study of 81 Principal American Markets.** 1925

Bennitt, Mark, comp. **History of the Louisiana Purchase Exposition.** 1905

Bowen, Eli. **The United States Post-Office Guide.** 1851

Bureau of Applied Social Research, Columbia University. **The People Look at Radio.** 1946

Burlingame, Roger. **Engines of Democracy:** Inventions and Society in Mature America. 1940

Burlingame, Roger. **March of the Iron Men:** A Social History of Union Through Invention. 1938

Burnham, W. Dean. **Presidential Ballots, 1836-1892.** 1955

Cochrane, Rexmond C. **Measures for Progress:** A History of the National Bureau of Standards. 1966

Cohn, David L. **The Good Old Days.** 1940

Cozens, Frederick W. and Florence Scovil Stumpf. **Sports in American Life.** 1953

Day, Edmund E. and Woodlief Thomas. **The Growth of Manufactures, 1899 to 1923.** 1928

Edwards, Richard Henry. **Popular Amusements.** 1915

Evans, Charles H., comp. **Exports, Domestic and Foreign, From the American Colonies to Great Britain, From 1697 to 1789, Inclusive;** Exports, Domestic, From the U.S. to All Countries, From 1789 to 1883, Inclusive. 1884

Federal Reserve System, Board of Governors. **All-Bank Statistics, United States, 1896-1955.** 1959

Flexner, Abraham. **Funds and Foundations:** Their Policies, Past and Present. 1952

Flint, Henry M. **The Railroads of the United States.** 1868

Folger, John K. and Charles B. Nam. **Education of the American Population.** 1967

Handel, Leo A. **Hollywood Looks At Its Audience:** A Report of Film Audience Research. 1950

Harlow, Alvin F. **Old Waybills:** The Romance of the Express Companies. 1934

Harrison, Shelby M. **Social Conditions in an American City:** A Summary of the Findings of the Springfield Survey. 1920

Homans, J. Smith, comp. **An Historical and Statistical Account of the Foreign Commerce of the United States.** 1857

Ingram, J. S. **The Centennial Exposition.** 1876

Institute of American Meat Packers and the School of Commerce and Administration of the University of Chicago. **The Packing Industry:** A Series of Lectures. 1924

Leech, D[aniel] D. T[ompkins]. **The Post Office Department of the United States of America.** 1879

Leggett, M. D., comp. **Subject-Matter Index of Patents for Inventions Issued by the United States Patent Office From 1790 to 1873, Inclusive.** 1874. Three vols.

Magazine Marketing Service. **M.M.S. County Buying Power Index.** 1942

Martin, Robert F. **National Income in the United States, 1799-1938.** 1939

McCullough, Edo. **World's Fair Midways.** 1966

Melish, John. **Surveys for Travellers, Emigrants and Others.** 1976

National Advertising Company. **America's Advertisers.** 1893

Peters, Harry T. **America On Stone:** The Other Printmakers to the American People. 1931

Peters, Harry T. **California On Stone.** 1935

Peters, Harry T. **Currier & Ives:** Printmakers to the American People. 1929/1931. Two vols.

Pownall, T[homas]. **A Topographical Description of the Dominions of the United States of America.** Edited by Lois Mulkearn. 1949

Reed, Alfred Zantzinger. **Present-Day Law Schools in the United States and Canada.** 1928

Reed, Alfred Zantzinger. **Training for the Public Profession of the Law.** 1921

Rogers, Meyric R. **American Interior Design.** 1947

Romaine, Lawrence B. **A Guide to American Trade Catalogs, 1744-1900.** 1960

Scammon, Richard M., comp. **America at the Polls:** A Handbook of American Presidential Election Statistics, 1920-1964. 1965

Smillie, Wilson G. **Public Health:** Its Promise for the Future. 1955

Thompson, Warren S. **Population: The Growth of Metropolitan Districts in the United States, 1900-1940.** 1947

Thorndike, E[dward] L. **Your City.** 1939

Truman, Ben[jamin] C. **History of the World's Fair.** 1893

U.S. Bureau of the Census, Department of Commerce. **Housing Construction Statistics: 1889 to 1964.** 1966

U.S. Census Office (12th Census). **Street and Electric Railways.** 1903

Urban Statistical Surveys. 1976

Wayland, Sloan and Edmund de S. Brunner. **The Educational Characteristics of the American People.** 1958

Woytinsky, W. S. **Employment and Wages in the United States.** 1953

U.S. Census Office (1st Census, 1790). **Return of the Whole Number of Persons Within the Several Districts of the United States.** 1802

U.S. Census Office (2nd Census, 1800). **Return of the Whole Number of Persons Within the Several Districts of the United States.** 1802

U.S. Census Office (3rd Census, 1810). **Aggregate Amount of Each Description of Persons Within the United States of America.** 1811

U.S. Census Office (4th Census, 1820). **Census for 1820.** 1821

U.S. Census Office (5th Census, 1830). **Abstract of the Returns of the Fifth Census.** 1832

U.S. Census Office (6th Census, 1840). **Compendium of the Enumeration of the Inhabitants and Statistics of the United States.** 1841

U.S. Census Office (7th Census, 1850). **The Seventh Census of the United States.** 1853

U.S. Census Office (8th Census, 1860). **Statistics of the United States in 1860.** 1866

U.S. Census Office (9th Census, 1870). **A Compendium of the Ninth Census.** 1872

U.S. Census Office (10th Census, 1880). **Compendium of the Tenth Census.** Parts I and II. 1883. Two vols.

U.S. Census Office (11th Census, 1890). **Abstract of the Eleventh Census.** 1894

U.S. Bureau of the Census (12th Census, 1900). **Abstract of the Twelfth Census of the United States.** 1904

U.S. Bureau of the Census (13th Census, 1910). **Thirteenth Census of the United States: Abstract of the Census.** 1913

U.S. Bureau of the Census (14th Census, 1920). **Abstract of the Fourteenth Census of the United States.** 1923

U.S. Bureau of the Census (15th Census, 1930). **Fifteenth Census of the United States: Abstract of the Census.** 1933

U.S. Bureau of the Census (16th Census, 1940). **Sixteenth Census of the United States: United States Summary.** 1943

U.S. Bureau of the Census (17th Census, 1950). **A Report of the Seventeenth Decennial Census of the United States: United States Summary.** 1953

U.S. Bureau of the Census (18th Census, 1960). **The Eighteenth Decennial Census of the United States: United States Summary.** 1964

U.S. Bureau of the Census (19th Census, 1970). **1970 Census of Population: United States Summary.** 1973. Two vols.